AF203952

Triumph Stag Owners Workshop Manual

by J H Haynes
Member of the Guild of Motoring Writers
and Bruce Gilmour

Models covered:
Triumph Stag hard top and soft top with the 2997 cc ohc
V8 engine. 1970 to 1978
Covers manual, overdrive and automatic transmission

ISBN 978 0 85733 603 3

© Haynes Group Limited 1979, 1986, 1987

All rights reserved. No part of this book may be reproduced or transmitted in any form or by any means, electronic or mechanical, including photocopying, recording or by any information storage or retrieval system, without permission in writing from the copyright holder.

(441-9N2)

Disclaimer

There are risks associated with automotive repairs. The ability to make repairs depends on the individual's skill, experience and proper tools. Individuals should act with due care and acknowledge and assume the risk of performing automotive repairs.

The purpose of this manual is to provide comprehensive, useful and accessible automotive repair information, to help you get the best value from your vehicle. However, this manual is not a substitute for a professional certified technician or mechanic.

This repair manual is produced by a third party and is not associated with an individual vehicle manufacturer. If there is any doubt or discrepancy between this manual and the owner's manual or the factory service manual, please refer to the factory service manual or seek assistance from a professional certified technician or mechanic.

Even though we have prepared this manual with extreme care and every attempt is made to ensure that the information in this manual is correct, neither the publisher nor the author can accept responsibility for loss, damage or injury caused by any errors in, or omissions from, the information given.

Haynes Group Limited
Haynes North America, Inc

www.haynes.com

Acknowledgements

Thanks are due to the Jaguar, Rover, Triumph subsidiary of BL Limited for the assistance given in the supply of technical material and illustrations, and to Mr H.M. Shaw who kindly loaned us his Triumph Stag (registration JJT 865N) to be used as the project car for this manual. The Champion Sparking Plug Company supplied the illustrations showing the various spark plug conditions and the bodywork repair photographs used in this manual were provided by Lloyds Industries Limited who supply 'Turtle Wax', 'Dupli-color Holts' and other Holts range products.

The section of Chapter 10 dealing with the suppression of radio interference, was originated by Mr. I.P. Davey, and was first published in *Motor* magazine.

Lastly, thanks are due to all those people at Sparkford who helped in the production of this manual, particularly, Martin Penny and Les Brazier who carried out the mechanical work and took the photographs respectively, Stanley Randolph who planned the layout of each page and David Neilson who edited the text.

About this manual

Its aims

The aim of this manual is to help you get the best value from your car. It can do so in several ways. It can help you decide what work must be done (even should you choose to get it done by a garage), provide information on routine maintenance and servicing, and give a logical course of action and diagnosis when random faults occur. However, it is hoped that you will use the manual by tackling the work yourself. On simpler jobs it may even be quicker than booking the car into a garage, and going there twice to leave and collect it. Perhaps most important, a lot of money can be saved by avoiding the costs the garage must charge to cover its labour and overheads.

The manual has drawings and descriptions to show the function of the various components so that their layout can be understood. Then the tasks are described and photographed in a step-by-step sequence so that even a novice can do the work.

Its arrangement

The manual is divided into twelve Chapters, each covering a logical sub-division of the vehicle. The Chapters are each divided into Sections, numbered with single figures, eg 5; and the Sections into paragraphs (or sub-sections), with decimal numbers following on from the Section they are in, eg 5.1, 5.2, 5.3 etc.

It is freely illustrated, especially in those parts where there is a detailed sequence of operations to be carried out. There are two forms of illustration; figures and photographs. The figures are numbered in sequence with decimal numbers, according to their position in the Chapter: eg Fig. 6.4 is the 4th drawing/illustration in Chapter 6. Photographs are numbered (either individually or in related groups) the same as the Section or sub-section of the text where the operation they show is described.

There is an alphabetical index at the back of the manual as well as a contents list at the front.

References to the 'left' or 'right' of the vehicle are in the sense of a person in the driver's seat facing forwards.

Whilst every care is taken to ensure that the information in this manual is correct no liability can be accepted by the authors or publishers for loss, damage or injury caused by any errors in, or omissions from, the information given.

Introduction to the Triumph Stag

Introduced in June 1970 at the top of the Triumph range, the Stag proved to be an immediate success.

With a completely new body design the car can be used as a convertible hardtop or soft-top coupe. When used as an open car it has the look of a sports car.

The 2997 cc V8 engine, based on two Dolomite engines put together, but with a shorter stroke, provides a quiet, smooth running power unit.

Front and rear independent suspension and power-assisted steering ensures a comfortable ride and good road holding qualities.

Both manual and automatic transmission models are available. When originally introduced, overdrive was available as an optional extra on manual transmission models, but since October 1972 it is fitted as standard.

Contents

1970 Triumph Stag

1976 Triumph Stag

Buying spare parts
and vehicle identification numbers

Buying spare parts

Spare parts are available from many sources, for example: Leyland garages, other garages and accessory shops, and motor factors. Our advice regarding spare part sources is as follows:

Officially appointed Leyland garages: This is the best source of parts which are peculiar to your car and otherwise not generally available (eg. complete cylinder heads, internal gearbox components, badges, interior trim etc). It is also the only place at which you should buy parts if your car is still under warranty as non-Leyland components may invalidate the warranty. To be sure of obtaining the correct parts it will always be necessary to give the storeman your car's engine and chassis number, and if possible, to take the 'old' part along for positive identification. Remember that many parts are available on a factory exchange scheme – any parts returned should always be clean! It obviously makes good sense to go straight to the specialists on your car for this type of part for they are best equipped to supply you.

Other garages and accessory shops: These are often very good places to buy material and components needed for the maintenance of your car (eg. oil filters, spark plugs, bulbs, fan belts, oils and greases, touch-up paint, filler paste etc). They also sell general accessories, usually have convenient opening hours, charge lower prices and can often be found not far from home.

Motor factors: Good factors will stock all of the more important components which wear out relatively quickly (eg. clutch components, pistons, valves, exhaust systems, brake cylinders/pipes/hoses/seals/shoes and pads, etc). Motor factors will often provide new or reconditioned components on a part exchange basis – this can save a considerable amount of money.

Vehicle identification numbers

The chassis, or commission number, as it is called at the factory, is stamped on a model identification plate located on top of the left-hand side of the front panel on cars from 1973. Upto 1973 the Commission number is stamped on a plate attached to the left-hand door pillar.

The engine number on earlier cars is stamped on the left-hand side of the block and can be seen between Nos 6 and 8 exhaust ports. On later models it is stamped on the engine casing at the rear (photo).

Manual gearboxes have the serial number stamped on the left-hand side of the clutch housing.

Automatic transmissions have the number stamped on a plate attached to the left-hand side of the casing.

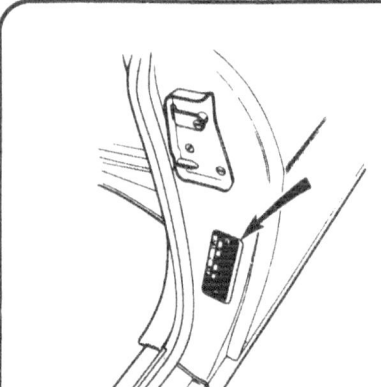
The vehicle identification plate is located on the left-hand door pillar on earlier cars

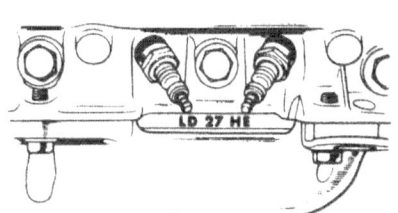
Location of engine number on earlier cars

Location of engine number on later cars

Tools and working facilities

Introduction

A selection of good tools is a fundamental requirement for anyone contemplating the maintenance and repair of a motor vehicle. For the owner who does not possess any, their purchase will prove a considerable expense, offsetting some of the savings made by doing-it-yourself. However, provided that the tools purchased meet the relevant national safety standards and are of good quality, they will last for many years and prove an extremely worthwhile investment.

To help the average owner to decide which tools are needed to carry out the various tasks detailed in this manual, we have compiled three lists of tools under the following headings: *Maintenance and minor repair, Repair and overhaul,* and *Special.* The newcomer to practical mechanics should start off with the *Maintenance and minor repair* tool kit and confine himself to the simpler jobs around the vehicle. Then, as his confidence and experience grows, he can undertake more difficult tasks, buying extra tools as, and when, they are needed. In this way, a *Maintenance and minor repair* tool kit can be built-up into a *Repair and overhaul* tool kit over a considerable period of time without any major cash outlays. The experienced do-it-yourselfer will have a tool kit good enough for most repair and overhaul procedures and will add tools from the *Special* category when he feels the expense is justified by the amount of use to which these tools will be put.

It is obviously not possible to cover the subject of tools fully here. For those who wish to learn more about tools and their use there is a book entitled *How to Choose and Use Car Tools* available from the publishers of this manual.

Maintenance and minor repair tool kit

The tools given in this list should be considered as a minimum requirement if routine maintenance, servicing and minor repair operations are to be undertaken. We recommend the purchase of combination spanners (ring one end, open-ended the other); although more expensive than open-ended ones, they do give the advantages of both types of spanner.

> Combination spanners - $\frac{7}{16}$ to $\frac{15}{16}$ in AF
> Adjustable spanner - 9 inch
> Engine sump/gearbox/rear axle drain plug key (where applicable)
> Spark plug spanner (with rubber insert)
> Spark plug gap adjustment tool
> Set of feeler gauges
> Brake adjuster spanner (where applicable)
> Brake bleed nipple spanner
> Screwdriver - 4 in long x $\frac{1}{4}$ in dia (flat blade)
> Screwdriver - 4 in long x $\frac{1}{4}$ in dia (cross blade)
> Combination pliers - 6 inch
> Hacksaw, junior
> Tyre pump
> Tyre pressure gauge
> Grease gun (where applicable)
> Oil can
> Fine emery cloth (1 sheet)
> Wire brush (small)
> Funnel (medium size)

Repair and overhaul tool kit

These tools are virtually essential for anyone undertaking any major repairs to a motor vehicle, and are additional to those given in the *Maintenance and minor repair* list. Included in this list is a comprehensive set of sockets. Although these are expensive they will be found invaluable as they are so versatile - particularly if various drives are included in the set. We recommend the $\frac{1}{2}$ in square-drive type, as this can be used with most proprietary torque wrenches. If you cannot afford a socket set, even bought piecemeal, then inexpensive tubular box spanners are a useful alternative.

The tools in this list will occasionally need to be supplemented by tools from the *Special* list.

> Sockets (or box spanners) to cover range in previous list
> Reversible ratchet drive (for use with sockets)
> Extension piece, 10 inch (for use with sockets)
> Universal joint (for use with sockets)
> Torque wrench (for use with sockets)
> 'Mole' wrench - 8 inch
> Ball pein hammer
> Soft-faced hammer, plastic or rubber
> Screwdriver - 6 in long x $\frac{5}{16}$ in dia (flat blade)
> Screwdriver - 2 in long x $\frac{5}{16}$ in square (flat blade)
> Screwdriver - 1$\frac{1}{2}$ in long x $\frac{1}{4}$ in dia (cross blade)
> Screwdriver - 3 in long x $\frac{1}{8}$ in dia (electricians)
> Pliers - electricians side cutters
> Pliers - needle nosed
> Pliers - circlip (internal and external)
> Cold chisel - $\frac{1}{2}$ inch
> Scriber (this can be made by grinding the end of a broken hacksaw blade)
> Scraper (this can be made by flattening and sharpening one end of a piece of copper pipe)
> Centre punch
> Pin punch
> Hacksaw
> Valve grinding tool
> Steel rule/straight edge
> Allen keys
> Selection of files
> Wire brush (large)
> Axle-stands
> Jack (strong scissor or hydraulic type)

Special tools

The tools in this list are those which are not used regularly, are expensive to buy, or which need to be used in accordance with their manufacturers' instructions. Unless relatively difficult mechanical jobs are undertaken frequently, it will not be economic to buy many of these tools. Where this is the case, you could consider clubbing together with friends (or a motorists' club) to make a joint purchase, or borrowing the tools against a deposit from a local garage or tool hire specialist.

The following list contains only those tools and instruments freely available to the public, and not those special tools produced by the vehicle manufacturer specifically for its dealer network. You will find occasional references to these manufacturers' special tools in the text of this manual. Generally, an alternative method of doing the job without the vehicle manufacturer's special tool is given. However, sometimes, there is no alternative to using them. Where this is the case and the relevant tool cannot be bought or borrowed you will have to entrust the work to a franchised garage

Valve spring compressor
Piston ring compressor
Balljoint separator
Universal hub/bearing puller
Impact screwdriver
Micrometer and/or vernier gauge
Carburettor flow balancing device (where applicable)
Dial gauge
Stroboscopic timing light
Dwell angle meter/tachometer
Universal electrical multi-meter
Cylinder compression gauge
Lifting tackle
Trolley jack
Light with extension lead

Buying tools

For practically all tools, a tool factor is the best source since he will have a very comprehensive range compared with the average garage or accessory shop. Having said that, accessory shops often offer excellent quality tools at discount prices, so it pays to shop around.

There are plenty of good tools around at reasonable prices, but always aim to purchase items which meet the relevant national safety standards. If in doubt, ask the proprietor or manager of the shop for advice before making a purchase.

Care and maintenance of tools

Having purchased a reasonable tool kit, it is necessary to keep the tools in a clean serviceable condition. After use, always wipe off any dirt, grease and metal particles using a clean, dry cloth, before putting the tools away. Never leave them lying around after they have been used. A simple tool rack on the garage or workshop wall, for items such as screwdrivers and pliers is a good idea. Store all normal spanners and sockets in a metal box. Any measuring instruments, gauges, meters, etc, must be carefully stored where they cannot be damaged or become rusty.

Take a little care when tools are used. Hammer heads inevitably become marked and screwdrivers lose the keen edge on their blades fom time to time. A little timely attention with emery cloth or a file will soon restore items like this to a good serviceable finish.

Working facilities

Not to be forgotten when discussing tools, is the workshop itself. If anything more than routine maintenance is to be carried out, some form of suitable working area becomes essential.

It is appreciated that many an owner mechanic is forced by circumstances to remove an engine or similar item, without the benefit of a garage or workshop. Having done this, any repairs should always be done under the cover of a roof.

Wherever possible, any dismantling should be done on a clean flat workbench or table at a suitable working height.

Any workbench needs a vice: one with a jaw opening of 4 in (100 mm) is suitable for most jobs. As mentioned previously, some clean dry storage space is also required for tools, as well as the lubricants, cleaning fluids, touch-up paints and so on which become necessary.

Another item which may be required, and which has a much more general usage, is an electric drill with a chuck capacity of at least $\frac{5}{16}$ in (8 mm). This, together with a good range of twist drills, is virtually essential for fitting accessories such as wing mirrors and reversing lights.

Last, but not least, always keep a supply of old newspapers and clean, lint-free rags available, and try to keep any working area as clean as possible.

Spanner jaw gap comparison table

Jaw gap (in)	Spanner size
0·250	$\frac{1}{4}$ in AF
0·275	7 mm AF
0·312	$\frac{5}{16}$ in AF
0·315	8 mm AF
0·340	$\frac{11}{32}$ in AF; $\frac{1}{8}$ in Whitworth
0·354	9 mm AF
0·375	$\frac{3}{8}$ in AF
0·393	10 mm AF
0·433	11 mm AF
0·437	$\frac{7}{16}$ in AF
0·445	$\frac{3}{16}$ in Whitworth; $\frac{1}{4}$ in BSF
0·472	12 mm AF
0·500	$\frac{1}{2}$ in AF
0·512	13 mm AF
0·525	$\frac{1}{4}$ in Whitworth; $\frac{5}{16}$ in BSF
0·551	14 mm AF
0·562	$\frac{9}{16}$ in AF
0·590	15 mm AF
0·600	$\frac{5}{16}$ in Whitworth; $\frac{3}{8}$ in BSF
0·625	$\frac{5}{8}$ in AF
0·629	16 mm AF
0·669	17 mm AF
0·687	$\frac{11}{16}$ in AF
0·708	18 mm AF
0·710	$\frac{3}{8}$ in Whitworth; $\frac{7}{16}$ in BSF
0·748	19 mm AF
0·750	$\frac{3}{4}$ in AF
0·812	$\frac{13}{16}$ in AF
0·820	$\frac{7}{16}$ in Whitworth; $\frac{1}{2}$ in BSF
0·866	22 mm AF
0·875	$\frac{7}{8}$ in AF
0·920	$\frac{1}{2}$ in Whitworth; $\frac{9}{16}$ in BSF
0·937	$\frac{15}{16}$ in AF
0·944	24 mm AF
1·000	1 in AF
1·010	$\frac{9}{16}$ in Whitworth; $\frac{5}{8}$ in BSF
1·023	26 mm AF
1·062	$1\frac{1}{16}$ in AF; 27 mm AF
1·100	$\frac{5}{8}$ in Whitworth; $\frac{11}{16}$ in BSF
1·125	$1\frac{1}{8}$ in AF
1·181	30 mm AF
1·200	$\frac{11}{16}$ in Whitworth; $\frac{3}{4}$ in BSF
1·250	$1\frac{1}{4}$ in AF
1·259	32 mm AF
1·300	$\frac{3}{4}$ in Whitworth; $\frac{7}{8}$ in BSF
1·312	$1\frac{5}{16}$ in AF
1·390	$\frac{13}{16}$ in Whitworth; $\frac{15}{16}$ in BSF
1·417	36 mm AF
1·437	$1\frac{7}{16}$ in AF
1·480	$\frac{7}{8}$ in Whitworth; 1 in BSF
1·500	$1\frac{1}{2}$ in AF
1·574	40 mm AF; $\frac{15}{16}$ in Whitworth
1·614	41 mm AF
1·625	$1\frac{5}{8}$ in AF
1·670	1 in Whitworth; $1\frac{1}{8}$ in BSF
1·687	$1\frac{11}{16}$ in AF
1·811	46 mm AF
1·812	$1\frac{13}{16}$ in AF
1·860	$1\frac{1}{8}$ in Whitworth; $1\frac{1}{4}$ in BSF
1·875	$1\frac{7}{8}$ in AF
1·968	50 mm AF
2·000	2 in AF
2·050	$1\frac{1}{4}$ in Whitworth; $1\frac{3}{8}$ in BSF
2·165	55 mm AF
2·362	60 mm AF

General dimensions, weight and capacities

Dimensions
Length	14 ft 5·75 in (4420 mm)
Width	5 ft 3·5 in (1612 mm)
Height (unladen)	4 ft 1·5 in (1258 mm)
Wheelbase	8 ft 4·0 in (2540 mm)

Weight (kerb)
Basic	2756 lbs (1250 kgs)
With optional extras	2826 lbs (1282 kgs)

Capacities
Fuel tank:	
1973 models on and 1972 left-hand drive models	12·75 gals (58·0 litres)
All other models	14·0 gals (63·5 litres)
Engine sump	8 pints (4·5 litres)
Manual gearbox	2·8 pints (1·6 litres)
with A type overdrive	3·75 pints (2·13 litres)
with J type overdrive	3·5 pints (2·0 litres)
Automatic transmission (with oil cooler):	
Type 35	14·25 pints (8·0 litres)
Type 65	9·5 pints (5·4 litres)
Rear axle	2·0 pints (1·13 litres)
Power steering reservoir	1·25 pints (0·7 litres)
Cooling system (with heater)	18·5 pints (10·5 litres)

Jacking and towing

Jacking
Two jacking points are provided under each body sill on both sides of the vehicle. These are for use with the jack supplied with the vehicle and should normally only be used for wheel changing in an emergency. When carrying out repairs, jack-up the vehicle under the rear axle or front suspension crossmember and then place addition axle-stands under the bodyframe sidemembers.

Towing
If, due to a mechanical breakdown, it is necessary for your vehicle to be towed, attach the tow rope by passing it through the aperture at the back of the bumper bracket.

If the vehicle is equipped with automatic transmission, do not exceed a towing distance of 20 miles (32 km) or at a speed greater than 30 mph (48 kph). If these conditions cannot be complied with, then disconnect or remove the propeller shaft. It is not recommended that any other vehicle is towed unless an approved towing kit has already been installed for regular caravan or trailer towing purposes.

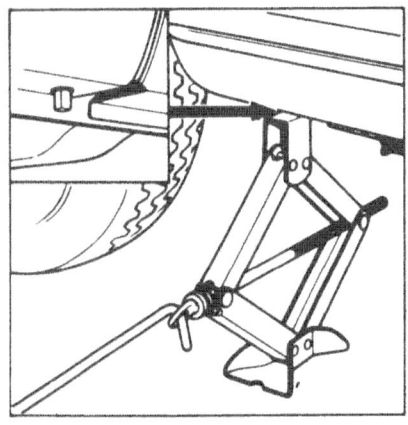

Jacking point

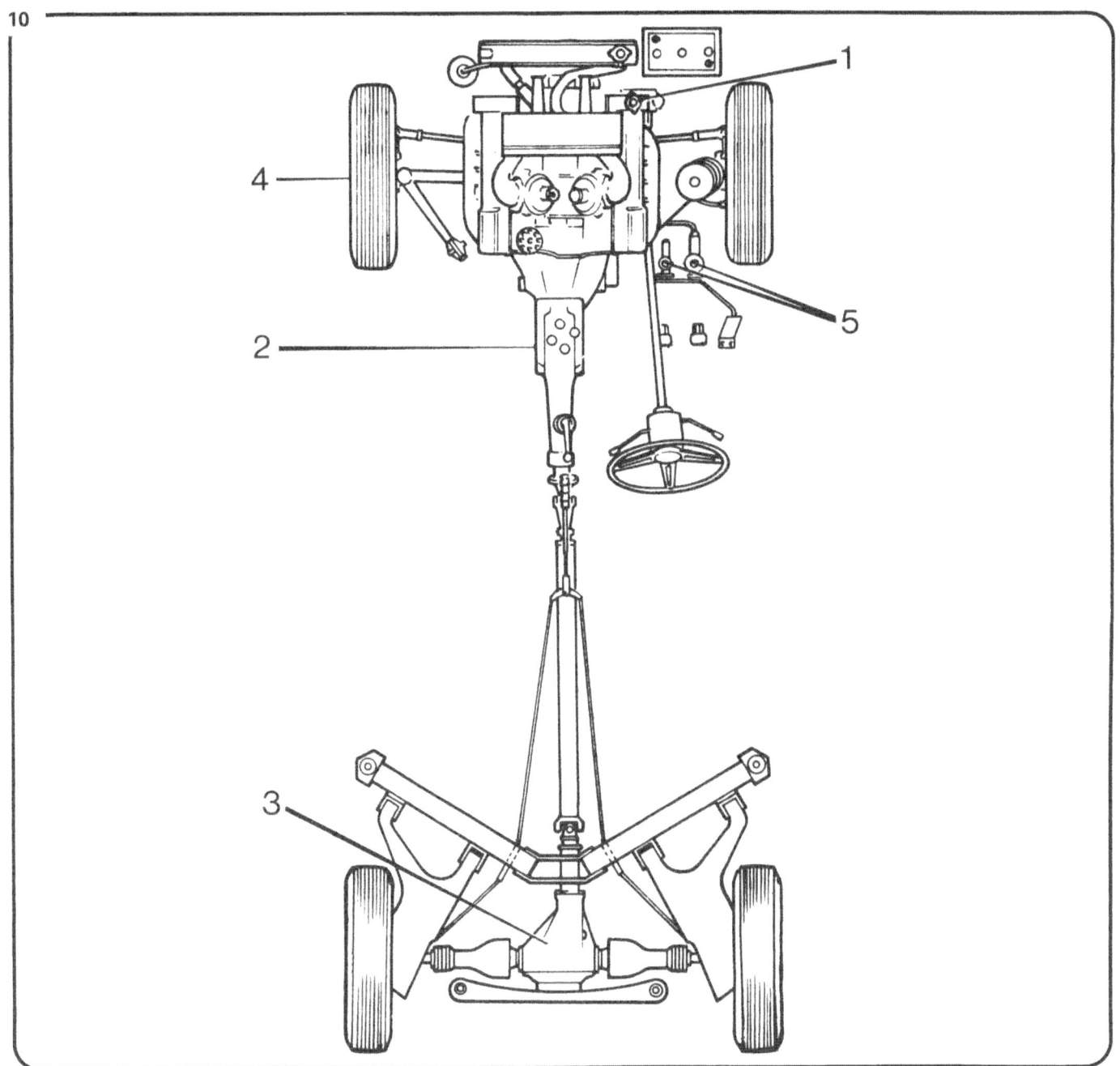

Recommended lubricants

Component	Castrol product
Engine (1)	Castrol GTX
Gearbox and overdrive (2)	Castrol Hypoy
Automatic transmission (2)	Castrol TQF
Rear axle (3)	Castrol Hypoy
Front wheel bearings (4)	Castrol LM Grease
Clutch and brake fluid (5)	Castrol Girling Universal Brake and Clutch Fluid
Power steering fluid	Castrol TQF

The above are general recommendations only. Different operating conditions require different lubricants. If in doubt, consult the Driver's Handbook supplied with your car, or your nearest Leyland dealer.

Routine maintenance

Maintenance is essential for ensuring safety and desirable for the purpose of getting the best in terms of performance and economy from your car. Over the years the need for periodic lubrication – oiling, greasing, and so on – has been drastically reduced if not totally eliminated. This has unfortunately tended to lead some owners to think that because no such action is required, components either no longer exist, or will last for ever. This is a serious delusion. It follows therefore that the largest initial element of maintenance is visual examination. This may lead to repairs or renewals.

Every 250 miles (400 km) or weekly

Check the tyre pressures
Check the tyres for wear or damage
Check the brake fluid level
Check all the lights
Check the windscreen wipers
Check the windscreen washer fluid lever
Check the engine oil level
Check the coolant level
Check the battery electrolyte level

Remove the cap (1) and check the brake fluid level

Checking the windscreen washer fluid level

Checking the engine oil level

Topping-up with engine oil

Topping-up the battery

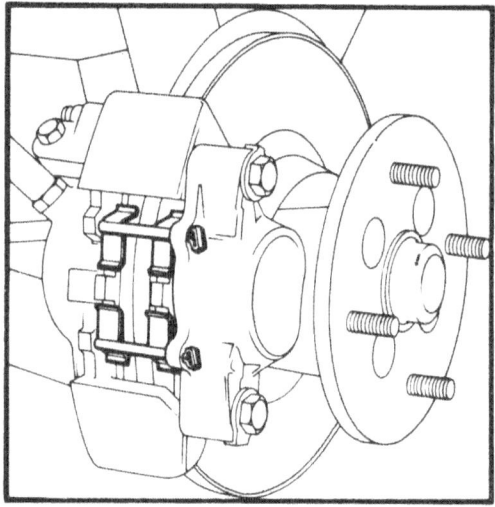

Check the front brake disc pads for wear

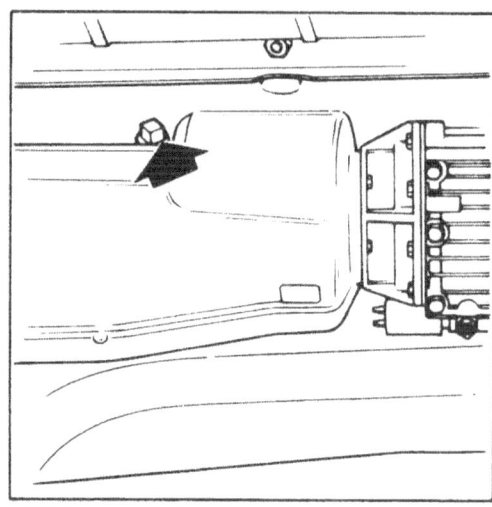

Manual gearbox filler/level plug

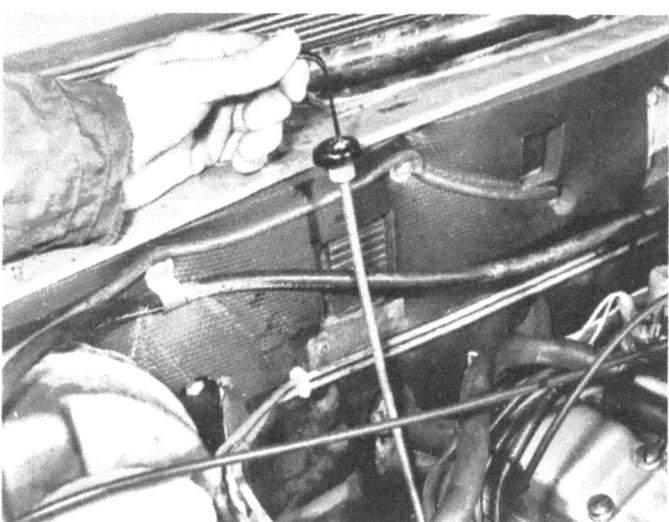

Check the automatic transmission fluid level

Topping-up the automatic transmission

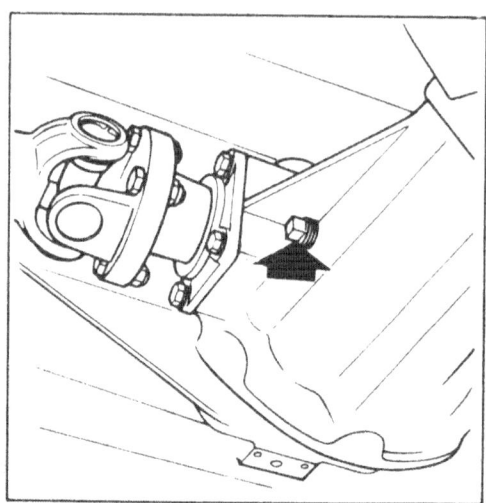

Rear axle differential filler/level plug

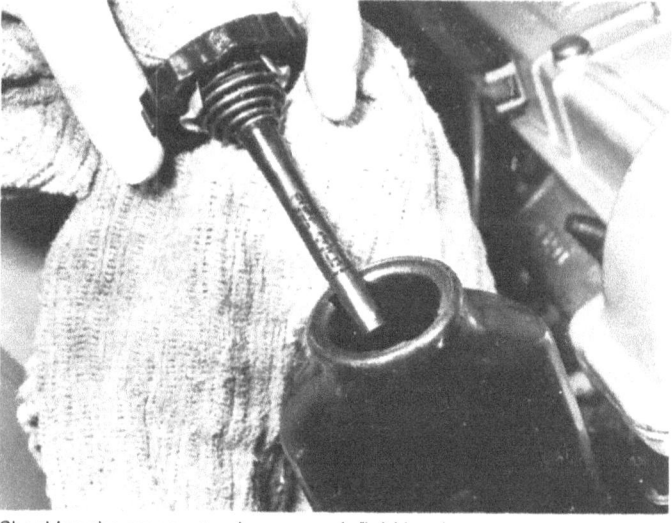

Checking the power steering reservoir fluid level

Every 3000 miles (5000 kms)

Check the tension of the drivebelts
Check the disc brake pad wear
Check the rear drum brake shoe lining wear
Check the level of the clutch fluid
Check the transmission oil level
Check the differential oil level
Check the power steering fluid level
Check the steering and suspension components for wear
Check the brake lines and hoses for damage
Check the condition of the seat belts
Check the exhaust system for leaks

Every 6000 miles (10 000 kms)

Top-up the carburettor dampers
Inspect the distributor points and renew, if necessary
Check the ignition timing
Check and adjust, if necessary, the carburettor idle speed
Clean and adjust the spark plugs
Renew the engine oil and filter
Grease the steering rack and pinion
Lubricate the handbrake components
Lubricate all body moving parts (door hinges, locks etc)

Every 12 000 miles (20 000 kms)

Clean the distributor cap and check for cracks and tracking
Renew the spark plugs
Check valve clearances
Renew the air cleaner element
Check the air intake temperature control system
Renew the fuel filters
Renew the carbon canister filter (early models only) in the evaporative control system
Check propeller shaft and axleshaft coupling bolts
Adjust the front hubs
Check oil level in air conditioning compressor (if fitted)

Every 50 000 miles (80 000 kms)

Drain the brake hydraulic system, renew all system seals and refill with fresh fluid.
Renew the evaporative control system carbon canister (later models)

Every 2 years

Drain and flush the cooling system and refill with antifreeze solution

Topping-up the power steering system

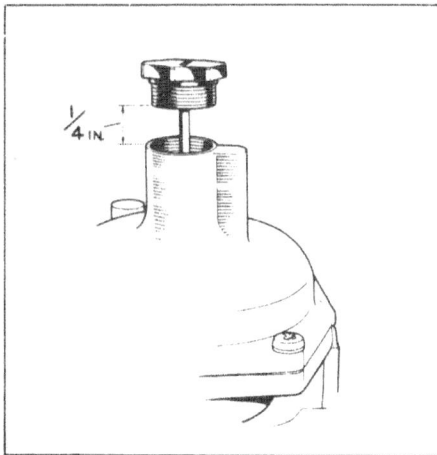

Check the damper oil level. When resistance is felt with the plug $\frac{1}{4}$ in (6 mm) above the dashpot the level is correct

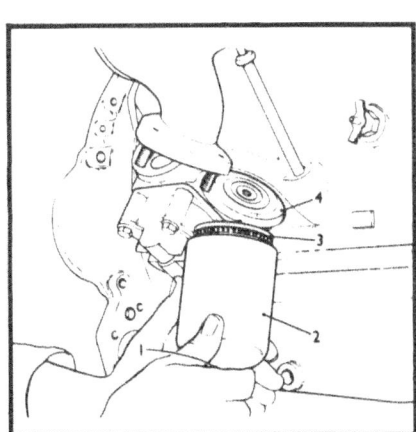

Renewing the oil filter element

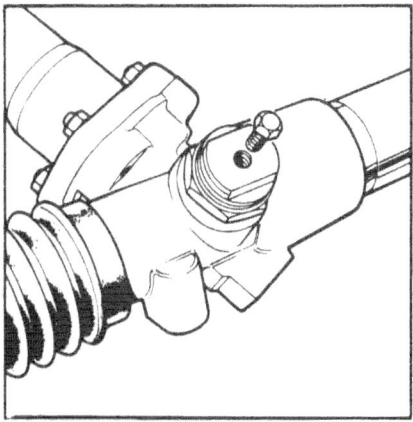

Lubricate the steering unit. Remove the sealing plug and fit a grease nipple

Chapter 1 Engine

Contents

Specifications

Type	90° V8, overhead camshafts
Bore	3.385 in (86 mm)
Stroke	2.539 in (64.5 mm)
Capacity	2997 cc

Compression ratio

Pre 1973 models	8.8 : 1
1973 on models	9.25 : 1

Firing order	See Chapter 4
No 1 cylinder location	RH bank-front

Valves

Clearance:

Inlet	0.008 to 0.010 in (0.15 to 0.20 mm)
Exhaust	0.016 to 0.018 in (0.41 to 0.46 mm)

Jackshaft

Journal diameter	1.5907 to 1.5912 in (36.982 to 36.995 mm)

Camshafts

Journal diameter	1.230 to 1.235 in (31.242 to 31.369 mm)

Connecting rods

Endfloat on crank	0.015 to 0.024 in (0.38 to 0.61 mm)
Small-end bush inside diameter	0.8572 to 0.8755 in (22.230 to 22.238 mm)

Pistons and piston rings

Diameter of top land	3.3630 to 3.3650 in (85.42 to 85.47 mm)
Cylinder bore	3.3853 to 3.3864 in (85.99 to 86.01 mm)
Grade F (grades are stamped on piston crown and cylinder block)	
Cylinder bore	3.3853 to 3.3858 in (85.99 to 86.00 mm)
Skirt diameter	3.3828 to 3.3833 in (85.92 to 95.94 mm)
Grade G (grades are stamped on piston crown and cylinder block)	
Cylinder bore	3.3859 to 3.3864 in (86.00 to 86.01 mm)
Skirt diameter	3.3834 to 3.3839 in (85.94 to 85.95 mm)
Number of rings	3
Ring groove width:	
Top	0.0812 to 0.0802 in (2.06 to 2.03 mm)
2nd	0.1196 to 0.1206 in (3.04 to 3.06 mm)
Oil control	0.157 to 0.158 in (3.99 to 4.01 mm)
Piston ring width:	
Top compression ring	0.0777 to 0.0787 in (1.97 to 2.00 mm)
2nd compression ring	0.1171 to 0.1181 in (2.97 to 3.00 mm)
Piston ring gap:	
Top compression ring	0.013 to 0.018 in (0.33 to 0.46 mm)
2nd compression ring	0.010 to 0.015 in (0.25 to 0.38 mm)
Oil control ring	
2 outer rings	0.015 to 0.055 in (0.38 to 1.40 mm)
3-part ring	Spring centre to butt
Gudgeon pins	
Length	2.915 to 2.920 in (74.04 to 74.17 mm)
Diameter	0.8749 to 0.8751 in (22.22 to 22.23 mm)

Crankshaft

Journal diameter	2.1260 to 2.1265 in (54.00 to 54.01 mm)
Crankpin diameter	1.750 to 1.7505 in (44.45 to 44.46 mm)
Maximum regrind – undersize	0.030 in (0.762 mm)
Maximum ovality and taper	0.002 in (0.05 mm)
Main and big-end bearings – undersize	−0.010, −0.020, −0.030 in (−0.25, −0.50, −0.76mm)
Crankshaft endfloat	0.003 to 0.011 in (0.07 to 0.28 mm)
Endfloat adjustment	Selective thrust washers on centre main bearing

Oil pump

Rotors endfloat (max)	0.004 in (0.1 mm)
Clearance between rotors (max)	0.010 in (0.25 mm)
Clearance between outer rotor and body (max)	0.008 in (0.2 mm)
Oil capacity	
Refill with new oil filter	9 pints (5.1 litre)
Refill without filter change	8 pints (4.5 litre)

Torque wrench settings

	lbf ft	kgf m
Alternator to timing cover	22	3.0
Alternator adjusting link	22	3.0
Camshaft bearing cap	14	1.9
Carburettor pedestal attachment	32	4.4
Sprocket to camshaft	10	1.4
Sprocket to jackshaft	38	5.2
Clutch to flywheel	22	3.0
Connecting rod bolt	45	6.2
Crankshaft pulley centre bolt	120	16.6
Cylinder head to block	55	7.6
Engine mounting bracket to block	22	3.0
Exhaust manifold attachment:		
Outer 4 sets	22	3.0
Inner 3 sets	34	4.7
Fan to hub unit	14	1.9
Flywheel to crankshaft	45	6.2
Jackshaft retaining plate	22	3.0
Inlet manifold attachment	20	2.8
Lifting eye to cylinder head	20	2.8
Main bearing caps to block	65	9.0
Oil filter to block	20	2.8
Oil pressure switch	7	1.0
Oil pump to block	22	3.0
Oil sump drain plug	25	3.5
Oil sump to block	20	2.8
Spark plugs	20	2.8
Timing cover attachment	20	2.8
Timing chain tensioner to block	10	1.4
Timing chain guides to block	20	2.8
Water pump cover	20	2.8

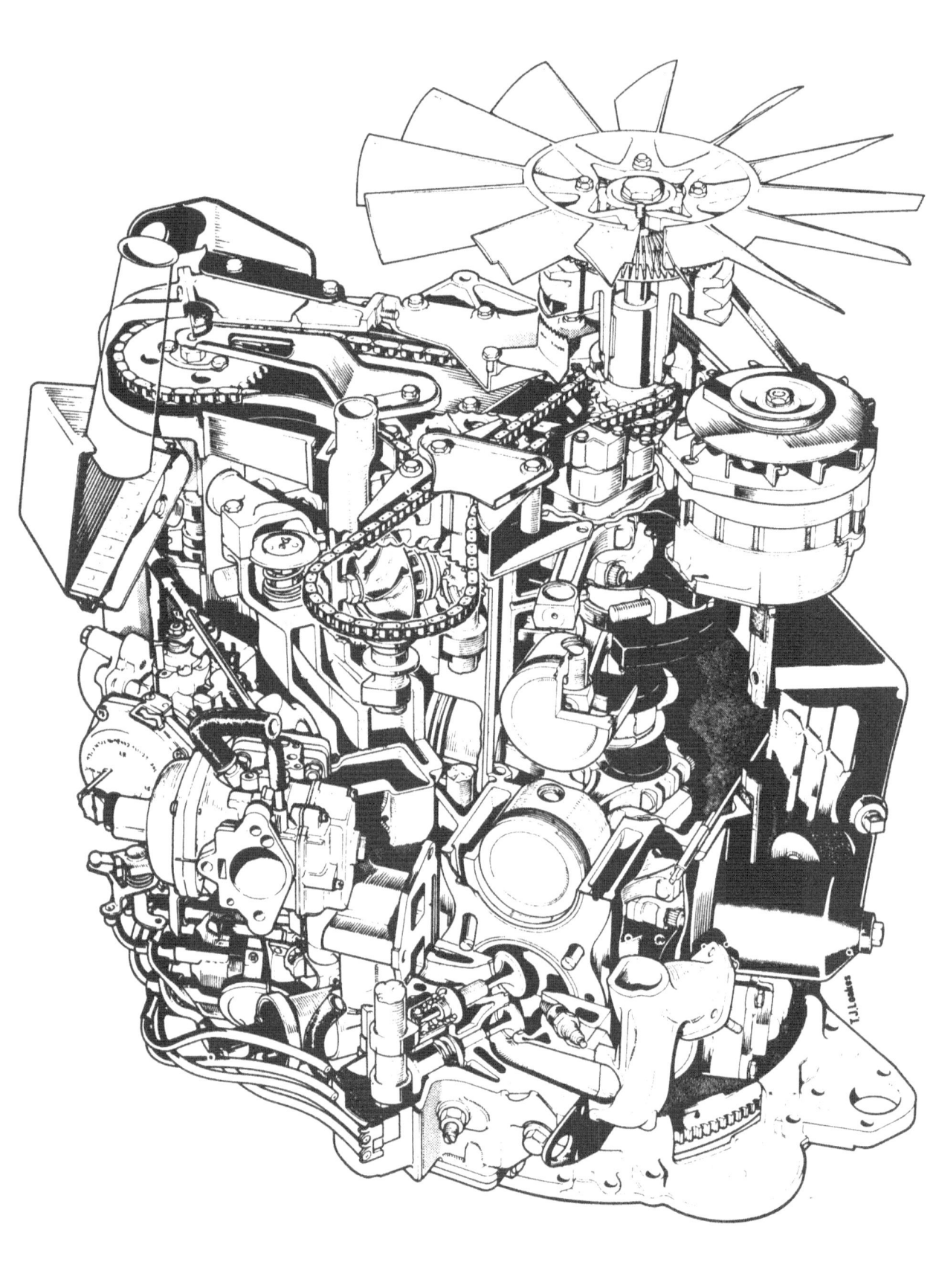

Fig. 1.1 Sectional view of the engine (Sec 1)

1 General description

The engine is a 3 litre, 90° V8 overhead cam type. The cylinder banks and crankcase are of cast iron and the cylinder heads are aluminium alloy and are of the crossflow type. The bottom half of the crankcase consists of a pressed steel sump. The forged steel crankshaft is supported in five renewable shell type main bearings.

The pistons are made from anodised aluminium. Two compression rings and a slotted oil control ring are fitted. The fully floating gudgeon pins are retained in the pistons by circlips. The connecting rods have renewable shell type big-end bearings.

At the front of the engine the two overhead camshafts are driven by separate timing chains, from the sprockets on the crankshaft. The left-hand chain also drives the jackshaft which is used to drive the water pump, distributor and oil pump.

The camshafts are supported directly in five bearings in the cylinder heads and operate the valves through bucket type tappets. Valve clearance adjustment is by means of steel pallets of different thickness.

The water pump is mounted centrally (at the front) between the cylinder banks and is driven by a skew gear on the jackshaft. The distributor, mounted on top of the crankcase at the rear, and the externally mounted oil pump are driven by a second skew gear on the jackshaft and a hexagon drive shaft.

Bolted to the rear end of the crankshaft is the flywheel to which is bolted the clutch assembly (manual transmission). On automatic transmission models a driveplate is bolted to the crankshaft.

The alternator and power steering pump are mounted on the right-hand side of the engine at the front and are driven by vee bolts from the crankshaft pulley.

2 Major operations possible with the engine fitted in the car

1   The following major operations can be carried out with the engine still in position in the car:

   (a) Removal and refitting of the camshaft
   (b) Removal and refitting of the cylinder heads
   (c) Removal and refitting of the jackshaft
   (d) Removal and refitting of the flywheel and the crankshaft rear oil seal (transmission must be removed)
   (e) Removal and refitting of the timing chains and sprockets
   *(f) Removal and refitting of the oil sump **
   *(g) Removal and refitting of the connecting rods and pistons **
* It will be necessary to remove the front crossmember for these operations.*

3 Methods of engine removal

The engine may be lifted out on its own after removal of the gearbox or in unit with the gearbox. It is recommended that the engine is lifted out on its own, unless a substantial crane or overhead hoist is available, because of the weight factor and also due to the fact that if the engine and gearbox are removed as a unit they have to be lifted out

at a very steep angle. It is also necessary to raise the front of the car (at least 18 inches) to ensure that there is sufficient ground clearance available.

4 Engine and gearbox assembly – removal

1   Assemble a selection of tools, rags and freeing fluid. It is essential to have a good hoist, axle-stands and a trolley jack available.
2   Open the bonnet and using a soft pencil mark the outline position of both hinges to act as a datum for refitting.
3   Remove the split pin retaining the bonnet stay (photo) and disconnect the stay. With the help of an assistant to take the weight of the bonnet, undo the bolts securing each hinge to the body, then lift off the bonnet and put it in a safe place where it will not get damaged.
4   Drain the cooling system as described in Chapter 2.
5   Place a container with a capacity of at least 8 pints (4.5 litres) under the engine sump and remove the oil drain plug. Allow the oil to drain out and then refit the plug (photo).
6   Slacken the clamp bolts and disconnect the cables from the battery terminals. Always remove the earth lead first and reconnect last. Remove the battery.
7   Remove the air cleaner assembly, refer to Chapter 3.
8   Undo the two securing clips and remove the top radiator hose, also the two clips securing the bottom radiator hose and remove it. Pull the overflow pipe off the connection on the radiator.
9   Undo the two bolts securing the radiator at the top, this releases the air intake duct which can now be lifted away (photo).
10 Remove the two nuts securing the radiator at the bottom and lift away the bottom fan guard which is also secured by these nuts.
11 Carefully lift out the radiator taking care not to damage the matrix on the fan blades.
12 Remove the centre bolt securing the crankshaft pulley and lift out the fan and Torquatrol unit. When unscrewing the centre bolt hold the pulley with a chain or strap wrench to prevent it from turning (photo).
13 Disconnect the hydraulic pipes from the power steering pump. Plug the ends of the pipes and open ports in the pump to prevent the ingress of dirt (photo).
14 Slacken the power steering pump mounting bracket to engine securing bolts and remove the pump drivebelt.
15 Remove the securing bolts and lift out the power steering pump and mounting bracket. Remove the bracket from the power steering pump and refit the bracket on the engine. This is necessary because the pump bracket incorporates the right-hand front lifting eye which is required when lifting out the engine.
16 Pull off the multi-connector and the two Lucar connectors at the rear of the alternator.
17 Slacken the alternator mounting bolts, take off the drivebelt then remove the earth strap from the alternator mounting bolt.
18 The crankshaft pulley can now be removed by sliding it off the front of the crankshaft (photo).
19 Disconnect the servo hose from the inlet manifold.
20 Undo the securing clips and pull the heater hoses from the heater connections at the bulkhead (photo).
21 Disconnect the throttle and choke cables from the carburettors. On automatic transmission modeis disconnect the downshift cable from the carburettor by removing the split pin securing the clevis pin in

4.3 Disconnect the stay from the bonnet

4.5 Oil sump drain plug

4.9 Lifting out the air intake duct

4.12 Hold the crankshaft pulley with a chain wrench and undo the centre bolt

4.13 Disconnect the hydraulic pipes from the power steering pump

4.18 Slide off the crankshaft pulley

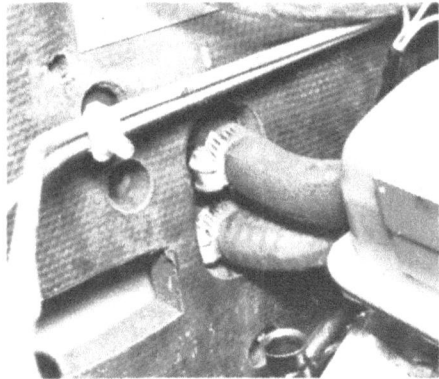

4.20 Disconnect the heater hoses at the bulkhead

4.21a Slacken the securing screw and then ...

4.21b ... pull out the throttle cable

4.21c Disconnecting the choke cable from the left-hand carburettor

4.21d Disconnect the downshift cable from the carburettors

4.31 Drain the gearbox (type 35 automatic transmission) by removing the filler/dipstick tube

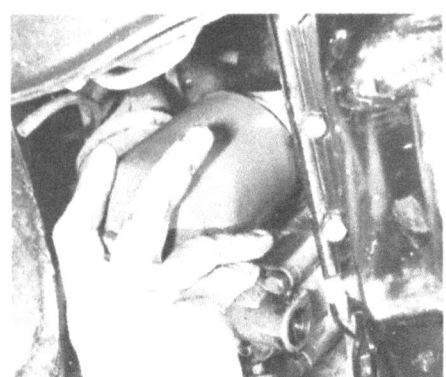

4.32 Removing the oil filter assembly

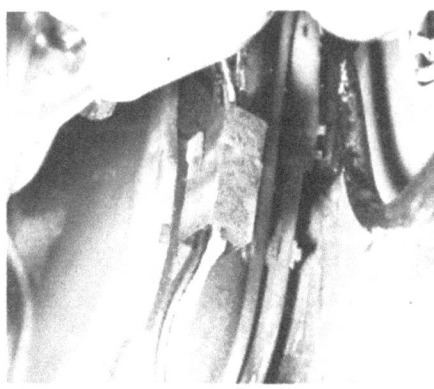

4.35 Gearbox wiring plug connector

4.36 Disconnect the wiring from the starter motor

the adjuster, then undo the nut securing the cable block to the carburettor (photos).

22 Remove the distributor cap, to avoid damage when removing the engine. Mark the spark plug leads so that they may be fitted in their original positions.

23 Detach the leads from the ignition coil and remove the two bolts securing the coil to the inlet manifold then lift away the coil. This will allow the downshift cable to be pulled clear of the engine (automatic transmission models).

24 Disconnect the fuel line from the fuel filter to the carburettor.

25 Disconnect the electrical leads from the water temperature switch by pulling off the Lucar connector.

26 Disconnect the oil pressure switch by pulling the Lucar connector from the terminal on the oil transfer adaptor on the right-hand side of the crankcase.

27 Disconnect the electrical lead from the windscreen washer and remove the reservoir and pump assembly by pulling it upwards from its mounting bracket.

28 Disconnect the ballast resistor.

29 Raise the front of the car at least 18 inches and support it on axle-stands or wooden blocks.

30 Drain the oil from the gearbox. On manual gearbox models, remove the drain plug, allow the oil to drain out into a suitable container and refit the drain plug. On automatic transmission models fitted with type 35 transmission, undo the filler/dipstick tube union and allow the oil to drain out. Cars fitted with type 65 transmission are provided with a drain plug.

31 Remove the bolt attaching the filler/dipstick tube (automatic transmission models) to the right-hand cylinder head and lift out the filler/dipstick tube (photo).

32 Undo the securing bolt and remove the oil filter assembly (photo).

33 Remove the three nuts securing the front exhaust pipes to the exhaust manifolds on each side of the engine. Slacken the clamp bracket nuts securing the intermediate pipes to the exhaust tail pipes. Undo the two bolts securing the front exhaust pipes to the gearbox mounting crossmember and remove the two front exhaust pipes, silencers and intermediate pipes. Note the gasket fitted between the manifold and front pipe flanges.

34 Remove the propeller shaft as described in Chapter 7.

35 Disconnect the electrical wiring to the gearbox at the plug connector on the left-hand side near the starter motor (photo).

36 Disconnect the battery cable and the two Lucar connectors from the starter motor (photo).

37 *Manual gearbox models:* Remove the clutch slave cylinder as described in Chapter 5, and the gearchange lever as described in Chapter 6.

38 *Automatic transmission models:* Disconnect the gear control rod by removing the spring retaining clips. Push the clips off the rod and then remove the control rod (photo). Disconnect the oil cooler pipes from the transmission and remove the rigid pipe by disconnecting it from the flexible hose (photos).

39 Disconnect the speedometer cable by removing the clamp plate securing bolt and then withdrawing the cable (photo). Collect the spacer. On cars fitted with overdrive the cable is attached by a knurled nut.

40 Position a trolley jack under the gearbox crossmember mounting and take the weight of the gearbox and engine assembly.

41 Sling the engine by the two front lifting eyes and just take the weight on the hoist (photo).

42 Remove the front engine mounting bolts, two each side (photo).

43 Remove the four nuts securing the gearbox mounting crossmember to the body, lower the gearbox slightly and collect the rubber washers, plain washers, nylon spacers and steel sleeves (photo).

44 Raise the engine at the front so that the engine sump will clear the front crossmember. It is advisable to free the brake pipe clips from the front crossmember and pull the brake pipe down so that the pipe will not get trapped between the sump and the crossmember.

45 Check that all electric wiring, cables and pipes have been disconnected from the engine/gearbox assembly and are tucked well of the way where they will not get caught up as the unit is lifted out of the engine compartment.

46 The complete unit can now be removed from the car. Carefully ease the assembly forward while at the same time raising the engine at the front and having an assistant lowering the trolley jack at the rear

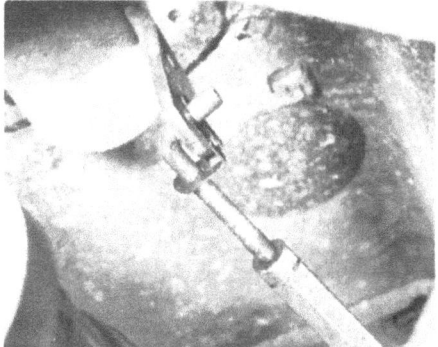
4.38a Remove the retaining clip and disconnect the gear control rod (automatic transmission)

4.38b Disconnect the oil cooler pipes and ...

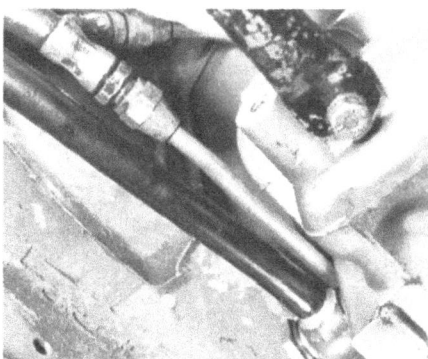
4.38c ... then remove the rigid pipe (automatic transmission)

4.39 Remove the speedometer cable clamp plate bolt and withdraw the cable

4.41 Sling the engine by the two front lifting eyes

4.42 Remove the front engine mounting bolts ...

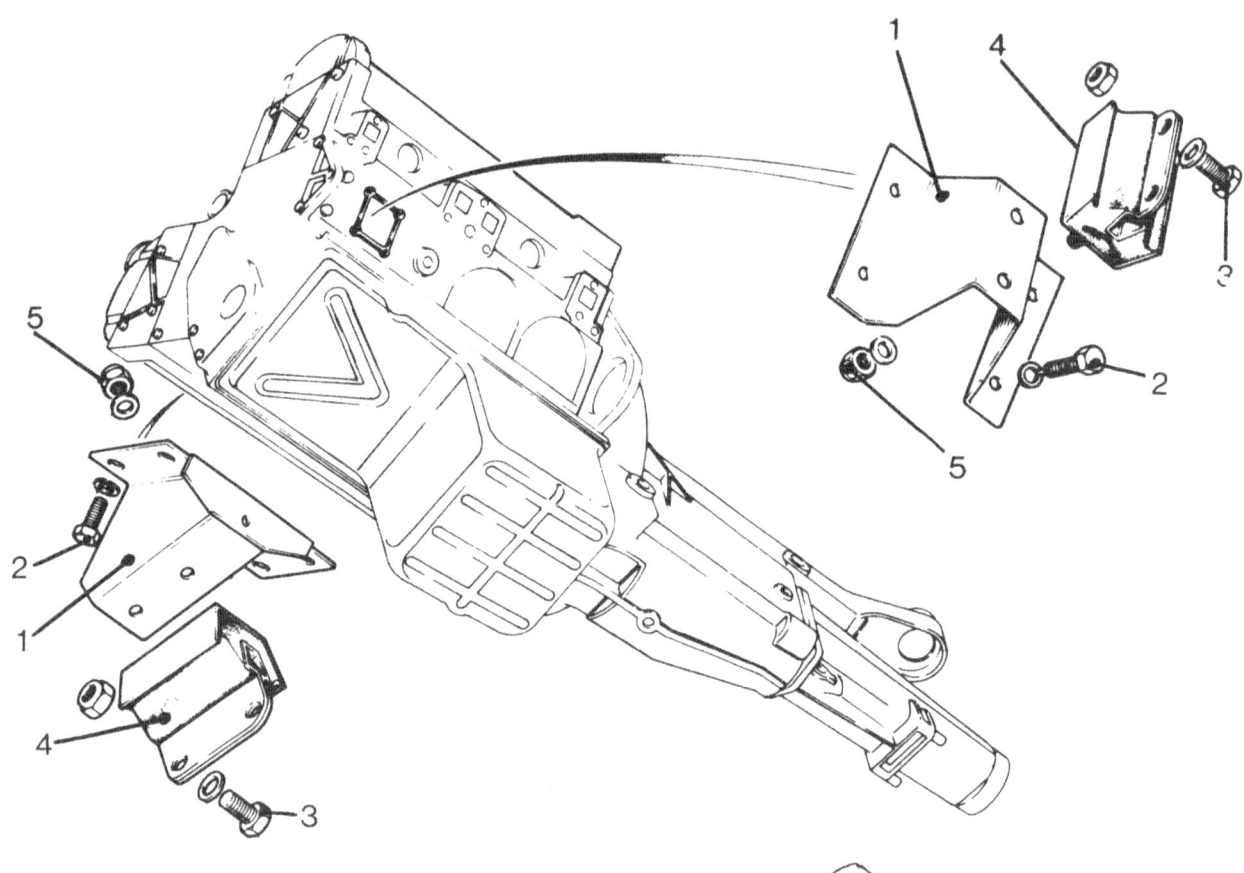

Fig. 1.2 Front engine mountings (Sec 4)

1 Bracket
2 Bracket to engine bolt
3 Engine to mounting bolt
4 Engine mounting
5 Mounting to bracket securing nut

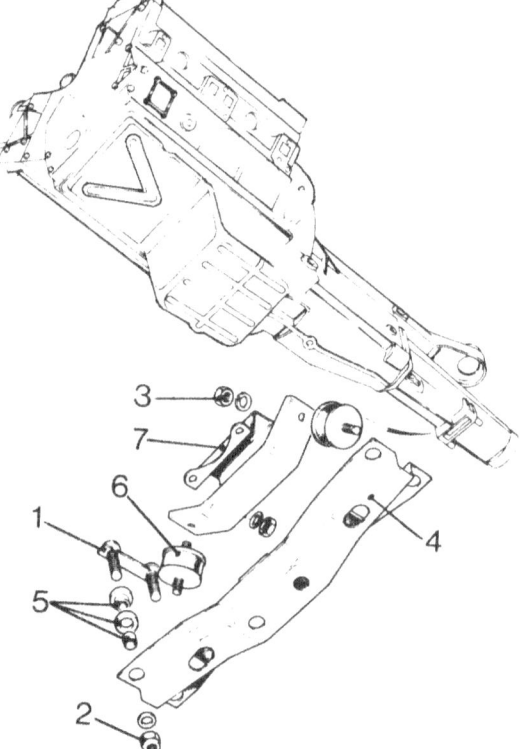

Fig. 1.3 Gearbox mounting crossmember (Sec 4)

1 Attaching bolts (in pairs)	5 Rubber washer, steel sleeve and nylon spacer
2 Nut	6 Flexible mountings
3 Nut	7 Mounting bracket
4 Crossmember	

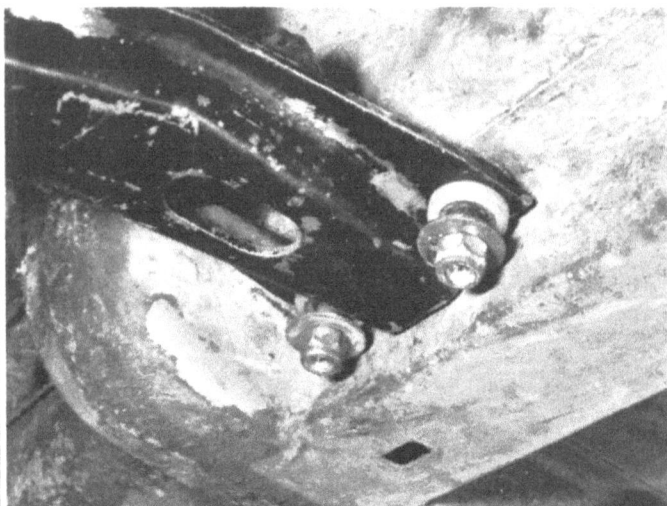

4.43 ... and the gearbox mounting crossmember to body bolts

of the gearbox. Proceed in this manner until the engine and gearbox assembly are suspended almost vertically in the engine compartment (photo).

47 Continue raising the assembly until it can be pulled clear of the car. Unless the hoist has a very high lift it will be necessary to manhandle the assembly over the front of the car. Make sure the front panel is well protected from any possible damage.

48 The gearbox can now be separated from the engine. Undo and remove the starter motor attaching bolts and lift away the starter motor. Undo and remove the bellhousing to engine bolts and on later models, the two gearbox anti-vibration straps. When separating the gearbox from the engine do not allow the weight of the gearbox to hang on the input shaft (first motion shaft) (photos).

49 On cars equipped with automatic transmission remove the torque converter to driveplate bolts, accessible working through the starter motor mounting aperture (photo).

5 Engine – removal as a separate unit

If the lifting equipment available is not suitable for removing the engine and gearbox as an assembly the engine can be removed on its own, but only after removal of the gearbox as described in Chapter 6, Section 2 or 28 as applicable. The remainder of the removal procedure is similar to that described in Section 4.

6 Dismantling the engine – general

1 It is best to mount the engine on a dismantling stand, but if one is not available, then stand the engine on a strong bench at a comfortable working height. Failing this, the engine can be stripped down on the floor.

2 During the dismantling process the greatest care should be taken to keep the exposed parts free from dirt. As an aid to achieving this, it is sound advice to thoroughly clean down the outside of the engine, removing all traces of oil and congealed dirt.

3 Use paraffin or a good grease solvent. The latter compound will make the job much easier, as, after the solvent has been applied and allowed to stand for a time, a vigorous jet of water will wash off all the solvent and the grease and filth. If the dirt is thick and deeply embedded, work the solvent into it with a stiff brush.

4 Finally, wipe down the exterior of the engine with a rag and only then, when it is quite clean, should the dismantling process begin. As the engine is stripped, clean each part in a bath of paraffin or petrol.

5 Never immerse parts with oilways in paraffin, ie. the crankshaft, but to clean, wipe down carefully with a petrol dampened rag. Oilways can be cleaned out with wire. If an air line is available all parts can be blown dry and the oilways blown through as an added precaution.

6 Re-use of old engine gaskets is a false economy and can give rise to oil and water leaks, if nothing worse. To avoid the possibility of

4.46 Raise the engine carefully so that it is almost vertical

4.48a Lifting away the starter motor

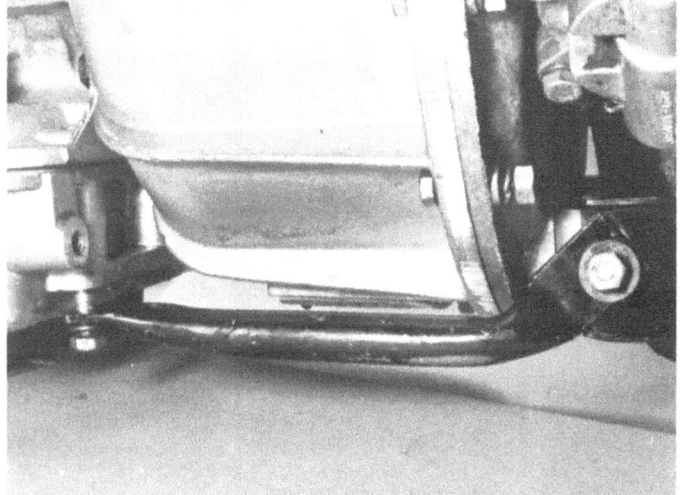

4.48b Separating the gearbox from the engine. The anti-vibration straps are not fitted on early models

4.49 Remove the torque converter to drive plate bolts (automatic transmission)

trouble after the engine has been reassembled always use new gaskets throughout.

7   Do not throw the old gaskets away as it sometimes happens that an immediate replacement cannot be found, and the old gasket is then very useful as a template. Hang up the old gaskets, as they are removed, on a suitable hook or nail.

8   To strip the engine it is best to work from the top downwards. The sump provides a firm base on which the engine can be supported in an upright position. When the stage where the sump must be removed is reached, the engine can be turned on its side and all other work carried out with it in this position.

9   Wherever possible, refit nuts, bolts and washers finger tight from where they were removed. This helps avoid later loss and muddle. If they cannot be refitted then lay them out in such a fashion that it is clear where they came from.

7   Cylinder heads – removal with engine in situ

1   Remove the bonnet as described in Chapter 12.
2   Drain the cooling system as described in Chapter 2.
3   Disconnect the earth strap from the battery negative terminal.
4   Remove the air cleaner assembly as described in Chapter 3.
5   Disconnect the throttle and choke cables from the carburettor, also the downshift cable on cars fitted with automatic transmission.
6   Mark the HT leads, so that they can be refitted in their original positions, and detach them from the spark plugs and the clips on the camshaft covers.
7   Release the clips securing the distributor cap to the distributor body and lift off the cap and HT leads. Detach the HT lead from the centre of the ignition coil and remove the distributor cap and leads from the engine compartment.
8   Disconnect the engine breather pipe from the right-hand camshaft cover and the vacuum advance pipe and union from the carburettor. The union has to be removed to provide access to the nut securing the carburettor pedestal to the inlet manifold.
9   Disconnect the fuel line from the fuel filter on the left-hand wing valance and the clip on the left-hand camshaft cover.
10   Pull the Lucar connectors from the temperature switch on the water transfer housing at the rear of the left-hand cylinder head.
11   Disconnect the lead from the windscreen washer pump and remove the windscreen washer pump and reservoir assembly by pulling it upwards from its mounting bracket on the right-hand wing valance.
12   Disconnect the leads from the ignition coil, undo the two bolts securing the coil to the inlet manifold and remove the coil. This is necessary to provide access to the inlet manifold bolt located under the coil.
13   Disconnect the heater hose from the rear of the left-hand cylinder head.
14   Remove the centre nut securing the carburettor pedestal to the inlet manifold and lift off the carburettors.
15   On cars with automatic transmission remove the bolt that secures the transmission filler/dipstick tube to the right-hand cylinder head.
16   If the car is not over a pit or on a ramp, jack-up the front of the car and support it on axle-stands or other suitable supports.
17   Undo the oil filter securing bolt and remove the oil filter assembly.
18   Undo the three nuts securing the front exhaust pipes to the exhaust manifold flanges on each side, pull the pipes clear of the manifolds and collect the gaskets.
19   Remove the three bolts securing the power steering mounting bracket to the left-hand cylinder head, take off the drivebelt and position the pump and bracket on the wheel arch. It is not necessary to disconnect the hydraulic pipes from the steering pump.
20   Remove the engine oil dipstick.
21   Remove the nuts securing the camshaft covers and lift off the covers.
22   Using a wrench on the crankshaft pulley securing bolt, turn the engine until the line marked on the camshaft flange is in alignment with the groove in the front camshaft bearing cap (Fig. 1.4).
23   Bend back the tabs on the lockplates and slacken the upper bolts securing the camshaft sprockets to the camshafts, then turn the engine until the lower bolts are accessible and release the tabs of the lockplates and remove the bolts.
24   Now turn the engine to the position set in paragraph 22 of this Section.

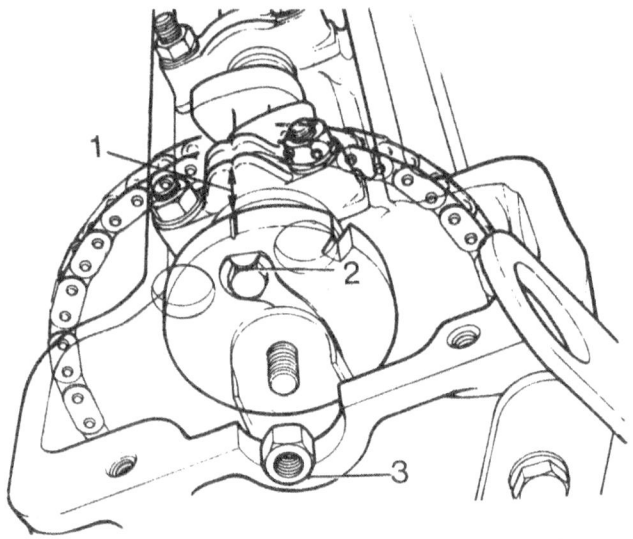

Fig. 1.4 Removing the camshaft sprocket (Sec 7)

1 Alignment marks   *3 Camshaft bearing nut*
2 Sprocket securing bolt

25   Using a nut from a camshaft bearing cap secure each camshaft sprocket to the support bracket on each side. Make sure the sprockets are tightened so that the timing chains cannot slacken and allow the chain tensioner to expand.
26   Now remove the other bolt and lockplate from each camshaft so that each sprocket is detached from the camshaft and attached to the support bracket.
27   Undo and remove the inlet manifold securing bolts and then lift off the inlet manifold.
28   Remove the two bolts securing the front cover to each cylinder head.
29   Slacken off the cylinder head nuts and bolts in the reverse sequence to that given in Fig. 1.5. Remove the nuts, bolts and thick washers then unscrew and remove the cylinder head holding-down studs using a screwdriver in the slot cut in the top of the studs. If the studs are very tight and difficult to remove, use a stud extractor or screw two nuts on and lock them against each other, then use a spanner on the lower nut to unscrew the stud.
30   Holding the exhaust manifold, rock the head to break the seal and then lift off the head and remove the cylinder head gasket.

8   Cylinder heads – refitting with engine in situ

Because of the angle at which the cylinder heads are fitted the cylinder head holding down studs are too long for use as guides when lifting the cylinder head into position with the engine in the car. Two slave studs, (2.5 x $\frac{7}{16}$ in UNC) are required. These can be made by cutting old holding-down studs and making a screwdriver slot in the top.

1   Turn the engine to position No 2 piston at TDC as indicated on the crankshaft pulley. Align the mark on the flanges of the camshafts with the groove on the No 1 camshaft bearing caps, refer to Fig. 1.4.
2   Ensure that all gasket faces are clean.
3   Fit the two slave studs into the G and H bolt hole positions (see Fig. 1.5) in the left-hand bank and then place the cylinder head gasket in position.
4   Fit the left-hand cylinder head. Screw in the cylinder head holding-down studs with a screwdriver, then remove the two slave studs. Fit the holding-down bolts, thick washers and nuts, and the two timing cover to cylinder head bolts. **Note**: *After fitting the cylinder head do not rotate the crankshaft or camshaft until the camshaft sprocket is refitted.*
5   Tighten the nuts and bolts, in the sequence shown in Fig. 1.5, to the specified torque given in the Specifications at the beginning of this Chapter.
6   Fit the inlet manifold gaskets to the left-hand cylinder, use a smear of grease to retain them in position, then fit the inlet manifold and tighten the securing bolts to the specified torque.

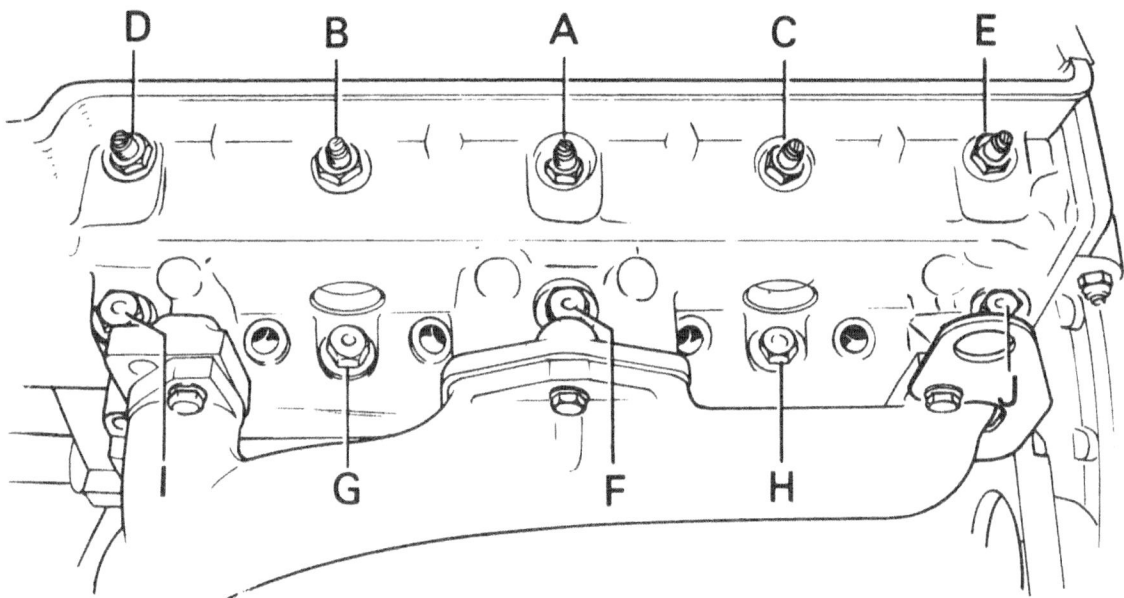

Fig. 1.5 Tightening sequence of cylinder head nuts and bolts (Sec 8)

7   Repeat the procedures described in paragraphs 1 to 4 above for the right-hand cylinder head.

8   Slide the inlet manifold gaskets into position between the manifold and the right-hand head and then fit the securing bolts. Tighten the bolts to the specified torque.

9   Tighten the right-hand cylinder head nuts and bolts; refer to paragraph 5 of this Section.

10 Using new lockplates fit the upper bolts that secure the sprocket to the camshaft. Turn the engine and fit the other camshaft sprocket securing bolt. Tighten the bolt and bend over the locking tab. Turn the engine till the first sprocket securing bolt is accessible, then tighten the bolt and bend over the locking tab.

11 Remove the nuts attaching the camshaft sprockets to the support brackets and refit them on the camshaft bearing caps. Refit the camshaft covers.

12 The remainder of the procedure is the reverse of the removal sequence described in Section 7. Refill the cooling system as described in Chapter 2. Refer to Chapter 11 for adjustment of power steering drivebelt tension.

13 Check the cylinder head holding-down nuts and bolts for tightness after 1000 miles (1600 km). With the engine cold, slacken off the nuts and bolts approximately $\frac{1}{16}$ of a turn, and retighten them to the specified torque in the sequence given in paragraph 5.

9   Engine – dismantling

1   Remove the carburettors as described in Chapter 3, Section 12.

2   Refer to Chapter 4, Section 7 and remove the ignition distributor.

3   Remove the camshaft cover securing screws and lift off the covers.

4   Turning the engine as necessary to gain access to the camshaft sprocket securing bolts, release the tabs of the locking plates and remove the securing bolts. Using a nut from a camshaft bearing cap, secure the camshaft sprocket to the support bracket on each bank.

5   Remove the twelve inlet manifold securing bolts and lift off the inlet manifold. Remove the two exhaust manifolds.

6   Slacken off the cylinder head securing bolts and nuts in the reverse sequence to that given in Section 8, paragraph 5, then remove the bolts and nuts. Do not forget the two bolts securing the front cover to each cylinder head.

7   Unscrew the five cylinder head holding-down studs on each bank, using a screwdriver in the slot cut in the head of the studs. If the studs will not unscrew with a screwdriver use some freeing fluid on them and then use a stud extractor, or two nuts locked together, to remove them.

8   Lift off the cylinder head and gaskets. If the head does not lift off, try to rock it to break the seal. Under no circumstances try to prise it away from the cylinder block with a screwdriver or similar tool, as damage may be done to the faces of the cylinder block and head. If the head will not free easily strike the head sharply with a plastic headed hammer, or a metal hammer with a block of wood to cushion the blow. Never strike the head with a metal hammer as this may result in the casing being fractured.

9   Remove the oil pump securing bolts and lift away the oil pump. The hexagon driveshaft will normally come away with the pump, but if it does not it can be withdrawn with a pair of long-nosed pliers.

10 Unscrew the oil transfer housing securing bolt and remove the housing and O-ring seal.

11 Remove the water pump as described in Chapter 2, Section 8.

12 Mark the position of the clutch assembly in relation to the flywheel, so that it can be refitted in its original position, then progressively slacken the clutch cover securing bolts. Remove the bolts and lift away the clutch cover assembly and clutch disc.

13 Remove the flywheel/driveplate securing bolts and lift off the flywheel/driveplate. Restain the flywheel/driveplate from turning while undoing the nuts, by locking the flywheel/driveplate with a screwdriver, or a wedge in mesh with the starter ring gear (photo). Undo the securing bolts and remove the flywheel housing.

14 Undo the front sump to timing chain cover bolts and the cover to

9.13 Use a wedge engaged in the starter ring gear to hold the driveplate

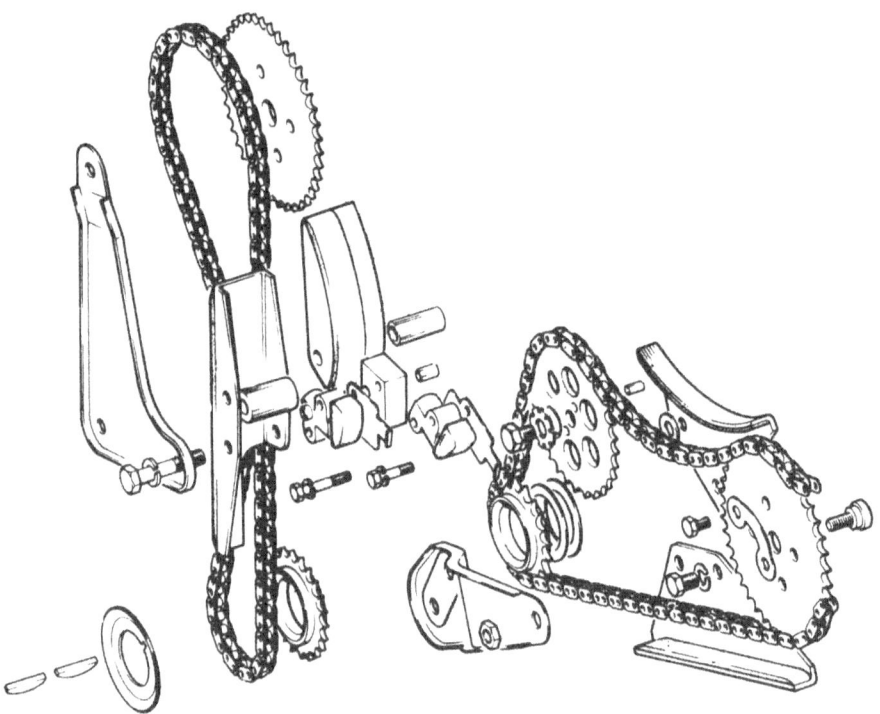

Fig. 1.6 Timing chains, sprockets, chain guides and chain tensioners (Sec 9)

cylinder block bolts, then remove the timing chain cover. The cover is located on two dowels and it may be necessary to tap the ccver with a soft faced hammer to free it. Do not prise off with a screwdriver or similar tool as the mating faces of the cover and cylinder block may get damaged.

15 Remove the two bolts securing the outer chain tensioner spacer and retainer to the cylinder block and lift away the tensioner, spacer and retainer.

16 Undo the bolts securing the outer chain guide and support bracket then remove the guide, bracket, complete with sprocket, and outer chain.

17 Remove the securing bolts and lift away the inner chain tensioner.

18 Remove the securing bolts and lift away the inner chain guide, support bracket complete with sprocket and inner chain (Fig. 1.6).

19 Remove the oil thrower from the front of the crankshaft and the crankshaft sprockets. Remove the Woodruff keys and any shims that may be fitted.

20 Using an Allen key, remove the jackshaft retaining plate securing bolts (photo) then lift away the retaining plate. Withdraw the jackshaft forward out of the crankcase.

21 Position the crankcase on its side and then remove the sump securing bolts and lift off the sump.

22 Undo the two securing bolts and remove the oil strainer.

23 Remove the nuts from the connecting rod big-end cap securing bolts and take off the caps, taking care to keep them in the right order and the correct way round. Normally the numbers 1 to 8 are stamped on adjacent sides of the big-end caps and the connecting rods, indicating which cap fits each rod (photo). If they are not numbered then with a sharp screwdriver or file, scratch marks across the cap and rod so that they can be fitted correctly at reassembly. It is most important that the caps are fitted on their original connecting rods and that the connecting rods and pistons are refitted in their original cylinders.

24 To remove the shell bearings, press the bearing opposite the groove in both the connecting rod and the connecting rod caps and the bearings will slide out (photo).

25 Withdraw the piston and connecting rod assemblies out through the top of the cylinder block. Refit the connecting rod caps to the connecting rods, if the bearings are not being renewed, as this will prevent the rods and caps from getting mixed up.

26 Undo the securing bolts and remove the crankshaft rear oil seal housing.

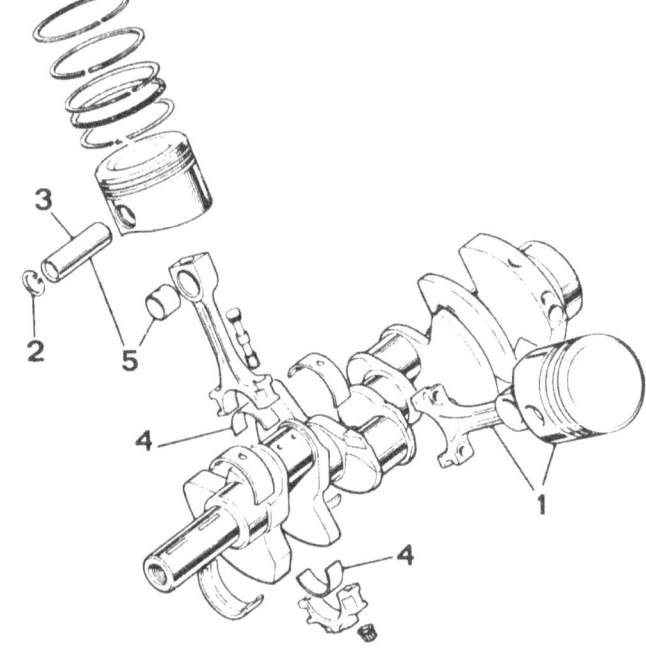

Fig. 1.7 Connecting rod and piston assembly (Sec 9)

1 *Piston and connecting rod*
2 *Circlip*
3 *Gudgeon pin*
4 *Big-end bearing*
5 *Small-end bush*

9.20 Removing the jackshaft retaining plate securing screws with an Allen key

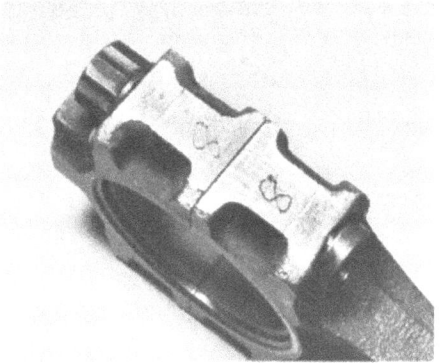

9.23 The numbers are usually stamped on the connecting rod and the cap

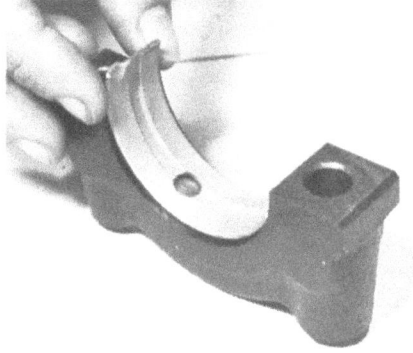

9.24 Removing connecting rod cap shell bearing

27 Unscrew the main bearing cap securing bolts and remove the caps. The caps are numbered 1 to 4 with number 5 bearing not numbered.

28 Remove the main bearing caps and the bottom half of each bearing shell, taking care to keep the bearing shells with their respective caps.

29 When removing the centre main bearing cap, note the bottom halves of the thrust washers, one half located on each side of the main bearing. Keep them with the centre main bearing cap, laying them along the correct side.

30 Lift out the crankshaft then remove the upper halves of the bearing shells and thrust washers. Place the shells and thrust washers with their respective main bearing caps in their relative fitted position. Take care not to get them mixed up.

10 Cylinder head and camshaft assembly – dismantling

1 Slacken the camshaft bearing caps evenly and progressively until the spring tension is released.

2 Remove the bearing caps and lay them out in order taking care not to mix one bank with the other.

Note: *The camshaft bearings are line-bored and must be refitted in their original positions.*

3 Lift out the camshafts.

4 Obtain a suitable container which can be conveniently divided into sixteen sections and number the sections.

5 Remove the tappet and pallet shim from each valve and place them in the appropriate section of the container.

6 Using a valve spring compression, compress each spring in turn and remove the split cotters, collar spring valve and spring seat. Keep all the parts in their respective sets and place them in the appropriate section of the container unless new items are to be fitted.

7 Remove the exhaust manifold securing bolts and take off the manifolds.

11 Pistons and connecting rods – dismantling

It is extremely important that all parts associated with each piston are kept together so that they can eventually be refitted (if suitable) in the same position.

1 To remove the gudgeon pin and free the piston from the connecting rod, remove one of the circlips at either end of the pin with a pair of circlip pliers.

2 Press out the pin from the rod and piston with your fingers.

3 If the pin shows reluctance to move, then on no account force it out, as this could damage the piston. Immerse the piston in a pan of boiling water for three minutes. On removal the expansion of the aluminium should allow the gudgeon pin to slide out easily.

4 Make sure the pins are kept with the same piston.

5 To remove the piston rings, slide them carefully over the top of the piston, taking care not to scratch the aluminium alloy. Never slide

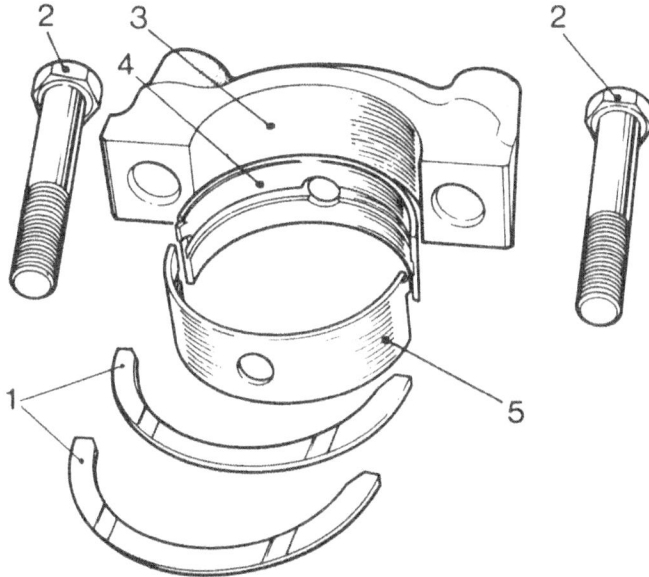

Fig. 1.8 Centre main bearing assembly (Sec 9)

1 Thrust washers
2 Securing bolts
3 Main bearing cap
4 Lower half of bearing
5 Upper half of bearing

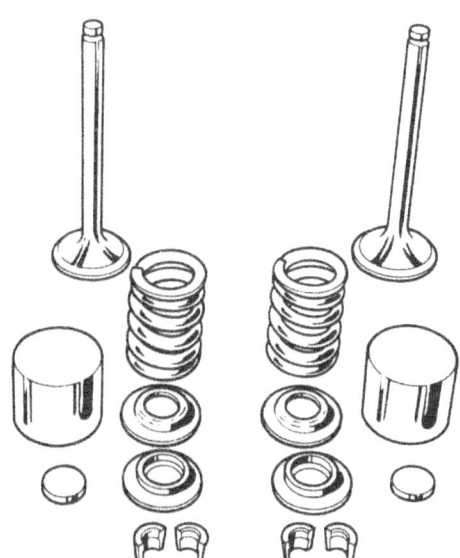

Fig. 1.9 Valves, valve springs and tappets (Sec 10)

them off the bottom of the piston skirt. It is very easy to break the iron piston rings if they are pulled off roughly, so this operation should be done with extreme caution. It is helpful to make use of an old hacksaw blade with the teeth ground off, or better still, an old 0.020 in (0.5080 mm) feeler gauge.

6   Lift one end of the piston ring to be removed, out of its groove, and insert the end of the feeler gauge under it.

7   Turn the feeler gauge slowly round the piston and, as the ring comes out of its groove, apply slight upward pressure so that it rests on the land above. It can then be eased off the piston with the feeler gauge stopping it from slipping into any empty groove, if it is any but the top piston ring that is being removed.

12 Oil pump – dismantling

1   Take out the hexagonal driveshaft then remove the screws which retain the pump cover.

2   Remove the rotors.

3   Take out the O-ring from the pump body.

4   To remove the relief valve, withdraw the split-pin in the pump body.

5   Take out the plug, spring and relief valve (Fig. 1.10).

Note: *If the plug is reluctant to come out, due to the O-ring sticking, it can be carefully driven out from inside the pump body.*

6   Remove the O-ring from the plug.

13 Cleaning, examination and storage of components – general

1   With the engine stripped down and all parts dismantled they must now be cleaned in petrol or proprietary solvents. Remove any traces of gasket material remaining using a blunt scraper but take care not to score out of the sealing surfaces.

2   Once the parts are cleaned, both before and after inspection, make sure that they stay clean by covering or wrapping them in polythene.

14 Crankshaft – examination and renovation

1   Examine the crankpins and main journal surfaces for signs of scoring or scratches. Check the ovality of the crankpins at different positions with a micrometer. If more than 0.001 inch (0.0254 mm) out of round, the crankpins will have to be reground. They will also have to be reground if there are any scores or scratches present. Also check the journals in the same fashion. If it is necessary to regrind the crankshaft and fit new bearings your local Triumph garage or engineering works will be able to decide how much metal to grind off and therefore, the correct undersize shells to fit.

2   Examine the spigot bearing in the rear end of the crankshaft for wear and renew if necessary. Using a suitable extractor remove the defective bearing. Clean out the bore in the crankshaft and using a suitable stepped drift, drive the new bearing in flush with the end of the crankshaft.

15 Big-end and main bearing shells – examination and renovation

1   Big-end bearing failure is often accompanied by a noisy knocking from the crankcase, and a slight drop in oil pressure. Main bearing failure is accompanied by vibration, which can be quite severe as the engine speed rises and falls, and a drop in oil pressure.

2   Bearings which have not broken up, but are badly worn will give rise to low oil pressure and some vibration. Inspect the big-ends, main bearings and thrust washers for signs of general wear, scoring, pitting and scratches. The bearings should be matt grey in colour. With lead-indium bearings, should a trace of copper colour be noticed, the bearings are badly worn as the lead bearing material has worn away to expose the indium underlay. Renew the bearings if they are in this condition, or if there is any sign of scoring or pitting.

3   The undersizes available are designed to correspond with the regrind sizes, ie – 0.010 in (0.2540 mm) bearings are correct for a crankshaft reground – 0.010 in (0.2540 mm) undersize. The bearings are in fact, slightly more than the stated undersize, as running clearances have been allowed for, during their manufacture.

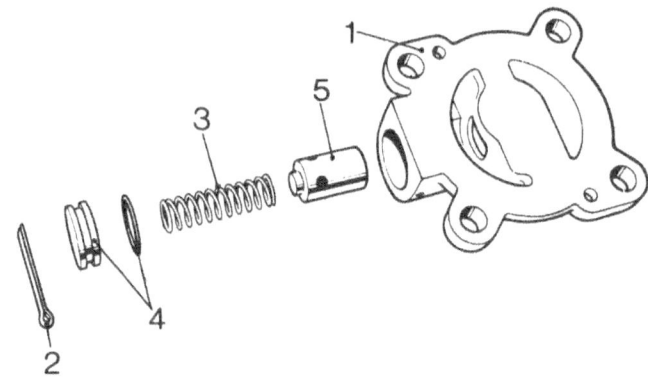

Fig. 1.10 Oil pump relief valve (Sec 12)

1 Oil pump cover	*4 Plug and O-ring*
2 Split pin	*5 Valve*
3 Spring	

16 Cylinder bores – examination and renovation

1   The cylinder bores must be examined for taper, scoring and scratches. Start by carefully examining the top of the cylinder bores. If they are at all worn, a very slight ridge will be found on the thrust side. This marks the top of the piston ring travel. The owner will have a good indication of the bore wear prior to dismantling the engine, or removing the cylinder head. Excessive oil consumption, accompanied by blue smoke from the exhaust, is a sure sign of worn cylinder bores and piston rings.

2   Measure the bore diameter just under the ridge with a micrometer, and compare it with the diameter at the bottom of the bore, which is not subject to wear. If the difference between the two measurements is more than 0.006 in (0.1524 mm) then it will be necessary to fit special pistons and rings or to have the cylinders rebored and to fit oversize pistons. If no micrometer is available, remove the rings from a piston and place the piston in each bore in turn about ¾ in (19 mm) below the top of the bore. If an 0.010 in (0.2540 mm) feeler gauge can be slid between the piston and the cylinder wall on the thrust side of the bore, then remedial action must be taken.

3   Pistons are available in an oversize 0.020 in (0.5080 mm). These are accurately machined to just below these measurements to provide correct running clearances in bores bored out to the exact oversize dimensions.

4   If the bores are slightly worn but not so badly worn as to justify reboring them, then special oil control rings and pistons can be fitted which will restore compression and stop the engine burning oil. Several different types are available, and the manufacturer's instructions concerning their fitting must be followed closely.

5   If new pistons are being fitted and the bores have not been reground, it is essential to slightly roughen the hard glaze on the sides of the bores with fine glass paper so the new piston rings will have a chance to bed in properly.

17 Pistons and piston rings – examination and renovation

1   If new rings are to be fitted to the old pistons, then the top ring should be stepped so as to clear the ridge left above the previous top ring. If a normal but oversize new ring is fitted, it will hit the ridge and break, because the new ring will not have worn in the same way as the old which will have worn in unison with the ridge.

2   Before fitting the rings on the pistons, each should be inserted approximately 2 in (50.8 mm) down the cylinder bore and the gap between the two ends of the ring measured with a feeler gauge. The correct value is given in the Specifications Section. It is essential that the gap should be measured at the bottom of the ring travel, as if it is measured at the top of a worn bore and gives a perfect fit, it could easily seize at the bottom. If the ring gap is too small, rub down the ends of the ring with a very fine file until the gap, when fitted, is correct. To keep the rings square in the bore for measurement, line up each in turn by inserting an old piston in the bore upside down and

using the piston to push the ring down about 2 in (50·8 mm). Remove the piston and measure the piston ring gap.

3   When fitting new pistons and rings to a rebored engine, the piston ring gap can be measured at the top of the bore as the bore will not taper. It is not necessary to measure the side clearance in the piston ring grooves with the rings fitted, as the groove dimensions are accurately machined during manufacture. When fitting new oil control rings to an old piston, it may be necessary to have the grooves widened by machining to accept the new wider rings — where this is the case follow the ring manufacturer's instructions.

4   Fit the rings to the piston and measure the gap between the ring and the wall of the groove. Refer to the Specifications at the beginning of this Chapter.

5   Check that the gudgeon pin is a good fit in the piston. The gudgeon pin should be a finger tight press fit but if any wear is detected the appropriate part must be renewed. Refer to the Specifications at the beginning of this Chapter.

18 Gudgeon pins and small-end bearings – examination and renovation

1   Examine the fit of the gudgeon pin in the small-end bearing. If any wear is detectable, new bearings and/or a new gudgeon pin will be required. Renewal of bearings is best left to a specialist since they require to be pressed in then reamered to suit the gudgeon pin size.

19 Jackshaft, camshaft and camshaft bearings – examination and renovation

1   With regard to the bearing and cam surfaces, both shafts are similar. There should be no signs of wear, but if very shallow scoring on the cams is noticed, the score marks can be removed by very gently rubbing with fine emery cloth. The greatest possible care must be taken to retain the original profile.

2   Examine the camshaft bearings for any signs of scoring or cracking. If they appear to be in first class condition, (and provided that no attention is required to the camshaft journals) they should be satisfactory for further use.

Note: *The bearings cannot be renewed. If their condition warrants replacement it will mean purchasing a new cylinder head complete with camshaft bearings.*

3   Examine the teeth on the jackshaft sprocket and renew if worn. Release the locking tabs on the sprocket retaining bolt, remove the bolt and take off the sprocket.

4   When fitting the new sprocket ensure that the mating faces of the shaft flange and the sprocket are smooth and clean and that the locat-ing dowel is not damaged. Fit the sprocket, tab washer and bolt (photos).

5   Tighten the bolt to the specified torque, then check the run-out of the sprocket using V-blocks and a dial test gauge. If V-blocks are not available the run-out can be checked when the jackshaft is fitted in the cylinder block. Excessive run-out will result in undue wear on the sprocket and chain.

20 Valves, valve seats and valve guides – examination and renovation

1   Examine the heads of the valves for pitting and burning, especially the heads of the exhaust valves. The valve seatings should be examined at the same time. If the pitting on valve and seat is very slight, the marks can be removed by grinding the seats and valves together with coarse, and then fine, grinding paste. Where bad pitting has occurred to the valve seats, it will be necessary to recut them and fit new valves. If the valve seats are so worn that they cannot be recut, then it will be necessary to fit new valve seat inserts. These latter two jobs should be entrusted to the local Triumph garage or engineering works. In practice, it is very seldom that the seats are so badly worn that they require renewal. Normally, it is the exhaust valve that is too badly worn for re-use. The owner can easily purchase a new set of valves and match them to the seats by valve grinding. Before commencing any operation on the valves and seats, decide which valves are going to be used in the reassembly then check them in the valve guides. If the valves are a very loose fit in the guides and there is the slightest suspicion of lateral rocking using a new valve, then new valve guides will have to be fitted. Renewal of valve guides requires special equipment and it is recommended that this work is left to the local Triumph garage or engineering works.

2   Whether new valves and seats are used or the original ones refitted, valve grinding should be carried out as follows:
smear a trace of coarse carborundum paste on the seat face and apply a suction grinder tool to the valve head. With semi-rotary motion, grind the valve head to its seat, lifting the valve occasionally to redistribute the grinding paste. When a dull matt even surface finish is produced on both the valve seat and the valve, then wipe off the paste and repeat the process with fine carborundum paste, lifting and turning the valve to redistribute the paste as before. A light spring placed under the valve head will greatly ease this operation. When a smooth unbroken ring of light grey matt finish is produced, on both valve and valve seat faces, the grinding operation is completed.

3   Scrape away all carbon from the valve head and the valve stem. Carefully clean away every trace of grinding compound, taking care to leave none in the ports or the valve guides. Clean the valves and valve seats with a paraffin soaked rag, then with a clean rag, and finally, if an air line is available, blow the valves, valve guides and valve ports clean.

19.4a Fitting the sprocket on the jackshaft

19.4b Lock the sprocket securing bolt with the tabwasher

21 Timing chains, sprockets and chain tensioners – examination and renovation

1   Examine the teeth on the camshaft, jackshaft and crankshaft sprockets for wear. Each tooth forms an inverted 'V' with the sprocket periphery, and if worn, the side of each tooth, ie one side of the inverted 'V' will be concave when compared with the other. If any sign of wear is present the sprockets must be renewed.

2   Examine the links of the chains for side slackness, and renew the chains if any slackness is noticeable when compared with a new chain. It is a sensible precaution to renew both chains if the engine is stripped down for overhaul. The rollers on a very badly worn chain may be slightly grooved.

3   Examine the chain tensioner slippers and the chain guides for wear, and if worn these items should be renewed. It is almost certain that if wear in the chains is such that new chains are required, the rubbing surfaces of the tensioner slippers and the guides will also need renewing.

4   Examine the tensioner plunger, cylinder and spring for wear or damage and renew parts as necessary (photo).

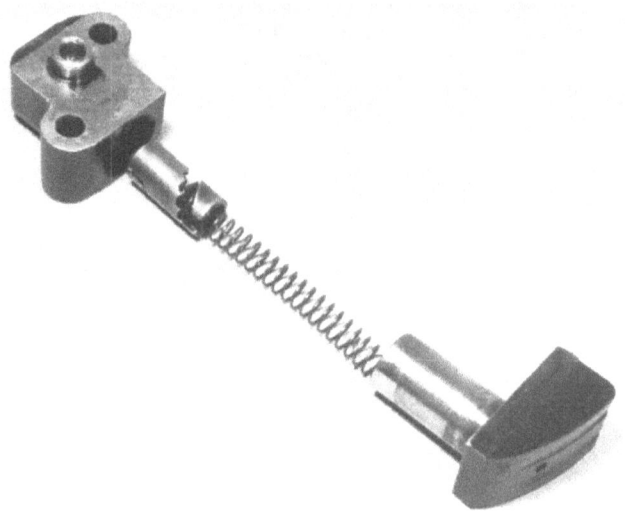

21.4 Examine the parts of the chain tensioner for wear

22 Tappets and pallet shims – examination and renovation

1   Even after a very high mileage the tappets and pallet shims should still be in satisfactory condition for re-use. Examine them for any signs of indentation, wear, scoring or cracking.

2   Using a micrometer, measure the thickness of the shims and keep a note of the dimensions of each one. When the valve clearances are being set you will undoubtedly need to purchase some new ones, but some of the existing ones may be suitable for re-use.

3   In the unlikely event of scoring of the surface of the tappets and pallet shims, it is permissible to lap the surface a little if the proper facilities are at hand. The important thing to remember is that the surfaces must be smooth, flat and parallel when they are assembled.

23 Flywheel/driveplate and starter ring gear – examination and renovation

On cars with automatic transmission the starter ring gear is welded to the driveplate and cannot be renewed separately.

1   If the flywheel clutch face is deeply scored, a new flywheel should be obtained or the surface skimmed using a lathe. The maximum allowable flywheel face run-out is 0·040 in (1 mm).

2   If the teeth on the flywheel starter ring are badly worn, or if some are missing, then it will be necessary to remove the ring. This is achieved by splitting the ring with a cold chisel. The greatest care should be taken not to damage the flywheel during this process. It is

sometimes advantageous to drill a $\frac{1}{4}$ inch (6 mm) hole at the intersection point of two teeth, and to strike this point with the cold chisel.

3   To fit a new ring heat it gently and evenly to a temperature of 170 to 175°C (338 to 347°F) in an oil bath or circulatory oven; do not exceed this temperature. With the ring at this temperature, fit it to the flywheel with the front of the teeth facing the flywheel register. The ring should be tapped gently down onto its register and left to cool naturally when the shrinkage of the metal on cooling will ensure that it is a secure and permanent fit. The maximum permissible gap between the flywheel and starter ring on one length of 6 in (15 cm) is 0·025 in (0·6350 mm).

24 Oil pump – examination, renovation and reassembly

1   Thoroughly clean all the components parts in petrol and then check the rotor endfloat and lobe clearances in the following manner:

2   Position the rotors in the pump and place the straight edge of a steel rule across the joint face of the pump. (Ensure that the chamfered edge of the outer rotor is at the driving end of the rotor pocket). Measure the gap between the bottom of the straight edge and the top of the rotors with a feeler gauge. If the measurement exceeds 0·004 in (0·1016 mm) then check the lobe clearances as described in the following paragraphs. If the lobe clearances are correct, then lap the joint face on a sheet of plate glass.

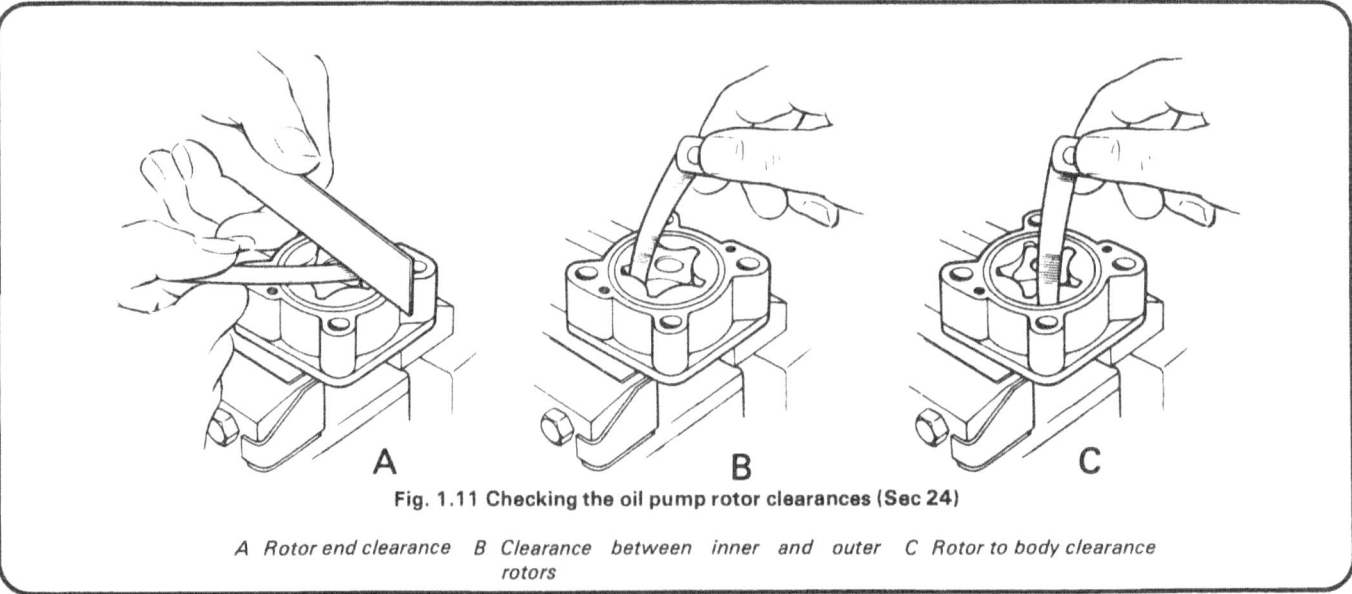

Fig. 1.11 Checking the oil pump rotor clearances (Sec 24)

A Rotor end clearance   B Clearance between inner and outer rotors   C Rotor to body clearance

3   Measure with a feeler gauge the gap between the inner and outer rotors. It should not be more than 0·010 in (0·2540 mm).
4   Then measure the gap between the outer rotor and the side of the pump body which should not exceed 0·008 in (0·2032 mm). It is essential to renew the pump if the measurements are outside these figures. It can be safely assumed that at any major reconditioning the pump will need renewal.
5   Reassembly is the reverse of the dismantling procedure described in Section 12.

25   Decarbonising

1   This can be carried out with the engine either in or out of the car. With the cylinder heads off, carefully remove with a wire brush and blunt scraper all traces of carbon deposits from the combustion spaces and the ports. The valve head stems and valve guides should also be freed from any carbon deposits. Wash the combustion spaces and ports down with petrol and scrape the cylinder head surface free of any foreign matter with the side of a steel rule, or a similar article.
2   Clean the pistons and top of the cylinder bores. If the pistons are still in the block it is essential that great care is taken to ensure that no carbon gets into the cylinder bores as this could scratch the cylinder walls or cause damage to the piston and rings. To ensure that this does not happen, first turn the crankshaft so that two of the pistons are at the top of their bores. Stuff rag into the other bores or seal them off with paper and masking tape. The waterways should also be covered with small pieces of masking tape to prevent particles of carbon entering the cooling system and damaging the water pump.
3   Remove all traces of carbon and press a little grease into the gap between the cylinder walls and the two pistons which are to be worked on. With a blunt scraper carefully scrape away the carbon from the piston crown, taking great care not to scratch the aluminium. Also scrape the carbon from the surrounding lip of the cylinder wall. When all carbon has been removed, scrape away the grease which will now be contaminated with carbon particles, taking care not to press any into the bores. To assist prevention of carbon build-up the piston crown can be polished with a metal polish. Turn the crankshaft so that the next two pistons are now at the top. Place rag or paper sealed with masking tape in the cylinders which have been decarbonised and proceed as described earlier, then repeat for the other four pistons.

26   Sump – examination and renovation

1   Thoroughly wash out the sump and wipe dry using a clean non-fluffy rag.
2   Inspect the casing for signs of cracking which could be caused by incorrect positioning of a jack or hitting a high object on the road surface. If a crack is evident, it may be repaired by welding using the service of a firm of specialists, otherwise obtain a new sump casting.
3   Check that the sealing faces are flat with no signs of scoring.

27   Engine reassembly – general

1   To ensure maximum life with minimum trouble from a rebuilt engine, not only must everything be correctly assembled, but all the parts must be spotlessly clean, all the oilways must be clear, locking washers and spring washers must always be fitted where indicated, and all bearing and other working surfaces must be thoroughly lubricated during assembly. Before assembly begins, renew any bolts or studs if the threads of which are in any way damaged, and whenever possible, use new spring washers.
2   Check the core plugs for signs of weeping and renew as necessary.
3   If a core plug is weeping then drive a punch through the centre of the plug.
4   Using the punch as a lever, prise out the old core plug.
5   Thoroughly clean the core plug orifice, coat the rim of the new plug with sealing compound and then drift the new plug squarely into position.
6   Apart from normal tools, a supply of clean rag, an oil can filled with engine oil (an empty plastic detergent bottle thoroughly cleaned and washed out, will invariably do just as well), a new supply of assorted spring washers, a set of new gaskets, a set of new oil seals and O-rings, a set of new valve springs and a torque wrench, should be collected together. You will also need new pallet shims as determined during the assembly stage of the cylinder head, and new big-end bearing cap nuts.

28   Cylinder heads and camshafts – reassembly and valve clearance checking and adjustment

After a major engine overhaul, it is recommended that the rebuild procedure is commenced with the cylinder heads since if there is a delay in obtaining the pallet shims, time-wasting can be prevented if other assembly work is still to be done.

1   Fit each valve in turn, wiping down and lubricating each stem as it is inserted into the same valve guide from which it was removed.
2   Fit the lower collar, spring, upper collar, and split collets. As with dismantling, a valve spring compressor will be required (photos).
Note: *Valve springs must be fitted with the closed coil towards the head.*
3   Repeat the procedure for the remaining valves.
4   Fit the tappets and pallet shims (photos) in their original positions.
5   Squirt a little engine oil in each of the camshaft bearings and caps then fit the camshafts (photo). Ensure that the caps are in the correct position – each is numbered (photos), then tighten the retaining nuts to the specified torque. Always tighten the nuts evenly in pairs, working along the length of the camshafts.
6   If the cylinder heads are on the bench, rotate the camshafts for the following stage by using a spanner on the hexagon in front of the rear camshaft bearing. If the heads are fitted on the engine the camshaft can be turned using a spanner on the crankshaft pulley securing bolt.
Caution: *The camshafts (or the crankshaft) must never be turned with the cylinder heads fitted to the engine when the timing chains are not fitted, as serious damage to the pistons and valves will result.*
7   Check the valve clearances, using feeler gauges, between the heel of the cam and the tappet. The correct gaps are given in the Specifications (photos).
8   If the measured gap is too large by, say, 0.008 in (0.203 mm) it means that the pallet shim fitted at the moment needs a replacement

28.2a Fit the lower collar ...

28.2b ... followed by the spring and upper collar

28.2c Compress the valve spring with a valve spring compressing tool ...

28.2d ... and fit the split cotters

28.4a Fit the pallet shim ...

28.4b ... and then the tappet

28.5a Fit the camshaft in the cylinder head ...

28.5b ... and then fit the bearing caps

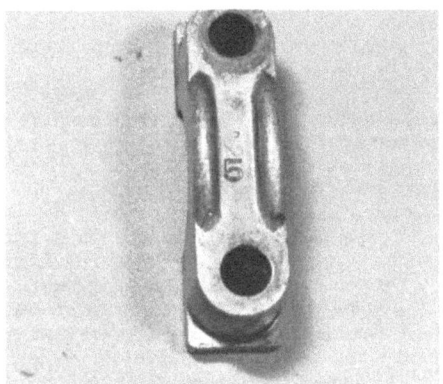

28.5c The camshaft bearing numbers are stamped on the caps

28.7 Checking the valve clearance

29.1 Fit the upper bearing shells in the crankcase ...

29.4 ... and the lower bearing shells in the caps

29.6 Note the milled face of the thrust washer

29.7 Fit the crankshaft in position

29.8 Lubricate the journals

which is 0.008 in thicker. Measure the existing pallet shim thickness with a micrometer, add the hypothetical 0.008 in (0.203 mm) to it and this is the thickness of pallet shim required.

9 If the measured gap is too small by, say, 0.003 in (0.076 mm), it means that the pallet shim fitted at the moment needs to be 0.003 (0.076 mm) thinner. Measure the existing pallet shim thickness, subtract the hypothetical 0.003 in from it and this is the thickness of pallet shims required).

10 When all the gaps have been checked, note the errors since it may be found that by interchanging some of the existing pallet shims that you will reduce the number which you have to purchase.

11 Remove the camshafts, fit the correct pallet shims, replace the camshafts and recheck the gaps. Do not forget to exercise care when removing and refitting the camshafts and to lubricate the bearings.

29 Crankshaft – refitting

Ensure that the crankcase is thoroughly clean and that all oilways are clear. A thin twist drill or a nylon pipe cleaner is useful for cleaning them out. If possible, blow them out with compressed air. Treat the crankshaft in the same manner and then inject engine oil into the crankshaft oilways.

1 If the old main bearing shells are to be renewed (it is false economy not to do so unless they are virtually new), fit the upper halves of the main bearing shells to their location in the crankcase, after wiping the locations clean (photo).

2 Note that at the back of each bearing is a tab which engages in the locating grooves in either the crankcase or the main bearing cap housings.

3 If new bearings are being fitted, carefully clean away all traces of the protective greases with which they are coated.

4 With the upper bearing shells securely in place, wipe the lower bearings cap housings and fit the lower shell bearings to their caps, ensuring that the right shell goes into the right cap if the old bearings are being refitted (photo).

5 Wipe the recesses either side of the centre main bearing which locates the thrust washers. Smear some grease onto the thrust washers and place the upper halves in position.

6 Note the milled faces of the thrust washers face outwards as shown in the photo.

7 Carefully lower the crankshaft into position (photo).

8 Generously lubricate the crankshaft journals (photo).

9 Fit the main bearing caps in position ensuring they locate correctly. The mating surfaces must be spotlessly clean or the caps will not seat correctly. As the bearing caps were assembled to the cylinder block and then line bored during manufacture, it is essential that they are returned to the same positions from which they were removed (photo).

10 Refit the main bearing cap bolts and washers and tighten the bolts to the specified torque given in the Specifications at the beginning of this Chapter (photo).

11 Test the crankshaft for freedom of rotation. Should it be stiff to turn or possess high spots, a most careful inspection must be made, preferably by a qualified mechanic, with a micrometer to get to the root of the trouble. It is very seldom that any trouble of this nature will be experienced when fitting the crankshaft.

12 Check the crankshaft endfloat with a feeler gauge measuring the longitudinal movement between the crankshaft and the centre main bearing cap. Endfloat should be between 0.003 to 0.011 in (0.07 to 0.28 mm). If the endfloat is incorrect, selective use of thrust washers must be made (photo).

30 Pistons and connecting rods – reassembly

1 If the old pistons are being re-used then they must be mated to the same connecting rod with the same gudgeon pin. If new pistons are being fitted, it does not matter which connecting rod they are used with, but the gudgeon pins should be fitted on the basis of selective assembly.

2 Because aluminium alloy, when hot, expands more than steel, the gudgeon pin may be a very tight fit in the piston when cold. To avoid damage to the piston, it is best to heat it in boiling water when the pin will slide in easily.

3 Lay the correct piston adjacent to each connecting rod and remember that the same rod and piston must go back into the same bore. If new pistons are being used, it is only necessary to ensure that the right connecting rod is placed in each bore.

4 Fit a gudgeon pin circlip in position at one end of the gudgeon pin hole in the piston.

5 Locate the connecting rod in the piston with the triangle mark on the piston crown towards the front of the engine, ie the timing cover end (photo). **NOTE**: *The connecting rods are offset and chamfered on one side only. The chamfered side is fitted next to the crankshaft, therefore each pair of connecting rods has the non-chamfered sides together when fitted on the crankpin. When the pistons are assembled to the connecting rods the chamfer on the big-end should be positioned as follows:*

Right-hand bank – in line with the front of the piston
Left-hand bank – away from the front of the piston

6 Slide the gudgeon pin in through the bore in the piston and through the connecting rod small-end until it rests against the previously fitted circlip. The pin should be a push fit requiring thumb pressure only.

7 Fit the second circlip in position. Repeat this procedure for all eight pistons and connecting rods.

8 Where special oil control pistons are being fitted, should the position of the top ring be the same as the position of the top ring on the old piston, ensure that a groove has been machined on the top of the new ring so no fouling occurs between the unworn portion at the top of the bore and the piston ring, when the latter is at the top of its stroke.

31 Piston rings – refitting

1 Check that the piston ring groove and oilways are thoroughly clean and unblocked. Piston rings must always be fitted over the head of the piston and never from the bottom.

2 The easiest method to use when fitting rings, is to wrap a 0.020 in (0.5080 mm) feeler gauge round the top of the piston and place the rings one at a time, starting with the bottom oil control ring over the feeler gauge.

29.9 The main bearing caps are numbered. Make sure they are fitted in their correct locations

29.10 Tighten the main bearing caps to the specified torque

29.12 Checking the crankshaft endfloat

30.5 The triangle mark on the piston points to the front when fitted in the cylinder

32.4 Fitting the piston and connecting rod assembly in the cylinder

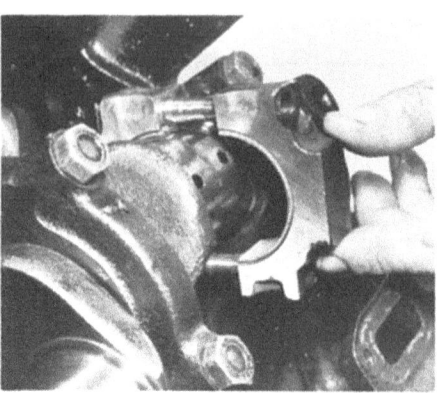

32.9 Fitting the connecting rod bearing cap

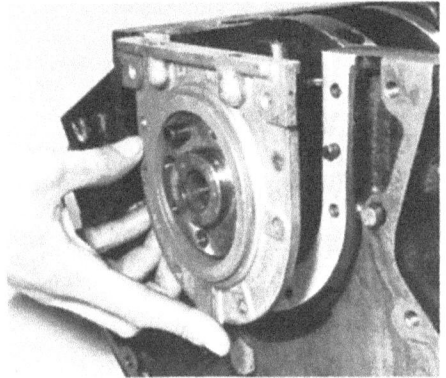

33.3 Fitting the rear oil seal housing

33.4 Place a new gasket on the crankcase and then fit the oil strainer

33.5a Position a new sump gasket on the crankcase ...

33.5b ... then fit the sump

34.1 Fit the driveplate housing

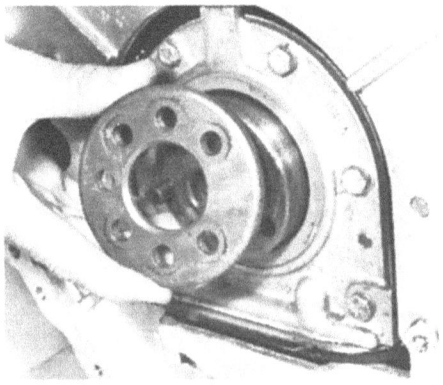

34.3a Position the driveplate spacer on the crankshaft ...

34.3b ... then fit the driveplate ...

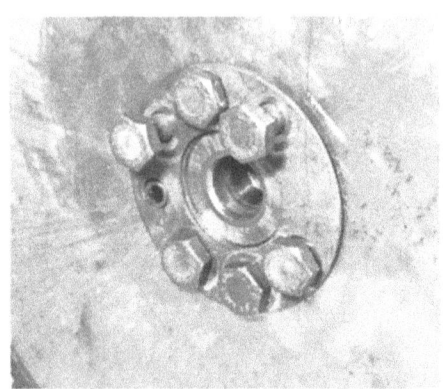

34.3c ... the driveplate washer and securing bolts

35.2 Slide the jackshaft into the block

3   The feeler gauge, complete with ring, can then be slid down the piston over the other piston ring grooves until the correct groove is reached. The piston ring is then slid gently off the feeler gauge into the groove.

4   An alternative method is to fit the rings by holding them slightly open with the thumbs and both index fingers. This method requires a steady hand and great care as it is easy to open or twist the ring too much and break it.

5   Ensure that the ends of the oil control expander are abutting but not overlapping.

6   Ensure that the oil scraper ring is fitted with the word 'Top' uppermost and the step lowermost.

32   Pistons and connecting rod assemblies – refitting

1   Check that the pistons and connecting rods are correctly assembled, refer to Section 30.

2   Wipe the cylinder bores clean and then oil the bores and piston rings.

3   Space the piston ring gaps evenly on the non-thrust side of the piston (inboard side) and then compress the rings with a piston ring clamp.

4   The pistons, complete with connecting rods, are fitted to their respective bores from the top of the cylinder block (photo). Make sure that the triangle on top of the piston is towards the front of the engine. Use the shaft of a hammer to tap the piston into the bore.

5   Wipe clean the connecting rod half of the big-end bearing cap and the underside of the shell bearing and fit the shell bearing in position with its locating tongue engaged with the corresponding rod.

6   If the bearings are nearly new and are being refitted, then ensure they are replaced in their locations on the correct rods.

7   Generously lubricate the crankpin journals with engine oil, and turn the crankshaft so that the crankpin is in the most advantageous position for the connecting rod to be drawn onto it.

8   Wipe clean the connecting rod bearing cap and back of the shell bearing and fit the shell bearing in position, ensuring that the locating tongue at the back of the bearing engages with the locating groove in the connecting rod cap.

9   Generously lubricate the shell bearing and offer up the connecting rod bearing cap to the connecting rod (photo)

10 Fit the connecting rod cap securing nuts and tighten them to the specified torque; refer to the Specifications at the beginning of this Chapter.

11 Insert a feeler gauge between each pair of big-ends to check the endfloat which should be between 0.015 and 0.024 in (0.38 to 0.61 mm).

12 When all the connecting rods have been connected to the crankshaft, rotate the crankshaft to ensure that there are no high spots causing binding.

33   Crankshaft rear oil seal, oil strainer and sump – refitting

1   Clean the mating faces of the seal housing and cylinder block.

2   Fit a new oil seal in the housing, with the rear face of the seal flush with the housing. Fit a new gasket on the cylinder block.

3   Locate the seal housing on the two dowels in the cylinder block (photo) then fit the housing to block securing bolts and tighten them to the specified torque.

4   Fit the oil strainer, using a new gasket, and the securing bolts (photo).

5   Clean the mating faces of the crankcase and oil sump (photos).

6   Fit a new gasket. Place the sump in position and fit the securing bolts and nuts. Do not tighten the bolts and nuts until the timing cover is fitted, refer to Section 36.

34   Flywheel housing and flywheel/driveplate – refitting

1   Ensure that the mating faces of the housing and cylinder block are clean then fit the housing, locating it on the two dowels in the block (photo).

2   Fit the bolts and tighten them to the specified torque.

3   *Automatic transmission:* Fit the spacer on the crankshaft and then the driveplate. The driveplate is located on a dowel in the crankshaft and can only be fitted in the one position. Fit the driveplate washer and new securing bolts (photos).

4   *Manual transmission:* Locate the flywheel on the dowel in the crankshaft and fit new securing bolts.

5   The driveplate/flywheel securing bolts have nylon inserts. Always use new bolts at reassembly to avoid the possibility of an oil leak from the cylinder block.

6   Tighten the driveplate/flywheel securing bolts to the specified torque.

35   Jackshaft, timing chains and cylinder heads – refitting

1   Turn the engine over by the flywheel to position No 2 piston (the front cylinder on the left-hand bank) at TDC. Check that the line on the flywheel is aligned with the line marked on the flywheel housing.

2   Lubricate the jackshaft bearings with engine oil then carefully slide the jackshaft into position taking care not to damage the bearing surfaces (photo).

3   Fit the jackshaft retaining plate and secure with the two Allen screws tightened to the specified torque (photo).

4   Fit the inner crankshaft sprocket and using a straight edge (a steel rule will do) check the alignment (Fig. 1.12) of the sprocket in relation

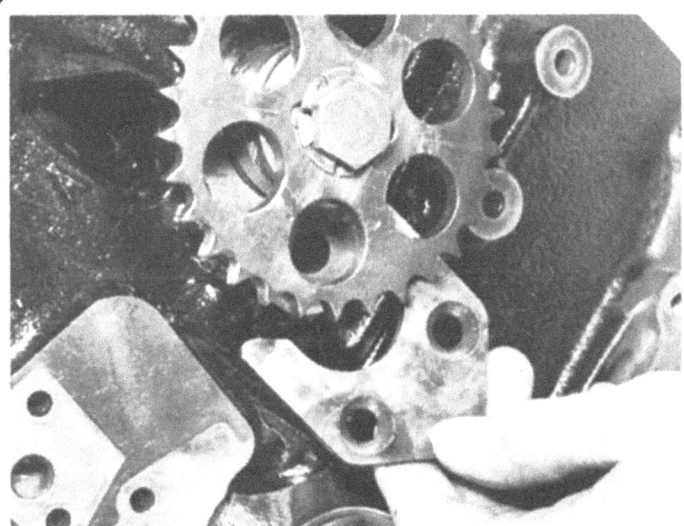

35.3 Fit the jackshaft retaining plate

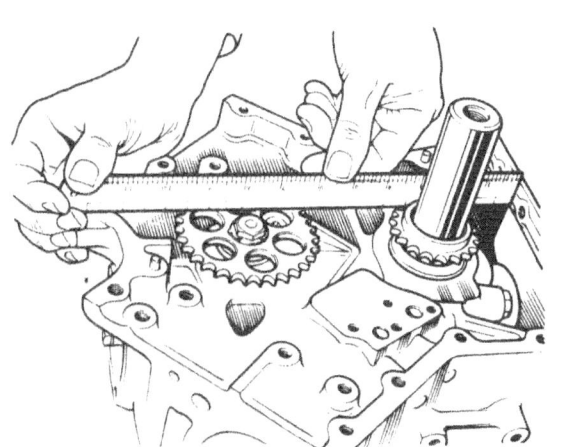

Fig. 1.12 Checking the alignment of the sprockets (Sec 35)

35.5 Fit the inner and outer sprockets on the crankshaft

35.6 Fit the inner chain tensioner

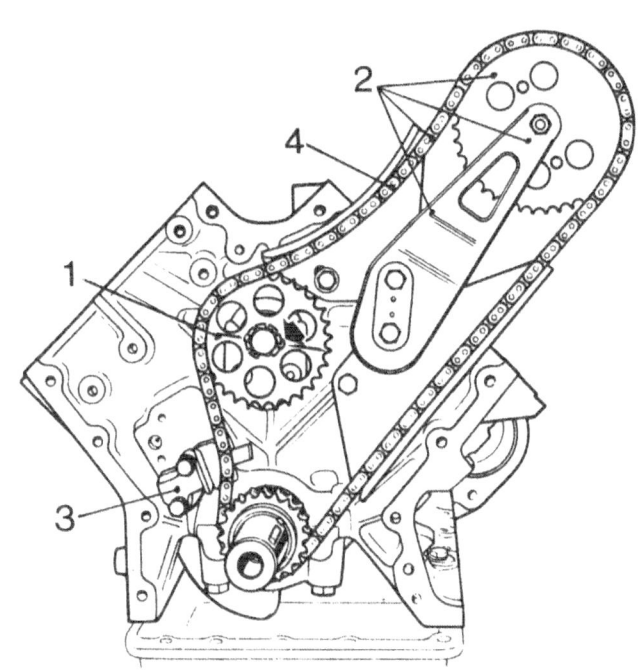

Fig. 1.13 Fitting the left-hand timing chain (Sec 35)

1 Jackshaft alignment marks with dowel arrowed
2 Timing chain, sprocket and support bracket
3 Inner chain tensioner
4 Curved chain guide

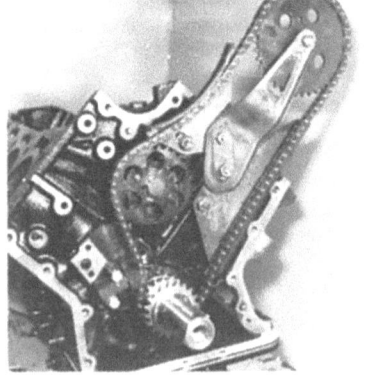

35.8 Left-hand chain fitted with support bracket and camshaft sprocket

35.12a Fitting the cylinder head hold-down studs ...

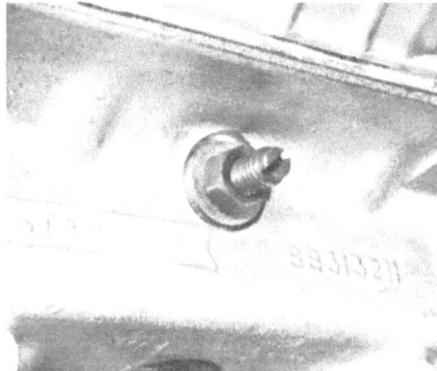

35.12b ... then the thick washer and nut

35.15 Bending over the locking tab to lock the camshaft sprocket securing bolt

35.17a Fitting a spacer to prevent the chain tensioner from releasing

35.17b A cut washer makes a good spacer

to the jackshaft sprocket. Fit shims, if necessary, behind the crankshaft inner sprocket to obtain correct alignment.

5 When the correct alignment is obtained, slide off the sprocket, fit the two Woodruff keys on the crankshaft and then refit the inner and outer sprockets (photo).

6 Fit the inner chain tensioner and restrictor plate and secure with two bolts. Fit the chain tensioner in the retracted position (photo).

7 Position the jackshaft so that the line marked on the sprocket slopes slightly down towards the left-hand bank with the dowel to the left-hand bank and No 2 piston on TDC (Fig. 1.13).

8 Fit the left-hand bank chain guides, the longer of the two timing chains and the support bracket with the camshaft chain guide or support bracket attaching bolts at this stage (photo).

9 Fit two of the left-hand cylinder head hold-down studs in the cylinder block to locate the cylinder head gasket and the cylinder head. When fitting the studs screw them in the full length of the threads, using a screwdriver.

10 Fit the cylinder head gasket.

11 Line up the mark on the camshaft flange with the groove on No 1 camshaft bearing cap and fit the left-hand cylinder head. **Note:** *The crankshaft or camshaft must not be turned while the head is fitted and the camshaft sprocket is disconnected.*

12 Fit the other studs, thick washers and nuts, then the cylinder head hold-down bolts and thick washers (photos).

13 Tighten the nuts and bolts. To prevent distorting the cylinder head the tightening sequence given in Section 8, paragraph 5 must be followed and the specified torque must not be exceeded.

14 Remove the left-hand camshaft sprocket from the support bracket and align the bolt holes with the holes in the camshaft flange by turning the sprocket, one tooth at a time, within the chain. Make sure the jackshaft sprocket does not move from its previously set position.

15 Fit the top camshaft bolt and lockplate, position the lockplate so that both holes are lined up, then tighten the top bolt and bend over the locking tab (photo).

16 Adjust the position of the support bracket so that the boss on the camshaft sprocket is centralised in the hole in the support bracket and tighten the bracket lower securing bolt.

17 Temporarily fit a spacer approximately 0.1 in (2.5 mm) thick between the body of the tensioner and the shoe to prevent the tensioner from releasing (photo). A plain washer cut out as shown (photo) makes a suitable spacer.

18 Place a 0.040 in (1 mm) feeler gauge between the shoe and the chain, then apply pressure with a screwdriver or similar tool, to the curved guide to tension the chain then tighten the bolts securing the curved chain guide and the support bracket. Remove the feeler gauge and the temporarily fitted spacer (photo).

19 Fit the outer chain tensioner, restrictor and spacer.

20 Fit the right-hand bank chain, chain guides and support bracket, with camshaft sprocket attached, together with the bolt spacers and bolts (photo). Do not tighten the bolts attaching the curved guide or support bracket at this stage.

21 Fit the water pump as described in Chapter 2, Section 8.

22 Now fit the right-hand cylinder head as described in paragraphs 10 to 13 for the left-hand head. Tighten the cylinder head hold-down nuts and bolts.

23 Clean the mating faces of the cylinder heads and inlet manifold. Apply a smear of grease to the joint faces of the cylinder heads and fit the inlet manifold gaskets in position.

24 Place the inlet manifold in position, taking care not to disturb the gasket and fit the securing bolts. Start all the bolts with the fingers before using a spanner as the threads in the cylinder heads are easily damaged. Tighten the bolts to the specified torque (photo).

25 Now carry out the operations described in paragraphs 13 to 19 on the right-hand bank.

26 Fit new camshaft cover gaskets and the rubber end grommets (photo). Renew the rubber sealing rings on the camshaft cover nuts. Refit the camshaft covers, securing nuts and the two screws at the front end.

36 Timing cover – refitting

1 Fit the oil slinger on the front end of the crankshaft with the dished face outwards (photo).

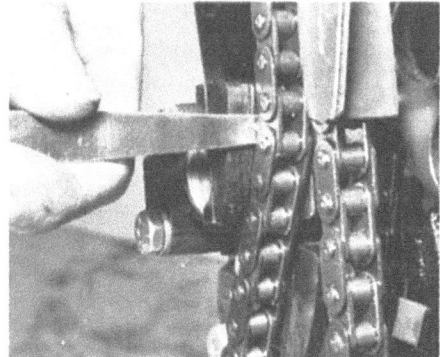

35.18 Using a feeler gauge between the chain and chain tensioner when adjusting the chain tension

35.20 Fit the right-hand chain, support bracket, chain guides and sprocket

35.24 Fitting the inlet manifold in position

35.26 Fit new rubber grommets on the cylinder heads

36.1 Slide the oil slinger on to the front of the crankshaft

2   Stick the three timing cover gaskets on the block with a smear of grease to hold them in position. Apply a little non-setting gasket cement on to the junction of the timing cover and sump gaskets (photo).

3   Tap a new oil seal evenly into the timing cover until the back face of the seal is flush with the front face of the cover (Fig. 1.14).

4   Fit the front cover taking care not to damage the cylinder head and sump gaskets. Use a piece of steel shim (or an old feeler gauge) to guide the timing cover between these gaskets. Tap the cover to locate it on the two dowels (photo).

5   Fit the timing cover securing bolts and the alternator mounting bracket. The cylinder head to front cover bolts should be fitted first, then the sump to cover bolts.

6   Tighten all the timing cover securing bolts and then all the sump bolts (photo).

7   The crankshaft pulley (photo) and the Torquatrol unit can now be fitted and secured with the centre bolt tightened to the specified torque. Use a chain or strap wrench, located in the middle groove of the pulley, to prevent the crankshaft from turning.

37 Oil transfer housing, oil pump and oil filter – refitting

1   Fit a new O-ring in the groove in the oil transfer housing, then fit the housing to the block. Ensure the housing is located on the dowel then fit the securing bolts (photos).

2   Fit a new O-ring seal in the groove in the oil pump. Ensure the cylinder block and pump mating faces are clean, then fit the oil pump and hexagonal drive shaft and the four securing bolts (photo).

3   Refit the oil filter assembly, using a new filter element and O-rings. Make sure that the filter bowl is correctly seated on the O-ring in the groove in the cylinder block (photo). Do not fully tighten the centre bolt as the filter has to be removed when refitting the engine in the car.

38 Engine – final assembly

1   Fit the ignition distributor as described in Chapter 4.

2   Fit the carburettors as described in Chapter 3 (photo).

36.2 Position the timing cover gaskets on the front of the block

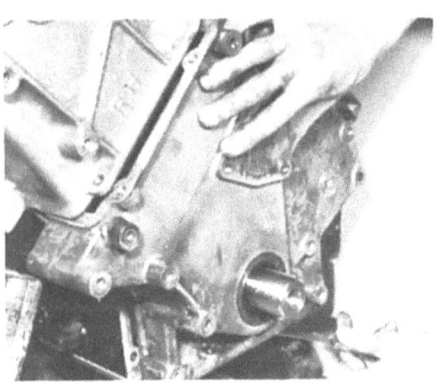

36.4 Using an old feeler gauge to guide the timing cover over the sump gasket

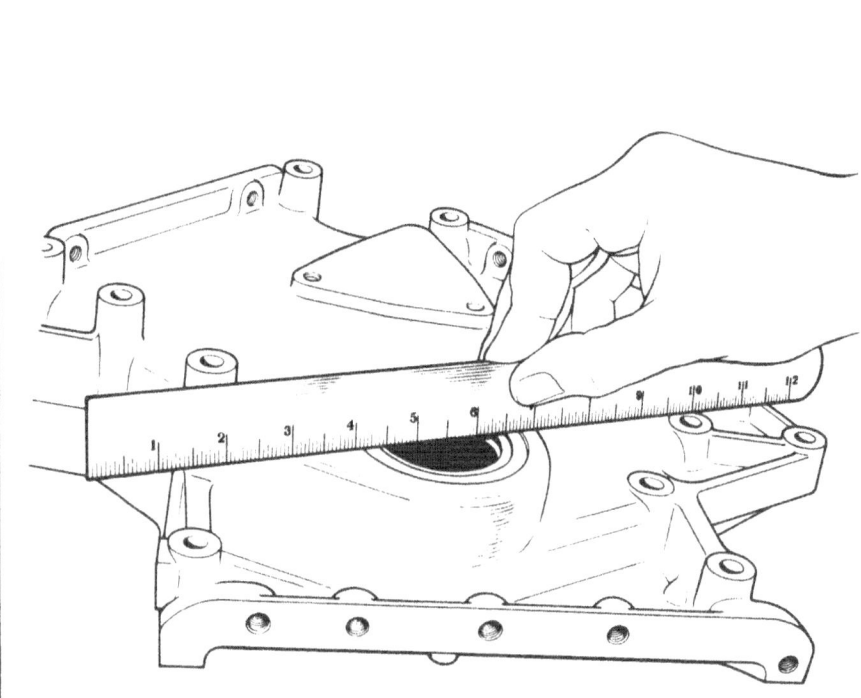

Fig. 1.14 Check that the oil seal is flush with the front face of the timing cover (Sec 36)

36.6 Tightening the timing cover to cylinder head bolts

36.7 Slide the pulley onto the crankshaft

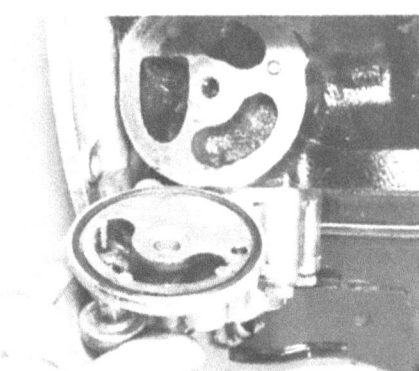

37.1a Fitting the oil transfer housing

37.1b The oil pressure switch is located on the oil transfer housing

37.2 Fitting the oil pump

37.3 Fit a new oil filter sealing ring in the groove in the block

38.2 Lowering the carburettors into position

Fig. 1.15 Oil filter assembly (Sec 37)

1 Centre bolt
2 Filter bowl
3 Element and O-ring

38.3 Fitting the alternator

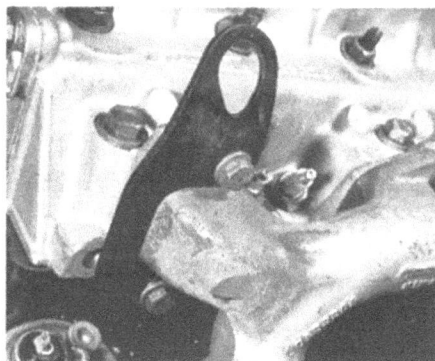

38.4a Do not forget the rear lifting eyes when fitting the right-hand exhaust manifold ...

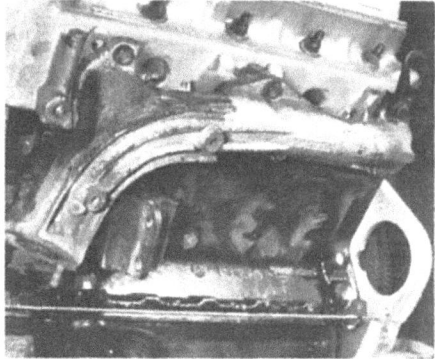

38.4b ... and the left-hand exhaust manifold

3   Fit the alternator and adjust the drivebelt tension as described in Chapter 10 (photo).

4   Fit the two exhaust manifolds. The manifolds are secured by seven bolts. There are no gaskets used between the manifolds and the cylinder heads. Do not forget the lifting eyes which are secured by the two rear bolts. Fit the hot air pre-heat shroud on the left-hand manifold (photos).

5   Fit the front lifting eyes. The right-hand lifting eye is part of the power steering pump mounting bracket which must be temporarily fitted (photos).

6   Fit the clutch assembly as described in Chapter 5.

7   Fit the engine mountings (photo).

8   Fit the heater pipes and by-pass hose.

39 Engine – refitting in car

1   If the engine/gearbox is being refitted as a unit the gearbox should now be refitted to the engine. Take care not to put any strain on the gearbox input shaft. On cars with automatic transmission fit the torque converter, then the driveplate and secure with the four bolts, working through the starter motor mounting opening.

2   Tighten all the gearbox to engine securing bolts, not forgetting the anti-vibration straps on later models.

3   Fit the starter motor.

4   Using a hoist, lift the combined assembly and move it into position above the engine compartment. Note the angle at which the engine is lowered into the engine compartment (photo). Remember that the front of the car must be raised by 18 inches as the engine is lowered. Place a trolley jack under the rear mounting so that the rear of the assembly can be rolled to the rear and then jacked-up into position.

5   Continue lowering the engine whilst raising and moving the trolley jack to the rear until the assembly is in position for the fitting of the mounting bolts.

6   Fit and tighten the front mounting bolts.

7   Fit the rubber washers, steel sleeves, nylon inserts, washers and

38.4c Fitting the warm air shroud on the left-hand manifold

38.5a Fit the left-hand front lifting eye

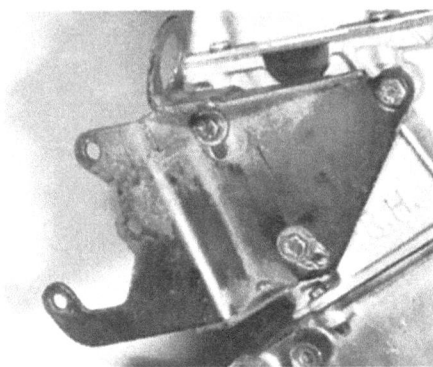

38.5b The power steering pump bracket is fitted temporarily

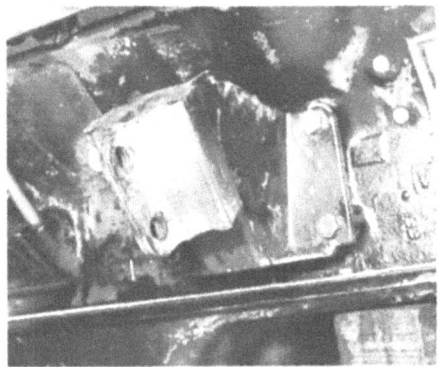

38.7 Right-hand front engine mounting

39.4 Lowering the engine into the engine compartment

nuts securing the rear mounting crossmember to the body. The four bolts securing the mounting crossmember are joined in pairs by a plate (see Fig. 1.3). When lifting the crossmember into position, the bolts may get pushed up into the car but they can be pushed down from inside the car without lifting the carpet. Should the bolt threads get damaged the carpet will have to be removed to renew the bolts.

8   The remainder of the items to be fitted are listed below and the refitting is the reverse of the removal procedure given in Section 4.

> *Electrical leads including engine earthing strap*
> *Exhaust pipes and silencers*
> *Speedometer drive connection*
> *Propeller shaft*
> *Gearshift linkage*
> *Fuel inlet pipe*
> *Throttle and choke linkage*
> *Downshift cable (automatic transmission)*
> *Clutch slave cylinder (manual transmission)*
> *Fan*
> *Brake servo pipe*
> *Distributor cap, coil and leads*
> *Air cleaner*
> *Radiator and all cooling system hoses*
> *Windscreen washer pump/reservoir*
> *Power steering pump, refer to Chapter 11 for adjustment of drive belt tension*
> *Bonnet*

9   Check that all leads, hoses and cable controls are securely connected. Fill the cooling system as described in Chapter 2. Refill the gearbox and engine with oil. Top-up the power steering reservoir with

automatic transmission fluid and bleed the system as described in Chapter 11.
10   If the engine was removed as a separate unit from the gearbox, the engine must be refitted first. The refitting procedure is similar to that described in this Section.

---

40 Engine – initial start-up after overhaul or major repair

1   Make sure the battery is fully charged and that all lubricants, coolants and fuel are replenished.
2   As soon as the engine fires and runs, keep it going at a fast tickover only (no faster) and bring it up to normal working temperature.
3   As the engine warms up, there will be odd smells and some smoke from parts getting hot and burning off oil deposits. Look for leaks of oil or water, which will be obvious if serious. Check also the clamp connections of the exhaust pipes to the manifolds as these do not always 'find' their exact gas tight position until the warmth and vibration have acted on them and it is almost certain that they will need tightening further. This should be done, of course, with the engine stopped.
4   When running temperature has been reached, adjust the idling speed as described in Chapter 3.
5   Stop the engine and wait a few minutes to see if any lubricant or coolant is dripping out when the engine is stationary.
6   Road test the car to check that the timing is correct and giving the necessary smoothness and power. Do not race the engine – if new bearings and/or pistons and rings have been fitted it should be treated as a new engine and run in at reduced revolutions for 1000 miles.
7   After 1000 miles, check the cylinder head for tightness as described in Section 8, paragraph 17.

41 Fault diagnosis – engine

Symptom	Reason/s
Engine will not turn over when starter switch is operated	Flat battery Bad battery connections Bad connections at solenoid switch and/or starter motor Starter motor jammed Defective solenoid Starter motor defective
Engine turns over normally but fails to fire and run	No spark at plugs No fuel reaching engine Too much fuel reaching the engine (flooding)
Engine starts but runs unevenly and misfires	Ignition and/or fuel system faults Incorrect valve clearances Burnt out valves
Lack of power	Ignition and/or fuel system faults Incorrect valve clearances Burnt out valves Worn out piston or cylinder bores
Excessive oil consumption	Oil leaks from crankshaft oil seal, camshaft cover gasket, drain plug gasket, sump plug washer, timing cover gaskets Worn piston rings or cylinder bores resulting in oil being burnt by engine (smoky exhaust is an indication) Worn valve guides
Excessive mechanical noise from engine	Incorrect valve clearances Worn crankshaft bearings Worn cylinders (piston slap)
Unusual vibration	Misfiring on one or more cylinders Loose mounting bolts

NOTE: *When investigating starting and uneven running faults do not be tempted into snap diagnosis. Start from the beginning of the check procedure and follow it through. It will take less time in the long run. Poor performance from an engine in terms of power and economy is not normally diagnosed quickly. In any event the ignition and fuel systems must be checked first before assuming any further investigation needs to be made.*

Chapter 2 Cooling system

Contets

Specifications

Type of system	Pressurised system with expansion tank. Pump and fan assisted

Water pump
Type	Centrifugal
Drive	From skew gear on jackshaft

Thermostat
Temperature stamped on thermostat:

82°C	Pre engine Nos LE20881/LF22050 and from engine No LF41212
88°C	From engine Nos LE20882/LF22051 up to engine No. LF41211

Starts to open:

82°C type	79·5 to 83·5°C (175 to 183°F)
88°C type	85 to 89°C (185 to 192°F)

Fully open

82°C type	93·5° to 96°C (200 to 205°F)
88°C type	99 to 102°C (210 to 215°F)

Pressure cap
Pressure cap opens at:

Pre Commission Nos. LD10195 and LE10001	13 lbf/in² (0·91 kgf/cm²)
From Commission Nos. LD10195 and LE10001	20 lbf/in² (1·41 kgf/cm²)

Cooling system capacity	18·5 pints (10·5 litres)

Torque wrench settings
	lbf ft	kgf m
Pump cover to block	20	2·8
Pump centre bolt (left-hand)	14	1·9
Transfer housing to cylinder head	20	2·8
Torquatrol unit to crankshaft	120	16·6
Fan to fan coupling	14	1·9

---

1 General description

The engine cooling water is circulated by a thermo-syphon, water pump assisted system, and the coolant is pressurised. This is primarily to prevent premature boiling in adverse conditions and also to allow the engine to operate at its most efficient running temperature, this being just under the boiling point of water. The overflow pipe from the radiator is connected to an expansion chamber which makes topping-up unnecessary. The coolant expands when hot, and instead of being forced down the overflow pipe and lost, it flows into the expansion chamber. As the engine cools the coolant contracts and, because of the pressure differential, flows back into the top tank of the radiator.

The system functions in the following manner: cold water in the bottom of the radiator circulates up the lower radiator hose to the water pump where it is pushed round the water passages in the cylinder block, helping to keep the cylinder bores and pistons cool.

The water then travels up into the cylinder head and circulates round the combustion spaces and valve seats absorbing more heat, and then, when the engine is at its proper operating temperature, travels out of the cylinder head, past the open thermostat into the upper radiator hose and so into the radiator header tank.

The water travels down the radiator where it is rapidly cooled by the in-rush of cold air through the radiator core, which is created by both the fan and the motion of the car. The water, now cold, reaches the bottom of the radiator, when the cycle is repeated.

When the engine is cold the thermostat (which is a valve which opens and closes according to the temperature of the water) restricts the circulation of the water in the engine.

Only when the correct minimum operating temperature has been reached, as shown in the specification, does the thermostat begin to open, allowing water to return to the radiator.

Two types of cooling system layout are used on Stag models. The earlier system operates at 13 lbf/in² (0·91 kgf/cm²) and can be identified by the pressure cap being located on the top of the radiator. Models from Commission No LD10195 operate at 20 lbf/in² (1·41 kgf/cm²) and has the pressure cap on top of the expansion tank which is located at the left-hand side of the radiator (Figs. 2.1 and 2.2).

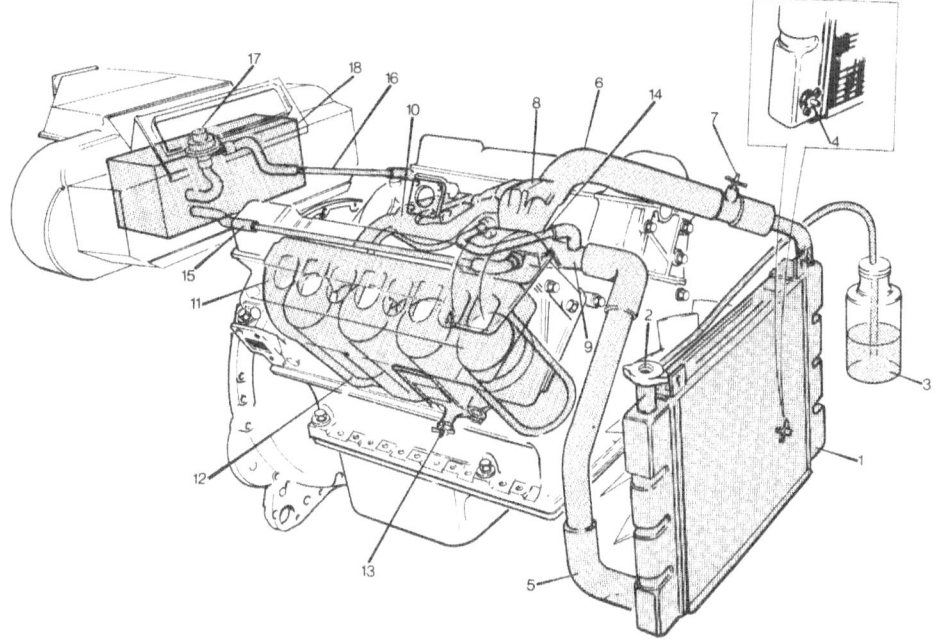

Fig. 2.1 Cooling system (Pre Commission No LD10195) (Sec 1)

1	Radiator	7	Air vent tap	13	Drain tap
2	Filler cap	8	Thermostat	14	By-pass hose
3	Expansion tank	9	Water pump	15	Heater inlet hose
4	Drain tap	10	Inlet manifold flow	16	Heater outlet hose
5	Bottom hose	11	Cylinder head flow	17	Heater valve
6	Top hose	12	Cylinder block flow	18	Heater assembly

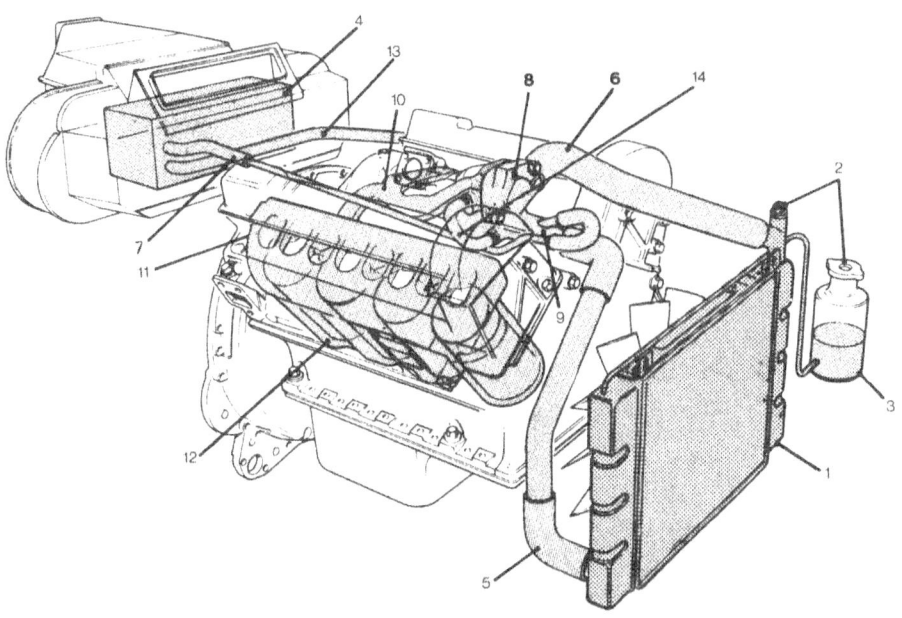

Fig. 2.2. Cooling system (From Commission No LD 10195) (Sec 1)

1	Radiator	6	Top hose	11	Cylinder head flow
2	Filler cap and plug	7	Heater inlet hose	12	Cylinder block flow
3	Expansion tank	8	Thermostat	13	Heater outlet hose
4	Heater assembly	9	Water pump	14	By-pass hose
5	Bottom hose	10	Inlet manifold flow		

The cooling system comprises the radiator, water pump, thermostat, interconnecting hoses and the waterways in the cylinder heads and block. The inlet manifold is heated by water from the pump.

The Torquatrol cooling fan limits the fan speed at high engine revolutions. Its aim is to reduce noise and engine load. The fan unit is mounted on the front of the crankshaft and is retained by the centre bolt which also secures the crankshaft pulley.

2 Cooling system – draining

When releasing the pressure in the cooling system of a hot engine, turn the filler cap slightly, using a rag over the cap for protection against any escaping steam. The sudden release of the cap (causing a drop in pressure) can result in the water boiling.

Earlier models
1   Remove the radiator filler cap.
2   If the system is filled with antifreeze, and it has been in use for less than two years, drain the coolant into a suitable container for re-use.
3   Open the two drain taps on the cylinder block and the one at the bottom of the radiator.

Later models
4   Remove the filler plug and the expansion tank cap (photos), then disconnect the bottom radiator hose from the radiator.

3 Cooling system – flushing

1   With time the cooling system will gradually lose its efficiency as the radiator becomes choked with rust scales, deposits from water and other sediment. To clear the system out, remove the radiator cap (or filler plug) and open the drain taps (if fitted) or remove the bottom hose and leave a hose running in the radiator filler orifice for ten to fifteen minutes.
2   Then close the drain taps or refit the bottom hose and refill with water and a proprietary cleansing compound. Run the engine for ten to fifteen minutes and then drain it and flush out thoroughly for a further ten minutes. All sediment and sludge should now have been removed.
3   In very bad cases the radiator should be reverse flushed. This can be done with the radiator in position, but it is more satisfactory to remove it.
4   Disconnect both radiator hoses from the radiator and insert a cold water pressure hose in the lower radiator outlet. Allow the water to flow until it runs clean from the upper radiator hose connection. If the radiator is removed and inverted, the reverse flushing action will be more searching.

4 Cooling system – filling

Earlier models
1   If opened for draining close the two taps on the cylinder block and the one on the radiator.
2   Open the tap on the top radiator hose.
3   Check that the valve to the heater unit is open, otherwise an air lock may form in the heater.
4   Fill the system slowly. If water only is to be used, rainwater should be used whenever possible.
5   If using anti-freeze use ethylene glycol base solutions with a suitable inhibitor for mixed metal engines.
6   Close the tap on the top radiator hose and fit the filler cap.

Later models
7   If removed for draining refit the bottom radiator hose and remove the filler plug.
8   Repeat the operations in paragraphs 3 to 5 above.
9   Fit the filler plug.
10 Half fill the expansion tank and fit the pressure cap.
11 Run the engine until it reaches the normal operating temperature; switch off and allow to cool, then top-up the expansion tank to half full.

5 Antifreeze mixture

1   Prior to the onset of cold winter weather, it is essential that antifreeze is added to the engine coolant if it has not been previously used.
2   If Castrol Antifreeze is not available, any antifreeze which conforms with specification 'BS 3151' or 'BS 3152' can be used. Never use an antifreeze with an alcohol base as evaporation is too high.
3   Castrol Antifreeze with an anti-corrosion additive can be left in the cooling system for up to two years, but after six months it is advisable to have the specific gravity of the coolant checked at your local garage, and thereafter, every three months.
4   Listed below are the amounts of antifreeze which should be added to ensure adequate protection down to the temperature given:

Amount of antifreeze	Protection to
4·74 pints (2·75 litre)	−12°C (10°F)
5·5 pints (3·25 litre)	−16°C (3°F)
6·5 pints (3·75 litre)	−20°C (−4°F)
9·25 pints (5·25 litre)	−36°C (−33°F)

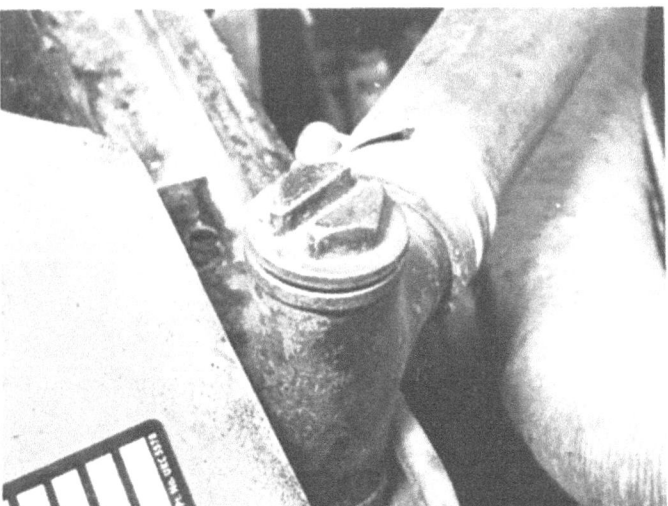

2.4a Remove the filler plug ...

2.4b ... and the expansion tank cap

6 Radiator – removal, servicing and refitting

1   To remove the radiator first drain the cooling system as described in Section 2.
2   Disconnect the radiator overflow pipe from the expansion tank.
3   Undo the hose clips holding the top and bottom hoses to the radiator and pull the hoses off their connections.
4   Remove the two securing nuts at the bottom of the radiator. The fan cowl will come away with the nuts.
5   Undo and remove the two bolts securing the radiator at the top. On later models using the temperature compensator type air cleaner it wil be necessary to remove the cold air duct by disconnecting the hose between the duct and the air cleaner and removing the securing screw from the centre of the duct.
6   Carefully lift up the radiator and tilt back slightly to allow for clearance of the fan blades. Great care must be taken whilst removing the radiator otherwise serious damage could result if the matrix is distorted or perforated.
7   With the radiator out of the car any leaks can be soldered up or repaired with a proprietary compound. Clean out the inside of the radiator by flushing as detailed in Section 3. When the radiator is out of the car it is advantageous to turn it upside-down for reverse flushing. Clean the exterior of the radiator by hosing down the radiator matrix with a strong jet of water to clean away road dirt, dead flies etc.
8   Inspect the radiator hoses for cracks, internal or external perishing and damage caused by overtightening of the securing clips. Renew the hoses as necessary. Examine the radiator hose securing clips and renew them if they are rusted or distorted.
9   Refitting is the reverse of the removal procedure. Fill the cooling system as described in Section 4.

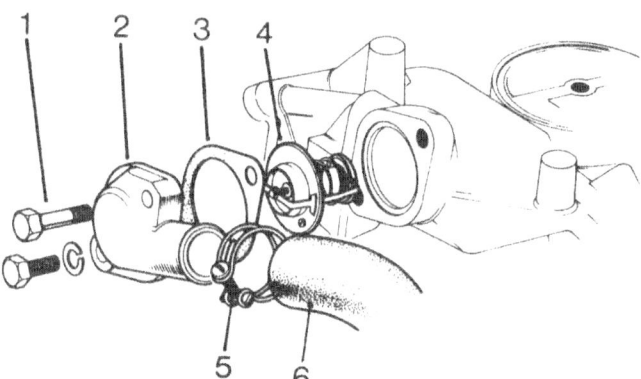

Fig. 2.3 Removing the thermostat (Sec 7)

1 Bolt
2 Thermostat housing
3 Gasket
4 Thermostat
5 Hose securing clip
6 Top hose

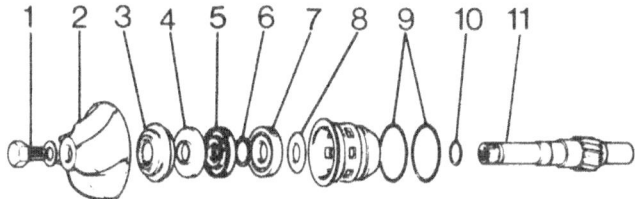

Fig. 2.4 Exploded view of water pump (Sec 8)

1 Centre bolt and washer
2 Impeller
3 Graphite seal
4 Water thrower
5 Oil seal
6 Circlip
7 Bearing
8 Oil thrower
9 Housing O-rings
10 Shaft O-ring
11 Shaft

7 Thermostat – removal, testing and refitting

1   To remove the thermostat, partially drain the cooling system (4 pints is enough), slacken the top radiator hose clip at the thermostat housing end and pull the hose off the elbow.
2   Unscrew the two set bolts and spring washers from the thermostat housing and lift the housing and paper gasket away. Take out the thermostat (Fig. 2.3).
3   Test the thermostat for correct functioning by suspending it by a length of string in a suitable container of cold water together with a thermometer.
4   Heat the water and note when the thermostat begins to open. This temperature is stamped on the flange of the thermostat, and is also given in the Specifications Section.
5   Discard the thermostat if it opens too early. Continue heating the water until the thermostat is fully open. Then let it cool down naturally. If the thermostat will not open fully in boiling water, or does not close down as the water cools, then it must be renewed.
6   If the thermostat is stuck open when cold this will be apparent when removing it from the housing.
7   Refitted the thermostat is a reversal of the removal procedure. Remember to use a new paper gasket between the thermostat housing elbow and the thermostat. Renew the thermostat housing elbow if it is badly corroded.

8 Water pump – removal, overhaul and refitting

Before attempting to remove the water pump from the block it must be appreciated that there is a likelihood that special tools will be required. These are identified as Triumph part numbers S4235A-10 and 4235A.

1   Remove the carburettors as described in Chapter 3.
2   Remove the inlet manifold. The procedure for this is given in Chapter 1, Section 7.
3   Slacken the securing clips and disconnect the bottom hose connection and the by-pass hose from the water pump. On later models also disconnect the heater pipe.
4   Remove the three bolts and flat washers securing the pump cover. Take the cover off (photo).
5   Remove the impeller retaining bolt (photo) by turning clockwise (ie left-hand threaded bolt) until

(a) *either the water pump is released from the jackshaft and can be lifted out or*
(b) *the centre bolt alone comes out*

6   If (b) applies, fit the impact tool S4235-10 and adaptor '4235A and drive out the pump.

8.4 Lift the water pump cover

8.5 Remove the impeller retaining bolt

8.25 Measuring the gap between the pump cover and block

9.4 The coolant temperature sender switch is located on the water transfer housing at the rear of the left-hand cylinder head

7 With the water pump removed from the block, drive the shaft out of the impeller. Make sure that the back of the impeller is adequately supported.

8 Drive out the driveshaft using a soft faced hammer.

9 Take off the O-ring, graphite seal, water thrower, oil seal and circlip in that order.

10 Carefully drive the bearing off the shaft.

11 Take off the oil thrower and remove the O-ring from the housing.

12 Discard the bearing, seals and O-ring. It is false economy not to do this even if they are in apparently serviceable condition.

13 Carefully examine the housing for cracks and corrosion. If cracked it must be renewed, but corrosion can be carefully dressed out with a fine file and emery paper; unless it is so severe that it will not permit the O-rings to seal properly. Make sure that no swarf remains after any local dressing.

14 Examine the shaft for wear. If this is present, or if there is any wear evident on the gears, the shaft should be renewed. It is permissible to carefully dress out any light scoring.

15 Check the impeller for corrosion and cracks. Light corrosion can be carefully dressed out but if any other defect is present, it too, must be renewed.

16 To reassemble, fit the oil thrower, concave side towards the gear.

17 Fit the bearing to the shaft then the circlip. The original one may be re-used if undamaged.

18 Now carefully press the shaft into the housing, then fit the oil seal inside the housing with the flat face towards the bearing.

19 Carefully press the water thrower to the shoulder of the shaft, concave side towards the bearing.

20 Fit the graphite seal, flat face downwards, into the housing.

21 Fit the shaft O-ring followed by the impeller. Torque tighten the left-hand threaded bolt to the specified torque; refer to the Specifications at the beginning of this Chapter.

22 Fit two new O-rings to the grooves in the housing, smaller one near the gear.

23 Smear a little rubber grease on the surface of the housing O-rings then fit the pump to the cylinder block. Turn the impeller anti-clockwise to engage the gears but do not use force either for turning, or pressing in. Don't forget to make sure that the cavity walls of the cylinder block are clean before fitting the pump.

24 Clean the mating faces of the pump cover and block, then loosely, but evenly, fit the cover bolts.

25 Using feeler gauges, measure the gap between the cover and block mating faces then select gaskets equal to this amount plus 0·010 to 0·025 in (0·25 to 0·5 mm). Gaskets are available in three thicknesses: 0·010, 0·020 and 0·030 in (0·254, 0·508 and 0·762 mm) (photo).

26 Fit the gaskets and cover then tighten the cover securing bolts evenly to the specified torque.

27 Reconnect the water hoses to the pump and fit the inlet manifold; refer to Chapter 1, Section 8.

28 Refit the carburettors as described in Chapter 3.

29 Refill the cooling system as described in Section 4.

9 Temperature gauge and sender unit – general

1 If the temperature gauge fails to work, either the gauge, the sender unit, the wiring, or the connections are at fault.

2 It is not possible to repair the gauge or the sender unit and they must be replaced by new units if at fault.

3 First check the wiring connections and if sound check the wiring for breaks using an ohmmeter. The sender unit and gauge should be tested by substitution.

4 The sender unit can be unscrewed from its location on the water transfer housing at the rear of the left-hand cylinder head after draining the cooling system (photo).

5 The temperature gauge can be removed as described in Chapter 10, Section 47.

10 Fan and Torquatrol unit – removal and refitting

1 Remove the radiator as described in Section 6.

2 If the fan only is to be removed, undo the four securing nuts and lift out the fan.

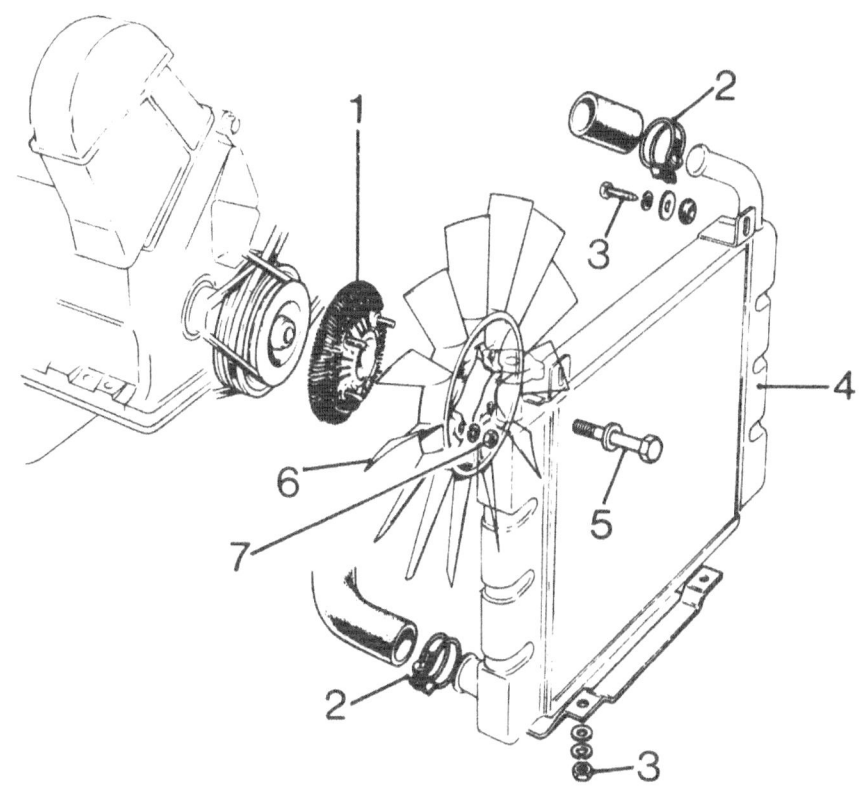

Fig. 2.5 Removing the fan and Torquatrol unit (Sec 10)

1 Torquatrol unit
2 Hose clip
3 Radiator securing bolt
4 Radiator
5 Centre bolt
6 Fan
7 Fan securing nut

3   To remove the Torquatrol unit undo the centre bolt securing the unit and the crankshaft pulley to the crankshaft and lift away the Torquatrol unit, then undo the fan securing nuts and separate the fan from the hub unit. When slackening off the centre bolt restrain the crankshaft from turning by holding it with a strap or chain wrench located in the centre groove of the crankshaft pulley.

4   Refitting is the reverse of the removal procedure. Tighten the fan securing nuts and the centre securing bolt to the specified torque.

11 Fault diagnosis – cooling system

Symptom	Reason/s
Heat generated in cylinder not being successfully disposed of by radiator	Insufficient water in cooling system Radiator core blocked or radiator grille restricted Bottom water hose collapsed, impeding flow Thermostat not opening properly Ignition advance and retard incorrectly set (accompanied by loss of power and perhaps, misfiring) Carburettors incorrectly adjusted (mixture too weak) Exhaust system partially blocked Oil level in sump too low Blown cylinder head gasket (water/steam being forced down the expansion tank overflow pipe under pressure) Engine not yet run-in Brakes binding
Too much heat being dispersed by radiator	Thermostat jammed open Incorrect grade of thermostat fitted allowing premature opening of valve Thermostat missing
Leaks in system	Loose clips on water hoses Top, bottom or expansion tank water hoses perished and leaking Radiator core leaking Thermostat gasket leaking Pressure cap spring worn or seal ineffective Blown cylinder head gasket (pressure in system forcing water/steam down overflow pipe) Cylinder wall or head cracked Expansion tank leaking

Chapter 3 Fuel and exhaust systems

Contents

Specifications

Air cleaner	Renewable paper element, later models fitted with temperature compensator system

Fuel pump

Make	SU
Type	AUF 30 electrically operated diaphragm
Maximum delivery	140 pints (80 litres) per hour
Cut-off pressure	2.7 lbf/in^2 (1.86 kgf/cm^2)

Fuel tank capacity

Pre-1973 models	14 gallons (63.5 litres – 16.5 US gallons)
From 1973 models on and 1972 left-hand drive models	12.75 gallons (58.0 litres – 15.3 US gallons)

Carburettors

Make	Twin side draught Stromberg	
Type	**UK**	**USA**
1970	175 CD2S	175 CDSE
1971	175 CDS or 175 CDSEV	175 CDSEV
1972 to 1973	175 CDSEV	175 CDSEV
1974 to 1977	175 CD2SEV	—
Main jet	0.100 in (2.54 mm)	0.100 in (2.54 mm)
Venturi	1.75	1.75
Needle		
1970/1	B1AQ	B1BF
1972 to 1977	B1AQ	B1AQ
Float height		0.629 to 0.669 in (16 to 17 mm)

Torque wrench settings

	lbf ft	kgf m
Carburettor adaptor attachment	32	4.4
Carburettor to adaptor	20	2.8

1 General description

The fuel system comprises a rear mounted fuel tank, an electrically operated fuel pump, located on the right-hand side of the luggage boot behind the trim panel, which delivers fuel to the two Stromberg carburettors. A fuel pump inertia cut-out switch is mounted on the left-hand side of the bulkhead (photo).

Various emission control equipment is fitted to some Stag models to meet the emission control regulations of certain territories. It is very important to appreciate that any adjustments made to the fuel system of cars so equipped will probably result in the car failing to meet the legal requirements in respect of air pollution, unless, special test equipment is used when making adjustments.

2 Air cleaner (early type) – removal, servicing and refitting

1 Disconnect the carburettor breather pipe from the rear of the air cleaner (Fig. 3.1).
2 Release the two clips at the front of the air cleaner and lift off the top cover.
3 Remove the air cleaner element.
4 Undo the six bolts securing the air cleaner base to the carburettor adaptor elbows. Lift off the base and collect the two gaskets.
Note: *If the air cleaner is being removed to provide access to other components it can be removed as a complete assembly with the adaptor elbows attached by removing the three bolts securing each elbow to the carburettors.*

1.1 Fuel pump inertia switch

5   Clean the dirt and dust from the filter element and the covers with a soft brush or air pressure from a tyre pump. The filter element should be cleaned after 6000 miles (9600 km) and renewed at 12 000 mile (19 000 km) intervals.
6   Refitting is the reverse of the removal procedure.

3   Air cleaner with temperature compensator system – description and servicing

1   This type of air cleaner is designed to maintain the air being drawn into the carburettors at an intake temperature above 20°C (68°F). The system is used to assist in reducing pollution emitted from the exhaust and consists essentially of a temperature sensor and air control valve. The non-return valve in the inlet manifold provides a delay factor when manifold vacuum is temporarily destroyed during sudden increase of engine speed.
2   The temperature sensor will actuate the flap valve in the air cleaner intake so that the correct mixture of hot air from the exhaust manifold and cold air entering the air cleaner inlet duct will be supplied to the carburettors at the specified temperature irrespective of the operating temperature of the engine itself (Fig. 3.3).
3   Regular maintenance of this type of air cleaner is not required beyond renewal of the element as described for the earlier type of air cleaner described in Section 2. However, in the event of a fault developing and evidence of increased exhaust fumes being emitted, carry out the following operations.
4   Inspect the condition and security of the hot air duct and the vacuum pipe to the sensor and vacuum capsule. Remove the cold air duct hose.
5   With the engine at the normal operating temperature, switch off the ignition and holding a mirror ro reflect the interior of the air cleaner intake duct, check the position of the valve. The valve should be closed to exhaust manifold heated air. If this is not the case check the valve linkage.
6   Disconnect the vacuum hose which connects the vacuum capsule to the inlet manifold. Suck the tube to actuate the vacuum capsule and check that the valve closes to the cold air intake. If this is not the case then the air cleaner must be renewed as an assembly.
7   With the engine cold, below 20°C (68°F), and using a mirror as previously described check that the valve is in the 'open to cold air' position A in Fig. 3.3.
8   Start the engine and run it at idling speed; the valve should close immediately to cold air and permit the exhaust manifold heated air to be drawn into the cleaner, B in Fig 3.3.
9   As the engine warms up observe that the flap valve gradually opens to permit the entry of cold air into the air cleaner.
10 If the valve does not operate correctly above 20°C (68°F), checked by using a thermometer adjacent to its location, remove and renew the sensor unit by prising off the retaining clip after removing the air cleaner.

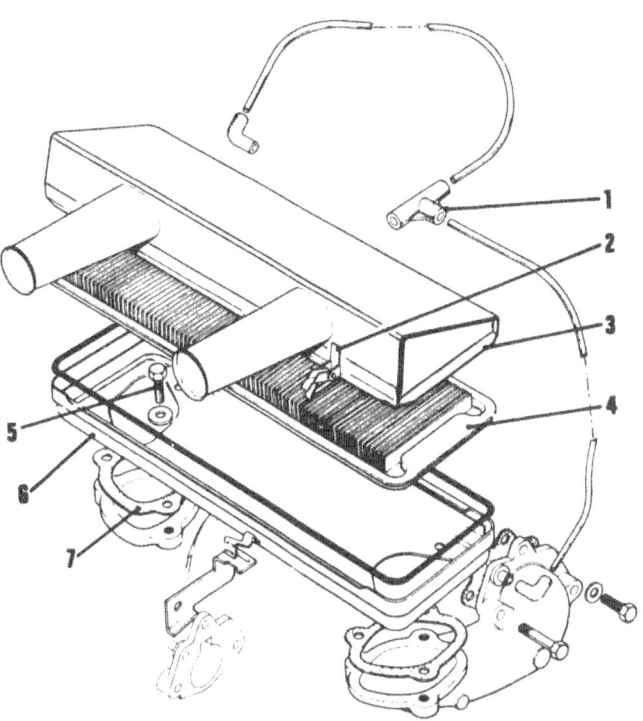

Fig. 3.1 Air cleaner – early type (Sec 2)

1 Carburettor breather pipe   5 Bolt
2 Clip   6 Air cleaner base
3 Top cover   7 Gasket
4 Paper element

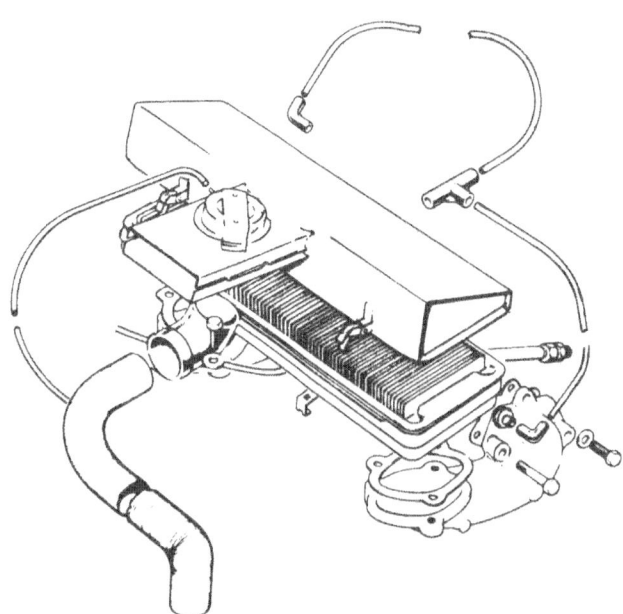

Fig. 3.2 Temperature compensator type air cleaner (Sec 3)

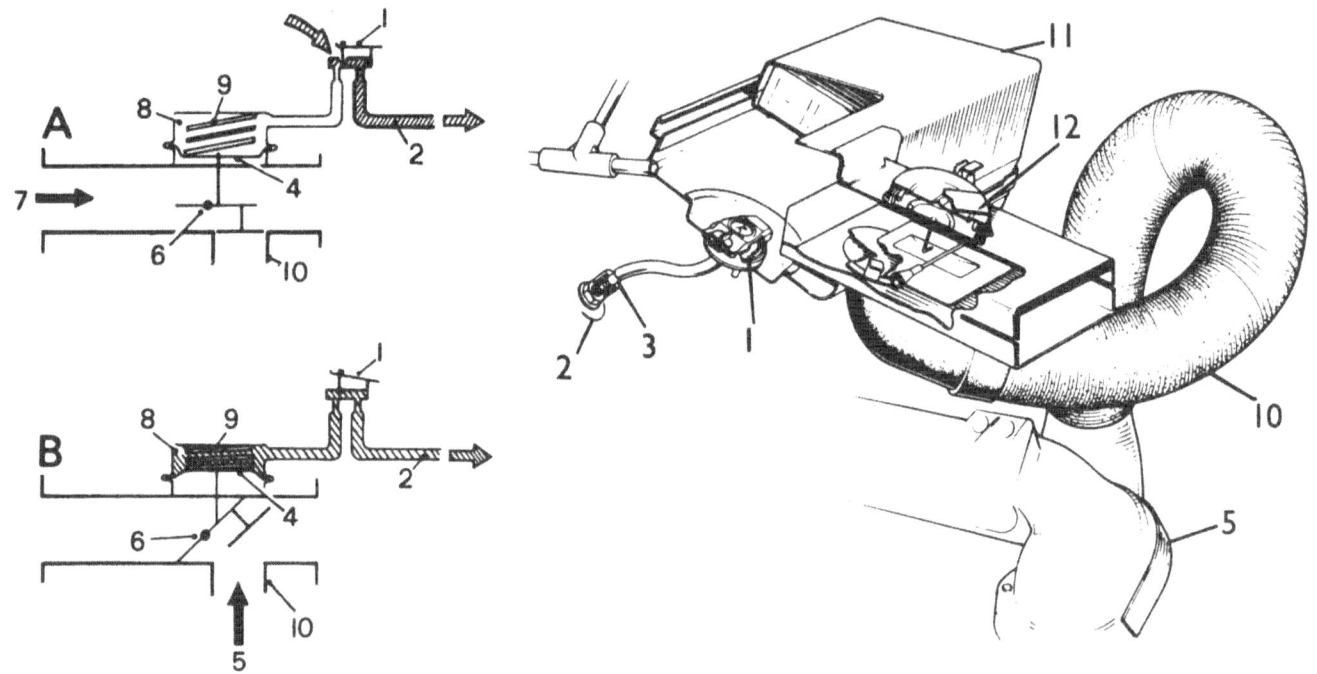

Fig. 3.3 Air cleaner temperature compensator system (Sec 3)

1 Temperature sensor	4 Vacuum capsule	7 Cold air duct	10 Cold air hose
2 Inlet manifold	5 Hot air duct	8 Vacuum side of motor	11 Air cleaner cover
3 Non-return valve	6 Flap valve	9 Spring	12 Motor housing

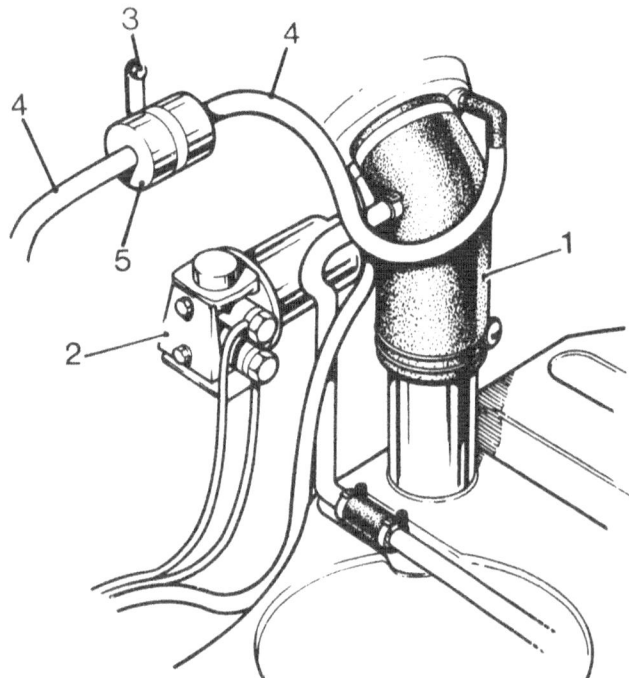

Fig. 3.4 Fuel pump and fuel line breather filter (Sec 4)

1 Filler
2 Fuel pump
3 Filter securing bolt
4 Filter inlet and outlet pipes
5 Filter

4 Fuel filters – renewal

1   The fuel line breather filter is located behind the right-hand trim panel in the luggage compartment.
2   When fitting the new filter the end marked IN must face the rear of the car (Fig. 3.4).

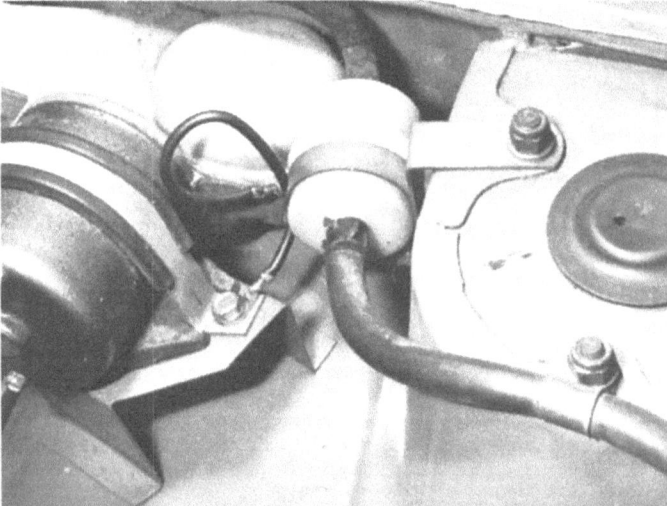

4.3 The main fuel filter is mounted on the left-hand turret

3   The fuel line main filter on early models is mounted on the left-hand camshaft cover; on later models the filter is attached to the rear stud on the left-hand turret (phcto).
4   When renewing the filter ensure that the end marked IN faces the rear of the car.
5   Both filters should be renewed every 6000 miles (10 000 km).

5 Fuel pump – description

1   The electrically operated fuel pump is located on the right-hand side of the luggage compartment behind the trim panel (photo).
2   The pump is secured to a flexible mounted bracket by two bolts.
3   The top connection is the outlet and the bottom connection is the inlet. The inlet connection leads into an air bottle provided by a chamber in the pump body.

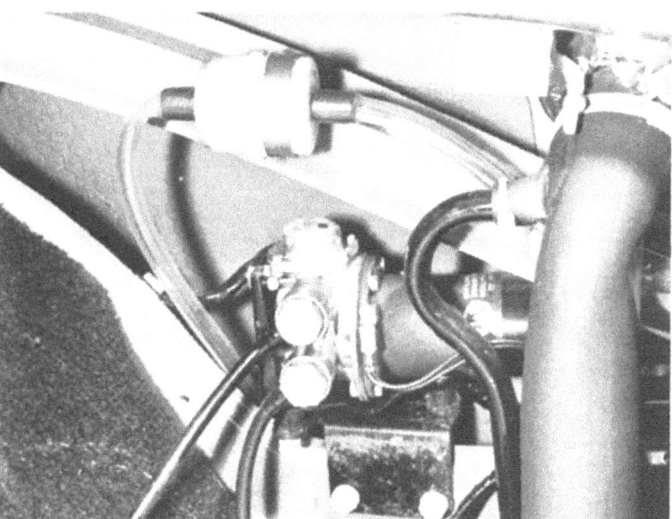

5.1 The fuel pump and fuel line breather filter

4   Smooth fuel delivery is achieved by an air cushion separated from the outlet chamber by a plastic diaphragm.

6   Fuel pump – testing

1   Disconnect the fuel inlet pipe from the fuel filter, and with a suitable container in position to catch the ejected fluid, switch on the ignition. A good flow of petrol should emerge from the pipe.
2   To check the fuel delivery pressure connect a low pressure gauge to the pipe and switch on the ignition. The gauge should record a pressure of approximately 2.7 lbf/in² (1.8 kgf/cm²).

7   Fuel pump – removal and refitting

1   Working in the luggage compartment, remove the floor carpet and the left-hand floor panel then slide out the right-hand floor panel.
2   Undo the securing screws and lift away the right-hand side trim panel.

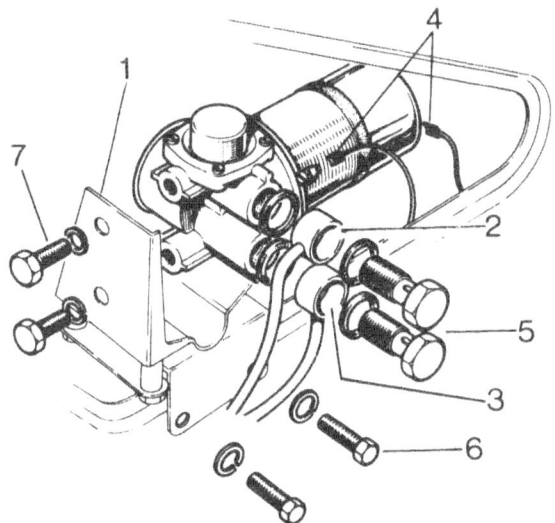

Fig. 3.5 Removing the fuel pump (Sec 7)

1   Mounting bracket   5   Banjo bolts
2   Outlet pipe   6   Bracket to body bolts
3   Inlet pipe   7   Pump to bracket bolts
4   Lucar connections

3   Disconnect the two electrical leads from the Lucar connectors (Fig. 3.5).
4   Disconnect the inlet and outlet fuel pipes from the pump by removing the two banjo bolts and the four fibre washers.
5   Remove the two bolts securing the flexible mounting bracket to the body and lift out the pump and mounting bracket assembly.
6   Undo the two pump to mounting bracket bolts and separate the pump from the bracket.
7   Refitting is the reverse of the removal procedure.

8   Fuel pump – dismantling, servicing and reassembly

1   Refer to Fig 3.6. Take off the sealing tape and rubber sealing band (1). Remove the plastic insulating sleeve, nut and Lucar connector (2) then withdraw the end cover.
2   Undo the screw (3) then lift the wire tags and remove the contact blade. Remove the screw and connector (4).
3   Separate the coil housing from the pump body after removing the six attaching screws (5). Unscrew the diaphragm anti-clockwise to release the spindle from the rocker mechanism then withdraw the assembly and remove the spring.
4   Remove the seal washer and nut, then using a knife, detach the lead washer (7). Remove the screw and condenser (8).
5   Remove the screw (9).
6   Tip the pedestal and remove the tag and spring washer (10) from the stud (12) then detach the pedestal from the coil housing.
7   Pull out the retaining pin and remove the rocker mechanism (11). Withdraw the stud (12).
8   Undo the two securing screws and remove the plate (13). Carefully lift out the cap, inlet valve, washers and filter (14), then the cap, outlet valve and washer (15).
9   Remove the bolt, spring washer, dished washer, cover (16) and gasket.
10 Dismantle the flow smoothing device, if necessary, by undoing the four securing screws and lifting off the cover (17), O-ring, diaphragm and washer.
11 Carefully wash the filter and clean all the parts with petrol, an old toothbrush is useful for this. Check the diaphragm for signs of deterioration and renew it if necessary. Check all parts for wear or damage and renew as necessary. Fit new O-ring and gaskets at assembly.
12 To reassemble the flow smoothing device, fit the washer, diaphragm, O-ring, and cover (17) and the four securing screws.
13 Fit the gasket and cover (16), then the securing bolt with dished washer and spring washer.
14 Insert the washer, outlet valve with the tongue towards the pump body and cap (15), then the washer, filter with concave side towards the coil housing, washer, inlet valve with tongue towards the coil housing and cap (14). Fit the plate (13) and two securing screws.
15 Fit the stud (12) then position the rocker mechanism and insert the retaining pin (11).
16 Fit the spring and coil housing tag on the stud (12) and position the contact pedestal to the coil housing, then fit the screw (9). Take care not to overtighten the screws and crack the pedestal.
17 Locate the condenser tag and contact earth tag on the screw (8) then fit the screw to the pump.
18 Fit a new lead washer (7) and nut, with the concave side towards the pedestal, then the seal washer.
19 Fit the spring (6) with the smaller diameter towards the diaphragm, then engage the diaphragm spindle to the contact trunnion and screw it in clockwise until the rocker mechanism does not throw out.
20 Fit the contact blade and two tags and secure with screw (3).
21 Adjust the contact blade to achieve the following condition:

(a) *Contact blade points slightly above the rocker mechanism points when closed*
(b) *When the points make or break each pair wipes across the centre line of the other*
(c) *When the rocker mechanism is withdrawn towards the coil housing, the contact blade must rest lightly on the ridge. Adjust by swinging the blade clear of the pedestal and bending it so that the blade rests lightly on the ridge (Fig 3.7). Do not bend the blade too much or the rocker mechanism travel will be restricted*

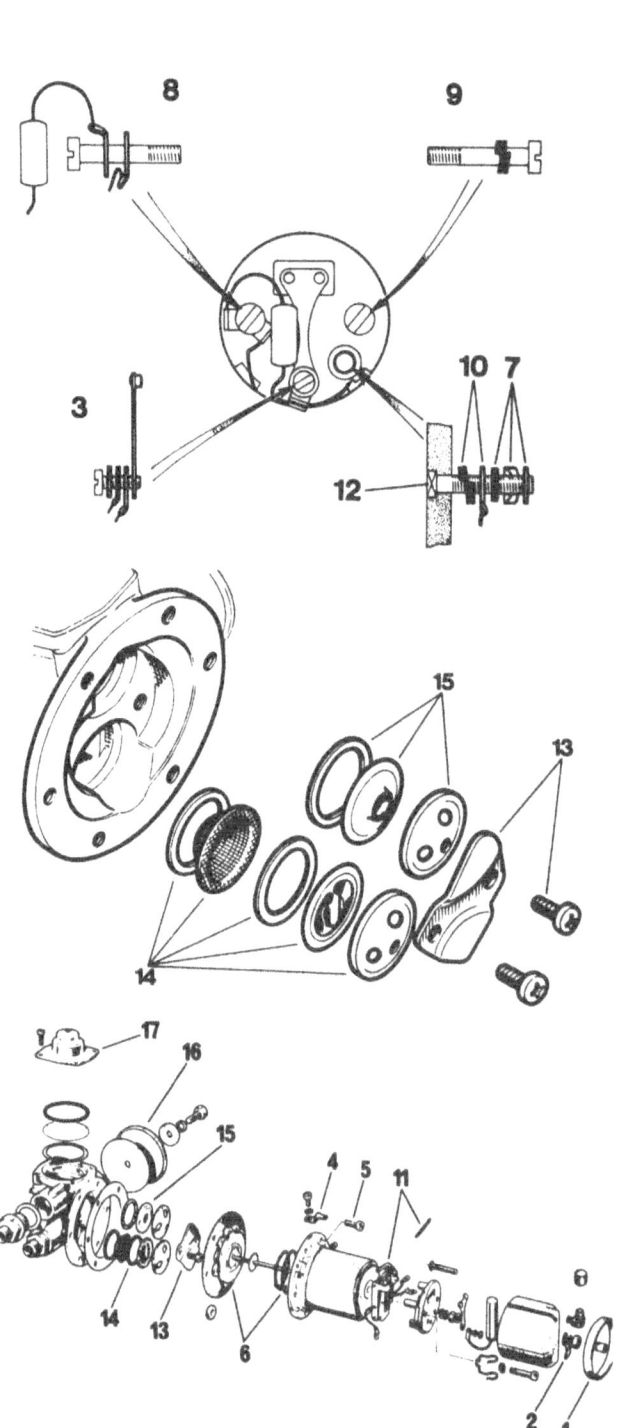

Fig. 3.6 Exploded view of fuel pump (Sec 8)

1	Sealing band	10	Tag and spring washer
2	Lucar connector	11	Rocker mechanism
3	Screw and contact blade	12	Stud
4	Screw and connector	13	Valve retaining plate
5	Screws	14	Inlet valve assembly
6	Diaphragm and spring	15	Outlet valve assembly
7	Lead washer	16	Cover
8	Screw and condenser	17	Cover
9	Screw		

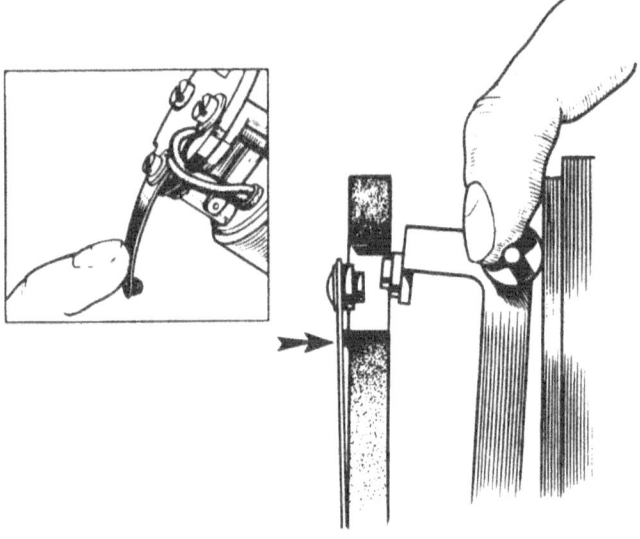

Fig. 3.7 Adjusting the contact blade (Sec 8)

22 Check that the lift of the contact blade tip, dimension A in Fig. 3.8, is 0.030 to 0.040 in (0.76 to 1.02 mm). Adjust, if necessary by bending the outer stop finger.

23 Check that gap B in Fig 3.8 is 0.065 to 0.75 in (1.65 to 1.91 mm). Adjust, if necessary, by bending the inner stop finger.

24 Hold the unit horizontal and press the diaphragm to ensure that the rocker mechanism will not throw over. Press and release the diaphragm while carefully unscrewing anti-clockwise until the rocker mechanism just throws over (Fig. 3.9). From this point unscrew to align the holes, then unscrew through a further four hole pitches to obtain the correct setting.

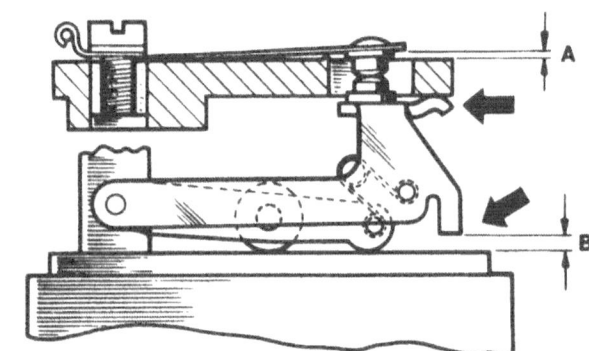

Fig. 3.8 Checking the lift of the contact blade (Sec 8)

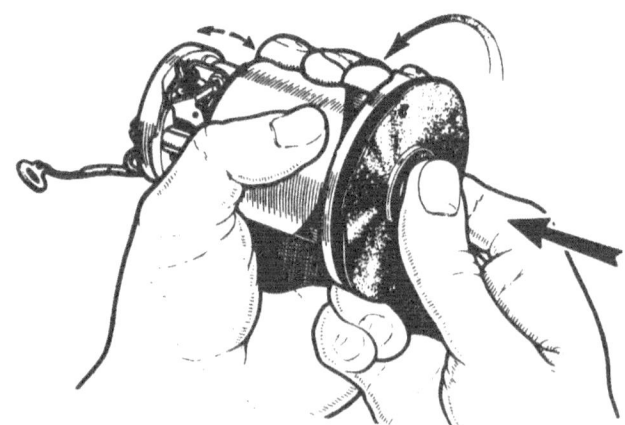

Fig. 3.9 Setting the rocker mechanism (Sec 8)

25 Assemble the gasket and coil housing to the pump body and fit the six securing screws.
26 Fit the Lucar earth connector (4), spring washer and securing screw.
27 Fit the end cover, shakeproof washer, Lucar connector, nut and insulating sleeve.
28 Fit the rubber sealing band (1) and wrap with sealing tape.
29 Check the delivery pressure, refer to Section 6.

9 Fuel tank – removal and refitting

1 Remove the battery earth strap and extinguish all naked lights in the vicinity.
2 Remove the fuel tank drain plug and drain the contents into a clean container.
3 Remove the luggage boot carpet and floor boards. Lift out the spare wheel.
4 Remove the right-hand side trim panel.
5 Disconnect the three electrical leads from the fuel level transmitter.
6 Disconnect the main fuel feed pipe at the tank union and the breather pipe at the rubber hose.
7 Slacken the lower clip that secures the fuel filler pipe to the tank.
8 Remove the four bolts which secure the tank to the mountings, then move the tank to disengage it from the filler pipe and lift away the tank.
9 Refitting is the reverse of the removal procedure.

10 Fuel level transmitter unit – removal and refitting

1 Disconnect the battery earth strap.
2 Remove the luggage boot carpet and floor boards.
3 Lift out the spare wheel.
4 Disconnect the three electrical leads from the transmitter unit.
5 Unscrew the sealing ring, then remove the gasket and lift the fuel level transmitter out of the tank.
6 Refitting is the reverse of the removal procedure. Always fit a new gasket.

11 Carburettors – description

All Stag models are equipped with twin Stromberg 175 CDSE or 175 CDSEV type carburettors of the variable jet type. This type of carburettor differs from fixed jet carburettors in that instead of having a number of jets for different conditions, only one variable jet is fitted to deal with all normal conditions. Also the cross-sectional areas of the air intake passage through the carburettor varies according to demands made by the engine. The fuel, which is drawn into the air passage through a jet orifice, is metered by a tapered needle which moves in and out of the jet, thus varying the effective size of the orifice. This needle is attached to, and moves with, the air valve piston which controls the variable choke opening. It is not centrally positioned in the orifice, but biased to one side which has the effect of improving atomization.

At rest, the air valve piston is right down, choking off the air supply and the tapered needle is fully home with the jet virtually cutting off the fuel outlet from the jet. For starting, the choke control is used.

The Stromberg carburettor incorporates a disc valve for cold starting which allows additional fuel to flow into the mixture stream. The disc valve itself incorporates several orifices which are progressively uncovered as the disc is moved when the choke control is pulled. The throttle butterfly is also opened a small amount. Also included in the Stromberg carburettor is a temperature controlled valve which weakens the mixture under light load and idling conditions when the engine is hot.

As soon as the engine fires, the suction from the engine for manifold depression is partially diverted to the upper side of the chamber in which the diaphragm attached to the air valve piston is positioned. This causes the valve to rise and provides sufficient air flow to enable the engine to run. As the throttle is opened further, manifold depression is reduced and now it is the speed of air through the venturi which causes the depression in the upper chamber, thus causing the piston to rise further. If the throttle is opened suddenly, the natural tendency of the air valve piston to rise – causing a weak mixture when it is least required (ie during acceleration) – is prevented by a hydraulic damper which delays the piston in its upward travel. The air intake is thus restricted and a proportionately larger quantity of fuel to air is drawn through.

Under constant speed running conditions the air valve position is balanced by air speed through the venturi, throttle opening and the light pressure of the diaphragm return spring.

The correct level of the petrol in the carburettor is determined by the level in the float chamber. When the level is correct, the float rises and by means of a lever resting on top of it, closes the needle valve in the cover of the float chamber. This closes off the supply of fuel from the pump. When the level in the float chamber drops as fuel is used in the carburettor, the float drops. As it does, the float needle is unseated, so allowing more fuel to enter the float chamber and restore the correct level.

On some later cars tamperproof carburettors are fitted so that the adjustments that can be carried out are limited in order to comply with local regulations in some territories. They can be identified by a capped sleeve fitted over the slow running adjustment screw. The only dismantling that should be carried out is limited to the following:

(a) *Removing the float chamber cover for access to the float and float chamber needle valve*
(b) *Removing the piston damper assembly*
(c) *Removing the top cover*
(d) *Removing the diaphragm*
(e) *Withdrawing the air valve*
(f) *Removing the needle assembly*

Any further dismantling should be avoided to prevent the possible breaking of anti-pollution exhaust emission regulations.

12 Carburettors – removal and refitting

1 Remove the air cleaner as described in Section 2.
2 Disconnect the vacuum advance pipe from the union on the right-hand carburettor. Remove the union to provide access to the nut securing the carburettor pedestal to the inlet manifold.
3 Disconnect the choke cables at the trunnions on the carburettors and release the outer cables from the securing clips.
4 Disconnect the throttle cable (and driveshaft cable on automatic transmission models).
5 Remove the nut securing the carburettors to the inlet manifold and lift the assembly from the centre stud.
6 Remove the O-ring seal from the inlet manifold.
7 Refitting is the reverse of the removal procedure. Fit a new O-ring seal. Use new gaskets between the carburettor elbow adaptors and the carburettors when refitting the air cleaner. Adjustment of the throttle cable is effected by positioning the locknuts on the carburettor linkage bracket so that all slackness in the inner cable is removed without impeding the closing of the throttle.

13 Carburettors – dismantling, overhaul and reassembly

Before commencing to dismantle a carburettor, whether it is for overhaul or examination it must be appreciated that a carburettor is a precision metering device which requires a great deal of care and attention in order for it to work properly. Where overhaul is concerned, the individual may well decide that a service-exchange item is preferable in view of the time and trouble saved. Generally speaking it is not advisable or even necessary for the carburettor to be dismantled for any other reason and here again the individual may well consider the job should be carried out by a Triumph dealer or carburettor specialist. For those people intending to do any work on the carburettor which will entail moving the metering needle, service tool No. S353 is essential. An airflow balancing meter is also a very useful device for timing and balancing, although listening carefully at the end of a rubber or plastic tube of about $\frac{1}{4}$ in (6 mm) diameter will usually be sufficient.

1 Remove the carburettors as described in Section 12 and separate them at the throttle levers. Undo the four bolts securing them to the pedestal and lift off the carburettors.
2 Unscrew the damper on the top cover.
3 Remove the bottom plug then drain the carburettor of residual

damper oil and petrol. Also remove the O-ring from the bottom plug.

4   Remove the six screws which secure the float chamber to the carburettor body, then take off the float chamber. This will probably be sticking to the body and very careful use of a penknife blade will be necessary. The float and needle valve can now be removed after carefully prising the spindle from the clip at each end.

5   Take out the four screws securing the top cover to the body, then lift off the cover and air valve return spring.

6   Remove the air valve complete with the diaphragm and metering needle. Take care not to damage the diaphragm if it is sticking to the carburettor body.

7   Remove the four screws from the diaphragm retaining ring, then separate the retaining ring, diaphragm and air valve.

8   Slacken the grubscrew in the stem of the air valve then insert special tool number S353 in the hollow stem of the air valve and turn approximately two turns anti-clockwise. Withdraw the needle and housing by pulling firmly with the fingers.

9   Remove the cold starting device after first taking out the two securing screws, and the adjacent idle trimming screw (if fitted).

10   Take out the two butterfly securing screws; then turn the spindle slightly and remove the butterfly.

11   Release the spindle return spring then withdraw the spindle and spring.

12   Using a small screwdriver or similar device hook the spindle seals out of the body but take care that the spindle bore is not scratched.

13   Wash all the parts in clean petrol then allow them to drain. Compressed air may be used provided that it is clean and dry. If ultrasonic cleaning facilities are available, all the internal parts should be cleaned using this method also.

14   When all the parts have been cleaned, lay them on a clean surface for inspection. Discard all the old seals and gaskets.

15   Examine the needle valve and seating, and if any ridging and grooving of the needle sealing face is detected, renew both items. Examine the diaphragm very carefully for minute cracks and any indication of bubbling or distortion. If in any doubt at all about the condition or if it is known to have been in service for more than two years or 24 000 miles (40 000 km), it should be renewed anyway. To examine the metering needle assembly it is preferable to use a watchmaker's eyeglass. The needle is unlikely to be bent unless damaged during removal but look for scoring or any signs of wear. If the needle is defective in any way it must be renewed or it will never be possible to set the carburettor correctly. If any evidence exists of contact between the needle and the carburettor body orifice it will almost certainly mean that a new carburettor is required since neither the body top cover nor the air valve are obtainable as spares. The body should otherwise be checked for cracks and distortion at the flange. Check the top cover, springs, starting device, float, float chamber, spindle and butterfly, renewing parts where appropriate.

16   If there is going to be any delay before reassembly is commenced, eg if new parts have to be purchased, store the remaining parts carefully in polythene bags.

17   When reassembling, first blow through all the ports and orifices in the carburettor body, the needle valve and the cold starting device.

18   Carefully tap the butterfly spindle seals into the body until the metal seal casings are flush with the body. The spindle can now be inserted, and the return spring loaded and fitted at the same time.

19   Insert the butterfly so that the two protruding spots are outboard and below the spindle. Refit and tighten the butterfly securing screws.

20   Fit the cold starting device to the carburettor body and tighten the screws.

21   Insert the metering needle housing assembly into the bottom of the air valve then fit the special tool number S353 in order to engage the threads of the needle assembly with the adjusting screw. Continue turning until the slot in the needle housing is aligned with the grubscrew (Fig. 3.11).

22   Tighten the grubscrew in this position. Note that it does not tighten on the housing but in the slot, thus ensuring that the needle remains biased by a spring in the needle housing towards the air cleaner side of the carburettor.

23   Position the diaphragm with the inner tag in the recess in the air valve, then fit the retaining ring. Fit and tighten the four screws, ensuring that the diaphragm is not distorted (Fig. 3.12).

24   Fit the air valve assembly to the carburettor body, locating the outer tag and the rim of the diaphragm in the complementary recesses of the body.

25   Fit the carburettor top cover with the bulge on the housing neck

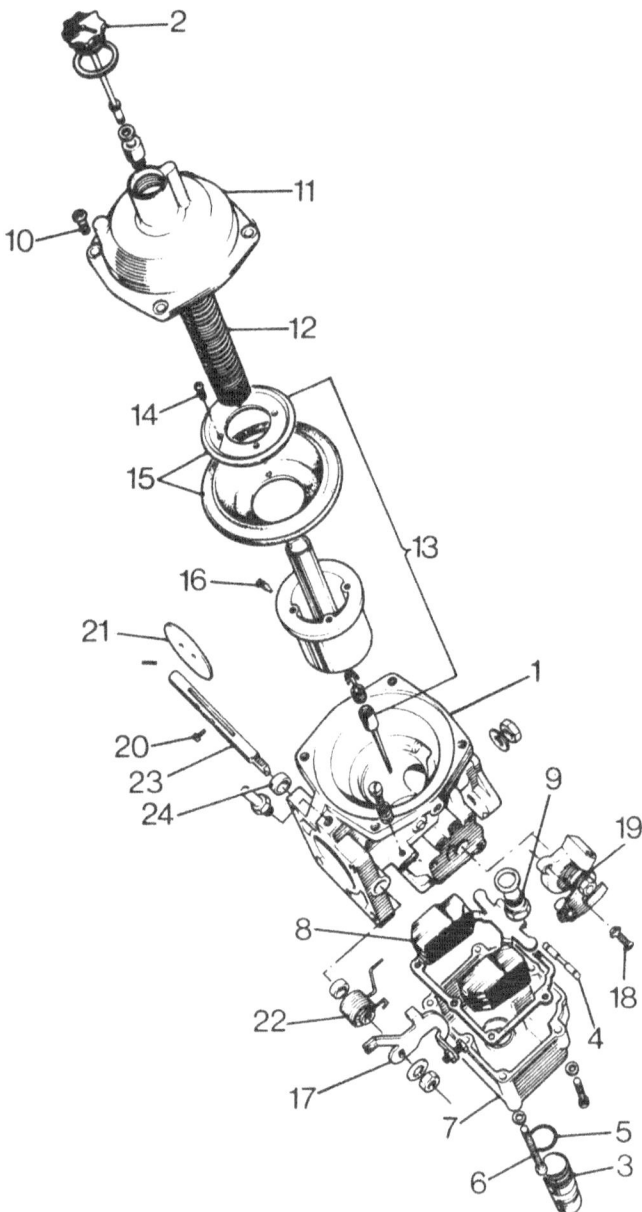

Fig. 3.10 Exploded view of Stromberg 175CDSE carburettor (Sec 13)

1	Carburettor body	13	Air valve assembly
2	Damper assembly	14	Screw
3	Plug	15	Diaphragm and retaining ring
4	Float pivot pin	16	Grub screw
5	O-ring	17	Stop lever
6	Screw	18	Screw
7	Float chamber	19	Cold start device
8	Float	20	Screw
9	Needle valve	21	Butterfly plate
10	Screw	22	Return spring
11	Top cover	23	Spindle
12	Spring	24	Spindle seal

towards the air intake.
26 Fit the cover screws, ensuring that they are tightened down evenly.
27 Screw in the float chamber needle valve using a new sealing washer then fit the float assembly by carefully levering the pivot pin into position.
28 Set the float height with the carburettor inverted, so that a dimension of 0.625 to 0.672 (16 to 17 mm) is obtained from the gasket face of the carburettor body to the highest point of the floats. Ensure that the float heights are equal, bending the tabs slightly to suit, but at the same time ensuring that the tab sits on the needle valve at right angles.

29 Now fit the float chamber itself. Tighten the screws down evenly to prevent distortion (Fig. 3.13).
30 Assemble a new O-ring to the bottom plug then screw in the plug.
31 When both carburettors are reassembled they can be refitted in the reverse order to removal, with the exception of the air cleaner.
32 Top up the piston damper dashpots using the damper as a dipstick until the threaded plug is 0.25 in (6 mm) above the dashpot when resistance is left. Use multigrade engine oil for this purpose.
33 Fit the idle trimming screw and spring; turn it fully clockwise but do not overtighten.
34 Now tune and balance the carburettors as described in Section 15.

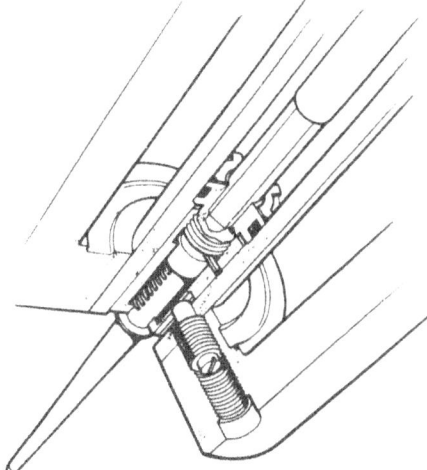

Fig. 3.11 Sectional view of the air valve and needle (Sec 13)

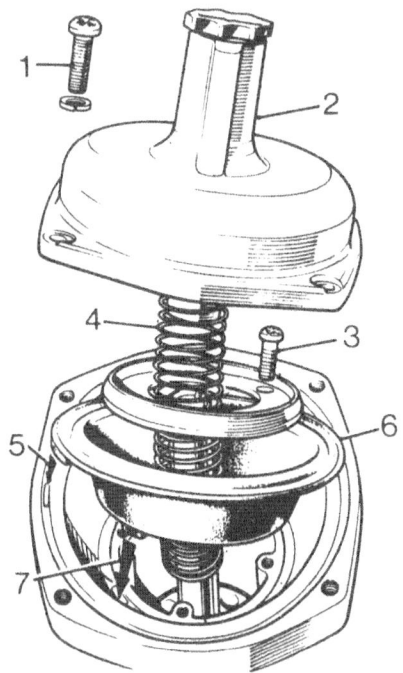

Fig. 3.12 Fitting the diaphragm and top cover (Sec 13)

1 Cover screw
2 Top cover
3 Retaining ring screw
4 Spring
5 Locating point in body
6 Diaphragm
7 Locating point in body

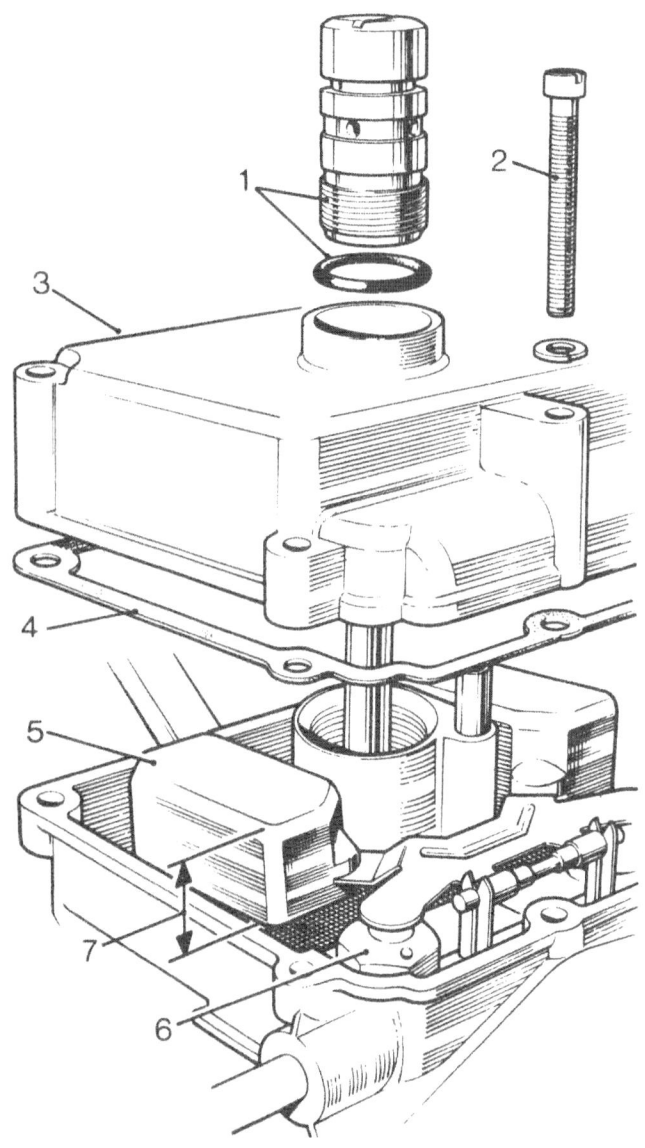

Fig. 3.13 Reassembly of the float chamber (Sec 13)

1 Plug and O-ring
2 Float chamber screw
3 Float chamber
4 Gasket
5 Float
6 Needle valve
7 Float setting dimension

14 Carburettor tuning and adjustment - general

Before attempting to tune and balance the carburettors, unless you have already stripped and overhauled them yourself, it is important that the reader is aware of the delicate nature of the job. In this respect it may well be considered worthwhile to entrust the job to a properly equipped Triumph garage. For those motorists intending to do the job themselves it is essential that service tool number S353 is purchased beforehand to enable the jet to be repositioned. An airflow balancing meter is also a very useful device for tuning and balancing although listening carefully at the end of a rubber or plastic tube of about $\frac{1}{4}$ in (6 mm) diameter will usually be sufficient. It is essential that before any attempt is made to balance the carburettors, ignition timing, tappet clearance, spark plugs and distributor contact breakers are checked and adjusted as necessary.

15 Carburettors – tuning and adjustments

Linkage adjustments
1   Run the engine until the normal operating temperature is reached.
2   Switch off the engine and remove the air cleaner.
3   Disconnect the throttle cable from the swivel pin.
4   Remove the plug and tamperproof sleeve from the idle screw on each carburettor, if fitted, refer to Section 11.
5   Disconnect the operating rod at the butterfly spindle lever (Fig. 3.14).
6   Run the engine and adjust the slow running adjusting screws to achieve an idling speed of 650 to 850 rpm (800 to 850 rpm in USA).

7   Check the airflow at each carburettor inlet, using either a flowmeter or by listening to the engine breathing with a length of flexible tubing placed against each air intake in turn (Fig. 3.15). A hissing sound can be heard which can be made to synchronize by careful adjustment of the control screws.
8   Adjust the length of the operating rod so that it will fit into the butterfly spindle lever without affecting the engine speed. Check that the gap of 0.030 to 0.060 in (0.76 to 1.52 mm) exists at A in Fig 3.16, then fit the rod and tighten the locknut.
9   Fit the inner throttle cable through the swivel pin and move the driving tag of the slave lever to the left-hand side of the slot in the operating lever then tighten the cable clamp screw.
10 Check that there is enough free travel in the linkage to allow fast idling, without disturbing the otherwise closed position of the throttle linkage, by inserting a 0.2 in (5 mm) rod through the slot in the operating lever and the hole in the mounting bracket.
11 Increase the engine speed to 1500 rpm and check the carburettors for balance with a flowmeter or by using a flexible rubber tube. Should the balance be uneven the operating rod will have to be re-adjusted.
12 To set the fast idle, pull out the choke knob fully and insert a $\frac{5}{16}$ in (7.9 mm) rod between the cam and its stop, see Fig. 3.17. Adjust the fast idle screw so that it just touches the edge of the cam. Repeat on the other carburettor. **Note:** *With the engine set to 1300 rpm that is the equivalent of approximately 1100 rpm when cold.*

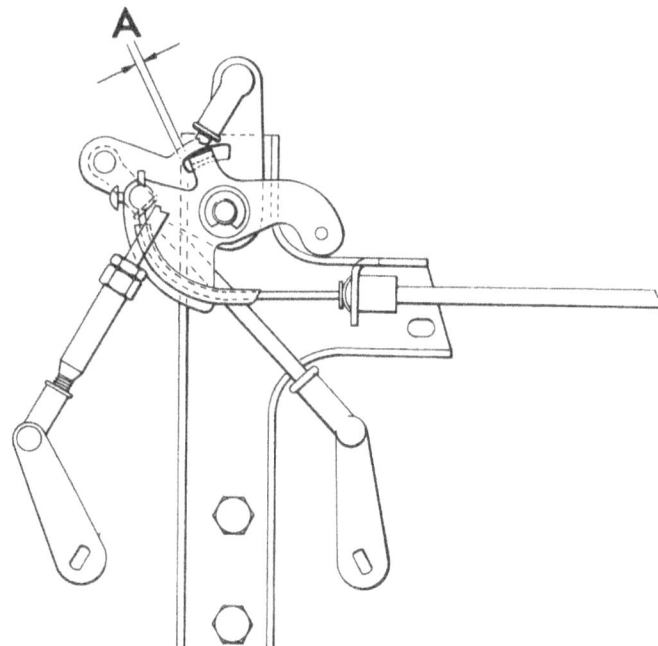

Fig. 3.16 Checking the linkage setting (Sec 15)

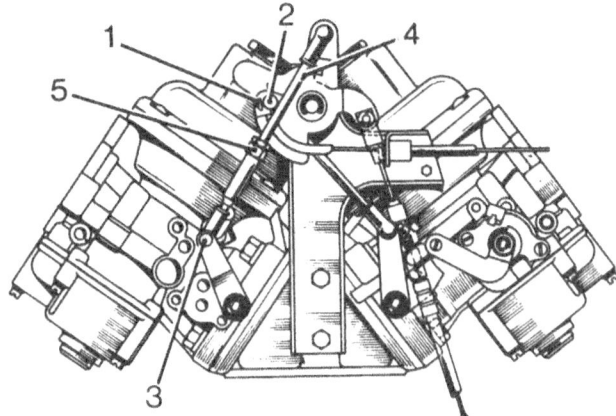

Fig. 3.14 Setting the control linkage (Sec 15)

1   *Throttle cable clamp screw*   4   *Operating rod*
2   *Throttle cable swivel pin*   5   *Operating rod locknut*
3   *Throttle spindle lever*

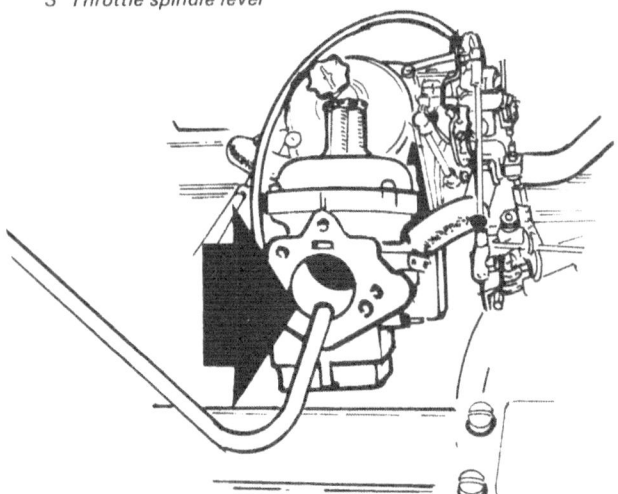

Fig. 3.15 Listening to the airflow hiss with flexible tube (Sec 15)

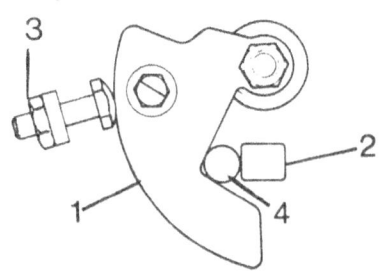

Fig. 3.17 Setting the fast idle (Sec 15)

1   *Fast idle cam*   3   *Fast idle screw and locknut*
2   *Fast idle cam stop*   4   *$\frac{5}{16}$ in (7.9 mm) rod*

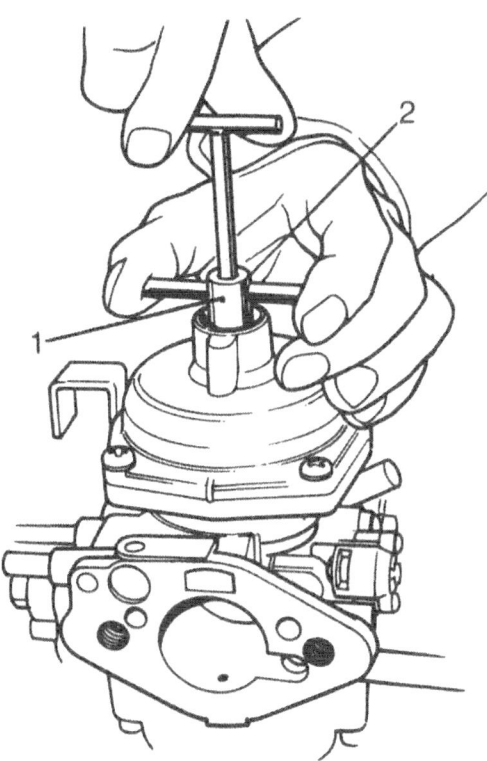

Fig. 3.18 Adjusting the needle adjusting screw using tool 'No S353' (Sec 15)

1 Outer part   *2 Inner part*

Mixture adjustment

13 Using a thin bladed screwdriver lift each carburettor air valve piston, in turn, approximately $\frac{1}{32}$ in (0.8 mm) and note the engine response as follows:

    (a) Engine speed increased immediately – mixture too rich
    (b) Engine speed decreases or stalls – mixture too weak.
    (c) Engine speed increases slightly then returns to normal – mixture setting correct.

14 Adjust the mixture if required by inserting tool number S353 into the hollow piston guide rod, after removing the damper, so that the inner part of the tool engages in a female hexagon in the needle adjusting screw.
15 Whilst holding the outer part of the tool firmly turn the inner part clockwise to richen the mixture or anti-clockwise to weaken the mixture (Fig. 3.18).
16 When the mixture setting is correct, top up the dashpots, if necessary, and refit the dampers.
17 Fit the air cleaner.
18 Check the idling speed and if necessary adjust the slow running speed to 650 to 850 rpm (800 to 850 rpm USA cars). Adjust each screw the same amount to avoid upsetting the balance of the carburettors.

Checking the CO level

19 Make a suitable Y piece to fit over the twin exhaust pipes, see Fig. 3.19.
20 Run the engine at the normal operating temperature and fit the Y piece to the exhaust.
21 With the engine running at the normal idling speed insert the probe of a gas analyser into the Y piece and allow a stabilising period of one and a half minutes then note the CO reading which should be less than 4.5%.
22 If the reading is not less than 4.5% after two minutes, run the engine at 2000 rpm for one minute and re-check.
23 If the CO level is still too high the mixture setting will have to be re-adjusted.

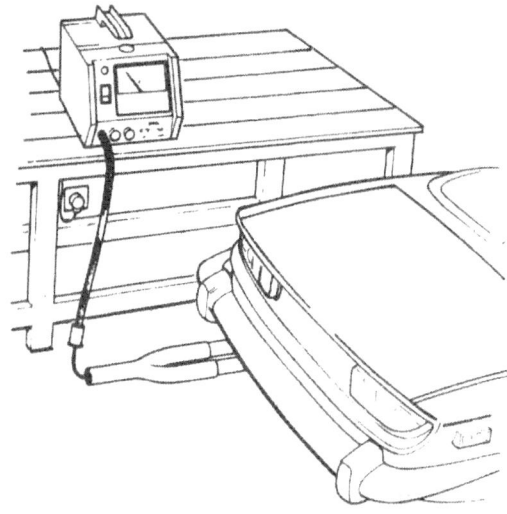

Fig. 3.19 Using a gas analyser to check the CO level (Sec 15)

24 On tamperproof carburettors fit a new sleeve and plug on the idle screw on both carburettors.

16 Evaporative emission control system – general

1 The evaporation of fuel from the tank is one of the main sources of pollution. To prevent this, the fuel tank is sealed. Air is allowed into the tank by the venting when the engine is running, to let the fuel flow out. When the engine is stopped, and fuel is evaporating, particularly when parked in the sun, the vapour is absorbed by an activated carbon canister.
2 When the engine is running air is drawn through the carbon canister to purge it of the absorbed fuel vapours and convey them to the inlet manifold, where they are drawn into the engine and burned.
3 Two types of expansion tank are used, the early type is shown in Fig. 3.20 and the later type in Fig. 3.21.
4 The carbon canister is located in the engine compartment. On pre-1973 models the canister can be lifted from its mounting and the base unscrewed to remove the filter, which should be renewed every 12 000 miles (20 000 km). On models from 1973 the filter is not renewable and the carbon canister must be renewed every 50 000 miles (80 000 km).
5 To renew the carbon canister, note the run of the pipes, then disconnect them from the top of the canister. Remove the bolt securing the canister to the mounting bracket (cars from 1973 disconnect the running-on valve connecting pipe), then lift out the canister.

17 Throttle cable – removal and refitting

1 Working inside the car, slide the clip from the top of the pedal arm.
2 Disconnect the other end of the cable from the carburettor linkage.
3 Pull the inner cable out and then remove the outer cable.
4 Feed the inner cable through the bulkhead from inside the car and connect the cable to the pedal arm.
5 Slide the outer cable over the inner cable to abut against the bulkhead.
6 Slide the inner cable through the collar on the linkage bracket and connect the cable to the linkage, and adjust so that there is no free play and no stress on the cable.
7 On cars equipped with automatic transmission, check the setting of the downshift cable as described in Chapter 6, Section 30.

18 Exhaust system – general

1 The exhaust system consists of two front pipes, two silencers, two intermediate pipes and two tail pipes. The front pipes are secured to

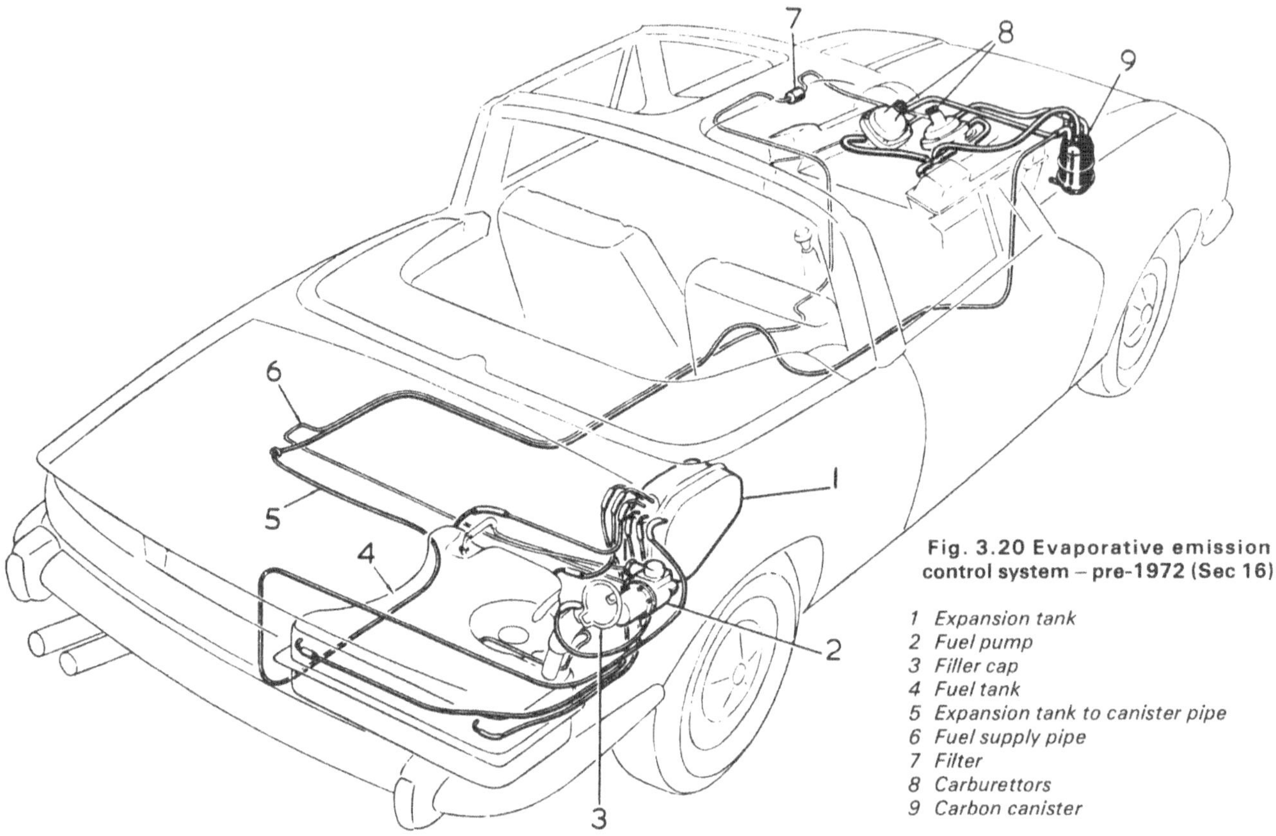

Fig. 3.20 Evaporative emission
control system – pre-1972 (Sec 16)

1 Expansion tank
2 Fuel pump
3 Filler cap
4 Fuel tank
5 Expansion tank to canister pipe
6 Fuel supply pipe
7 Filter
8 Carburettors
9 Carbon canister

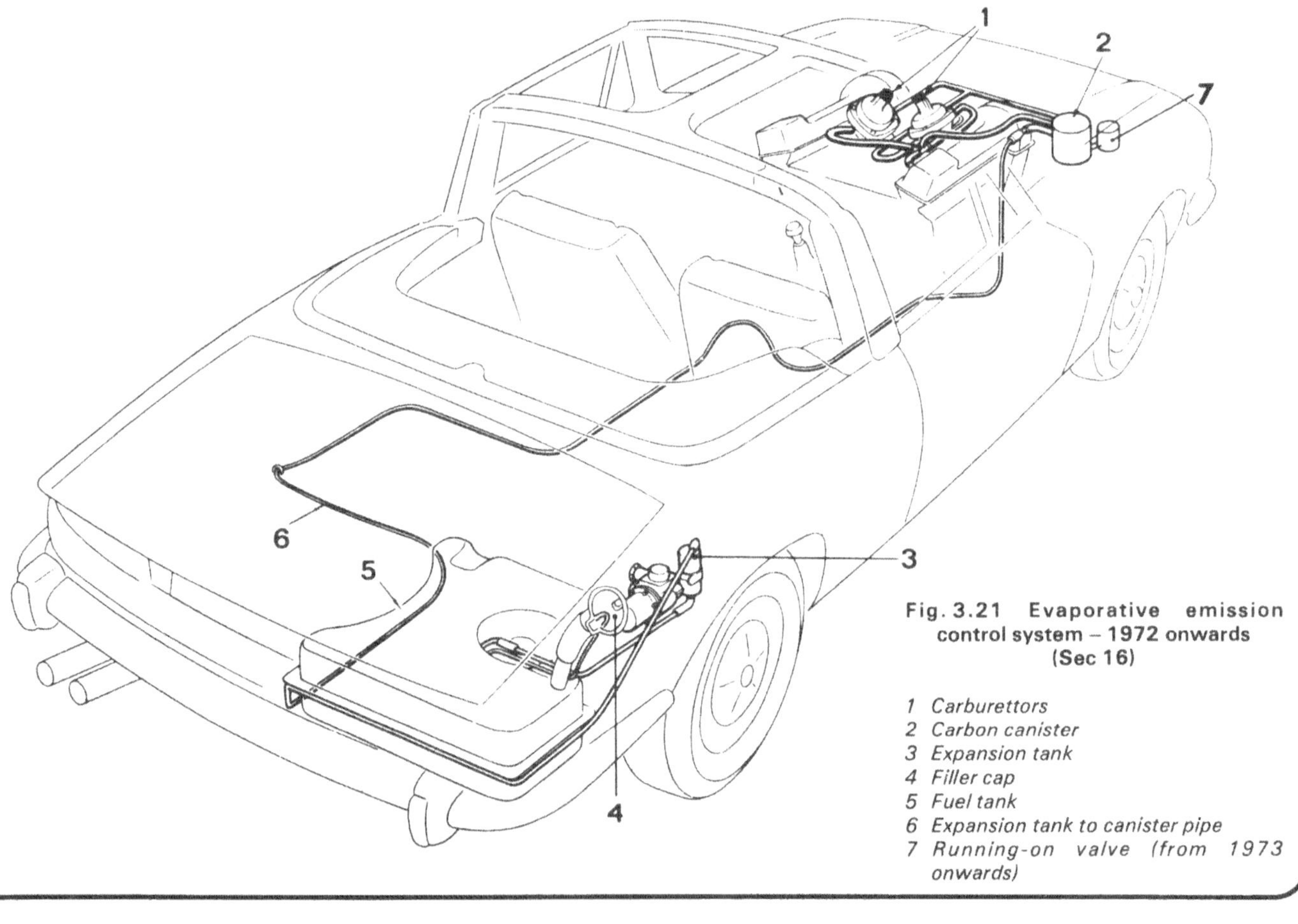

Fig. 3.21 Evaporative emission
control system – 1972 onwards
(Sec 16)

1 Carburettors
2 Carbon canister
3 Expansion tank
4 Filler cap
5 Fuel tank
6 Expansion tank to canister pipe
7 Running-on valve (from 1973
onwards)

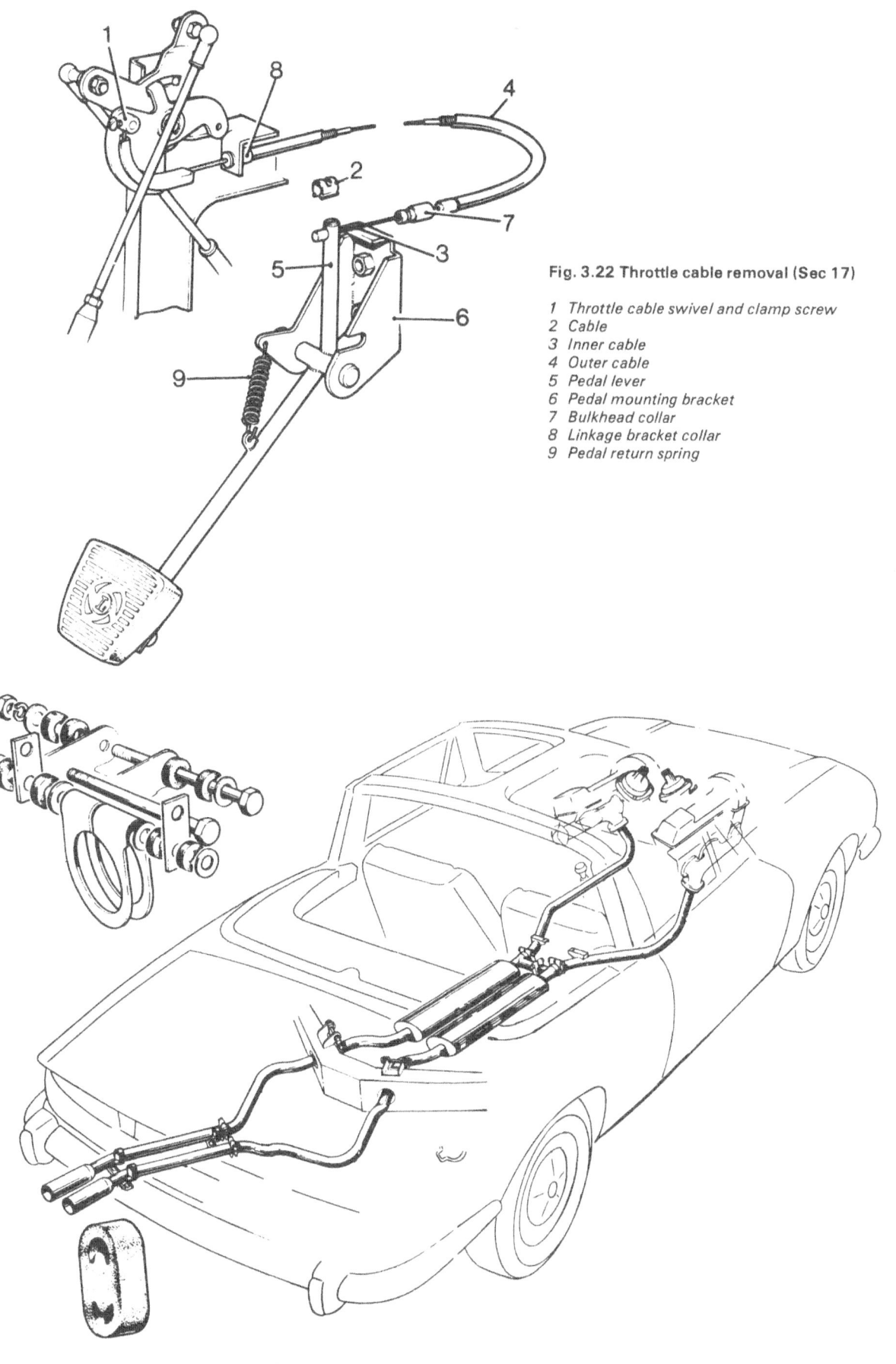

Fig. 3.22 Throttle cable removal (Sec 17)

1 Throttle cable swivel and clamp screw
2 Cable
3 Inner cable
4 Outer cable
5 Pedal lever
6 Pedal mounting bracket
7 Bulkhead collar
8 Linkage bracket collar
9 Pedal return spring

Fig. 3.23 Component parts of the exhaust system (Sec 18)

18.1a Front exhaust pipe attaching bracket

18.1b Intermediate to tail exhaust pipe clamps

18.1c Rubber hangers supporting the tail pipes

the gearbox mounting crossmember and the tail pipes are supported by rubber hangers. The silencers are joined together at the front by a clamp (photos).

2   When any one section of the exhaust system needs renewing it often follows that the whole system is best renewed. Always use new gaskets.

3   It is most important when fitting exhaust that the twists and contours are carefully followed and that each connecting joint overlaps the correct distance. Any stresses or strain imparted, in order to force the system to fit the hanger rubbers, will result in early fractures and failures.

4   When fitting a new part or complete system it is well worth removing the whole system from the car and cleaning up all the joints so that they fit together easily. The time spent struggling with obstinate joints whilst flat on your back under the car is eliminated and the likelihood of distorting or even breaking a section is greatly reduced. Do not waste a lot of time trying to undo rusted and corroded clamps and bolts. Cut them off. New ones will be required anyway if they are that bad.

19 Choke cable – removal and refitting

1   Disconnect the battery negative lead.

2   Disconnect the inner and outer choke cables from both carburettors.

3   Working inside the car, remove the choke control knob by depressing the spring-loaded pin. Remove the choke control bezel.

4   Pull off and remove the three heater control knobs, then unscrew and remove the heater control panel.

5   On automatic transmission models, prise off and remove the selector gate panel.

6   Prise up and remove the front console panel.

7   Remove the two screws securing the rear console panel, then move the console to gain access to the choke cable.

8   Disconnect the choke switch wiring, then pull the cable through into the car and remove the choke switch.

9   Refitting is the reverse of the removal procedure, but check for correct operation of the choke on completion.

20 Fault diagnosis – carburation and fuel system

Unsatisfactory engine performance and excessive fuel consumption are not necessarily the fault of the fuel system or carburettor. In fact they more commonly occur as a result of ignition faults. Before acting on the fuel system it is necessary to check the ignition system first. Even though a fault may lie in the fuel system it will be difficult to trace unless the ignition is correct.

The table below therefore, assumes that the ignition system is in order.

Symptom	Reason/s
Smell of petrol when engine is stopped	Leaking fuel lines or unions Leaking fuel tank
Smell of petrol when engine is idling	Leaking fuel line unions between pump and carburettor Overflow of fuel from float chamber due to wrong level settting or ineffective needle valve or punctured float
Excessive fuel consumption for reasons not covered by leaks or float chamber faults	Worn needle Sticking needle
Difficult starting, uneven running, lack of power, cutting out	One or more blockages Float chamber fuel level too low or needle sticking Fuel pump not delivering sufficient fuel Intake manifold gaskets leaking, or manifold fractured

Chapter 4 Ignition system

Contents

Specifications

Spark plugs
Type	Champion N 11Y or N 12Y
Gap	0.024 to 0.026 in (0.625 to 0.660 mm)

Distributor
Type	Lucas 35 D8
Points gap	0.014 to 0.016 in (0.36 to 0.41 mm)
Rotation	Anti-clockwise (viewed on rotor)
Dwell angle:	
Single contact breaker type	26° to 28°
Double contact breaker type	$29\frac{1}{2}°$ to $33\frac{1}{2}°$ (USA 34° to 38°)
Condenser capacity	0.18 to 0.25 mfd

Firing order
Firing order	1-2-7-8-4-5-6-3 (RH bank – odd numbers, LH bank – even numbers)

Ignition timing (static)
Static	
Pre-engine No LF20001	14° BTDC
From engine No LF20001	12° BTDC
USA models	10° BTDC
Stroboscopic	
Pre-engine No LF 20001	14° BTDC at 750 ± 100 rpm
From engine No LF 20001	12° BTDC at 750 ± 100 rpm

Ignition coil
Type:	
Pre-engine No LF 20250	Lucas 16 C6
From engine No LF 20250 to engine No LF 28553	Lucas 15 P6
From engine LF 28554	Lucas 15 C6

Ballast resistor
Type:	
Pre-engine No LF 20001	Lucas 3 BR
From engine No LF 20001	High resistance wire in engine wiring harness

Torque wrench settings
	lbf ft	kgf m
Distributor to block	10	1.4
Spark plugs	20	2.8

1 General description

In order that the engine may run correctly, it is necessary for an electrical spark to ignite the fuel/air charge in the combustion chamber at exactly the right moment in relation to engine speed and load. The ignition system is based on supplying low tension voltage from the battery to the ignition coil where it is converted to high tension voltage by virtue of contact breaker operation. The high tension voltage is powerful enough to jump the spark plug gap in the cylinder many times a second under high compression pressure, providing that the ignition system is in good working order and that all adjustments are correct.

The ignition system comprises two individual circuits known as the low tension circuit and the high tension circuit.

The low tension (or primary) circuit comprises the lead from the positive terminal of the 12 volt battery, the ignition/starter switch, a ballast resistor wire, the primary winding of the 6 volt ignition coil, the contact breaker points of the distributor (which are bridged by the condenser) and an earth connection. Since the negative terminal of the battery is also earthed, current will flow in the low tension circuit when the distributor contacts are closed and a magnetic field will be set up in the primary winding of the coil.

The high tension (or secondary) circuit comprises the secondary winding of the ignition coil (one end of which is connected internally to the output terminal of the primary winding), the heavily insulated ignition lead from the centre of the coil to the centre of the distributor cap, the rotor arm, the spark plug leads and the spark plugs.

When the contacts open, the magnetic field in the primary coil winding collapses rapidly and induces a voltage in the secondary winding. At this instant, the distributor rotor is bridging the coil output terminal and one of the spark plug connections in the distributor cap, and a spark therefore jumps the electrode gap. The condenser across the contacts serves the dual purpose of assisting the rapid collapse of the magnetic field in the primary winding and acts as a spark suppressor for the contacts.

The whole cycle is repeated when the contacts open again which will be when the distributor has turned through 45°, but this time the next spark plug in the ignition sequence will fire.

During the starting sequence, the ballast resistor or resistor wire in series with the coil primary winding is by-passed so that the full battery voltage (which will be low anyway due to the high current drawn by the starter motor) is passed to the 6 volt coil. In this way a bigger secondary voltage will be induced and therefore a bigger spark will result.

Whilst the above sequence is apparently satisfactory, in that the distributor can be physically set to provide a spark when it is needed, some variation of ignition timing is required to obtain optimum efficiency under varying conditions of engine load and speed. A centrifugal advance mechanism is used inside the distributor body which will give an increasing amount of spark advancement (ie, firing earlier in the cycle) as the engine speed increases. Additionally, a vacuum device is fitted, which is operated by the depression in the inlet manifold, and will give additional spark advancement at low and moderate throttle openings eg, when the car is cruising. At wide throttle openings, eg, when hill climbing, there is less suction in the inlet manifold and hence there will be little or no additional advancement. The combination of the two devices will provide a wide range of ignition advancement or retardation according to the engine requirements at any particular time.

2   Contact breaker points – adjustment

1   To adjust the contact breaker points to the correct gap, first pull off the two clips securing the distributor cap to the distributor body, and lift away the cap. Clean the cap inside and out with a dry cloth. It is unlikely that the eight segments will be badly burned or scored, but if they are the cap will have to be renewed.
2   Push in the carbon brush located in the top of the cap once or twice to make sure that it moves freely.
3   Lift away the rotor and gently prise the contact breaker points open to examine the condition of their faces. If they are rough, or dirty, it will be necessary to remove them for resurfacing, or for new points to be fitted.
4   Presuming the points are satisfactory, or that they have been cleaned and refitted, check the gap between the points by turning the engine over until the contact breaker arm is on the peak of one of the eight cam lobes and proceed as follows:

Models with external adjusting nut
5   Disconnect the distributor lead from the coil and connect a test lamp as shown in Fig. 4.1.
6   Press the adjustment nut inwards and rotate it anti-clockwise until the test lamp lights, then rotate the nut a further half turn.
7   Slowly turn the adjustment nut clockwise until the light just goes out. This is the datum point.
8   Now continue turning the nut clockwise through exactly five flats from the datum point to obtain the correct contact breaker gap.

Models without adjustment nut
9   With the contact breaker arm on the peak of one of the cam lobes, slacken the contact plate securing screw. Adjust the gap by inserting a 0.015 in (0.38 mm) feeler gauge between the points (photo), then insert a screwdriver in the notch at the end of the plate and turn the screwdriver as necessary to obtain the correct gap.

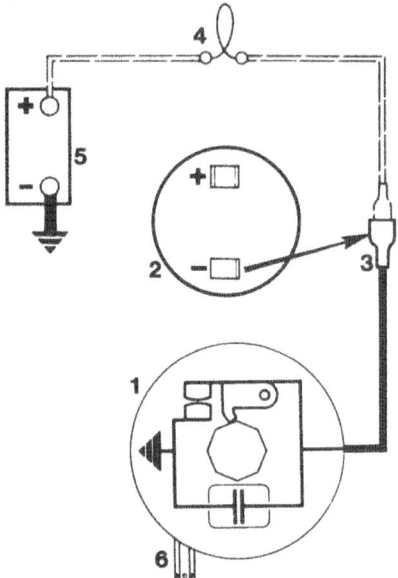

Fig. 4.1 Test lamp circuit for adjusting contact breaker points gap (Sec 2)

1 Distributor   4 Bulb
2 Coil   5 Battery
3 Distributor to coil lead   6 Adjustment nut

2.9 Checking the contact breaker gap using a feeler gauge

10   Retighten the securing screw, turn the engine over and recheck the gap.

All models
11   Refit the rotor arm and distributor cap, then clip the spring blade retainers into position.
12   A more accurate points setting is obtained by using a dwell angle meter and it is recommended that your Leyland dealer carries out this operation.

3   Contact breaker points – removal, cleaning and refitting

1   If the contact breaker points are burned, pitted or badly worn, they must be removed and either renewed or their faces ground smooth.
2   Remove the distributor cap and rotor.

3 Unscrew the terminal nut (Fig. 4.2) and remove the nylon insulator, the condenser lead and the low tension lead from the terminal pin.
4 Remove the securing screw, spring washer and plain washer, then lift out the contact set.
5 To reface the points, rub their faces on a fine carborundum stone, or on fine emery paper. It is important that the faces are rubbed flat and parallel to each other so that there will be complete face to face contact when the points are cleaned. One of the points will be pitted and the other will have deposits on it.
6 It is necessary to completely remove the built-up deposits, but not necessary to rub the pitted point right down to the stage where all the pitting has disappeared, though obviously if this is done it will prolong the time before the operation of refacing the points has to be repeated.
7 Refitting the contact breaker assembly is the reverse of the removal procedure. Before refitting the rotor and distributor cap adjust the points gap as described in Section 2.

4 Condenser – removal, testing and refitting

1 The purpose of the condenser, (sometimes known as a capacitor) is to ensure that when the contact breaker points open there is no sparking across them which would waste voltage and cause wear.
2 The condenser is fitted in parallel with the contact breaker points. If it develops a short circuit, it will cause ignition failure as the points will be prevented from interrupting the low tension circuit.
3 If the engine becomes very difficult to start or begins to miss after several miles running and the breaker points show signs of excessive burning, then the condenser must be suspect. A further test can be made by separating the points by hand with the ignition switched on. If this is accompanied by a flash it is indication that the condenser has failed.
4 Without special equipment the only sure way to diagnose condenser trouble is to replace a suspected unit with a new one and note if there is any improvement.
5 To remove the condenser from the distributor, remove the distributor cap and the rotor arm.
6 Loosen the outer nut from the contact stud and pull off the condenser lead.
7 Undo the mounting bracket screw and remove the condenser.
8 Refitting is simply a reversal of the removal process. Take particular care that the condenser lead does not short circuit against any portion of the breaker plate.

5 Distributor – lubrication

1 It is important that the distributor cam is lubricated with petroleum jelly at the specified mileages and that the breaker arm, governor weights and cam spindle bush are lubricated with engine oil every 6000 miles (10 000 km)
2 Great care should be taken not to use too much lubricant, as any excess that finds it way into the contact breaker points could cause burning and misfiring.
3 To gain access to the cam spindle, lift away the rotor arm. Drop no more than two drops of engine oil onto the felt pad. This will run down the spindle when the engine is hot and lubricate the bearings.
4 To lubricate the automatic timing control allow a few drops of oil to pass through the hole in the contact breaker base plate through which the eight sided cam emerges. Apply not more than one drop of oil to the pivot post and remove any excess.

6 Ignition timing – checking and adjustment

1 Check the contact breaker gap and adjust or clean the points as necessary.
2 Disconnect the lead from the distributor at the negative terminal of the coil.
3 Using a 12 volt bulb of up to 5 watt rating (eg, parking lamp or luggage compartment lamp bulb), connect it between the distributor/coil lead and the battery positive terminal, see Fig. 4.1.
4 Turn the engine over so that No 2 piston (front left-hand bank) is coming up to TDC (top dead centre) on the compression stroke. This can be ascertained by removing the No 2 spark plug and feeling the

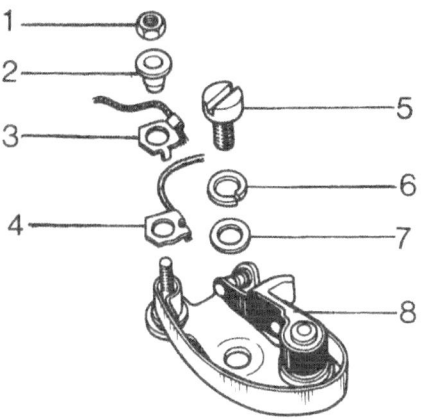

Fig. 4.2 Removing the contact breaker points (Sec 3)

1 Terminal nut
2 Nylon insulator
3 Condenser lead
4 LT lead
5 Screw
6 Spring washer
7 Plain washer
8 Contact breaker set

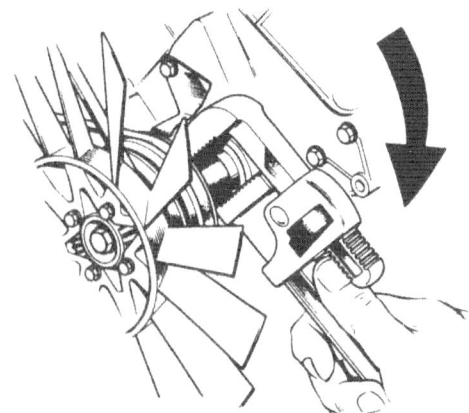

Fig. 4.3 Using a pipe wrench on the crankshaft pulley to turn the engine (Sec 6)

pressure being developed in the cylinder.
5 Continue turning the crankshaft to approximately 24 degrees BTDC (before top dead centre), notch on crankshaft pulley opposite the 24 mark on the timing scale bolted to the front cover. The test lamp will now be illuminated. Turn the crankshaft slowly in the same direction until the light goes out.
6 If the timing is correct, the notch on the crankshaft pulley will be opposite the specified static timing mark on the timing scale; refer to the Specifications at the beginning of this Chapter.
7 If the timing requires adjusting, set the notch on the crankshaft pulley opposite the specified timing mark on the timing scale, then slacken the two distributor securing bolts. These bolts are difficult to get at and a bent spanner as shown in Fig. 4.4 is required.
8 With the securing bolts slackened off rotate the distributor body anti-clockwise past the point at which the lamp illuminates, then rotate the distributor slowly and carefully clockwise until the light just goes out. Now tighten the distributor securing bolts without allowing the distributor body to move.
9 Recheck the timing as described in paragraphs 4 to 6 above.
10 Remove the test lamp and reconnect the lead to the ignition coil.
11 The timing can be checked more accurately with the engine running and using a stroboscopic timing light. Make sure the engine idling speed is as given in the Specifications.
12 Clean the timing mark on the crankshaft pulley and the timing scale on the front cover. Mark the specified setting with quick drying white paint or chalk.
13 Run the engine to the normal operating temperature.

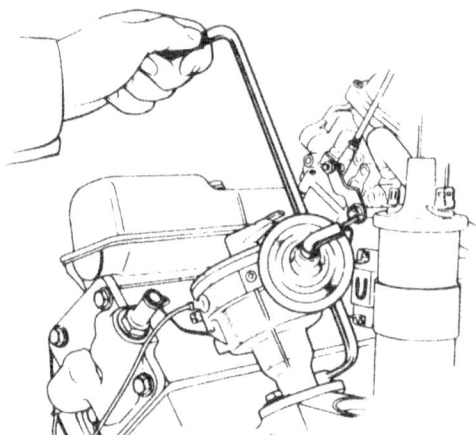

Fig. 4.4 Using a bent spanner to slacken the distributor securing bolts (Sec 6)

14 Disconnect the vacuum pipe from the distributor and plug it.

15 Connect the timing light between No 2 spark plug and No 2 HT lead in accordance with the manufacturer's instructions.

16 Start the engine and point the stroboscope at the white marks. They will appear stationary and if the ignition timing is correctly set they will be in alignment. If they are not directly opposite each other, slacken the distributor securing bolts and turn the distributor body one way or the other until the marks line up. Tighten the securing bolts and recheck the setting.

17 If the engine speed is increased, the white mark on the crankshaft pulley will move away from the fixed point, indicating that the centrifugal advance mechanism is operating. If the vacuum pipe is reconnected, the movement of the timing mark in relation to the fixed point will be greater when the engine speed is increased. This indicates that the vacuum advance is operating.

7 Distributor – removal and refitting

1 Detach the two plastic clips securing the spark plug leads to the camshaft covers and disconnect the leads from the spark plugs. Pull out the HT lead from the centre of the coil.

2 Release the distributor cap retaining clips and lift away the distributor cap and HT leads.

3 Disconnect the low tension lead from the distributor and pull off the vacuum tube from the vacuum unit in the distributor.

4 Rotate the crankshaft until the notch on the pulley aligns with the O-mark on the scale on the front cover (photo).

5 Mark the fitted position of the distributor in relation to a similar marking on the cylinder block and also mark the position of the rotor to the distributor body.

6 Remove the two distributor securing bolts and carefully withdraw the distributor from the block.

7 If the same distributor is not being refitted, make a sketch of the

markings and distributor position so that they can be transferred to the new one.

8 When refitting, first align the pulley marking as described in paragraph 4.

9 Refit the distributor making sure that the marks are aligned and that the rotor is in the correct position.

10 Tighten the securing bolts, then reconnect the vacuum tube and low tension lead.

11 Check the ignition timing as described in Section 6.

12 Refit the distributor cap and HT leads.

13 If the distributor is removed without first marking its fitted position it should be refitted as follows.

14 Turn the engine over until No 2 piston is coming up to TDC on the compression stroke. This can be ascertained by removing No 2 cylinder spark plug and feeling the pressure developing in the cylinder.

15 Continue turning the crankshaft until the notch on the crankshaft pulley is opposite the TDC mark (O-mark) on the scale on the front cover.

16 Insert the distributor into its location in the cylinder block so that the vacuum unit is adjacent to the coil, then carefully engage the drive gear with the skew gear on the jackshaft, so that the rotor is pointing towards the outer coil securing bolt when the distributor is in the fitted position (photos).

17 Repeat the procedures described in paragraphs 10 to 12.

8 Distributor (single contact breaker type) – dismantling, overhaul and reassembly

1 Remove the distributor from the engine as described in Section 7.

2 Remove the rotor arm and the contact breaker assembly as described in Section 3. Remove the condenser.

3 Undo the moving plate earth lead screw and washer, then unscrew the locknut and remove the washer and spring. Lift out the moving plate (Fig. 4.5).

4 Undo the two screws securing the vacuum unit to the distributor body and remove the vacuum unit and rubber grommet.

5 Unscrew the adjustment nut and remove the plastic friction strip and spring.

6 Undo the two securing screws and lift out the base plate.

7 Using a suitable pin punch tap out the drivegear retaining pin, then remove the drivegear and thrust washer.

8 Withdraw the shaft and remove the spacer.

9 The controls springs can now be removed, but take care not to stretch and distort them.

10 Take the felt pad from the top of the cam spindle, then undo and remove the cam spindle screw and separate the cam spindle from the action plate.

11 Lift off the centrifugal weights.

12 Remove the rubber O-ring from the body and clean all the mechanical parts in petrol.

13 Check the fit of the centrifugal weights, if the pivots or holes are worn the weights should be renewed. Renew the springs if they appear to be stretched when compared with a new spring.

14 Examine the driving gear teeth for wear and renew if necessary. Check the fit of the driveshaft in the housing; if excessive wear is

7.4 Crankshaft timing mark aligned with the O-mark on the timing scale

7.16a Fit the distributor with the vacuum unit next to the coil

7.16b In the fitted position the rotor should be pointing towards the coil outer securing bolt

evident the parts must be renewed as an assembly as they are not supplied separately.

15 Check the metal contact on the rotor for security and burning. Small burn marks can be dressed out with a smooth file or very fine emery cloth but if badly burned it must be renewed.

16 Check the condition of the points and renew if necessary.

17 Check the distributor cap for signs of tracking, indicated by a thin black line between the segments. Renew the cap if any sign of tracking is found.

18 Check that the carbon brush moves freely in the centre of the distributor cap.

19 When reassembling, first fit a new O-ring in the body.

20 Lubricate the action plate sliding surfaces and cam surfaces with a little petroleum jelly, also the cam spindle bearing, weight pivots and driveshaft.

21 Locate the centrifugal weights on the action plate. Fit the cam spindle, either way round, to the weights and secure with the cam spindle screw. Insert the felt pad and lubricate it with a few drops of engine oil.

22 Fit the control springs, taking care not to stretch them so that the length is increased.

23 Fit the spacer and insert the shaft into the body. Fit the thrust washer, then the drivegear and securing pin.

24 If a new shaft is being fitted, insert the shaft and drill the hole for the drivegear securing pin so that the shaft endfloat will be between 0.007 and 0.012 in (0.18 and 0.31 mm).

25 Fit the contact breaker baseplate and two securing screws.

26 Fit the plastic strip and sping in position then screw in the adjustment nut.

27 Assemble the vacuum unit and rubber grommet to the distributor body and fit the two securing screws.

28 Fit the moving plate to the pivot post and vacuum unit and then the spring, washer and locknut.

29 Attach the moving plate earth lead and securing screw.

30 Refit the contact breaker assembly, refer to Section 2 and adjust the points gap.

31 Refit the condenser and rotor.

32 Refit the distributor to the engine, refer to Section 7.

9 Distributor (double contact breaker type) – dismantling, overhaul and reassembly

1 Remove the distributor from the engine as described in Section 7.

2 Remove the rotor and contact breaker assemblies as described in Section 3. Remove the condenser.

3 Undo the baseplate earth lead screw and remove the lead.

4 Remove the screw that secures the vacuum unit control rod to the contact breaker bearing plate.

5 Undo and lift out the remaining two baseplate securing screws.

6 Remove the vacuum unit securing screws and lift away the vacuum unit, carefully easing out the rubber grommet.

7 The contact breaker bearing plate and the baseplate assembly can now be lifted out of the distributor body. If necessary the plates can be separated by a twisting movement.

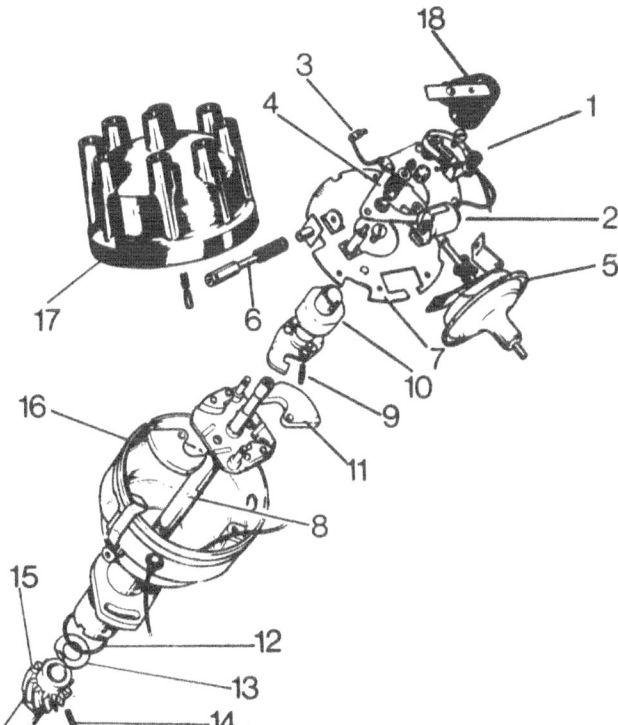

Fig. 4.5 Exploded view of single contact breaker distributor (Sec 8)

1	Contact breaker set	10	Cam
2	Condenser	11	Weight
3	Earth lead	12	O-ring
4	Moving plate	13	Thrust washer
5	Vacuum unit	14	Drivegear retaining pin
6	Adjustment nut	15	Drivegear
7	Baseplate	16	Distributor body
8	Shaft	17	Distributor cap
9	Spring	18	Rotor

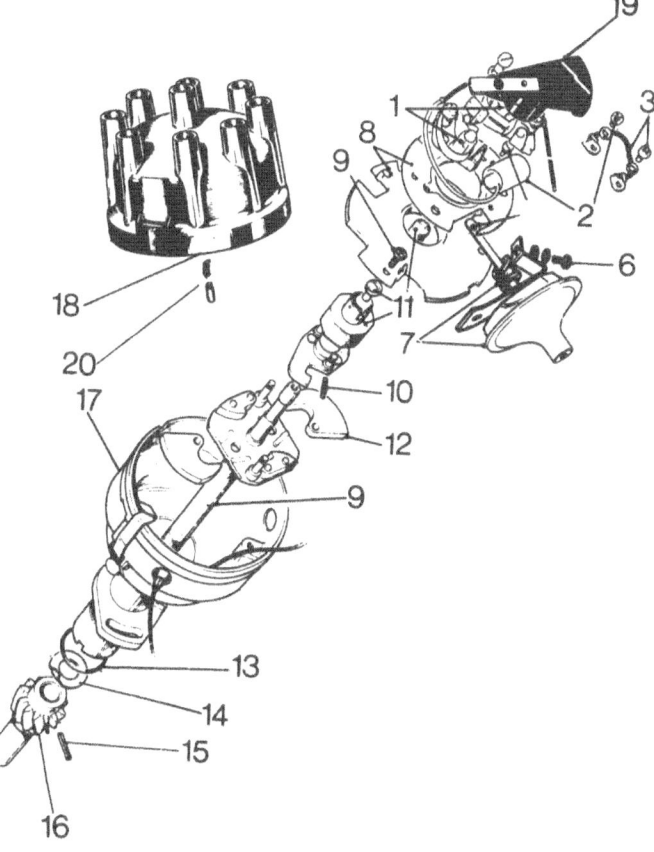

Fig. 4.6 Exploded view of double contact breaker distributor (Sec 9)

1	Contact breakers	11	Cam spindle, securing screw and felt pad
2	Condenser and securing screw	12	Weights
3	Earth lead and screw	13	O-ring
4	Vacuum control rod and screw	14	Thrust washer
5	Baseplate securing screw	15	Roll pin
6	Vacuum unit securing screws	16	Drivegear
7	Vacuum unit and rubber grommet	17	Distributor body
8	Moving plate and baseplate assembly	18	Cap
9	Shaft and action plate	19	Rotor
10	Control spring	20	Carbon brush and spring

8   The rest of the dismantling procedure and the inspection of the dismantled parts is the same as described for the single contact breaker distributor, refer to Section 8, paragraphs 7 to 18.

9   For reassembling refer to Section 8 and carry out the operations described in paragraphs 19 to 25.

10 The remainder of the assembly procedure is the reverse of the dismantling sequence described in paragraphs 2 to 7 above.

11 Refit the distributor to the engine, refer to Section 7.

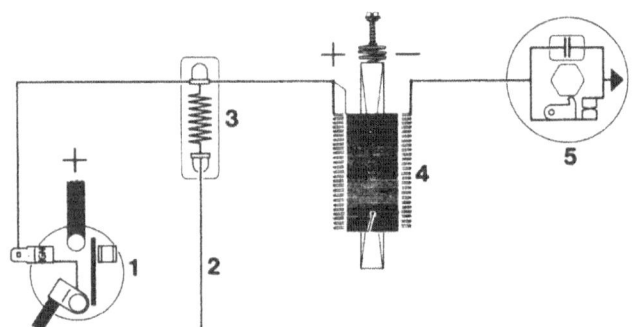

Fig. 4.7 Ballast resistor circuit (Sec 10)

1 Starter motor solenoid   4 Coil
2 Normal ignition current   5 Distributor
3 Ballast resistor

10 Ignition coil and ballast resistor – general

1   A ballast resistor system is fitted. The resistor is fitted in series in the normal supply to the 6 volt coil, to assist cold starting. When the starter switch is operated the resistor is by-passed and a full 12 volts is supplied direct to the coil from the starter solenoid. With the engine running the ballast resistor is in circuit with the coil so allowing the coil to operate at its normal voltage (Fig. 4.7).

2   Pre engine No LF 20001 the resistor is a separate unit attached to the side of the coil mounting bracket. From engine No LF 20001 the resistor is incorporated in the wiring harness as a high resistance wire.

3   It is particularly important that all electrical connections are kept clean and dry to obtain full benefit of this system.

11 Spark plugs and HT leads

1   The correct functioning of the spark plugs is vital for the correct running and efficiency of the engine.

2   At intervals of 6000 miles (9600 km) the plugs should be removed, examined, cleaned and if worn excessively, renewed. The condition of the spark plug will also tell much about the overall condition of the engine.

3   If the insulator nose of the spark plug is clean and white with no deposits, this is indicative of a weak mixture, or too hot a plug. (A hot plug transfers heat away from the electrode slowly – a cold plug transfers it away quickly).

4   The plugs fitted as standard cannot be improved upon (see Specifications). If the top and insulator nose are covered with hard black looking deposits, then this is indicative that the mixture is too rich. Should the plug be black and oily, then it is likely that the engine is fairly worn, as well as the mixture being too rich.

5   If the insulator nose is covered with light tan to greyish brown deposits, the mixture is correct and it is likely that the engine is in good condition.

6   If there are any traces of long brownish tapering stains on the outside of the white portion of the plug, then the plug will have to be renewed, as this shows that there is a faulty joint between the plug body and the insulator, and compression is being allowed to leak away.

7   Plugs should be cleaned by a sandblasting machine, which will free them from carbon more thoroughly then cleaning by hand. The machine will also test the condition of the plugs under compression. Any plug that fails to spark at the recommended pressure should be renewed.

8   The spark plug gap is of considerable importance, as if it is too

large or too small, the size of the spark and its efficiency will be seriously impaired. The spark plug gap should be set to 0.025 inch (0.635 mm) for the best results.

9   To set it, measure the gap with a feeler gauge, and then bend open, or close, the outer plug electrode until the correct gap is achieved. The centre electrode should never be bent as this may crack the insulation and cause plug failure if nothing worse.

10 When refitting the plugs, remember to use a new plug washer, and refit the leads from the distributor in the correct firing order.

11 The plug leads require no routine attention other than being kept clean and wiped over regularly. At intervals of 12 000 miles (19 000 km), however, pull each off the plug in turn and remove them from the distributor by unscrewing the knurled moulded terminal knobs. Water can seep down into these joints giving rise to a white corrosive deposit which must be carefully removed from the brass washer at the end of each cable through which the ignition wires pass.

12 Ignition system – fault diagnosis

By far the majority of breakdown and running troubles are caused by faults in the ignition system either in the low tension or high tension circuits.

There are two main symptoms indicating ignition faults: either the engine will not start or fire, or the engine is difficult to start and misfires. If it is a regular misfire, (ie, the engine is running only on six or seven cylinders, the fault is almost sure to be in the secondary, or high tension, circuit. If the misfiring is intermittent, the fault could be in either the high or low tension circuits. If the car stops suddenly, or will not start at all it is likely that the fault is in the low tension circuit. Loss of power and overheating, apart from faulty carburation settings, are normally due to faults in the distributor or incorrect timing.

Engine fails to start

1   If the engine fails to start and the car was running normally when it was last used, first check there is fuel in the petrol tank. If the engine turns over normally on the starter motor and the battery is evidently well charged, then the fault may be in either the high or low tension circuits. First check the HT circuit. **Note:** *If the battery is known to be fully charged, the ignition light comes on, and the starter motor fails to turn the engine,* **check the tightness of the leads of the battery terminals,** *and also the secureness of the earth lead to its* **connection to the body.** *It is quite common for the leads to have worked loose, even if they look and feel secure. If one of the battery terminal posts gets very hot when trying to work the starter motor this is a sure indication of a faulty connection to the terminal.*

2   One of the commonest reasons for bad starting is wet or damp spark plug leads and distributor. Remove the distributor cap. If condensation is visible internally, dry the cap with a rag and also wipe over the leads. Refit the cap.

3   If the engine still fails to start, check that current is reaching the plugs, by disconnecting each plug lead in turn at the spark plug end, and holding the end of the cable about $\frac{3}{16}$ in (5 mm) away from the cylinder block. Spin the engine on the starter motor.

4   Sparking between the end of the cable and the block should be fairly strong with a regular blue spark. (Hold the lead with rubber to avoid electric shocks). If current is reaching the plugs, then remove them and clean and regap them to 0.025 inch (0.635 mm). The engine should now start.

5   If there is no spark at the plug leads take off the HT lead from the centre of the distributor cap and hold it to the block as before. Spin the engine on the starter once more. A rapid succession of blue sparks between the end of the lead and the block indicates that the coil is in order and that the distributor cap is cracked, the rotor arm faulty, or the carbon brush in the top of the distributor cap is not making good contact with the spring on the rotor arm. Possibly the points are in bad condition. Clean and reset them as described in Section 2.

6   If there are no sparks from the end of the lead from the coil, check the connections at the coil end of the lead. If it is in order start checking the low tension circuit.

7   Use a 12v voltmeter or a 12v bulb and two lengths of wire. With the ignition switch on and the points open test between the low tension wire to the coil (it is marked (+) and earth). No reading indicates a break in the supply from the ignition switch. Check the connections at the switch to see if any are loose. Refit them and the

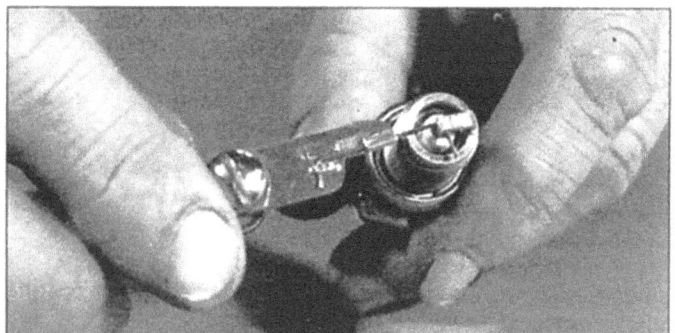

Electrode gap check - use a wire type gauge for best results

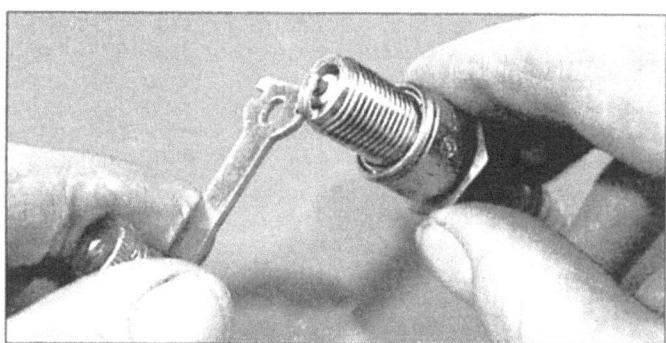

Electrode gap adjustment - bend the side electrode using the correct tool

Normal condition - A brown, tan or grey firing end indicates that the engine is in good condition and that the plug type is correct

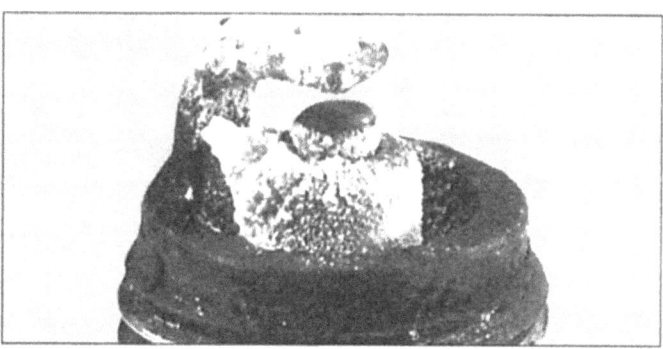

Ash deposits - Light brown deposits encrusted on the electrodes and insulator, leading to misfire and hesitation. Caused by excessive amounts of oil in the combustion chamber or poor quality fuel/oil

Carbon fouling - Dry, black sooty deposits leading to misfire and weak spark. Caused by an over-rich fuel/air mixture, faulty choke operation or blocked air filter

Oil fouling - Wet oily deposits leading to misfire and weak spark. Caused by oil leakage past piston rings or valve guides (4-stroke engine), or excess lubricant (2-stroke engine)

Overheating - A blistered white insulator and glazed electrodes. Caused by ignition system fault, incorrect fuel, or cooling system fault

Worn plug - Worn electrodes will cause poor starting in damp or cold weather and will also waste fuel

engine should run. A reading shows a faulty coil or condenser, or broken lead between the coil and the distributor.

8   Take the condenser wire off the points assembly and with the points open, test between the moving point and earth. If there now is a reading, then the fault is in the condenser. Fit a new one and the fault is cleared.

9   With no reading from the moving point to earth, take a reading between earth and the (-) terminal of the coil. A reading here shows a broken wire which will need to be renewed between the coil and distributor. No reading confirms that the coil has failed and must be renewed, after which the engine will run once more. Remember to refit the condenser wire to the points assembly. For these tests it is sufficient to separate the points with a piece of dry paper while testing with the points open.

Engine misfires

10   If the engine misfires regularly run it at a fast idling speed. Pull off each of the plug caps in turn and listen to the note of the engine. Hold the plug cap in a dry cloth or with a rubber glove as additional protection against a shock from the HT lead.

11   No difference in engine running will be noticed when the lead from the defective circuit is removed. Removing the lead from one of the good cylinders will accentuate the misfire.

12   Remove the plug lead from the end of the defective plug and hold it about $\frac{3}{16}$ inch (5 mm) away from the block. Re-start the engine. If the sparking is fairly strong and regular the fault must lie in the spark plug.

13   The plug may be loose, the insulation may be cracked, or the points may have burnt away giving too wide a gap for the spark to jump. Worse still, one of the points may have broken off.

14   If there is no spark at the end of the plug lead, or if it is weak and intermittent, check the ignition lead from the distributor to the plug. If the insulation is cracked or perished, renew the lead. Check the connections at the distributor cap.

15   If there is still no spark, examine the distributor cap carefully for tracking. This can be recognised by a very thin black line running between two or more electrodes, or between an electrode and some other part of the distributor. These lines are paths which now conduct electricity across the cap thus letting it run to earth. The only answer is a new distributor cap.

16   Apart from the ignition timing being incorrect, other causes of misfiring have already been dealt with under the section dealing with the failure of the engine to start. To recap – these are that:

(a) The coil may be faulty giving an intermittent misfire
(b) There may be a damaged wire or loose connection in the low tension circuit
(c) The condenser may be short circuiting
(d) There may be a mechanical fault in the distributor (broken driving shaft or contact breaker spring)

17   If the ignition timing is too far retarded, it should be noted that the engine will tend to overheat, and there will a quite noticeable drop in power. If the engine is overheating and the power is down, and the ignition timing is correct, then the carburettor should be checked, as it is likely that this is where the fault lies.

Chapter 5 Clutch

Contents

Specifications

Type .... Diaphragm spring, single dry plate

Driven plate
Diameter .... 9 in (228·6 mm)
Number of damper springs 6

Clutch operation .... Hydraulic

Torque wrench settings

	lbf ft	kgf m
Clutch to flywheel	22	3·0
Slave cylinder mounting bolts	20	2·8
Master cylinder mounting bolts	20	2·8

1 General description

The clutch is fitted in order that the engine may run without being mechanically connected to the transmission. It enables the engine torque to be progressively applied to the gearbox so that the car can move off gradually from rest, and then for the gear to be changed easily as the speed increases or decreases.

The clutch comprises a steel cover which is bolted and dowelled to the rear face of the flywheel and contains the pressure plate and clutch disc or driven plate.

The pressure plate, diaphragm spring, and release plate are all attached to the clutch assembly cover.

The clutch disc is free to slide along the splined first motion shaft and is held in position between the flywheel and the pressure plate by the pressure of the diaphragm spring.

Friction lining material is riveted to the clutch disc which has a spring cushioned hub to absorb transmission shocks and to help ensure a smooth take off.

The clutch is actuated hydraulically. The pendant clutch pedal is connected to the clutch master cylinder and hydraulic fluid reservoir by a short pushrod. The master cylinder and hydraulic reservoir are mounted on the engine side of the bulkhead in front of the driver.

Depressing the clutch pedal moves the piston in the master cylinder forwards, so forcing hydraulic fluid through the clutch hydraulic pipe to the slave cylinder.

The piston in the slave cylinder moves forward on the entry of the fluid and actuates the clutch release arm by means of a short pushrod. The opposite end of the release arm is forked and is located behind the release bearing.

As this pivoted clutch release arm moves backwards it bears against the release bearing pushing it forwards to bear against the release plate, so moving the centre of the diaphragm spring inwards. The spring is sandwiched between two annular rings which act as fulcrum points. As the centre of the spring is pushed in, the outside of the spring is pushed out, so moving the pressure plate backwards and disengaging the pressure plate from the clutch disc.

When the clutch pedal is released, the diaphragm spring forces the pressure plate into contact with the high friction linings on the clutch disc and at the same time pushes the clutch disc a fraction of an inch forwards on its splines so engaging the clutch disc with the flywheel. The clutch disc is now firmly sandwiched between the pressure plate and the flywheel so the drive is taken up.

As the friction linings on the clutch disc wear the pressure plate automatically moves closer to the disc to compensate. There is therefore no need to periodically adjust the clutch.

2 Clutch hydraulic system – maintenance and bleeding

1   Maintenance consists of checking the fluid level in the master cylinder reservoir at regular intervals and topping up if necessary with the specified fluid.
2   Inspect the hoses for deterioration and the master and slave cylinders for leakage. Should the latter be evident, then overhaul the component and renew the seals as described later in this Chapter.
3   Bleeding will normally only be required if some part of the hydraulic system has been disconnected.
4   Gather together a clean jar, a length of rubber tubing which fits tightly over the bleed nipple in the slave cylinder and a tin of hydraulic brake fluid. An assistant will be required.
5   Check that the master cylinder is full. If it is not, fill it and cover the bottom two inches (50 mm) of the jar with hydraulic fluid (Fig. 5.2).
6   Remove the rubber dust cap from the bleed nipple on the slave cylinder, and with a suitable spanner open the bleed nipple one turn.
7   Place one end of the tube securely over the nipple and insert the other end in the jar so that the tube orifice is below the level of the fluid.

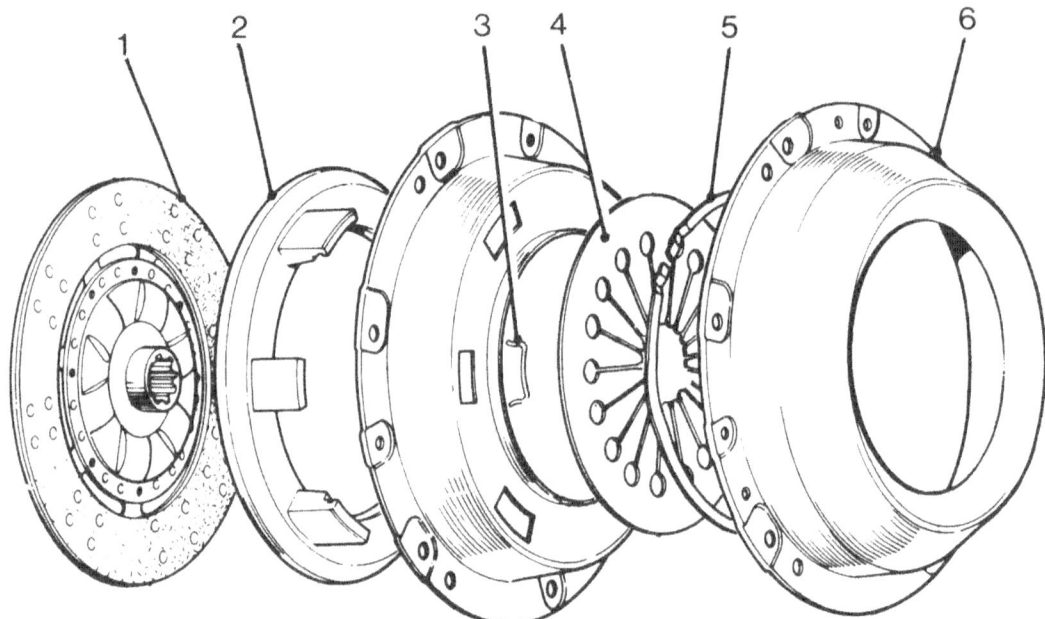

Fig. 5.1 Exploded view of clutch assembly (Sec 1)

1 Driven plate   2 Pressure plate   3 Spring clip   4 Diaphragm spring   5 Retaining ring   6 Outer cover assembly

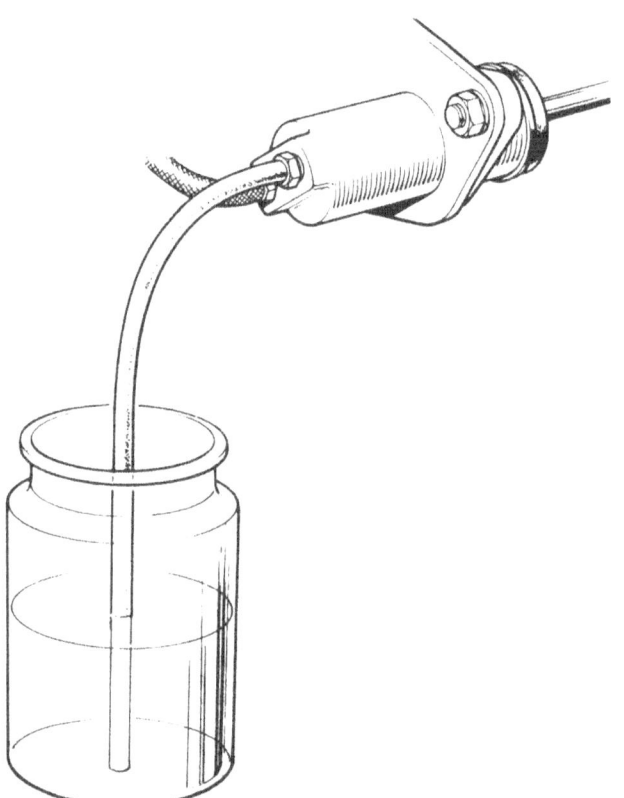

Fig. 5.2 Bleeding the hydraulic system (Sec 2)

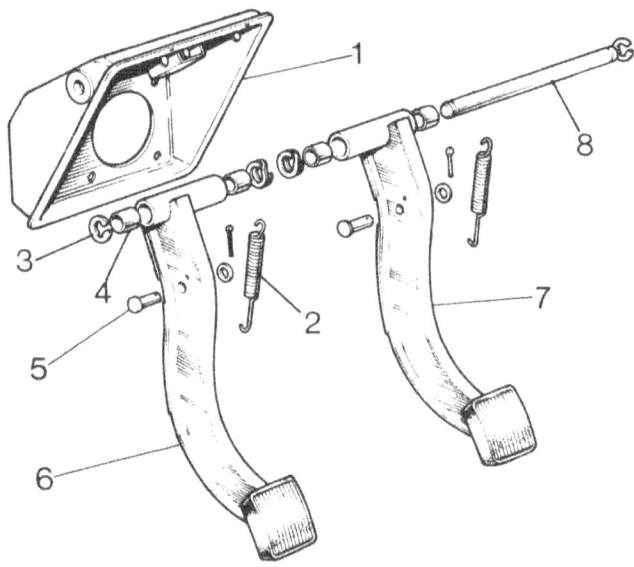

Fig. 5.3 Exploded view of clutch and brake pedal assembly (Sec 3)

1 Pedal assembly mounting bracket	*5 Clevis pin*
	6 Clutch pedal
2 Return spring	*7 Brake pedal*
3 Circlip	*8 Cross-shaft*
4 Bush	

8   The assistant should now depress the clutch pedal fully and then release it, repeating until air bubbles cease to emerge from the end of the tubing. He should also check the reservoir frequently to ensure that the hydraulic fluid does not disappear so letting air into the system.

9   When no more air bubbles appear, tighten the bleed nipple on the downstroke.

10 Refit the rubber dust cap over the bleed nipple. Discard the fluid which has been expelled.

3   Clutch and brake pedal assembly – removal, inspection and refitting

1   Disconnect the leads from the brake light switch.

2   Remove the split pins from the clevis pins attaching the clutch and brake pedals to their respective pushrods and withdraw the clevis pins.

3   Remove the pedal bracket to bulkhead securing bolts and lift away the pedal assembly.

4   Disconnect the clutch and brake pedal return springs.

5   Remove the retaining circlip, withdraw the pedal cross-shaft and remove the pedals and bushes (Fig. 5.3).

6   Inspect all the parts for wear or damage and renew as necessary.
7   Refitting is the reverse of the removal procedure.

4   Clutch – removal

1   Remove the gearbox as described in Chapter 6.
2   Mark the clutch cover and flywheel so that the clutch may be refitted in its original position, unless it is to be renewed. The clutch cover, pressure plate and diaphragm spring assembly must be renewed as a unit if it is found to be faulty.
3   Remove the clutch assembly by unscrewing the six bolts holding the cover to the rear face of the flywheel. Unscrew the bolts diagonally half a turn at a time to prevent distortion to the cover flange.
4   With the bolts and spring washers removed, lift the clutch assembly off the locating dowels. The driven plate or clutch disc will fall out at this stage as it is not attached to either the clutch cover assembly or the flywheel.

5   Clutch – refitting

1   It is important that no oil or grease gets on the clutch disc friction linings, or the pressure plate and flywheel faces. It is advisable to refit the clutch with clean hands and to wipe down the pressure plate and flywheel faces with a clean dry rag before assembly begins.
2   Place the clutch disc against the flywheel with the longer end of the hub facing outwards away from the flywheel. On no account should the clutch be refitted the reverse way round, as on reassembly it will be found quite impossible to operate the clutch with the friction disc in this position.
3   Refit the clutch cover assembly loosely on the dowels. Refit the six bolts and spring washers and tighten them finger-tight so that the clutch disc is gripped but can still be moved.
4   The clutch disc must now be centralised so that when the engine and gearbox are mated, the gearbox input shaft splines will pass through the splines in the centre of the driven plate hub.
5   Centralisation can be carried out quite easily by inserting a round bar or long screwdriver through the hole in the centre of the clutch, so that the end of the bar rests in the small hole in the end of the crank-shaft containing the input shaft bearing bush. Moving the bar sideways or up and down will move the clutch disc in whichever direction is necessary to achieve centralisation.
6   Centralisation is easily judged by removing the bar and viewing the driven plate hub in relation to the hole in the reverse bearing. When the hub appears exactly in the centre of the release bearing hole all is correct. Alternatively, if an old Triumph input shaft can be borrowed this will eliminate all the guesswork as it will fit the bush and centre of the clutch hub exactly, obviating the need for visual alignment.
7   Tighten the clutch bolts firmly in a diagonal sequence to ensure that the cover plate is pulled down evenly, and without distortion of the flange.
8   Mate the engine and gearbox, bleed the slave cylinder if the pipe was disconnected and check the clutch for correct operation.

6   Clutch – dismantling and reassembly

1   In the normal course of events, clutch dismantling and reassembly is the term used for simply fitting a new clutch pressure plate and friction disc. Under no circumstances must the diaphragm clutch unit be dismantled. If a fault develops in the pressure plate assembly an exchange replacement unit must be fitted.
2   If a new clutch disc is being fitted, it is false economy not to renew the release bearing at the same time. This will preclude having to renew it at a later date when wear on the clutch linings is still very small.

7   Clutch – inspection

1   Examine the clutch disc friction linings for wear or loose rivets and the disc for rim distortion, cracks and worn splines.
2   It is always best to renew the clutch driven plate as an assembly to preclude further trouble, but, if it is wished to merely renew the linings

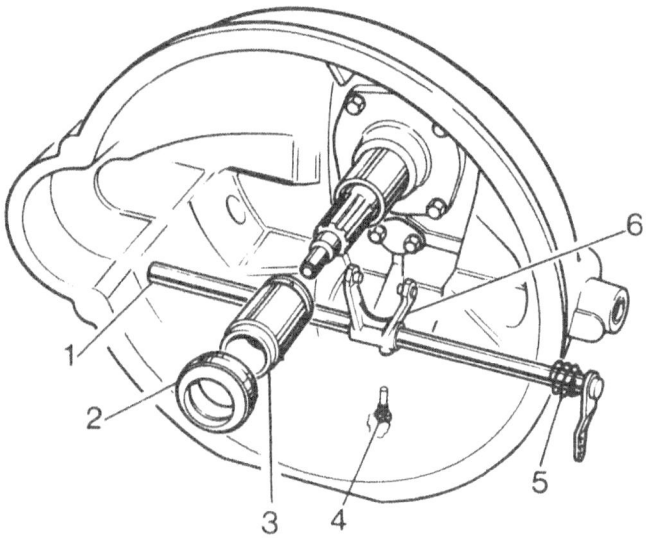

Fig. 5.4 Exploded view of clutch release mechanism (Sec 8)

1 Cross-shaft   *4 Pin-bolt*
2 Release bearing   *5 Anti-rattle spring*
3 Sleeve   *6 Fork*

the rivets should be drilled out, and not knocked out with a centre punch. The manufacturers do not advise that the linings only are renewed and personal experience indicates that it is far more satisfactory to renew the driven plate complete than to try to economise by fitting only new friction linings.
3   Check the machined faces of the flywheel and the pressure plate. If either is badly grooved it should be machined until smooth, or replaced with a new item. If the pressure plate is cracked or split it must be renewed.

8   Clutch release mechanism – removal and refitting

1   Remove the gearbox as described in Chapter 6.
2   Remove the locking wire from the pin-bolt then unscrew the pin-bolt (Fig. 5.4).
3   Push out the cross-shaft and collect the release fork and anti-rattle spring.
4   Slide off the release bearing and sleeve assembly
5   As the sleeve is pressed into the bearing the two parts may be separated by placing the bearing on the top of the opened jaws of a bench vice and using a drift of suitable diameter, tap out the sleeve.
6   Inspect the cross-shaft, the fork and sleeve for excessive wear and fit new parts as necessary.
7   Hold the outer track of the release bearing and rotae the inner track. If it feels rough during rotation fit a new bearing.
8   Refitting is the reverse of the removal procedure. Smear a little high melting point grease on the inside of the sleeve and also on the cross-shaft, do not over-grease. Do not forget to lock the pin-bolt with soft iron wire.

9   Clutch slave cylinder – removal and refitting

1   The clutch slave cylinder is mounted on a bracket attached to the bellhousing (Fig. 5.5).
2   Before removing the slave cylinder take off the clutch master cylinder reservoir cap and place a piece of thin polythene over the top of the reservoir. Screw the cap down tightly over the polythene.
3   Extract the split pin, washer and clevis pin from the clutch pushrod yoke and withdraw the pushrod from the slave cylinder.
4   Undo the two bolts holding the slave cylinder to the bracket on the bulkhead.
5   Wipe the area clean of dust and dirt where the hydraulic pipe is connected to the slave cylinder and disconnect the hydraulic pipe from the slave cylinder by releasing the union with an open ended spanner

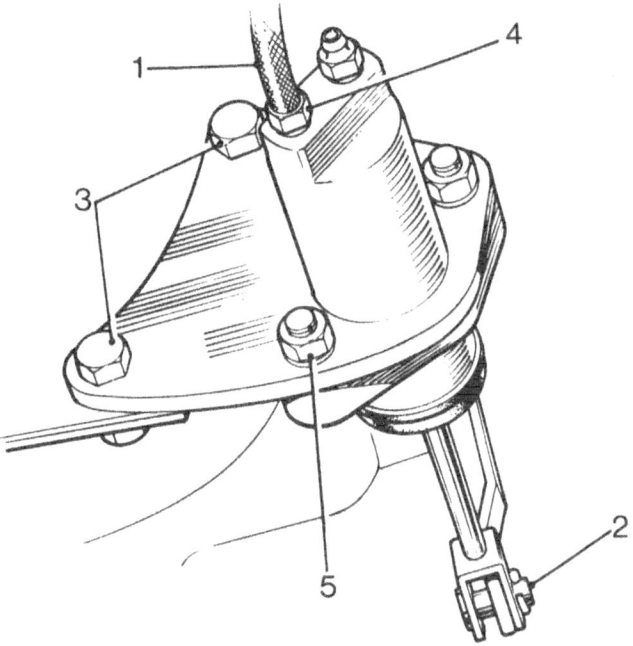

Fig. 5.5 Removing the clutch slave cylinder (Sec 9)

1 Pressure hose	4 Union
2 Clevis pin	5 Bracket to slave cylinder
3 Bracket to bellhousing bolts	bolts

and rotating the slave cylinder. Take care not to kink or twist the flexible hose. The polythene over the reservoir will prevent any loss of fluid from the master cylinder when the hydraulic pipe is disconnected.

6   Refitting is the reverse of the removal procedure. After refitting, remove the polythene from the reservoir and top up the system with the correct grade of hydraulic fluid and then bleed the system as described in Section 2.

10 Clutch slave cylinder – dismantling, examination and reassembly

1   Clean the outside of the slave cylinder before dismantling.

2   Pull off the rubber dust cover and by shaking hard, the piston, seal, filler block and the spring should come out of the cylinder bore (Fig. 5.6).

3   If they prove stubborn carefully use a foot pump air jet on the hydraulic hose connection and this should remove the internal parts, but do take care as they will fly out. We recommend placing a pad over the dust cover end to catch the parts.

4   Wash all the internal parts with either brake fluid or methylated spirits and dry using a non-fluffy rag.

5   Inspect the bore and piston for signs of deep scoring which, if evident, means a new cylinder should be fitted.

6   Carefully examine the rubber components for signs of swelling, distortion, splitting, hardening or other wear although it is recommended new rubber parts are always fitted after dismantling.

7   Reassembly is a straight reversal of the dismantling procedure but note the following points:

    (a) *As the component parts are refitted to the slave cylinder bore smear them with clean hydraulic fluid*

    (b) *When refitting the piston seal ensure that it is positioned the correct way round as shown*

11 Clutch master cylinder – removal and refitting

1   Drain the fluid from the clutch master cylinder reservoir by attaching a rubber tube to the slave cylinder bleed nipple; undo the screw at the base of the nipple one turn, and then pump the fluid out into a suitable container by means of operating the clutch pedal. Note

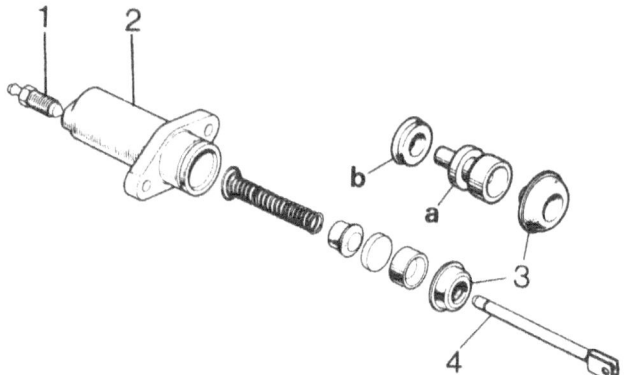

Fig. 5.6 Exploded view of clutch slave cylinder (Sec 10)

1 Bleed screw	4 Pushrod
2 Slave cylinder	a Piston
3 Dust cover	b Seal

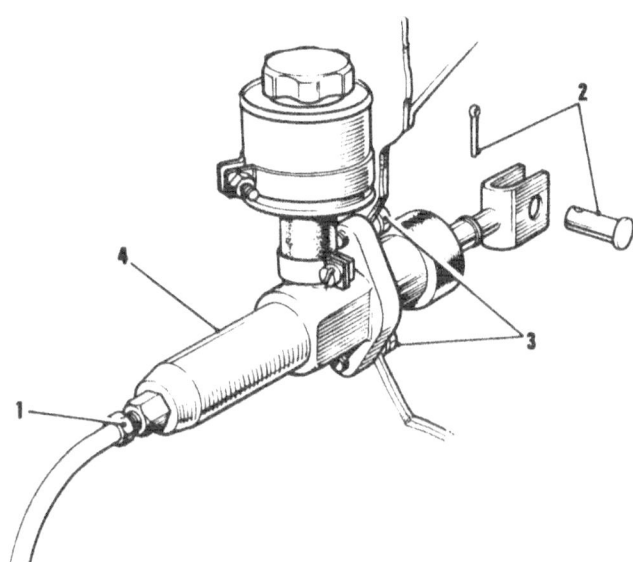

Fig. 5.7 Removing the clutch master cylinder (Sec 11)

1 Pressure pipe union	bolts
2 Split pin and clevis pin	4 Master cylinder
3 Master cylinder mounting	

that the pedal must be held against the floor at the completion of each stroke and bleed nipple tightened before the pedal is allowed to return. When the pedal has returned to its normal position loosen the bleed nipple and repeat the process, until the clutch master cylinder is empty.

2   Place a rag under the master cylinder to catch any hydraulic fluid that may be spilt. Unscrew the union nut from the end of the hydraulic pipe where it enters the clutch master cylinder and gently pull the pipe clear (Fig. 5.7).

3   From inside the car extract the split pin from the pushrod yoke to pedal clevis pin and lift away the washer and clevis noting which way round the clevis is fitted.

4   Unscrew the two bolts holding the clutch master cylinder to the bulkhead, lift away the two nuts, bolts and spring washers.

5   Remove the master cylinder and reservoir taking care not to allow any hydraulic fluid to come into contact with the paintwork as it acts as a solvent. Unscrew the filler cap and drain any hydraulic fluid into a container.

6   Refitting is the reverse of the removal procedure. It will be necessary to bleed the hydraulic system as described in Section 2.

12 Clutch master cylinder – dismantling, examination and reassembly

1   Refer to Fig. 5.8. Pull back the dust cover to expose the circlip which must be removed so that the pushrod complete with the pushrod stop can be pulled out of the master cylinder.
2   By shaking hard, the piston with the seal, dished washer and seal should come out of the cylinder bore. Also the spring and rod retainer may be removed.
3   If they prove stubborn carefully use a foot pump air jet on the hydraulic pipe connection and this should remove the internal parts, but do take care as they will fly out. We recommended placing a pad over the pushrod end to catch the parts.
4   Separate the spring retainer and secondary seal from the piston.
5   Thoroughly clean the parts in brake fluid or methylated spirits. After drying them, inspect the seals for signs of distortion, swelling, splitting or hardening although it is recommended new rubber parts are always fitted after dismantling as a matter of course.
6   Inspect the bore and piston for signs of deep scoring which, if evident, means a new cylinder should be fitted. Make sure that the by-pass ports are clear by poking gently with a piece of thin wire.
7   As the parts are refitted to the cylinder bore make sure they are thoroughly wetted with hydraulic fluid.
8   Fit the secondary seal to the piston and the spring retainer to the spring.
9   Insert the large end of the spring into the cylinder bore followed by the primary seal ensuring that the lip is inserted first. Great care must be taken not to turn back the lip on the seal.
10 Refit the dished washer, concave side adjacent to the rubber seal, and the piston into the cylinder bore.
11 Insert the pushrod and guide into the rubber dust cover and fit the pushrod complete with stop plate into position on the master cylinder. Refit the circlip holding the components into the cylinder bore and finally refit the dust cover.

13 Fault diagnosis – clutch

There are four main faults to which the clutch and release mechanism are prone. They may occur by themselves or in conjunction with any of the other faults. They are clutch squeal, slip, spin and judder.

Clutch squeal
1   If on taking up the drive or when changing gear, the clutch squeals, this is sure indication of a badly worn clutch release bearing.
2   As well as regular wear due to normal use, wear of the clutch release bearing is much accentuated if the clutch is ridden or held down for long periods in gear, with the engine running. To minimise wear of this component the car should always be taken out of gear at traffic lights and for similar hold ups.
3   The clutch release bearing is not an expensive item, but difficult to get at.

Clutch slip
4   Clutch slip is a self-evident condition which occurs when the clutch friction plate is badly worn, oil or grease have got onto the flywheel or pressure plate faces, or the pressure plate itself is faulty.
5   The reason for clutch slip is that due to one of the faults above, there is either insufficient pressure from the pressure plate, or insufficient friction from the friction plate to ensure solid drive.
6   If small amounts of oil get onto the clutch, they will be burnt off under the heat of the clutch engagement, and in the process, gradually darken the linings. Excessive oil on the clutch will burn off leaving a carbon deposit which can cause quite bad slip, or fierceness, spin and judder.
7   If clutch slip is suspected, and confirmation of this condition is required, there are several tests which can be made.
8   With the engine in second or third gear and pulling lightly up a moderate incline, sudden depression of the accelerator pedal may cause the engine to increase its speed without increase in road speed. Easing off on the accelerator will then give a definite drop in engine speed without the car slowing.
9   In extreme cases of clutch slip the engine will race under normal acceleration conditions.

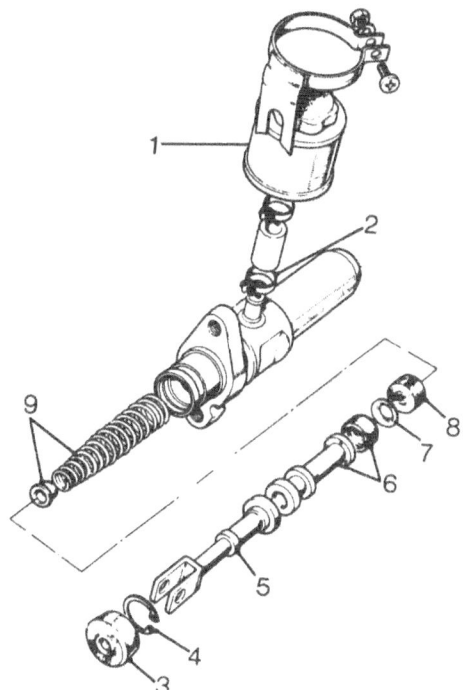

Fig. 5.8 Exploded view of clutch master cylinder (Sec 12)

1 Reservoir	6 Piston and seal
2 Hose clip	7 Dished washer
3 Dust cover	8 Primary seal
4 Circlip	9 Spring and spring retainer
5 Pushrod	

10 If the slip is due to oil or grease on the linings a temporary cure can sometimes be effected by squirting carbon tetrachloride into the clutch housing. The permanent cure is, of course, to renew the clutch driven plate and trace and rectify the oil leak.

Clutch spin
11 Clutch spin is a condition which occurs when there is a leak in the clutch hydraulic actuating mechanism; there is an obstruction in the clutch either in the primary gear splines or in the operating lever itself; or the oil may have partially burnt off the clutch linings and have left a resinous deposit which is causing the clutch disc to stick to the pressure plate or flywheel.
12 The reason for clutch spin is that due to any, or a combination of, the faults just listed, the clutch pressure plate is not completely freeing from the centre plate even with the clutch pedal fully depressed.
13 If clutch spin is suspected, the condition can be confirmed by extreme difficulty in engaging first gear from rest, difficulty in changing gear, and very sudden take up of the clutch drive at the full depressed end of the clutch pedal travel as the clutch is released.
14 Check the clutch master and slave cylinders and the connecting hydraulic pipe for leaks. Fluid in one of the rubber boots fitted over the end of either the master or slave cylinder is a sure sign of a leaking piston seal.
15 If these points are checked and found to be in order then the fault lies internally in the clutch, and it will be necessary to remove the clutch for examination.

Clutch judder
16 Clutch judder is a self-evident condition which occurs when the gearbox or engine mountings are loose or too flexible; or when there is oil on the face of the clutch friction plate.
17 The reason for the clutch judder is that, due to one of the faults just listed, the clutch pressure plate is not freeing smoothly from the friction disc, and is snatching.
18 Clutch judder normally occurs when the clutch pedal is released in first or reverse gears, and the whole car shudders as it moves backwards or forwards.

Chapter 6 Manual gearbox, overdrive and automatic transmission

---

Contents

Specifications

Part A – Manual gearbox

Type . . . .   Four forward speeds (all with synchromesh) and one reverse gear

Gear ratios
1st . . . .   2.99 : 1
2nd . . . .   2.10 : 1
3rd . . . .   1.38 : 1
4th . . . .   1.00 : 1
Reverse . . . .   3.36 : 1

Oil capacity . . . .   2.8 pints (1.6 litres)

Layshaft
Endfloat . . . .   0.007 to 0.012 in (0.18 to 0.3 mm)
Adjustment . . . .   Selective thrust washers

Mainshaft
Endfloat of 1st, 2nd and 3rd gears on bushes . . . .   0.004 to 0.008 in (0.1 to 0.2 mm)
Endfloat of 1st, 2nd and 3rd gear bushes and thrust washers . . . . .   0.003 to 0.009 in (0.8 to 0.23 mm)

Part B – A-type overdrive

Type . . . .   Laycock de Normanville A-type overdrive providing an additional ratio
to 3rd and 4th gears

Overdrive gear ratios
3rd . . . .   1.13 : 1
4th . . . .   0.82 : 1

Oil capacity . . . .   3.75 pints (2.13 litres)

Part C – J-type overdrive

Type	Laycock de Normanville J-type overdrive providing an additional ratio to 3rd and 4th gears

Overdrive gear ratios

3rd	1.10 : 1
4th	0.79 : 1

Oil capacity . . . .

3.5 pints (2.0 litres)

Part D – Automatic transmission

Type	Borg-Warner 35 up to Commission No LD 41993. Borg-Warner 65 from Commission No LD 41994

Converter reduction

Type 35	Infinitely variable between 1:1 and 1:2
Type 65	Infinitely variable between 1:1 and 1.91 : 1

Gear ratios

3rd	1 : 1
2nd	1.45 : 1
1st	2.39 : 1
Reverse	2.09 : 1

Fluid capacity (including oil cooler)

Type 35	14.25 pints (8.0 litres)
Type 65	9.5 pints (5.4 litres)

Torque wrench settings		
Manual gearbox	lbf ft	kgf m
Mainshaft rear flange nut	120	16.6
Top cover bolts	20	2.8
Reverse lever fulcrum	24	3.3
Front cover bolts	20	2.8
Extension housing bolts	20	2.8
Drain and filler plugs	24	3.3
Bellhousing to engine bolts	30	4.1
Gearbox to crossmember	20	2.8
Gearbox crossmember to body	20	2.8
Overdrive units		
Adaptor to gearbox	20	2.8
Overdrive to adaptor	20	2.8
Automatic transmission		
Torque converter to driveplate	30	4.1
Sump bolts	15	2.1
Filler/dipstick tube union	18	2.5
Torque converter housing to engine	30	4.1

Part A – Manual gearbox

1 General description

The gearbox has four forward speeds and one reverse speed with synchromesh action on all forward speeds. Gears are selected by means of a remote control assembly mounted on top of the gearbox. A Laycock de Normanville overdrive unit, operating on third and top gear, is fitted as an optional extra on cars before 1972. Overdrive is standard on all cars from 1972 (refer to Part B or C of this Chapter).

The clutch driven plate slides on the splines of the first motion shaft which is in constant mesh with the layshaft gear. This constant mesh layshaft gear is splined to the layshaft hub which is able to revolve at all times, including when no gears have been selected. The laygear hub assembly is supported at each end in needle roller bearings. Thrust washers are fitted at each end of the layshaft to take up excessive endfloat of the laygear.

The mainshaft carries the four forward gears and their respective synchromesh assemblies. The front of the shaft is supported in a needle roller bearing located in an annulus in the rear of the first motion shaft. The rear end of the mainshaft is splined to the flange to which is connected the propeller shaft universal joint coupling flange. Various thickness thrust washers are fitted onto the mainshaft to control the endfloat of the bushes and gear assemblies on the mainshaft.

2 Gearbox with overdrive – removal and refitting

The best method of removing the gearbox is to separate the gearbox away from the underside of the car leaving the engine in position. It is recommended that during the final stages of removal the assistance of a second person is obtained especially if an overdrive unit is fitted to the rear of the gearbox.

1 Disconnect the battery earth terminal, raise the car and put on axle-stands if a ramp is not available. The higher the car is off the ground the easier it will be to work underneath.
2 Undo the gearbox drain plug and drain the oil into a clean container. When all oil has drained out refit the drain plug. On later models, a drain plug is not fitted and so cannot be drained until removed.
3 Drain the cooling system and disconnect the top hose from the radiator. Disconnect both heater hoses from the heater.
4 Slacken the locknut and remove the gear lever knob. On cars with overdrive prise off the gear lever knob cap and disconnect the leads from the overdrive switch, then remove the gear lever knob.
5 Lift up the rear edge of the console tray and remove the front section. Remove the two securing screws and lift out the rear section of the console tray (Fig. 6.2).

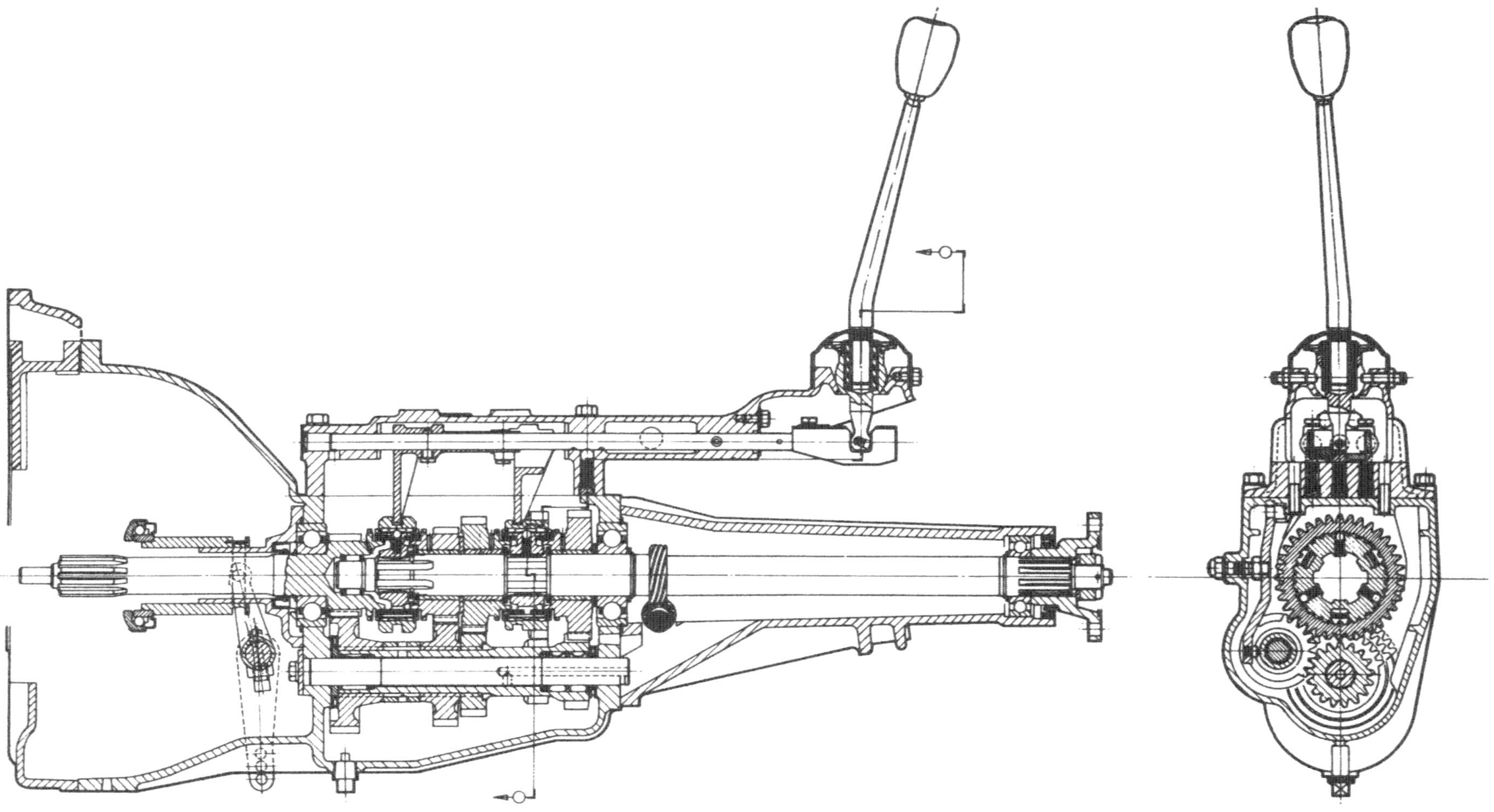

Fig. 6.1 Sectional view of gearbox (Sec 1)

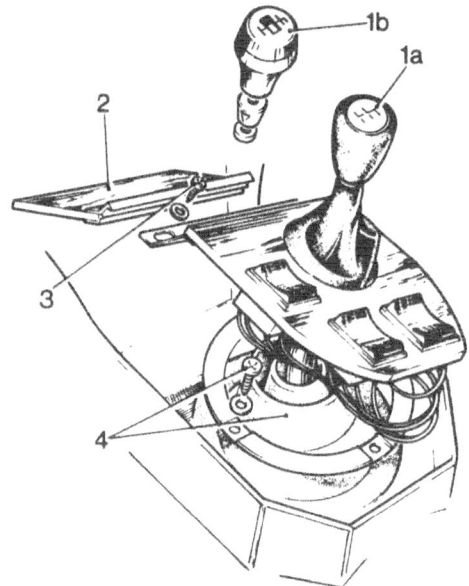

Fig. 6.2 Removing the console tray (Sec 2)

1a Gear lever knob   3 Retaining screws
1b Overdrive gear lever knob   4 Rear section of console tray
2 Front section console tray

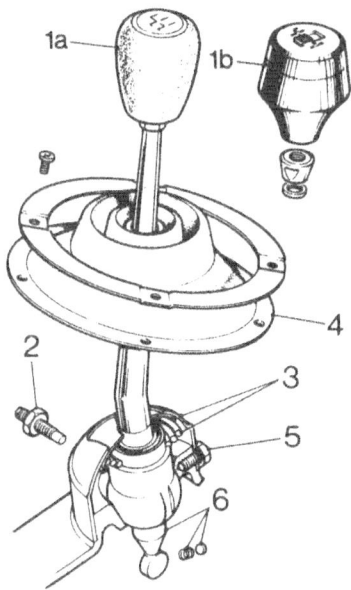

Fig. 6.3 Removing the gear lever (Sec 2)

1a Gear lever knob   4 Rubber gaiter
1b Overdrive gear lever knob   5 Cover securing bolt
2 Adjuster pin and locknuts   6 Plunger and spring
3 Gear lever cover and spring

6   Remove the four attaching screws and lift out the rubber gaiter.
7   Withdraw the overdrive switch lead (if fitted) through the gear lever.
8   Position the gear lever in neutral and remove the bolt at the rear of the gear lever cover (Fig. 6.3).
9   Slacken the adjuster pin locknuts. Depress and turn the gear lever cover, then remove the cover, plate and spring.
10 Withdraw the gear lever taking care not to lose the plunger and spring located in the striker end of the gear lever.
11 Loosen the five bellhousing to engine bolts accessible from the

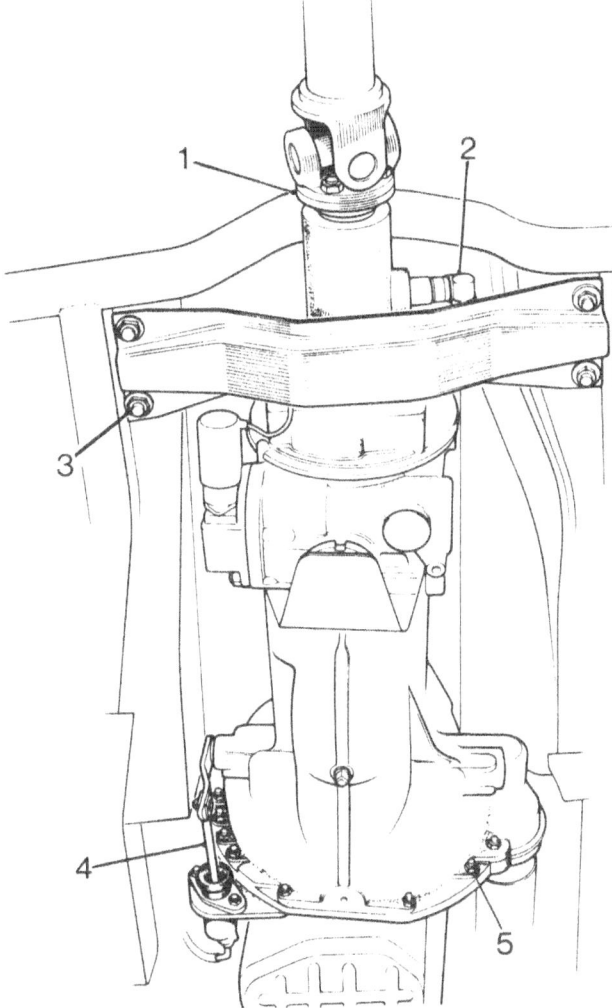

Fig. 6.4 Gearbox removal (Sec 2)

1 Flange coupling   4 Clutch slave cylinder pushrod
2 Speedometer cable   5 Bellhousing to engine bolts
3 Crossmember to body bolt

engine compartment.
12 Working under the car disconnect the wiring to the reverse light switch and overdrive (if fitted) at the block connector on the left-hand side, near the starter motor.
13 Disconnect the speedometer from the side of the gearbox or overdrive unit (if fitted). Note that a spacer is fitted on overdrive units.
14 Disconnect the exhaust pipes from the exhaust manifolds by undoing the three nuts securing each flange. Note that there is a gasket fitted between each flange and manifold. Slacken the two clamp nuts securing the silencer pipes to the rear intermediate pipes. Undo the bolts securing the exhaust pipe to the gearbox mounting and remove the front exhaust pipes and silencers.
15 Scribe a line across the gearbox drive flange and the front universal joint flange to ensure the propeller shaft is refitted in the same position, relative to the gearbox, at reassembly. Undo the four propeller shaft universal joint coupling flange bolts at the rear of the gearbox. Lower the end of the propeller shaft to the ground. Disconnect the clutch slave cylinder pushrod yoke from the clutch cross-shaft in the bellhousing. Note into which hole in the cross-shaft lever the clevis pin fits. Use string or wire to retain the piston in the slave cylinder.
16 Using a jack to support the gearbox, remove the four nylon nuts securing the gearbox rear mounting plate to the body (Fig. 6.4).
17 Unclip the brake pipe from the rear of the front cross-member, then lower the gearbox, ensuring that the engine sump does not trap

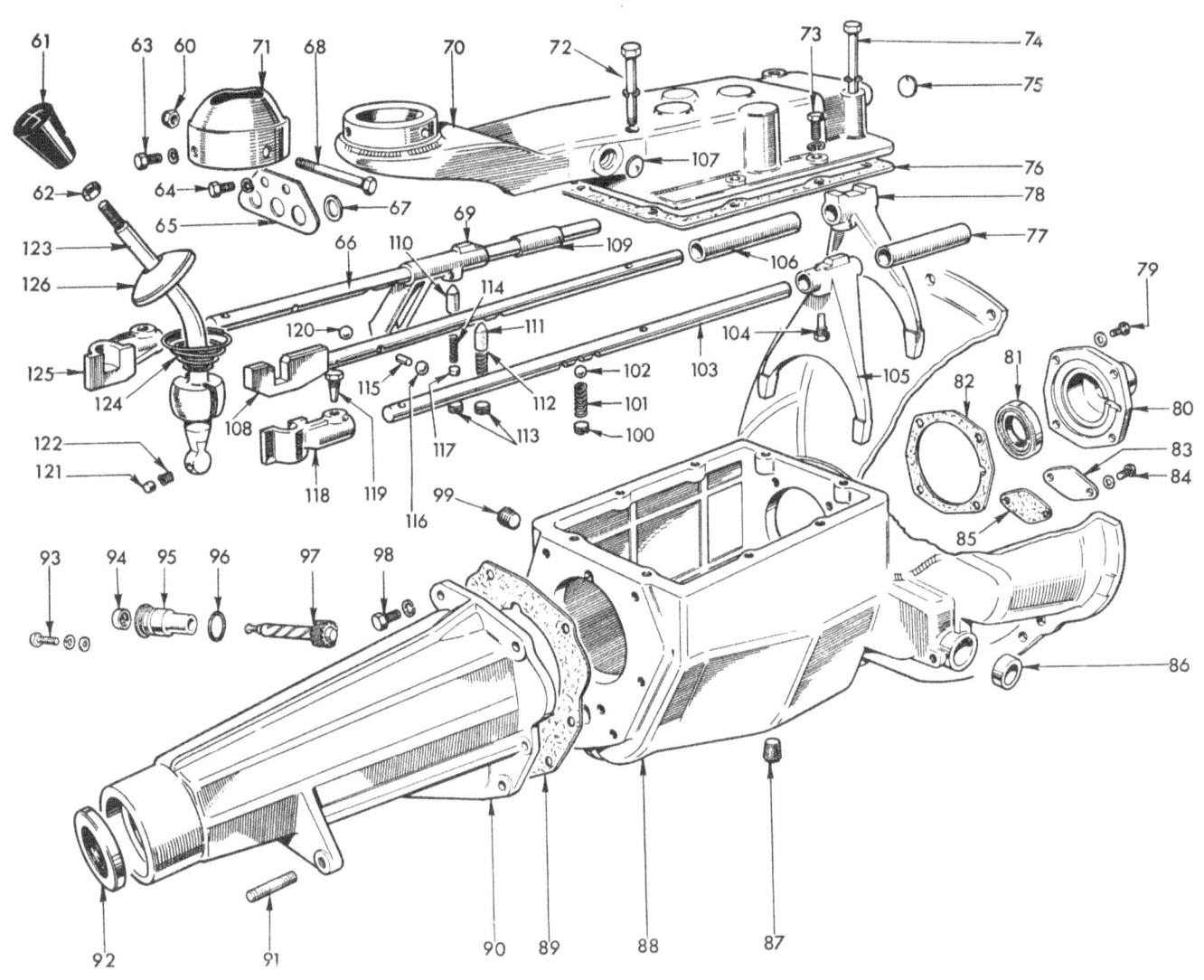

Fig. 6.5 Gearbox external components and selector system parts (Sec 3)

60	Nyloc nut	83	Countershaft cover plate	105	1st/2nd selector fork
61	Knob	84	Setscrew	106	Distance tube
62	Locknut	85	Gasket	107	Welch plug
63	Setscrew	86	Bush	108	Top/3rd selector shaft
64	Setscrew	87	Drain plug	109	Distance tube
65	Retaining plate	88	Casing	110	Plunger
66	Reverse selector shaft	89	Gasket	111	Plunger
67	Rubber sealing ring	90	Extension housing	112	Spring
68	Cross bolt	91	Stud	113	Plug
69	Reverse actuator	92	Oil seal	114	Spring
70	Top cover	93	Setscrew	115	Interlock plunger
71	Cap	94	Seal	116	Ball – interlock
72	Bolt	95	Speedometer pinion housing	117	Distance piece
73	Bolt	96	Rubber O-ring	118	Selector – 1st/2nd
74	Bolt	97	Speedometer drive pinion	119	Peg bolt
75	Welch plug	98	Bolt	120	Ball – interlock
76	Gasket	99	Level plug	121	Ball – anti-rattle
77	Distance tube	100	Plug	122	Spring
78	Top/3rd selector fork	101	Spring	123	Lever
79	Wedglok bolts	102	Ball – detent	124	Spring
80	Front cover	103	1st/2nd selector shaft	125	Selector – reverse
81	Oil seal	104	Peg bolt	126	Cap disc
82	Gasket				

the brake pipe against the cross-member. Keep lowering the jack slowly until the weight of the engine and gearbox is taken by the crossmember then remove the jack.

18 On later models remove the two nuts securing the engine to gearbox anti-vibration straps.

19 Undo the bellhousing bolts securing the gearbox to the engine and take the weight of the gearbox. Do not, under any circumstances, allow it to hang on the first motion shaft. Carefully withdraw the gearbox to the rear and when the first motion shaft is clear of the clutch assembly lower the gearbox and remove it from under the car.

20 Refitting the gearbox is the reverse sequence to removal. Refill the gearbox with the recommended grade of oil. For refill capacity see the Specifications at the beginning of this Chapter. Do not forget to refill the cooling system.

3 Gearbox – dismantling into major assemblies

1 Undo the eight $\frac{1}{2}$ AF bolts that hold the remote control and top cover onto the top of the gearbox (photo). Lift away the bolts and spring washers noting that the four longer bolts are to the front and rear of the top cover.

2 Lift away the remote control and top cover from the top of the gearbox noting the gasket.

3 Remove the bolt retaining the speedometer drivegear housing and carefully prise out the speedometer pinion and housing.

4 Refer to Figs. 6.5 and 6.6. Extract the split pin from the slotted nut (42) and undo the nut from the end of the mainshaft (32). Lift away the nut (42) followed by the plain washer (41).

5 Carefully tap the flange (40) using a soft-faced hammer, from the rear of the gearbox extension.

6 Using a pair of circlip pliers or a small screwdriver remove the circlip (39) from the end of the mainshaft.

7 Undo the bolts (98) holding the extension housing (90) to the rear of the gearbox and remove the bolts and spring washers. Carefully tap the extension housing with a soft-faced hammer to break the joint and remove the extension housing and gasket.

8 Using a suitable puller withdraw the speedometer drivegear from the mainshaft.

9 If an overdrive is fitted to the gearbox, undo the $\frac{1}{2}$ AF nuts which hold the overdrive unit to the end of the gearbox casing. This should be done in a diagonal manner as there are strong springs which will automatically separate the two parts and if the pressure is not even, the mating flanges could be strained. Remove the nuts and spring washers (photo).

10 Under the action of the strong springs in the front of the overdrive unit, the overdrive unit will automatically separate, this being controlled by the two long studs situated on either side of the unit (photo).

11 Note that there are eight springs in the front of the overdrive unit and that the upper and lowermost rows have springs of slightly longer length than the remainder (photo). Although the four inner springs look as if they are longer they are merely further forward.

12 Cut the locking wire securing the square headed bolt which locates the clutch release fork to the cross-shaft (photo).

13 Undo and completely remove the square headed bolt.

14 Pull the release bearing forwards, so disengaging it from the clutch release fork and completely remove it.

15 To release the cross-shaft, undo the bolt which locks it in position situated on the right-hand side of the clutch housing on the cross-shaft bush housing.

16 Pull the shaft from the side of the bellhousing and at the same time pull the release fork from the shaft. The release fork can be a tight fit on the shaft but with care it can be removed.

17 Undo the four bolts that hold the front cover to the front of the gearbox casing (photo). Lift away the bolts and spring washers.

18 Remove the front cover and its gasket making a note that there is a small cut-out on the gasket and front cover which matches an oil hole in the gearbox casing by the ball race.

19 Undo the two bolts that hold the layshaft cover plate to the front of the gearbox (photo). Lift away the bolts, spring washer, cover plate and gasket.

20 On gearboxes fitted with overdrive unit an adaptor plate is fitted to the rear end. Undo the six adaptor plate retaining bolts (photo).

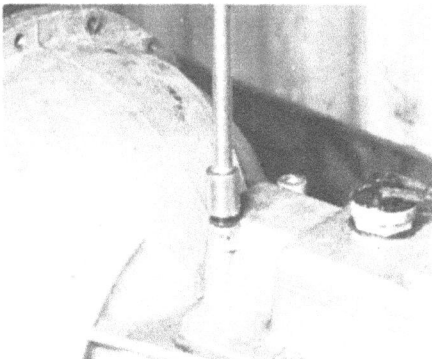

3.1 Removing the gearbox cover bolts

3.9 Removing the overdrive securing nuts

3.10 Overdrive released from the gearbox

3.11 Overdrive spring identification

3.12 Cutting the clutch release fork bolt locking wire

3.17 Removing the gearbox front cover bolts

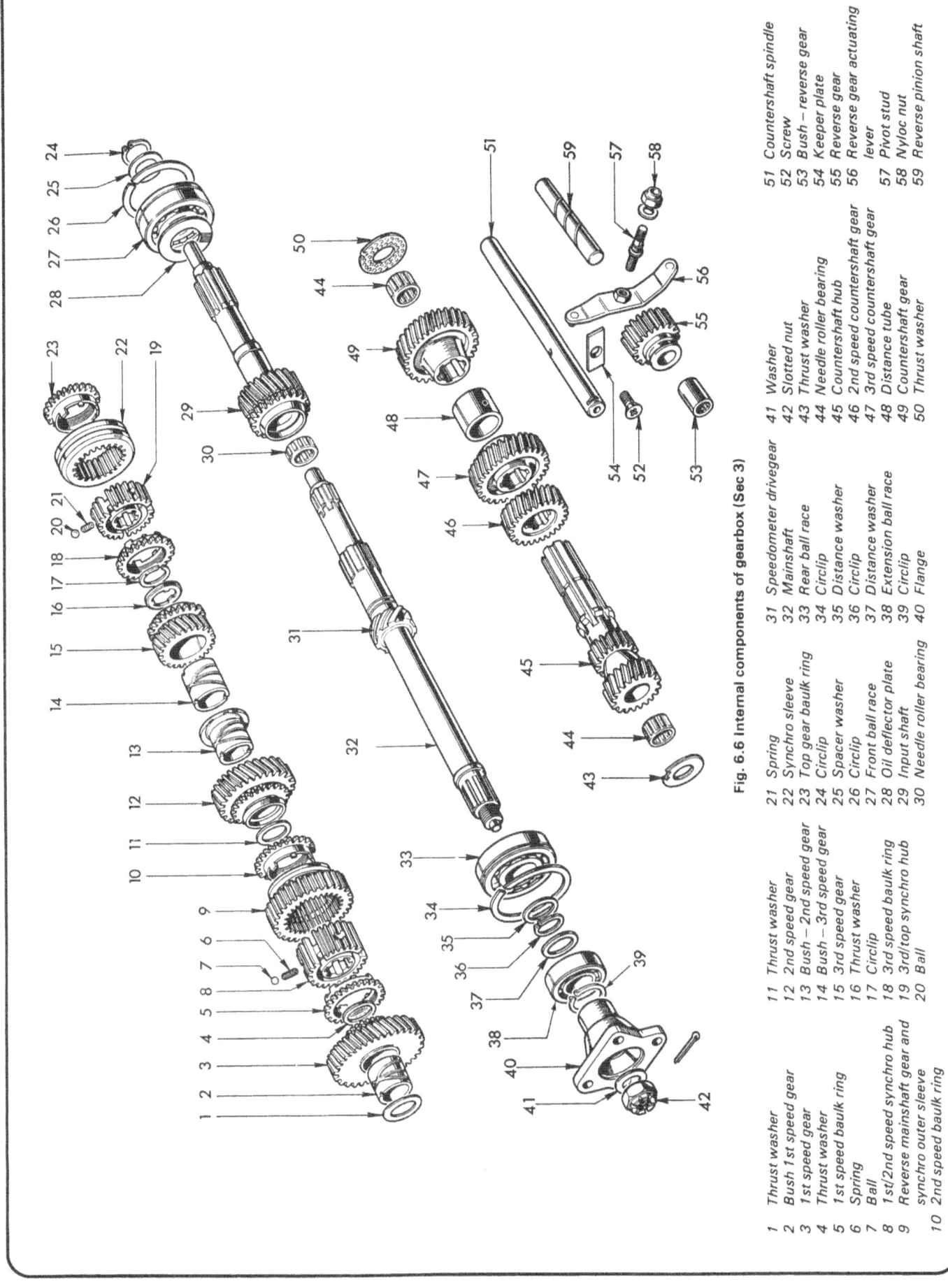

Fig. 6.6 Internal components of gearbox (Sec 3)

1 Thrust washer
2 Bush 1st speed gear
3 1st speed gear
4 Thrust washer
5 1st speed baulk ring
6 Spring
7 Ball
8 1st/2nd speed synchro hub
9 Reverse mainshaft gear and synchro outer sleeve
10 2nd speed baulk ring
11 Thrust washer
12 2nd speed gear
13 Bush – 2nd speed gear
14 Bush – 3rd speed gear
15 3rd speed gear
16 Thrust washer
17 Circlip
18 3rd speed baulk ring
19 3rd/top synchro hub
20 Ball
21 Thrust washer
22 Synchro sleeve
23 Top gear baulk ring
24 Circlip
25 Spacer washer
26 Circlip
27 Front ball race
28 Oil deflector plate
29 Input shaft
30 Needle roller bearing
31 Speedometer drivegear
32 Mainshaft
33 Rear ball race
34 Circlip
35 Distance washer
36 Circlip
37 Distance washer
38 Extension ball race
39 Circlip
40 Flange
41 Washer
42 Slotted nut
43 Thrust washer
44 Needle roller bearing
45 Countershaft hub
46 2nd speed countershaft gear
47 3rd speed countershaft gear
48 Distance tube
49 Countershaft gear
50 Thrust washer
51 Countershaft spindle
52 Screw
53 Bush – reverse gear
54 Keeper plate
55 Reverse gear
56 Reverse gear actuating lever
57 Pivot stud
58 Nyloc nut
59 Reverse pinion shaft

3.19 Removing the layshaft cover plate

3.20 Removing rear adaptor plate

3.22 Layshaft keeper plate

3.23 Ejecting the layshaft

3.26 Driving out the first motion shaft bearing

3.28 Withdrawing overdrive cam

3.29 Extracting mainshaft circlip

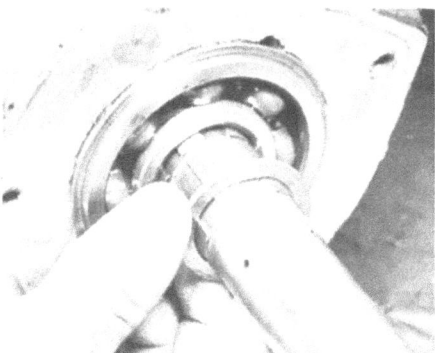

3.31 Removing mainshaft bearing washer

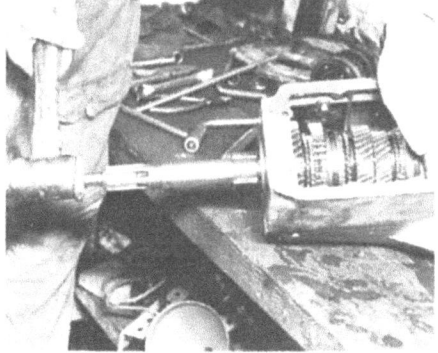

3.32 Driving mainshaft forward

21 Gently tap the end of the adaptor plate to release it from the gearbox.

22 Undo the large Phillips head screw which holds the keeper plate in position. The keeper plate locks the layshaft spindle and reverse pinion shaft to the gearbox. Lift away the Phillips screw and slide out the keeper plate (photo).

23 Obtain a piece of metal rod of approximately the same diameter as the layshaft but longer, insert the rod in the layshaft hole in the bellhousing and push out the layshaft so it emerges from the rear of the gearbox (photo).

24 Note that there is a milled slot in the layshaft spindle which must be to the rear so that the keeper plate, which was previously removed, may engage in the slot.

25 Withdraw the metal rod that was used to remove the layshaft spindle and allow the layshaft assembly to drop to the bottom of the gearbox.

26 The first motion shaft should next be removed. Using a metal drift gently tap the first motion shaft bearing outwards, through the front of the gearbox casing (photo).

27 Lift the first motion shaft complete with bearing from the front of the gearbox.

28 Turning to the rear of the gearbox, slide off the cam that drives the pump in the overdrive unit (if fitted) (photo).

29 With a pair of circlip pliers, extract the circlip from its groove in the mainshaft (photo).

30 With a screwdriver ease the circlip over the mainshaft splines.

31 Slide the distance washer from the face of the bearing inner track and remove from the mainshaft (photo).

32 To remove the rear mainshaft bearing use a soft-faced hammer and drive the mainshaft into the gearbox as shown in the photo, until the bearing is at the rear of the mainshaft splines. Note that the bearing circlip on the outer race periphery is still in position.

33 Carefully ease the bearing rearwards using two open-ended spanners and tapping the mainshaft into the gearbox. Continue this operation until the bearing is completely free of the splines and lift away the bearing (photo).

34 If difficulty is experienced in levering the bearing along the mainshaft place the gearbox on its end with the mainshaft vertical.

3.33 Levering out mainshaft rear bearing

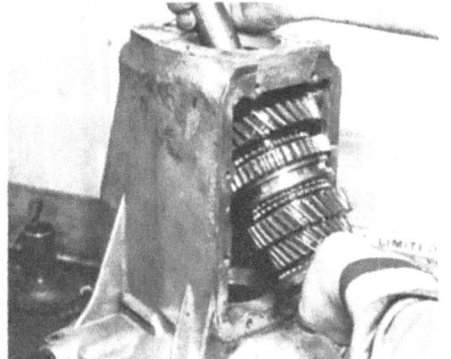

3.35 Withdrawing mainshaft assembly

3.36 Removing reverse idler shaft

3.38 Extracting lay gear rear thrust washer

3.39 Extracting lay gear front thrust washer

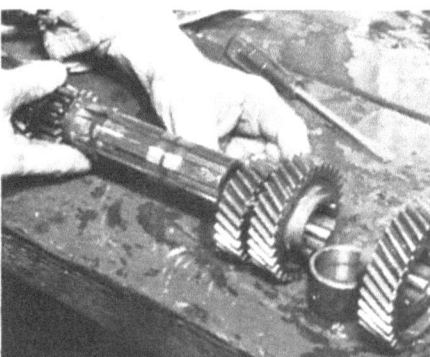

3.40 Dismantling lay gear

35 The mainshaft assembly may now be lifted through the gearbox as shown in the photo.

36 Withdraw the reverse idler shaft from the rear of the gearbox. Note the slot in the rear of the shaft into which engages the keeper plate (photo).

37 Lift away the reverse idler gear having made a note of which way round it fits.

38 Lift out the laygear rear thrust washer (photo).

39 Lift out the laygear front thrust washer (photo) and finally remove the complete laygear assembly.

40 The laygear may be dismantled by sliding off the gears and bushing from the splined layshaft hub (photo).

4 Gearbox – examination and renovation

1 Carefully clean and then examine all the component parts for general wear, distortion, slackness of fit, and damage to machined faces and threads.

2 Examine the gearwheels for excessive wear and chipping of the teeth. Renew them as necessary. If the laygear endfloat is above the permitted tolerance of 0.012 inch (2.59 mm) the thrust washers must be renewed. New thrust washers will almost certainly be required on any car that has completed more than 50 000 miles (80 000 km).

3 Examine the layshaft for signs of wear, particularly where the laygear needle roller bearing bears.

4 The four synchroniser rings are bound to be badly worn and it is false economy not to renew them. New rings will improve the smoothness and speed of the gearchange considerably.

5 The needle roller bearing and cage located between the nose of the mainshaft and the annulus in the rear of the shaft is also liable to wear, and should be renewed as a matter of course.

6 Examine the condition of the three ball bearing assemblies, one on the first motion shaft, one on the mainshaft and the third in the tail of the gearbox extension. Check them for noisy operation, looseness between the inner and outer races, and general wear. Normally they should be renewed on a gearbox that is being rebuilt.

7 Examine the mainshaft bushes and fit them on the mainshaft to

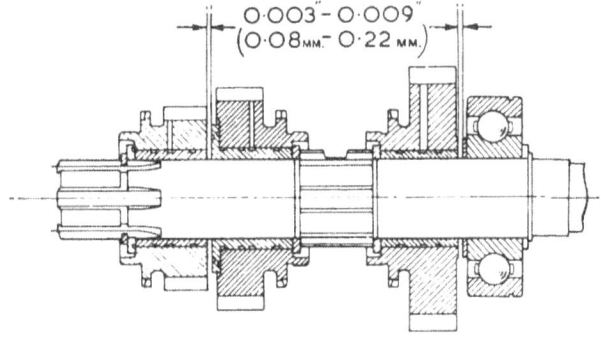

$$0.003'' - 0.009''$$
$$(0.08\text{mm} - 0.22\text{mm})$$

Fig. 6.7 Sectional view through mainshaft assembly showing endfloat of mainshaft bushes (Sec 4)

check for overall endfloat.

8 Fit the inner thrust washer, two bushes, thrust washer and finally the circlip. With a feeler gauge measure the endfloat between the inner thrust washer and the adjacent bush. This should be between 0.003 and 0.009 inch (0.076 and 0.229 mm). If outside these figures experiment with alternative thrust washers until the endfloat is correct (Figs. 6.7, 6.8 and 6.9).

9 To dismantle the synchromesh units, first wrap a piece of clean rag completely round a unit and then pull off the outer synchro sleeve. The cloth will catch the spring loaded balls and springs which are bound to fly out. Compare the length of the old springs with the new and renew any that are worn. Note that an interlock plunger and ball is fitted to the second speed synchromesh hub.

10 Parts of the remote control gearchange are bound to be worn on any high mileage model and this is dealt with in Section 8.

11 Later type gearboxes have a laygear with roller bearings in each end which are retained by circlips. On early models the roller bearings

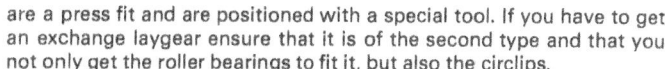

are a press fit and are positioned with a special tool. If you have to get an exchange laygear ensure that it is of the second type and that you not only get the roller bearings to fit it, but also the circlips.

12 If the gearbox is to be left for any time it is a good idea to wire the respective components of the laygear together, in their respective order so as to avoid confusion later on.

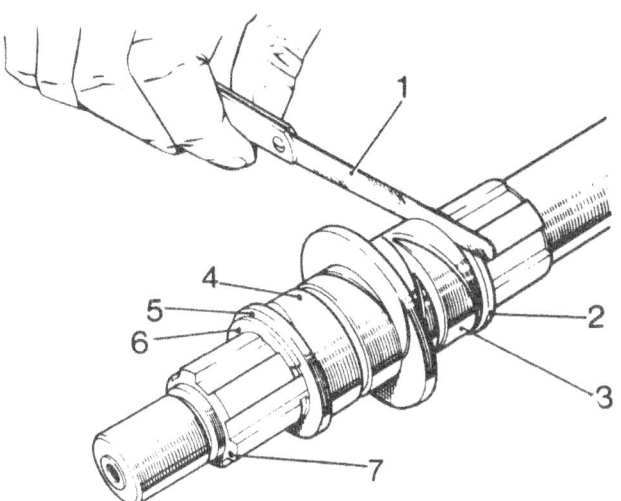

Fig. 6.8 Measuring bush endfloat on mainshaft (Sec 4)

1 Feeler gauge	5 Thrust washer
2 Thrust washer	6 Circlip
3 2nd gear bush	7 Mainshaft
4 3rd gear bush	

5 First motion shaft – dismantling and reassembly

1 The first motion shaft may be dismantled by first removing the circlip from its groove in the shaft (photo).
2 Slide off the spacer washer from the face of the race inner track and place the first motion shaft on the top of the vice with the outer track of the race resting on soft faces (photo).
3 Using a soft-faced hammer, drive the first motion shaft through the race inner track. The strain placed on the bearing does not matter, as the bearing would not be removed unless it was being renewed.
4 Lift away the race from the first motion shaft followed by the oil deflector plate.
5 The component parts of the first motion shaft are shown in the photo.
6 To assemble the first motion shaft first fit the circlip to the bearing race outer track (photo).
7 Slide the oil deflector plate onto the first motion shaft and then the bell race with the circlip away from the constant mesh gears.
8 Place the race against soft metal on the top of the jaws of a vice and using a soft drift located in the spigot bearing hole, drive the shaft into the bearing.
9 Refit the spacer washer and finally the circlip. Ensure that the circlip seats correctly in its groove.

6 Mainshaft – dismantling and reassembly

1 Place two pieces of soft metal in the jaws of a firm bench vice ready for holding the mainshaft.
2 Place the end of the mainshaft between the soft faces of the vice so that it is parallel with the bench top.
3 Commence dismantling the mainshaft by sliding off the third and fourth gear synchromesh hub and the conical synchromesh ring (photo). Note which way round it fits on the mainshaft.
4 Using a pair of circlip pliers, remove the circlip that holds the third gear in position (photo).
5 This can be a little difficult to remove so an assistant working with two screwdrivers will probably make this operation easier. With one end of the circlip released from the groove gradually work the way round until it is free of the groove and then ease it along the splines of the mainshaft.
6 Remove the third gear thrust washer from the mainshaft, Note which way round it fits as there is a flange on the inside (photo).
7 Slide the third speed gear and bush from the mainshaft (photo). Note that in the recess of the third gear is a spline.
8 Remove the second speed gear and second speed bush (photo). Note that there is a thrust washer inside the cone portion of the second speed gear.
9 Remove the first and second gear synchroniser hub which also

Fig. 6.9 Measuring gear endfloat on bushes (Sec 4)

1 Bush	2 Gear

5.1 Removing circlip from first motion shaft

5.2 Removing spacer from first motion shaft

5.5 First motion shaft components

5.6 Installing circlip to first motion shaft outer track

6.3 Removing 3rd/4th synchro from mainshaft

6.4 Removing 3rd gear circlip from mainshaft

6.6 Removing 3rd gear thrust washer from mainshaft

6.7 Removing 3rd gear and bush from main-shaft

6.8 Removing 2nd gear and bush from main-shaft

6.9 Removing 1st/2nd synchro unit from main-shaft

6.10 Removing 1st gear, bush and thrust washer from mainshaft

6.13 Assembling 1st/2nd synchro unit to mainshaft

6.14 Assembling 2nd gear bush and spacer to mainshaft

6.15 Correct mating of synchro hub and ring

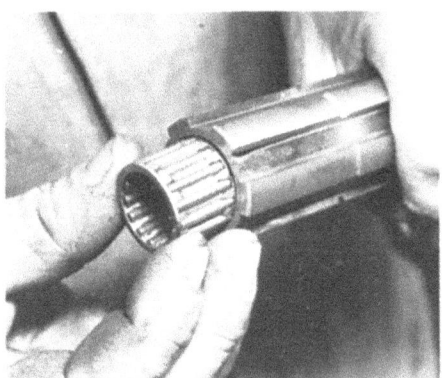
7.1 Inserting a layshaft needle roller bearing

incorporates the reverse gear machined on its periphery. Also remove the two grooved synchromesh rings (photo).

10 Remove the mainshaft from the vice and slide off the first gear and bush from the longer end of the mainshaft. Note that there is a thrust washer between the mainshaft larger diameter splines and the first gear bush (photo).

11 Dismantling the mainshaft is now complete.

12 Assemble to the longer end of the mainshaft, the thrust washer, followed by the first gear bush, the first gear, with the conical end towards the first thrust washer, and then the second thrust washer.

13 Next mount the longer end (tail end) of the mainshaft between the soft jaws of a vice and fit from the shorter end the synchromesh ring followed by the first and second gear selector hub which incorporates on its forward periphery (part nearest the first gear) the reverse gear teeth (photo).

14 Continue building the front end of the mainshaft by fitting the synchromesh cone followed by a spacer, then second gear followed by the second gear bush which should be positioned with the raised lip on the end nearest to the front of the shaft (photo).

15 Ensure that when refitting the synchromesh rings the tongue on the ring mates with the recess in the synchromesh hub as shown in the photo.

16 Refit the third gear, the third gear bush and the thrust washer so that the end of the spacer abuts inside the recess in the forward end of the gear.

17 Fit the spring circlip into position on the front of the mainshaft.

18 Do not fit the 3rd/4th synchro components until the mainshaft has been installed in the gearbox casing.

---

7 Gearbox – reassembly

1 To reassemble the layshaft gear first grease the two needle roller bearings, and insert them into the ends of the shaft (photo).

2 Lubricate the hub splines and slide the second gear, third, distance tube and layshaft gear onto the splines. The photo shows the gears positioned the correct way round for refitting. They have been previously wired together to ensure they are not separated.

3 Fit the front thrust washer for the layshaft gear in place in the gearbox casing having first coated the gearbox casing with grease to retain the thrust washer (photo). Do not fit the rear thrust washer at this stage.

4 Carefully insert the layshaft into the bottom of the gearbox ensuring that the thrust washer does not slip out. The largest gearwheel on the layshaft goes towards the bellhousing end of the gearbox casing (photo).

5 Stick the smaller thrust washer to the rear end of the gearbox casing, ensuring the tongue in the washer seats in the groove, at the same time it will be necessary to lift the laygear up slightly (photo).

7.2 Laygear ready for refitting

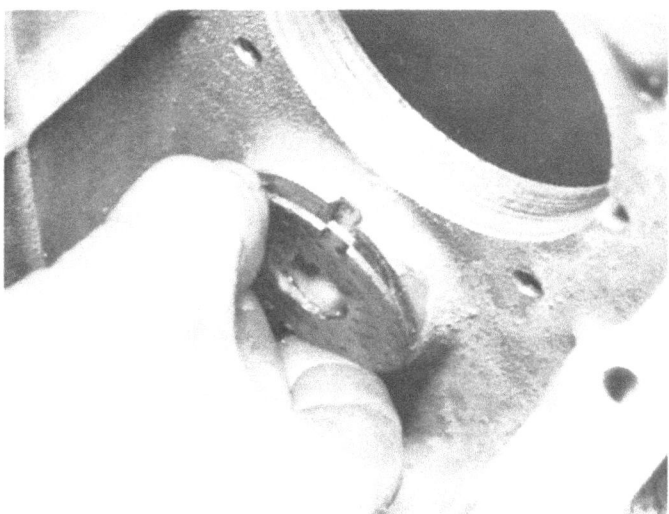

7.3 Fitting layshaft front thrust washer

7.4 Fitting lay gear

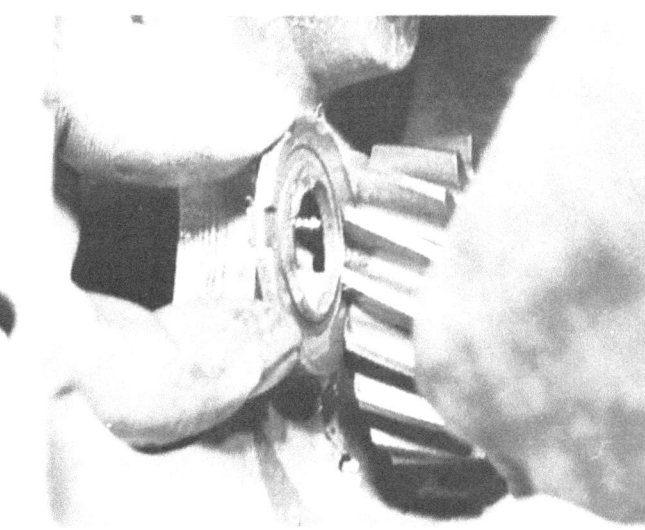

7.5 Fitting layshaft rear thrust washer

6   Temporarily fit the layshaft and using feeler gauges check the end-float of the layshaft which should be 0.007 to 0.012 in (0.18 to 3.0 mm) measured between the rear thrust washer and the gear, Any excessive endfloat may be reduced by selective assembly of thrust washers. Remove the layshaft again.

7   Insert the reverse idler gear into the casing, locating the end of the actuating lever into its location groove on the rear of the gear. Slide the reverse gear shaft into position so that the milled notch is at the rear of the gearbox.

8   Insert the tail end of the mainshaft through the large cut-out for the bearing in the rear of the gearbox casing.

9   Position the third and top synchromesh unit onto the front end of the mainshaft before the front end finally passes into the gearbox. Do not forget the synchro ring.

10   Push the rear bearing onto the mainshaft as far as it will go. The circlip should be towards the rear of the bearing.

11   It is not possible to tap home the rear bearing of the tail end of the mainshaft without a support on the front end of the mainshaft, because otherwise this gearwheel hits the third gear on the countershaft, which could mean chipped gear teeth. Invert the gearbox so that the flange of the clutch bellhousing is on the bench and position wood blocks under the end of the mainshaft so that it is well supported.

12   Using a soft metal drift, tap the rear main bearing down on the mainshaft by alternately tapping the inner and outer tracks.

13   Continue tapping the bearing tracks until the bearing is fully positioned onto the mainshaft so that there is approximately $\frac{3}{16}$ inch (4.76 mm) between the inner race of the bearing on the tail end of the mainshaft and the groove which holds the circlip.

14   Once the bearing is fully on in this position, the supports inside the bellhousing which are supporting the front or the nose of the mainshaft can be removed, and the bellhousing allowed to rest flange downwards on the bench. It is now necessary to drive the outer race of the bearing fully into the rear of the gearbox casing until the circlip on the outer race track is adjacent to the face of the casing.

15   With the gearbox still in the inverted position fit the spacer and lock in position with the circlip (photo).

16   Well lubricate the needle roller bearings in the annulus of the first motion shaft. Fit the top gear baulk ring onto the end of the first motion shaft and insert it into the casing (photo).

17   Using a soft-faced hammer, carefully drive the first motion shaft into position with the circlip hard up against the gearbox face (photo).

18   Position the gearbox casing on the bench with a wooden block under the rear end of the gear casing. The laygear should now drop into mesh with mainshaft end first motion shaft gears. Insert the layshaft (photo) until the milled slot is flush with the machined face at the rear of the casing. Turn it until the slot faces the slot in the reverse idler shaft.

19   Locate the keeper plate in the milled slots of the layshaft and reverse idler spindle and refit the Phillips head screw. This should be

7.15 Fitting mainshaft rear bearing spacer and circlip

7.16 Fitting first motion shaft

7.17 Driving first motion shaft into final position

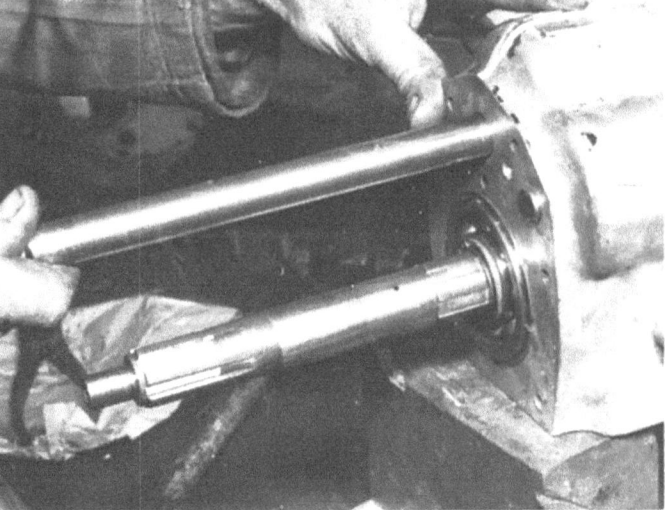

7.18 Fitting layshaft

done up as tightly as possible.

20 Fit the layshaft plate and new gasket to the front of the gearbox and secure with two bolts and copper washers. To assist the gasket to seal, coat with gasket cement and also apply a little to the bolt threads.

21 The front cover should be fitted next. Note that there is a cut-out which should be positioned to the left when looking at the first motion shaft. Use a new gasket. Fit and tighten the end cover securing bolts.

22 Ensure that there are no burrs on the mating faces of the speedometer drivegear and mainshaft. Fit the drivegear with the four spots on the edge facing the gearbox and using a suitable piece of tubing drive the gear home.

23 Now fit the gasket to the rear end of the gearbox using gasket cement to ensure an oil tight joint. On overdrive models fit the overdrive adaptor plate, whilst on standard models fit the gearbox extension.

24 Fit the six bolts and flat washers and tighten securely.

Overdrive models

25 Fit a new gasket to the rear of the gearbox casing adaptor plate suitably coated with cement.

26 Splines on the mainshaft have to go through sets of splines inside the overdrive. It is therefore essential to line up these splines in relation to one another. A torch will assist here.

27 Secure the overdrive unit in the vertical position and insert the eight springs. It is important that these are correctly positioned whereby the four inner springs, although they are set higher than the outer springs, are in fact shorter.

28 Now slide the cam, which operates the hydraulic pump in the overdrive unit, into place on the tail end of the mainshaft. The lowest part of the cam (indicated in photo A) must abut the spring loaded plunger (indicated in photo B). In this latter photo the cam has been removed from the mainshaft and placed against the plunger to show how they fit together. Place a piece of wire around the head of the plunger rod so that the spring can be compressed whilst the two units are being assembled.

29 With an assistant to help, lower the gearbox to the overdrive unit. Pull on the wire so as to compress the spring and when the gearbox adaptor plate is nearly in position withdraw the wire.

30 Refit the nuts and spring washers to the overdrive to adaptor plate studs and tighten in a diagonal manner so as to compress the eight springs.

All models

31 For a conventional gearbox refit the circlip to the end of the mainshaft.

32 Carefully tap on the flange using a soft-faced hammer until it is in position on the mainshaft.

33 Refit the plain washer and the castellated nut and tighten the nut securely. Lock the nut with a new split pin.

34 Refit the speedometer pinion and housing assembly so that the recess aligns with the hole in the rear extension and secure with the plain washer, spring washer and bolt.

35 Ensure that all gears are in their neutral position and, using an oil can, well lubricate all moving parts of the selector mechanism and synchromesh units.

36 Carefully lower the remote control and top cover with a new gasket fitted onto the top of the gearbox housing. Take care that all the selector forks are locating correctly in their grooves, especially the reverse selector fork (photo).

37 Refit the eight bolts with spring washers noting that the four longer bolts fit the front and rear of the top cover only. Tighten securely in a diagonal manner.

8 Top cover and remote control assembly – overhaul

1 The components of the top cover and remote control assembly are shown in Fig. 6.5.

2 To remove the assembly undo the eight bolts that hold the remote control and top cover onto the top of the gearbox. Lift away the bolts and spring washers noting that the four longer bolts are to the front and rear of the top cover.

3 Lift away the remote control and top cover from the top of the gearbox noting the gasket placed between the two parts.

4 Turn the cover over and unscrew the plugs and lift away the distance piece, spring, plungers and ball bearing.

5 Undo the peg bolts holding the selector forks to the selector rods.

6 Check that the selectors are in the neutral position and withdraw the third/top gear selector shaft. As the shaft is being removed, collect the interlock plunger and ball bearings as they are released.

7 Lift away the third/top selector fork and distance tube from the top cover.

8 Repeat operations in paragraphs 6 and 7 for the first/second and also reverse gear selector shafts.

9 Undo the two retaining plate setscrews and remove together with spring washers, and lift away the retaining plate.

10 Lift away the three sealing rings from their recess in the casing.

11 The selectors may be removed from their respective shafts by undoing the peg bolts.

12 Inspect all parts for signs of wear and, if evident, new parts should be fitted. The seals should be renewed every time the assembly is dismantled.

13 To reassemble, first fit the selectors to their respective shafts and secure with peg bolts.

14 Install new O-ring seals into their recesses in the rear cover and fit the retaining plate. Refit the two bolts and spring washers.

15 Place the interlock plunger in the third/top selector shaft and insert the shaft into the top cover. Engage the selector fork, distance tube and secure the fork with a peg bolt.

16 Refit the interlock ball bearing between the reverse and third/top selector shaft bores retaining the ball with grease.

17 Insert the reverse selector shaft into the top cover, engaging it with the reverse actuator and distance tube. Fit the peg bolt to the selector fork.

18 Check that the reverse and third/top selector shafts are in neutral and fit the second interlock ball retaining the ball with grease.

19 Insert the first/second selector shaft into the top cover, passing the shaft through the first/second selector fork and distance tube.

20 Lubricate all moving parts and refit to the top of the gearbox, using a new gasket.

9 Speedometer drivegear housing and pinion oil seals – renewal

1 Disconnect the speedometer cable and remove the speedometer

7.28a Lowest point of overdrive cam

7.28b Overdrive pump plunger

7.36 Fitting gearbox top cover

drivegear housing and pinion assembly securing bolt. Prise the assembly out of the gearbox rear extension.

2   Remove the drivegear pinion from the housing and discard the O-ring and inner oil seal (Fig. 6.10).

3   Reassemble the drivegear pinion in the housing using a new O-ring and inner oil seal.

4   Refit the drivegear housing and pinion assembly so that the recess aligns with the hole in the rear extension and fit the securing bolt.

5   Reconnect the speedometer cable.

---

10 Reverse light switch – removal and refitting

---

1   Disconnect the electrical leads from the switch.

2   Unscrew the switch from the gearbox top cover and collect the shims (Fig. 6.11).

3   Refit the switch using the same shims collected at removal.

4   Reconnect the leads to the switch terminals.

5   Select reverse gear and check that the reverse lamp is working. If the lamp does not light remove shims, as necessary, until the lamp lights.

6   Place the gear lever in the neutral position and check that the lamp extinguishes. If the lamp does not extinguish add shims as necessary.

7   Repeat operations 5 and 6 until the reverse lamp lights when reverse gear is selected and does not light when the gear lever is in neutral.

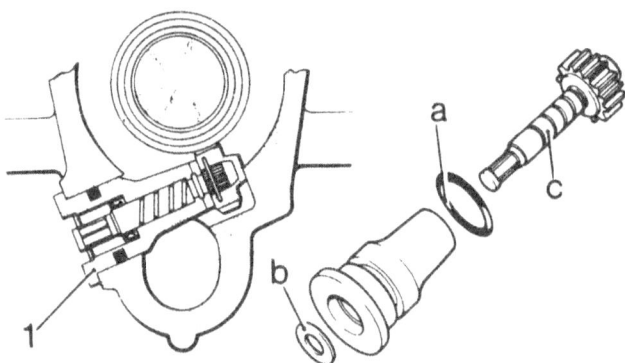

Fig. 6.10 Speedometer drivegear housing and pinion oil seals assembly (Sec 9)

1   Housing and pinion assembly
a   O-ring
b   Inner oil seal
c   Pinion gear

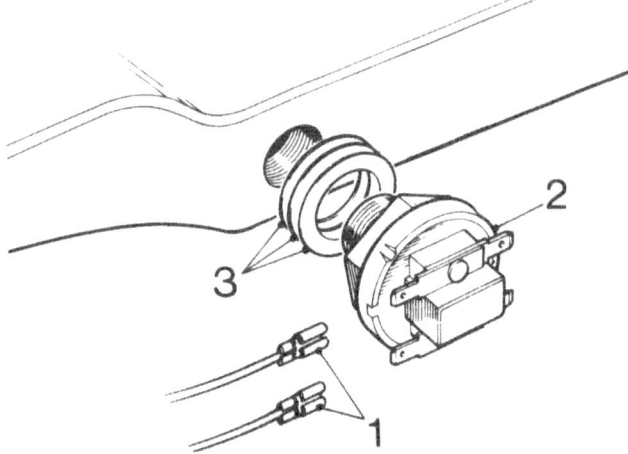

Fig. 6.11 Removing the reverse light switch (Sec 10)

1 Electrical leads   2 Switch   3 Shims

Part B – A-type overdrive

---

11 General description

The overdrive unit is attached to the extension on the rear of the gearbox by eight studs and nuts, and takes the form of an hydraulically operated epicyclic gear. Overdrive operates on third and fourth speeds to provide fast cruising at lower engine revolutions. The overdrive 'in-out' switch actuates a solenoid attached to the side of the overdrive unit. In turn the solenoid operates a valve which opens the hydraulic circuit which pushes the cone clutch into contact with the annulus when overdrive is engaged.

During high speed motoring, the engine speed is decreased with the engagement of overdrive so that with continual use of the unit there will be a considerable increase in engine life with a corresponding decrease in engine wear together with improved fuel economy.

A special switch called an inhibitor switch is incorporated in the electrical circuit and prevents the engagement of overdrive in reverse, first or second gears. The switch is located on the top of the gearbox top cover.

The normal minimum engagement speeds are top gear 40 mph (64 km/h) and third gear 30 mph (48 km/h) whilst the minimum disengagement speed in top is under the control of the driver who must take care not to over rev the engine at high speeds. For third speed the disengagement should occur at a maximum of 70 mph (112 km/h).

The overdrive unit operates in the following manner: (numbers in brackets refer to Fig. 6.15). The operating gears in the overdrive are of epicyclic design and comprise a sunwheel (52) which meshes with three planet gears carried in a circular metal carrier (54). These planet gears mesh with an annulus (60) which has internal teeth. The planet carrier (54) is attached to the input shaft which is the output shaft of the gearbox. The annulus (60) is an integral part of the output shaft.

When the driver selects overdrive, hydraulic pressure is built up by a plunger type pump (19, 20, 21) which operates from a cam (18) splined to the input shaft, ie. the output shaft from the gearbox. The hydraulic pressure built up by the pump forces the two pistons (34) against bridge pieces (38) which are themselves attached to the thrust ring (36). The thrust ring is pushed forwards by the pistons (34) so engaging the clutch (51) with the brake ring (45), with sufficient force to hold the sunwheel (52) firmly at rest.

The planet carrier (54) is now able to rotate with the input shaft allowing the planet wheels in the planet carrier assembly (54) to rotate about their own axes so driving the annulus (60) at a faster speed than the input shaft is rotating.

Oil is drawn by the pump through a wire mesh filter (25) and delivers it to the operating valve (12-18) through an hydraulic accumulator (74-78), the amount of pressure being controlled by a pressure relief valve built into the accumulator. The oil is free to pass between the gearbox and overdrive unit and there is one common level for both units. The oil level is indicated by a 'level' plug on the side of the gearbox.

Whenever the oil is drained, the two drain plugs, one on the underside of the gearbox and the other on the underside of the overdrive unit, must be removed but it is usual practice not to change the oil during normal servicing but to top up. Only recommended grades of oil must be used and it is important that under no circumstances must oil anti-friction additives be used otherwise the overdrive will not operate properly.

Cleanliness is very important so do not remove the drain plug without first wiping the surrounding area. Whenever the oil is drained for service/repair work on either the gearbox or the overdrive always clean the mesh filter (25).

The overdrive is normally a very reliable unit and trouble is usually due to either the solenoid sticking; a fault in the hydraulic system due to dirt ingress; insufficient oil; or incorrect solenoid operating lever adjustment.

---

12 Overdrive – removal and refitting

---

1   It is unnecessary to remove the overdrive from the car in order to attend to the following: the hydraulic lever setting; the relief valve; the non-return valve; the solenoid; and the operating valve.

2   If the unit as a whole requires overhaul it must be removed from

the car together with the gearbox as described earlier in this Chapter.

3   To separate the overdrive from the gearbox undo the eight nuts from the $\frac{1}{4}$ inch (6.35 mm) diameter studs (noting the extra length of two of the studs) to separate the main overdrive casing from the gearbox. Carefully pull the overdrive off the end of the mainshaft.

4   To mate the overdrive and gearbox, start by placing the overdrive in an upright position and then line up the splines of the clutch and planet carrier by eye, turning them anti-clockwise only, with the aid of a long thick screwdriver. Make certain that the spring clip is correctly positioned in the groove in the mainshaft and that it does not protrude above the mainshaft splines.

5   Under normal circumstances, if everything is in line the gearbox mainshaft should enter the overdrive easily. If trouble is experienced do not try and force the components together but separate them and re-align the components. Place the gearbox in top gear while refitting.

6   As the mainshaft is fed into the overdrive, gently rotate the input shaft to and fro to help mate the mainshaft to the splines. At the same time make certain that the lowest portion of the cam on the mainshaft will rest against the pump and that as the gearbox and overdrive come together, the end of the mainshaft enters into the needle roller bearing in the tailshaft.

7   The remainder of the refitting procedure is a straightforward reversal of the removal sequence.

13 Overdrive – overhaul

1   It is not recommended that the overdrive unit is overhauled by the home mechanic due to the need for special tools.

2   The unit is very long lasting and when wear does eventually take place it is preferable to remove it as described in the preceding Section and to replace it with a new or reconditioned unit.

3   However, any faults which may occur should be diagnosed by reference to Section 35 and remedial action or adjustment carried out by referring to Sections 14, 15, 16 and 17.

14 Overdrive unit – operating lever adjustment

1   If the overdrive does not engage, or will not release when it is switched out, providing the solenoid is not at fault the trouble is likely to be that the operating lever is out of adjustment. Adjustment can be made without removing the overdrive, but it will probably be necessary to support the gearbox weight with a suitable jack, then remove the gearbox crossmember and lower the jack to provide proper access. It

has been found that a short $\frac{7}{16}$ in AF ring spanner ground down to reduce its thickness, is suitable for slackening the nut on the clamp bolt described in paragraph 5.

2   To one end of a shaft passing through the overdrive casing is attached a setting lever having a $\frac{3}{16}$ inch (4.76 mm) hole in its outer end as shown in Fig. 6.12. The other end of the shaft is attached to a solenoid lever as shown in Fig. 6.13.

3   Switch on the ignition and set the overdrive switch to energize the solenoid. The hole in the setting lever should align with a similar hole in the casing which will indicate that the operating valve is fully open. To check this try and insert a $\frac{3}{16}$ inch (4.76 mm) diameter rod through both holes. (A suitable size round nail, filed square at the end and bent at 90° will suffice for this job). If it is not possible adjustment is necessary. Switch off the ignition.

4   Undo the three solenoid housing cover retaining bolts and lift away the cover.

5   Slacken the clamp bolt nut (1) on the operating lever (2) and rotate the shaft until the rod is able to pass into the hole in the casing.

6   Approximately 0.008 inch (0.203 mm) endfloat should be allowed for on the shaft. Push the solenoid plunger fully home, at the same time holding the fork of the lever against the collar in the plunger.

7   Tighten the clamp bolt so securing the lever to the shaft, then check the shaft endfloat. If a dial test indicator is not available, a gauge plate will have to be made up so that feeler gauges can be used. The shaft endfloat is governed by the longitudinal position of the lever on the shaft and must be repositioned if necessary whilst maintaining the radial position already determined.

8   Still continuing to push the plunger hard home in the solenoid, set the adjustable stop (3), until there is a gap of 0.150 to 0.155 inch (3.81 to 3.94 mm) between the end of the plunger and the stop. A suitable gap gauge can be made from a piece of wood or metal, since feeler gauges are impractical.

9   Remove the rod and energise the solenoid. Check the alignment of the two setting holes with feeler gauges inserted between the stop and the plunger.

10 Operate the switch several times checking with the test rod to ensure that the adjustment remains correct.

11 Measure the current consumed by the solenoid switch which, with the operating arm correctly set should be about 2 amps. If a reading of 15-20 amps is obtained it is an indication that the solenoid plunger is not moving sufficiently to switch to the holding coil from the operating coil. If very fine adjustment will not remedy this condition, fit a new solenoid and plunger.

12 Refit the solenoid housing cover and tighten the three retaining bolts.

15 Overdrive operating valve – removal, inspection and refitting

1   It will be seen from referring to Fig. 6.15, that the operating valve components (14-17) are located in the top of the main casing (1). To

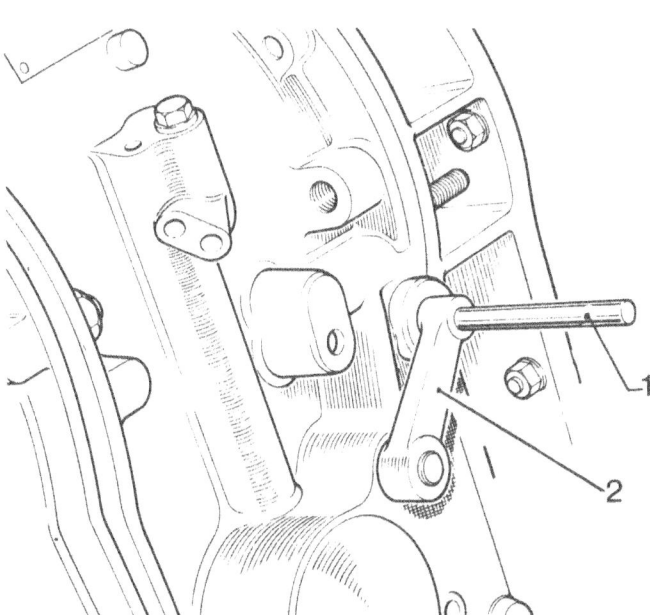

Fig. 6.12 Setting lever pinned to the casing (Sec 14)

1 $\frac{3}{16}$ in (4·76 mm) diameter rod   2 Setting lever

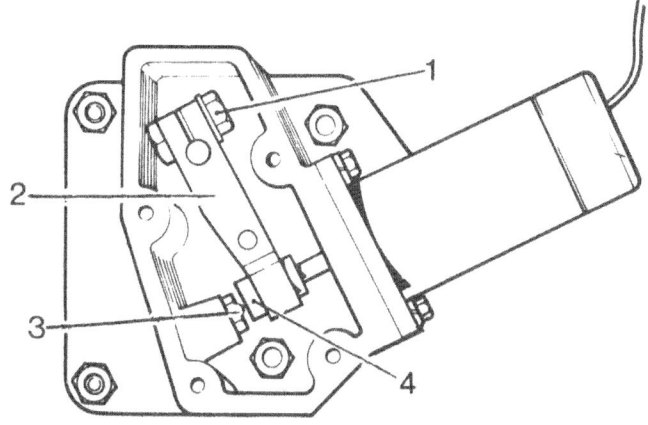

Fig. 6.13 Setting of operating lever (Sec 14)

1 Locking nut   3 Adjustment stop locknut
2 Operating lever   4 Plunger

gain access to the valve with the unit in the car the console tray must be removed.

2　Switch on the ignition but do not start the engine. Activate the overdrive control switch several times so as to operate the solenoid, thus releasing any residual oil pressure. Wipe the area around the valve plug free of dust.

3　Unscrew and remove the operating valve plug (16) and copper washer (17). Using a paper clip which has been straightened and the end bent to a small hook withdraw the spring (15). The plunger (14) may be removed using a small magnet or magnetised screwdriver. Also remove the ball bearing (13).

4　Using the other end of the paper clip with a slight kink in it carefully insert it into the centre of the valve (12) and withdraw the valve.

5　Clean the removed parts in petrol and allow to dry. Locate the small drilling near to the base of the valve (12) and check that it is free of dirt.

6　Inspect the ball bearing (13) for signs of pitting which, if evident, indicate that a new ball bearing should be obtained.

7　If the ball bearing is satisfactory re-seat it by placing the ball bearing on a block of soft wood. Invert the valve and place on top of the ball bearing and lightly tap the end. If it is tapped too hard the drilling in the side of the valve or in the end may be closed.

8　Reassembling the valve is the reverse sequence to removal.

16 Hydraulic oil pressure – checking

1　Check that the oil level is correct.
2　Lift the front console tray and remove the rubber grommet.
3　Switch on the ignition and select top gear. Engage and disengage the overdrive six times.
4　Remove the operating valve plug and fit a pressure gauge suitable for reading up to 500 lbf/in² (35 kgf/cm²) (Fig. 6.15).
5　Raise the rear wheels and chock the front wheels. Run the engine with and without overdrive and note the pressure recorded on the gauge which should be 480 to 500 lbf/in² (33 to 35 kgf/cm²). Lack of oil pressure with overdrive selected may indicate a fault in the pump

Fig. 6.14 Fitting hydraulic pressure test gauge (Sec 16)

non-return valve. Lack of oil pressure when the overdrive is not selected may indicate a fault in the operating valve.

6　Stop the engine then switch on the ignition, select top gear and engage and disengage the overdrive six times to dissipate the oil pressure.

7　Remove the pressure gauge, fit the operating valve plug, rubber grommet and front console tray.

Fig. 6.15 Exploded view of A-type overdrive (Sec 11, 15 and 17)

1	Main casing	41	Adaptor plate	77	Piston ring
2	Stud (⅜ in) adaptor plate attachment	42	Adaptor plate to overdrive unit joint washer	78	Accumulator spring
3	Stud (¼ in) adaptor plate attachment	43	Adaptor plate to overdrive unit nut	79	Solenoid bracket assembly
5	Stud – rear casing attachment	44	Adaptor plate to overdrive unit lock washer	80	Solenoid bracket to main casing joint washer
6	Stud – solenoid bracket attachment	45	Brake clutch ring	81	Solenoid bracket to main casing setscrew
7	Taper plug	46	Thrust washer at front of sunwheel (standard)	82	Solenoid bracket to main casing plain washer
8	Oil pump plunger guide peg	47	Thrust washer at front of sunwheel (selected size)	83	Solenoid bracket to main casing lockwasher
9	Valve operating shaft	48	Clutch thrust ring ball bearing	84	Solenoid bracket to main casing nut
10	Cam lever	49	Front bearing location circlip	85	Solenoid bracket to main casing dowel
11	Welch plug	50	Rear bearing location circlip	86	Distance collar
12	Operating valve	51	Clutch sliding member assembly	87	Solenoid operating lever
13	Operating valve steel ball	52	Sunwheel assembly	88	Solenoid operating lever to shaft retaining bolt
14	Operating valve plunger	53	Thrust washer at rear of sunwheel	89	Solenoid operating lever to shaft plain washer
15	Operating valve spring	54	Planet carrier assembly	90	Solenoid operating lever to shaft nut
16	Operating valve plug	55	Uni-directional cage	91	Operating lever stop adjustment screw
17	Operating valve plug copper washer	56	Roller set	92	Operating lever stop adjustment screw locknut
18	Oil pump operating cam	57	Uni-directional inner member	93	Solenoid bracket cover plate
19	Oil pump plunger assembly	58	Uni-directional cage spring	94	Cover plate to bracket joint washer
20	Oil pump plunger spring	59	Thrust washer at rear of free wheel	95	Cover plate to bracket screw
21	Oil pump body	60	Annulus assembly	96	Cover plate to bracket screw lockwasher
22	Pump body plug	61	Front ball bearing annulus	97	Solenoid
23	Pump to casing setscrew	62	Annulus endfloat adjustment washer (various sizes)	98	Solenoid rubber cover
24	Pump to casing lockwasher	63	Rear ball bearing annulus	99	Solenoid to solenoid bracket joint washer
25	Oil filter	64	Rear casing assembly	100	Solenoid to solenoid bracket setscrew
26	Magnet	65	Rear casing attachment stud	101	Solenoid to solenoid bracket lockwasher
27	Drain plug	66	Rear casing to main casing nut	102	Speedometer driven gear
28	Drain plug washer	67	Rear casing to main casing lockwasher	103	Bearing assembly
29	Non-return valve steel ball	68	Rear casing oil seal	104	Bearing O-ring
30	Non-return valve plunger	69	Coupling flange	105	Speedometer driven gear to casing retaining screw
31	Non-return valve spring	70	Flange to annulus attachment washer	106	Speedometer driven gear to casing retaining screw copper washer
32	Non-return valve washer	71	Flange to annulus attachment slotted nut		
33	Non-return valve plug	72	Flange to annulus slotted nut split pin		
34	Operating piston	73	Accumulator housing assembly		
35	Operating piston O-ring	74	Accumulator housing O-ring		
36	Clutch thrust ring	75	Spacer tube assembly		
37	Clutch spring	76	Accumulator piston assembly		
38	Bridge piece				
39	Tab washer securing bridge pieces to clutch thrust wing				
40	Nut securing bridge pieces to clutch thrust wing				

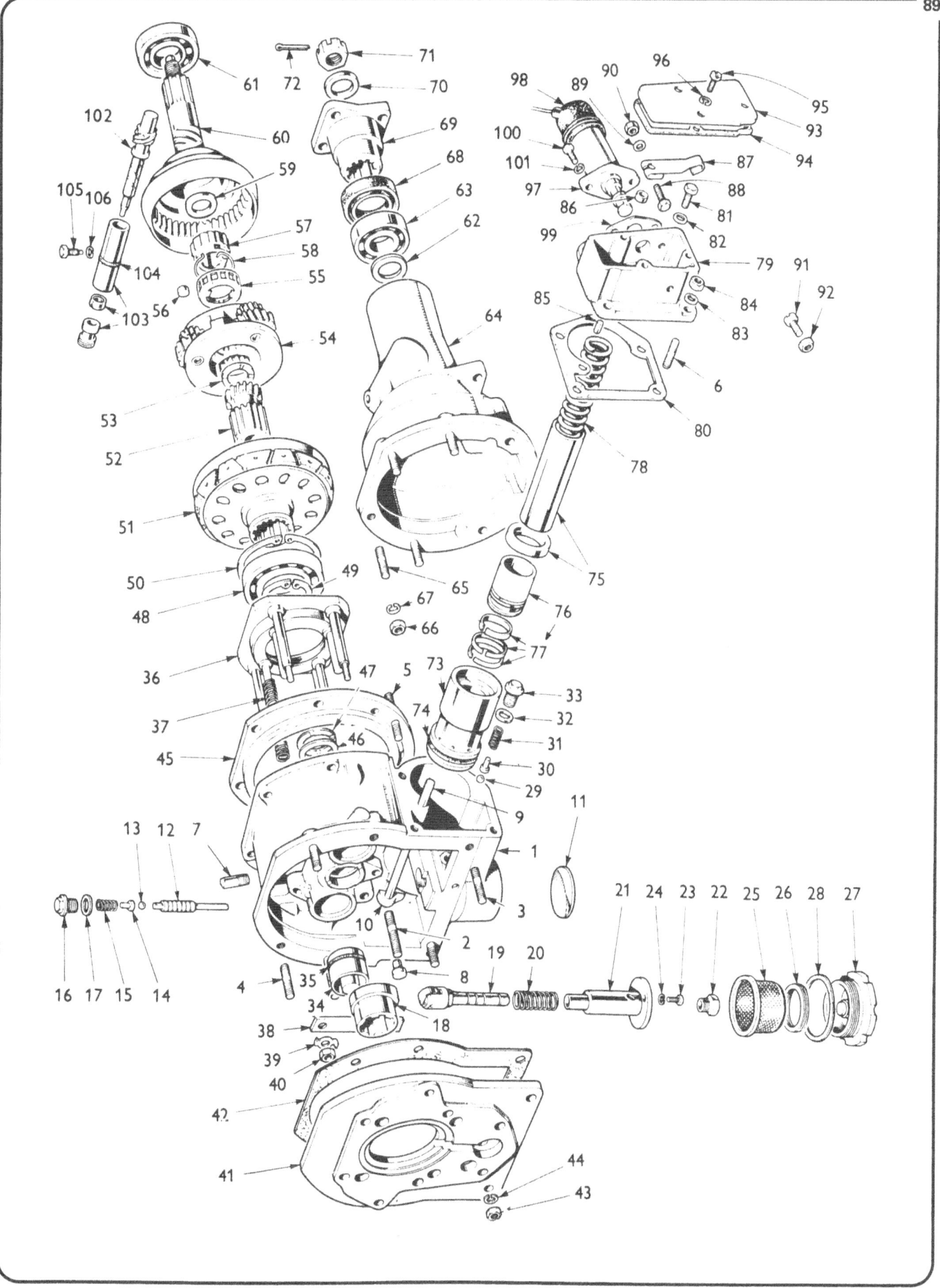

17 Pump non-return valve – removal, inspection and refitting

1   It will be seen that by referring to Fig. 6.15. the pump non-return valve components (29-33) are situated in the solenoid side of the main casing (1). To gain access to the valve first drain the oil from the unit by undoing and removing the drain plug (27).

2   It is recommended that whenever the drain plug is removed the filter (25) and three magnetic rings (26) be cleaned before refitting.

3   Undo the three bolts, spring washers (96), cover plate (93) and gasket (94).

4   Undo the solenoid retaining bolts (100) and lift away the bolts, spring washers (101) and the solenoid by disconnecting the solenoid plunger from the yoke of the operating valve lever (87).

5   Slacken the clamp bolt nut (90) and withdraw the operating lever (87) from the end of the valve operating shaft (9) followed by the distance collar (86).

6   Remove the nuts (84) and spring washers (83) from the two short studs that secure the solenoid bracket assembly (79) to the main casing (1). Also undo the two setscrews (painted red) (81) so as to release the accumulator spring (78) tension. Do not remove the two setscrews first. Lift away the solenoid bracket (79) followed by the spring (78) and spacer tube assembly (75).

7   The pump non-return valve is positioned in the cavity of the main body casing once the solenoid bracket assembly (79) is removed. Undo and remove the hexagonal plug (33) and washer (32) followed by the spring (31), plunger (30) and ball bearing (29).

8   Wash all valve parts in petrol and allow to dry. Ensure that the valve is clear of any foreign matter. Inspect the ball bearing for signs of pitting; if evident, a new bearing should be obtained.

9   Insert the ball bearing using a soft metal drift and a hammer, to re-set it. Insert the plunger (30), spring (31) and plug (33) with a new copper washer (32), fitted under its head. Check that the copper washer seats on its location correctly to ensure no oil leaks.

10   Insert the accumulator spring (78) into the tube (75) and fit the accumulator tube (75) into the recess in the accumulator sleeve (73) still in the main casing.

11   Fit a new O-ring over the operating shaft (9) if one was originally fitted and, using a new joint washer (80), refit the solenoid bracket (79), ensuring that the accumulator spring (78), locates over the dowel (85) on the bracket.

12   Tighten the two screws (81) with spring washers (82) evenly and then the nuts (84) with spring washers onto the two short studs (6).

13   Slide the distance collar (86) onto the lever shaft (9).

14   Refit the operating lever (87) to the lever shaft and lightly tighten the locknut (90).

15   Fit a new joint washer (99) to the solenoid bracket (79) and insert the solenoid plunger into the yoke in the operating lever.

16   Secure the solenoid (97) to the bracket with the two bolts (100) and spring washers (101).

17   It will now be necessary to set the solenoid operating lever and full details of this are given in Section 12 of this Chapter.

18   Fit a new cover plate gasket (94) and then the cover plate (93). Secure with three bolts (95) and spring washers (96).

19   Top up the level of oil in the gearbox and overdrive unit.

Part C – J type overdrive

18 General description

The overdrive unit is attached to the rear of the gearbox by eight studs and nuts, and takes the form of an hydraulically operated epicyclic gear. Overdrive operates on third and fourth speeds to provide fast cruising at lower engine revolutions. The overdrive 'in-out' switch on the top of the gear change lever actuates a solenoid attached to the side of the overdrive unit. In turn the solenoid operates a valve which opens the hydraulic circuit which pushes the cone clutch into contact with the annulus when overdrive is engaged.

During high speed motoring, the engine speed is decreased with the engagement of overdrive so that with continual use of the unit there will be a considerable increase in engine life with a corresponding decrease in engine wear. Fuel consumption will be reduced considerably, also.

A special switch called an inhibitor switch is incorporated in the electrical circuit and prevents the engagement of overdrive in reverse, first or second gears. The switch is fitted to the gearbox. Overdrive can be engaged or disengaged at any speed, but 30 mph in top gear is about the minimum. It should be operated without using the clutch pedal and at any required throttle opening since the unit is designed to be engaged and disengaged when transmitting full power. The only precaution necessary is to avoid disengaging overdrive third gear into direct third gear at road speeds in excess of 78 mph (125 km/h), as this would over-rev the engine.

The overdrive gears are epicyclic and comprise a central sunwheel meshing with three planet gears which in turn mesh with an internally toothed annulus gear. The planet carrier is attached to the input shaft and the annulus gear is integral with the output shaft. All gears are maintained in constant mesh.

Power is transmitted from the gearbox mainshaft to the inner member of a one way clutch and then to the outer member when direct drive is being used. The outer member of the one way clutch forms part of the combined annulus and output shaft, and the gear train is inoperative.

A spring loaded cone clutch engages with the friction surface on the annulus and therefore the clutch rotates with the annulus and output shaft. The sunwheel is splined to the clutch member; hence the whole gear train is locked, and over-run and reverse torque can be transmitted. Due to the helix angle of the sunwheel gearteeth, additional load is imparted during over-run and reverse as the sunwheel reacts against the cone clutch.

When overdrive is engaged, hydraulic pressure causes the clutch to move. It disengages from the annulus and engages with the brake ring in the overdrive casing. The sunwheel, to which the clutch is attached, is therefore held stationary. The planet carrier now rotates with the input shaft and the annulus is therefore driven by the planet wheels as they rotate about their own axes. Since the output speed is greater than the input shaft speed, the outer member of the one-way clutch over-runs the inner member to permit this drive.

The hydraulic pressure required to operate the hydraulic cone clutch is developed from an integral plunger type pump. Oil is drawn from an air-cooled sump and passed, via a pressure filter, to the clutch operating pistons. When overdrive is selected, a solenoid valve operates and allows oil to pass, via a damping orifice, to the relief valve. This allows a controlled bleed of pressure back to the oil sump but maintains a high system pressure. Smooth engagement of overdrive is assured by the combined effect of the orifice and a spring dashpot within the relief valve. When overdrive is switched out, the solenoid is de-energised and the relief valve opens fully. The system pressure now falls to about 20 psi but the relief valve does not immediately open since the relief valve pressure is restricted by the orifice. Therefore a smooth disengagement of overdrive is assured.

A tapping at the inlet to the relief valve is utilized for the purpose of lubricating the one-way clutch, gears and bearings.

Note: *The procedure given in Sections 19, 20, 21, 22 and 23 can be carried out without removing the overdrive from the car.*

19 Hydraulic oil pressure – checking

1   Initially check that the oil level is correct then remove the plug adjacent to the solenoid and fit a pressure gauge suitable for reading up to 550 lbf/in² (38.7 kgf/cm²) Fig. 6.19).

2   Raise the rear wheels and adequately chock the front wheels. Run the engine and transmission in top gear at an indicated speed of 25 mph and check that a pressure of 20 lbf/in² (1.4 kgf/cm²) (approximately) is recorded.

3   Now engage overdrive and check that the pressure rises to 510 to 550 lbf/in² (35.8 to 38.7 kgf/cm²) and then returns to around 20 lbf/in² (1.4 kgf/cm²) when overdrive is switched out.

20 Solenoid valve – removal and checking

1   Remove the solenoid using a 1 in (25 mm) AF spanner. Do not use a wrench on the solenoid valve body, or irreparable damage may result.

2   Do not attempt to dismantle the solenoid valve as it is a sealed unit. Examine the O-rings and sealing washer, and renew them if they are damaged in any way.

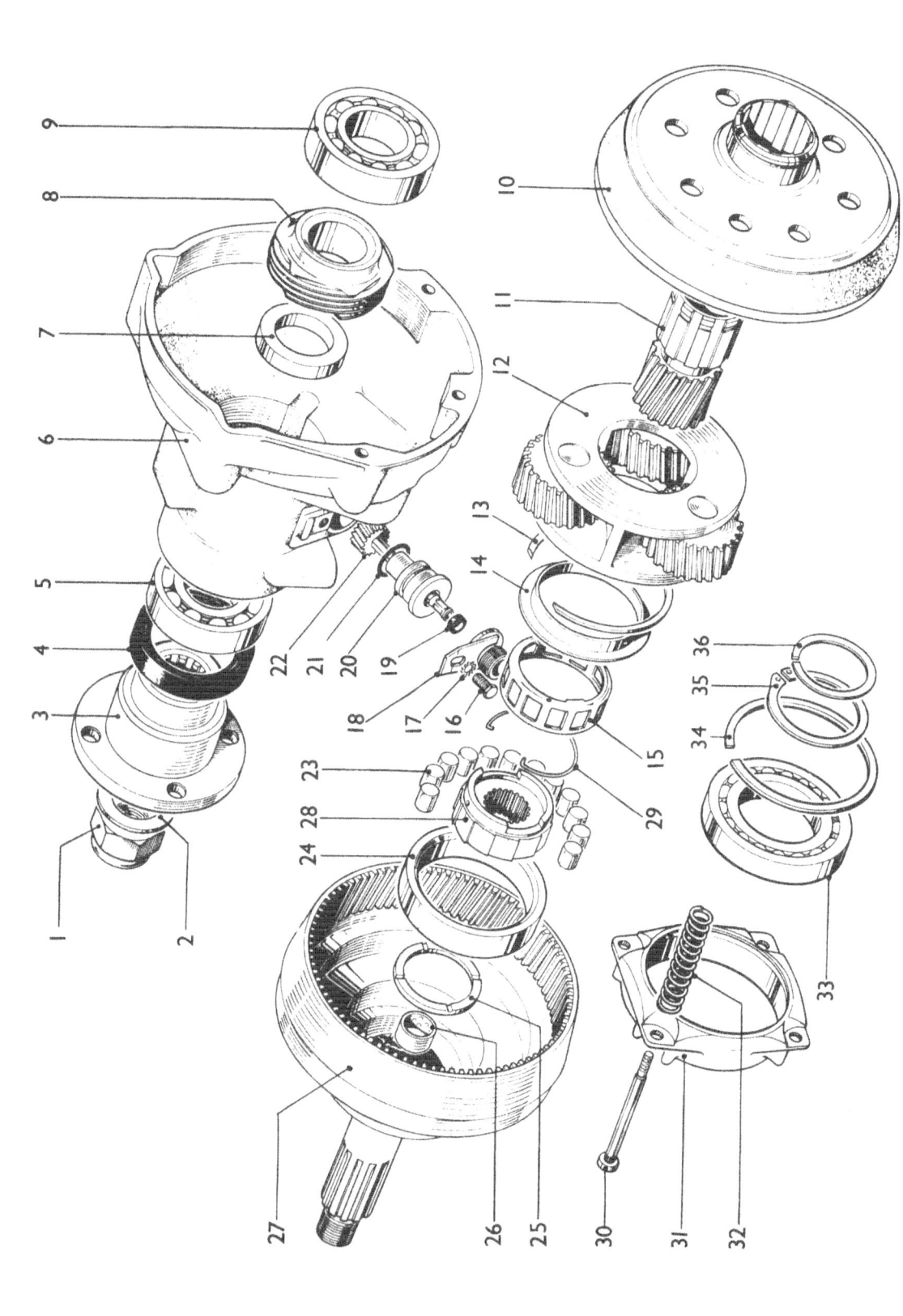

Fig. 6.16 Exploded view of J-type overdrive rear casing and gears (Sec 18)

1 Nyloc nut
2 Washer
3 Flange
4 Oil seal
5 Annulus rear bearing
6 Rear casing

7 Spacer
8 Speedometer gear
9 Annulus front bearing
10 Clutch sliding member
11 Sunwheel
12 Planet carrier assembly

13 Circlip
14 Oil thrower
15 One-way clutch cage
16 Bolt
17 Star washer
18 Speedometer gear clamp

19 Oil seal
20 Speedometer gear housing
21 O-ring
22 Speedometer driven gear
23 One-way clutch rollers
24 One-way clutch roller track

25 Thrust washer
26 Mainshaft bush
27 Annulus
28 One-way clutch hub
29 One-way clutch spring
30 Thrust pin

31 Thrust ring
32 Clutch springs
33 Thrust race
34 Circlip
35 Sliding member circlip
36 Sunwheel circlip

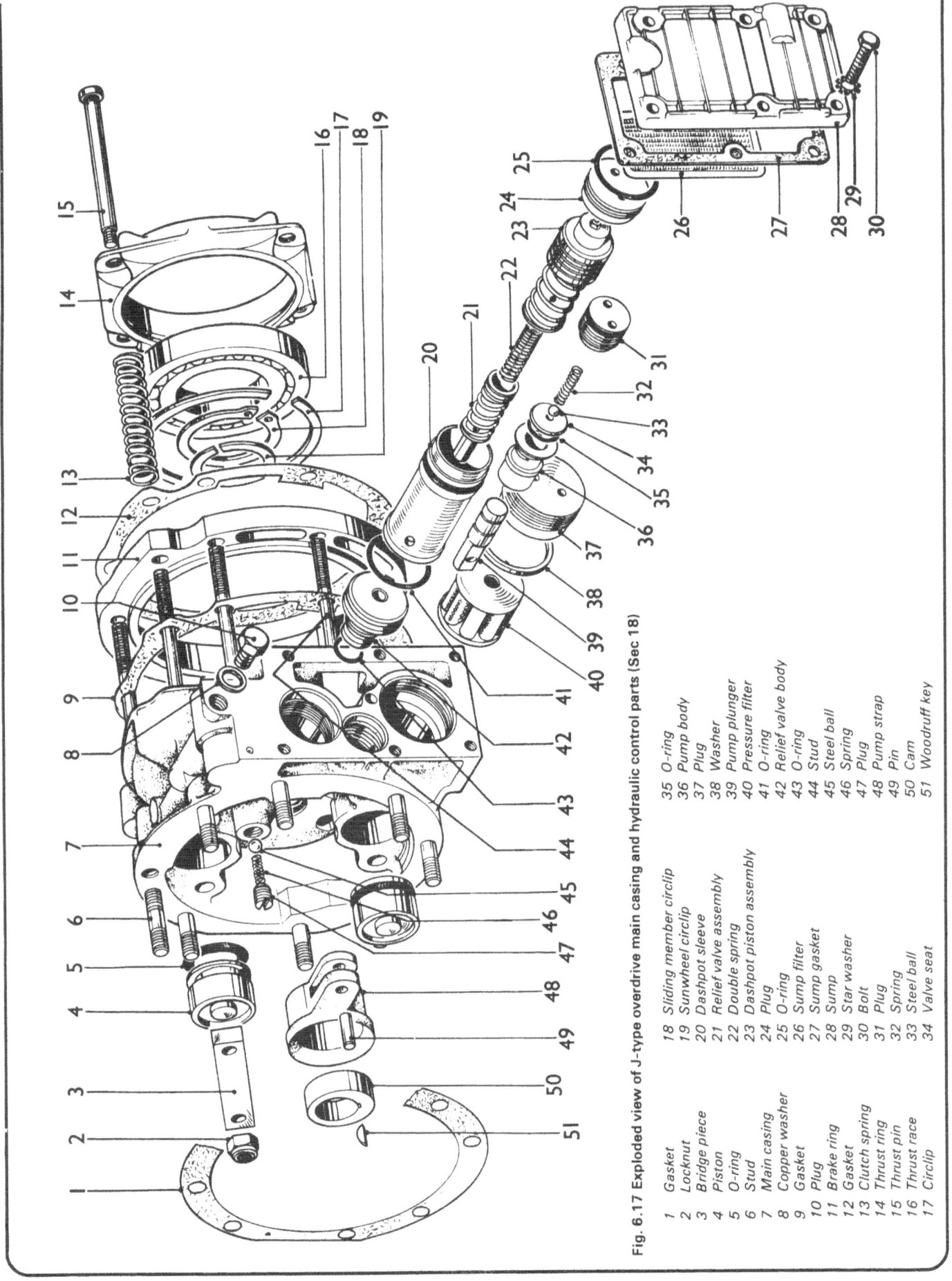

Fig. 6.17 Exploded view of J-type overdrive main casing and hydraulic control parts (Sec 18)

1	Gasket	18	Sliding member circlip	35	O-ring
2	Locknut	19	Sunwheel circlip	36	Pump body
3	Bridge piece	20	Dashpot sleeve	37	Plug
4	Piston	21	Relief valve assembly	38	Washer
5	O-ring	22	Double spring	39	Pump plunger
6	Stud	23	Dashpot piston assembly	40	Pressure filter
7	Main casing	24	Plug	41	O-ring
8	Copper washer	25	O-ring	42	Relief valve body
9	Gasket	26	Sump filter	43	O-ring
10	Plug	27	Sump gasket	44	Stud
11	Brake ring	28	Sump	45	Steel ball
12	Gasket	29	Star washer	46	Spring
13	Clutch spring	30	Bolt	47	Plug
14	Thrust ring	31	Plug	48	Pump strap
15	Thrust pin	32	Spring	49	Pin
16	Thrust race	33	Steel ball	50	Cam
17	Circlip	34	Valve seat	51	Woodruff key

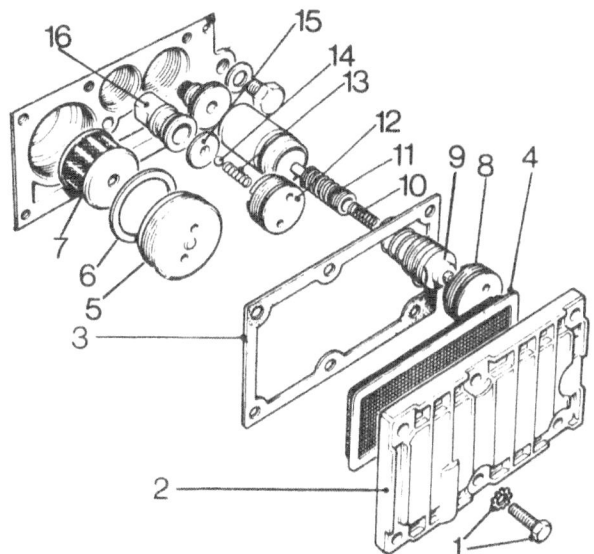

Fig. 6.18 Items accessible with the overdrive fitted (Sec 18)

1	Sump bolt and washer	9	Dashpot assembly
2	Sump	10	Residual pressure spring
3	Sump gasket	11	Relief valve piston assembly
4	Sump filter	12	Non-return valve plug
5	Pressure filter plug	13	Spring
6	Aluminium washer	14	Ball
7	Pressure filter element	15	Valve seat
8	Relief valve plug	16	Valve body

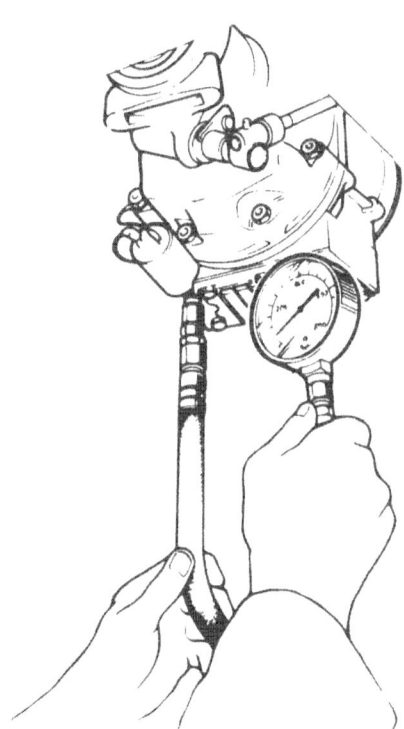

Fig. 6.19 Using a gauge to check the oil pressure (Sec 19)

3   Using a 12 volt battery and an ammeter, check that the unit operates at a current of approximately 2 amps. It will not be possible to hear the solenoid move, but a clean brass pin or piece of copper wire can be inserted at the end to detect movement of the valve stem. If the solenoid draws the correct current but does not move, the operating valve may be cleaned in paraffin to remove any deposits. If

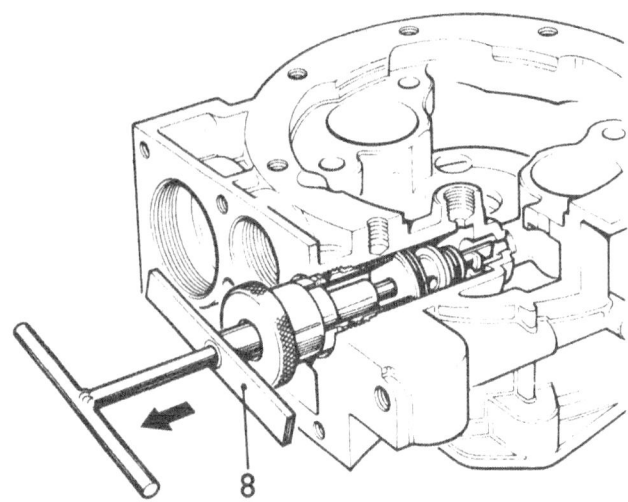

Fig. 6.20 Using tool number 'L401' to withdraw the relief valve and dashpot sleeve (Sec 21)

this does not cure the fault, or if no current is drawn, the solenoid must be renewed.
4   To check the electrical control system to the solenoid, connect the line solenoid feed connection to a 12 volt test lamp, the other terminal of which is earthed. With the ignition on and top gear engaged, check that the lamp illuminates when overdrive is selected. If there is no illumination of the lamp trace through the wiring and check the overdrive inhibitor switch.

21 Relief valve and dashpot assembly – removal, repair and refitting

Before attempting to carry out any work on the relief valve it must be appreciated that if the relief valve body is to be removed it will be necessary to purchase 'Churchill' tool number L401A.

1   Drain the overdrive unit but if the car has been in recent use take care that the hot oil does not burn the hands. Remove the overdrive sump and gauge filter.
2   Using a suitable locally manufactured tool, or alternatively 'Churchill' tool number L354, remove the relief valve plug.
3   Now withdraw the dashpot piston complete with its component springs and cup, followed by the residual pressure spring. Using a pair of long nosed pliers the relief valve piston can also be withdrawn. At this stage it is advisable to clean the control orifice, which can be done using a clean dry air line. This will need to be done with the solenoid removed. Under no circumstances should a wire or pin be inserted into the orifice since even the slightest damage, scoring or burring can impair its calibration.
4   If it is intended to remove the relief body and sleeve, insert the special tool number L401A into the exposed relief valve bore, taking care not to damage or score any working parts, and withdraw the relief valve body together with the dashpot sleeve (Fig. 6.20).
5   *Do not dismantle the preset dashpot and piston assemblies or the operating datum will be disturbed.* Examine all parts for freedom of movement, scoring, corrosion, cracks etc. Check the residual pressure spring and O-rings for damage. Renew any defective or suspect parts.
6   When refitting, make sure that all the parts are clean and lightly oiled. Insert the relief valve body in the bore and using the relief valve outer sleeve push fully home, making sure that the O-ring is nearest to the outside of the casing.
7   Now position the relief valve spring and piston assembly into the dashpot cup taking care that the residual pressure spring is correctly located. Position the components in the relief valve outer sleeve and at the same time engage the relief valve piston in its housing.
8   Finally fit the base plug and tighten it flush with the casing to a torque of 16 lbf ft (2.21 kgf m).

22 Hydraulic pump non-return valve – removal, cleaning and refitting

1   Drain the overdrive oil and remove the sump and gauge filter as described in the previous Section.
2   Using a locally manufactured tool, or alternatively 'Churchill' tool number L354, remove the pump plug taking care not to lose the non-return valve spring and ball. Withdraw the pump valve seat.
3   If it is required to remove the pump body, rotate the propeller shaft until the pump plunger is at the top of its stroke and very carefully withdraw the pump body by hooking a piece of clean wire into the now exposed inlet port.
4   Clean and inspect all parts, looking particularly for damage or corrosion to the ball and valve seat. Examine the O-rings for condition and renew any defective or suspect parts.
5   When refitting, fit the body (if previously removed) then place the spring in the recess in the plug and carefully balance the ball on the spring. The return seat can then be placed on the ball and plug, torque tightened to a value of 16 lbf ft (2.21 kgf m).

23 Pressure filter – removal, cleaning and refitting

1   Drain the overdrive unit of oil; then remove the sump and gauze filter, as previously described.
2   Using a locally manufactured tool, or 'Churchill' tool number L354 remove the pressure filter plug. The filter element will come away with the plug but take care not to lose the aluminium washer which locates on the shoulder of the filter bore.
3   Wash the filter element in petrol or paraffin and allow it to dry.
4   When refitting, check that the aluminium washer is undamaged and renew if necessary, then torque tighten the plug to a value of 16 lbf ft (2.21 kgf m).

24 Overdrive unit – removal and refitting

1   Initially raise the rear wheels and run the transmission normally. Engage overdrive, then disengage with the clutch pedal depressed. (This releases the spline loading between the planet carrier and one-way roller clutch).
2   Remove the gearbox and overdrive from the car by reference to the gearbox removal procedure in Section 2 of this Chapter.
3   Remove the gearbox from the overdrive in the normal way.
Note: *If difficulty is experienced, remove the plug adjacent to the solenoid, energize the solenoid then force clean oil from an oil gun through the plug orifice. This will require the use of a locally manufactured adaptor or 'Churchill' tool number L402. De-energise the solenoid once the two units have started to separate.*
4   When refitting, first use a screwdriver to rotate the inner member of the one-way clutch (ie, the innermost set of splines) in an anti-clockwise direction until they align with the splines in the planet carrier.
5   Check that the oil pump cam and sungear spring ring are correctly located on the mainshaft of the gearbox.
6   Rotate the gearbox mainshaft to get the peak of the pump cam lowermost. This will assist with the engagement of the pump strap.
7   Select first gear on the gearbox.
8   With a new face gasket in position, offer up the overdrive to the gearbox.
9   Rotate the output shaft clockwise whilst applying slight end pressure until the splines engage.
10 Check that the pump strap assembly rides smoothly on to the cam and that the overdrive can be pushed fully to the adaptor plate face without excessive force. **Note**: *If a gap of approximately $\frac{5}{8}$ in (16 mm) remains, it means that the planet carrier and one-way roller clutch splines have become disengaged. If this occurs, re-align them as detailed in paragraph 4, of this Section.*
11 Fit and tighten the eight gearbox/overdrive nuts.

25 Overdrive - overhaul

1   It is not recommended that the overdrive unit is overhauled by the home mechanic due to the need for special tools.

2   Any faults which may occur should be diagnosed by reference to Section 35 and if applicable remedial action or adjustment carried out by referring to Section 19, 20, 21, 22 and 23.

Part D   Automatic transmission

26 General description

Two models of automatic transmission are available as an optional extra. Early cars are equipped with the Borg-Warner model 35 and later cars have the Borg-Warner model 65 fitted. Both types are very similar with the 65 model being a lighter version of the 35 model.

The automatic transmission system comprises two main components: (1) a three-element hydrokinetic torque converter coupling capable of torque multiplication at an infinitely variable ratio between 2:1 and 1:1 or 1:91 and 1:1 depending on type; (2) a torque/speed responsive and hydraulically operated epicyclic gearbox comprising a planetary gear set providing three forward ratios and one reverse ratio.

Due to the complexity of the automatic transmission unit, if performance is not up to standard, or overhaul is necessary, it is imperative that this be left to the local main agents who will have the special equipment and knowledge for fault diagnosis and rectification.

The content of this Chapter is therefore confined to supplying general information and any service information and instruction that can be used by the owner.

27 Transmission fluid level – checking

1   It is important that transmission fluids manufactured only to the correct specification, such as Castrol TQF are used.
2   Every 6000 miles (9600 km) or more frequently if wished, check the automatic transmission fluid level. With the engine at its normal operating temperature move the selector to the 'P' position and allow to idle for two minutes. Remove the dipstick, wipe it clean and with the engine idling insert the dipstick and quickly withdraw again. If necessary add enough of the clean correct grade fluid to bring the level to the 'High' mark. The difference between the two dipstick graduations is 1 pint (0.57 litres).

28 Transmission – removal and refitting

1   Any suspected fault must be referred to the main agent before the unit is removed, as with this type of transmission the fault must be diagnosed, using special equipment, before the assembly is removed from the car.
2   As the automatic transmission is heavy it is best if the car is raised from the ground on ramps but it is possible to remove the unit if the car is placed on high axle-stands or other suitable supports.
3   Disconnect the battery.
4   Drain the cooling system. Disconnect the radiator top hose and the heater hoses at the heater.
5   Disconnect the downshift cable from the throttle linkage (Fig. 6.22).
6   Remove the gearbox drain plug (type 65) or the filler dipstick tube (type 35) and drain the oil into a suitable container. The torque converter cannot be drained.
7   Undo the three nuts securing each front exhaust pipe to the exhaust manifolds. Slacken the clamps securing the silencers to the intermediate exhaust pipes then remove the bolt securing the exhaust pipes to the gearbox crossmember and withdraw the exhaust front pipes and silencers from under the car.
8   Remove the bolts attaching the propeller shaft to the rear axle coupling flange and withdraw the propeller shaft from the gearbox.
9   Disconnect the wiring to the gearbox at the block connector on the left-hand side near the starter motor.
10 Disconnect the oil cooler pipes from the transmission. Have a container ready to catch the oil that will drain out (Fig. 6.23).
11 Remove the two nuts securing the engine to the transmission anti-vibration straps (later models).

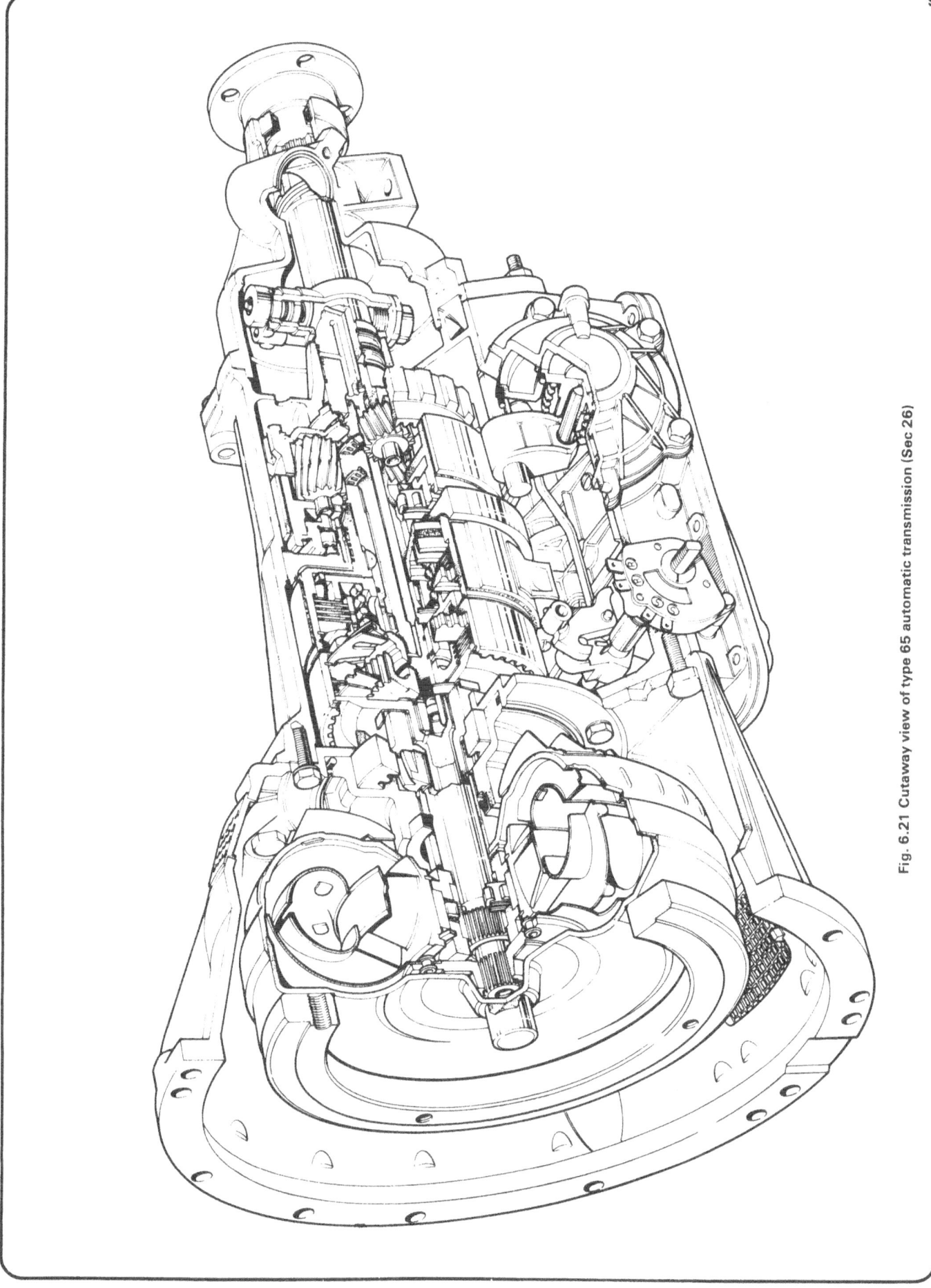

Fig. 6.21 Cutaway view of type 65 automatic transmission (Sec 26)

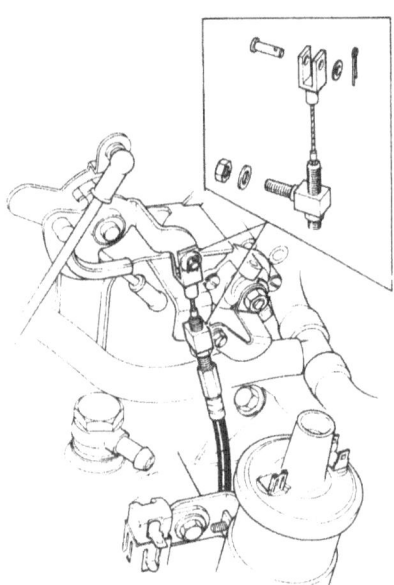

Fig. 6.22 Disconnect the downshift cable (Sec 28)

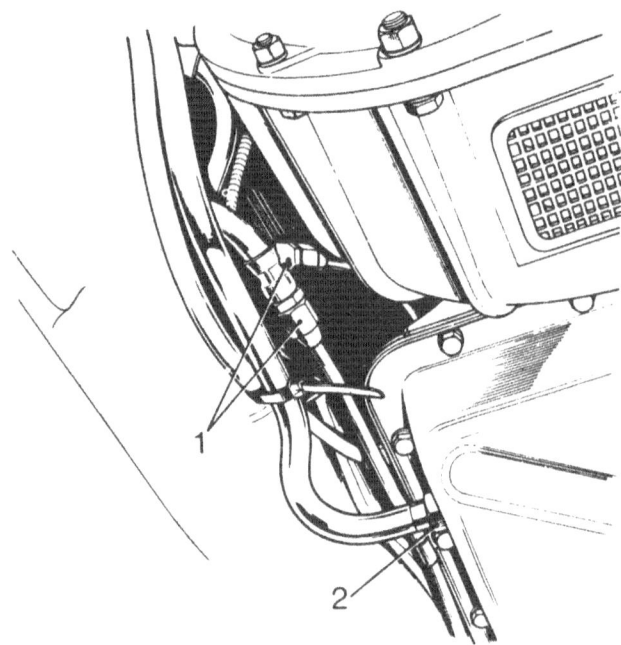

Fig. 6.23 Disconnect the oil cooler pipes (Sec 28)

1 Oil cooler pipes   2 Filler/dipstick tube union

12 Disconnect the speedometer cable. Remove the securing clip and disconnect the gear control linkage.
13 Position a jack under the torque converter housing and take the weight of the engine and transmission.
14 Remove the four bolts and nylon spacers securing the rear mounting crossmember to the body (Fig. 6.24).
15 Unclip the brake pipe from the rear of the front crossmember and then slowly lower the jack until the weight of the engine and transmission is taken by the front edge of the sump against the front crossmember. Make sure the brake pipe is not trapped between the sump and crossmember.
16 Remove the six bolts securing the gearbox to the converter housing and pull the gearbox rearwards clear of the torque converter and lower it to the ground.

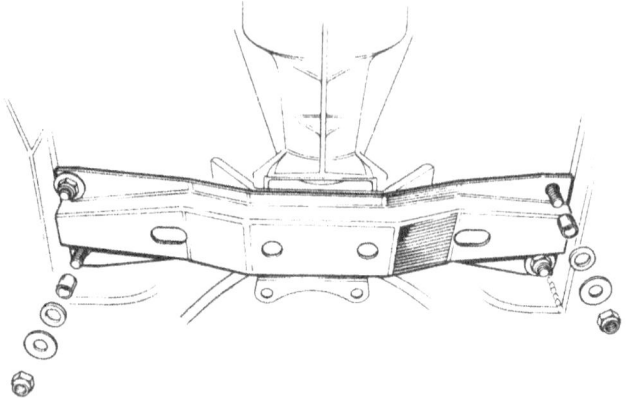

Fig. 6.24 Removing the transmission to body bolts (Sec 28)

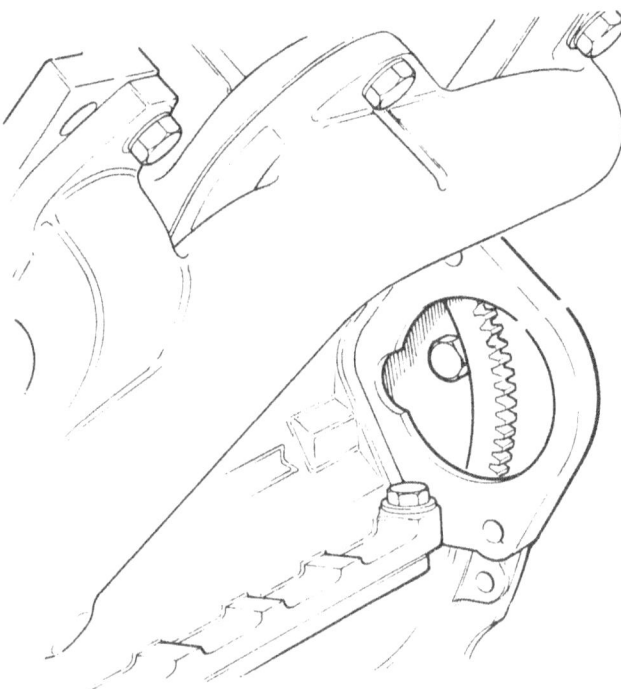

Fig. 6.25 Converter to driveplate bolts (arrowed) are accessible through starter motor aperture (Sec 29)

17 Refitting the gearbox is the reverse of the removal procedure. Align the slots in the front pump driving gear with the drive fingers of the converter hub and then insert the input shaft into the torque converter. Have an assistant turn the crankshaft, if necessary, to align the splines. Fill the transmission with the correct grade of fluid. Don't forget to fill the cooling system.

29 Torque converter – removal and refitting

1   Remove the gearbox as described in Section 28.
2   Unscrew the bolts securing the torque converter housing to the engine and remove the housing.
3   Remove the starter motor as described in Chapter 10.
4   Working through the starter motor aperture loosen the converter attaching bolts progressively. Turn the engine over to bring each bolt opposite the aperture (Fig. 6.25).
5   Remove the attaching bolts and lift the converter off the driveplate.
6   Refitting the torque converter is the reverse of the removal procedure.

30 Downshift cable – adjustment

Before the cable is adjusted it is necessary to confirm that it is the cable that is maladjusted not some other fault. Generally, if difficulty is experienced in obtaining 2nd to 1st downshift in the 'kick-down' position at just below 31 mph it is an indication that the outer cable is too short. If there is a bumpy or delayed shift at low throttle opening it is an indication that the outer cable is too long.

During production of the car the adjustment is set by a crimped stop on the carburettor end of the inner cable and it is unusual for this setting to change expect at high mileages when the inner cable can stretch.

1   Apply the handbrake firmly and chock the front wheels for safety reasons.
2   Run the engine until it reaches normal operating temperature. Adjust the engine idle speed to approximately 750 rpm with the selector in the 'D' position.
3   Stop the engine and with an open spanner loosen the locknut. Adjust the outer cable to $\frac{1}{16}$ (1.5 mm) on type 35 transmissions, or $\frac{1}{32}$ in (0.8 mm) on type 65 transmissions, from the stop by turning the outer cable collar in the trunnion block. Tighten the locknut (Fig. 6.26).
4   Should the crimped stop have moved or a new cable have been installed (supplied with loose crimped stop), it will be necessary to remove the transmission sump pan.
5   Reset the engine idle to normal speed with the selector in the 'N' position. Stop the engine.
6   Wipe the area around the drain plug and sump. Place a clean container of at least 8 pints (4.5 litres) capacity under the pan drain plug. Undo the plug and allow the oil to drain into the container, (type 65 transmissions). On type 35 transmissions, the oil is drained by removing the filler/dipstick tube union from the sump.
7   Undo and remove the fifteen sump pan retaining bolts and spring washers. Take care not to damage the joint between the transmission casing and sump pan.
8   Refer to Fig. 6.27 and check that the position of the downshift cam is in the idling position as shown in the illustration.
9   Adjust the length of the outer cable so as to remove all the slack from the inner cable.
10 Refer to Fig. 6.28 and check the position of the downshift cam with the throttle pedal in the 'kick-down' position as shown in the illustration.
11 Refit the sump pan joint, sump pan and bolts with spring washers. Tighten the bolts in a diagonal pattern.
12 Refill the transmission with the correct grade of hydraulic fluid or use the fluid that was drained originally if it is clean with no streaks, showing signs of contamination.

31 Selector linkage – adjustment

1   Carry out this adjustment with the car on ramps or raised on axle-stands or other suitable supports.
2   Push off the retaining clip rearwards and disconnect the selector rod from the selector lever.
3   Position the selector lever in position N and the transmission selector lever in N position which is the second position from P.
4   Loosen the locknut and adjust the selector rod length. Tighten the locknut and fit the retaining clip.
5   Check that the selector lever moves easily in each one of the five selector positions.

32 Starter/inhibitor/reverse lamp switch – removal and refitting

Type 35 transmission
1   Refer to Section 28 and lower the rear end of the engine and transmission so that the engine sump rests against the front cross-members as described in paragraphs 3, 4, 7 and 12 to 15 inclusive.
2   Disconnect all four leads from the switch.
3   Loosen the locknut and unscrew the switch.
4   Refitting is the reverse of the removal procedure. Coat the switch threads with sealing compound.

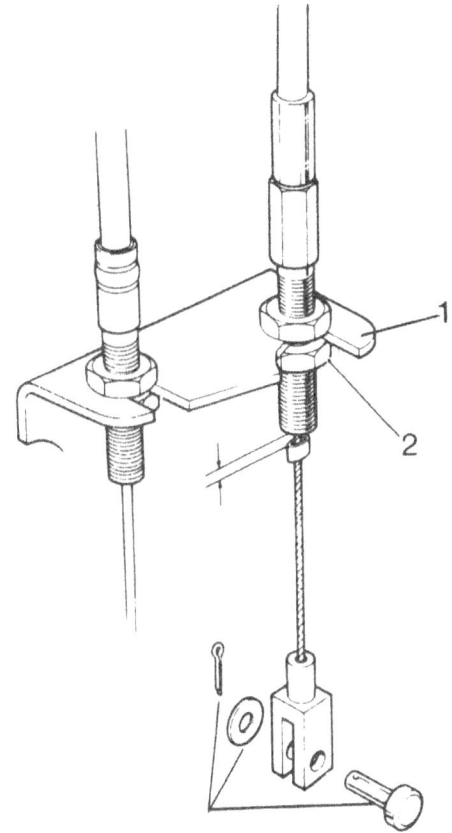

Fig. 6.26 Adjusting the downshift cable (Sec 30)

1 Linkage bracket   2 Adjustment locknut   3 Clevis pin assembly

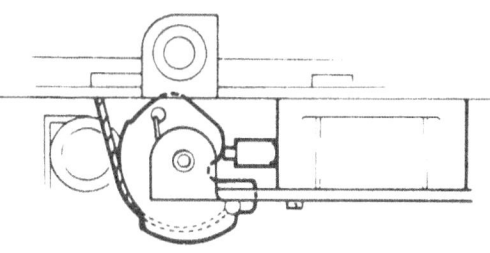

Fig. 6.27 Position of the downshift cam at engine idle position (Sec 30)

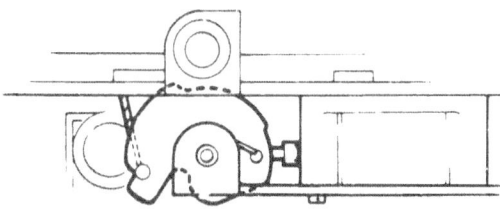

Fig. 6.28 Position of the downshift cam at kickdown (Sec 30)

Type 65 transmission
5   Raise the car on ramps or axle-stands.
6   Select P and apply the handbrake.
7   Take off the thread protector from the switch cover (if fitted).
8   Disconnect the four switch leads.
9   Undo the switch securing bolt and remove the switch.
10 Refitting the switch is the reverse of the removal procedure.

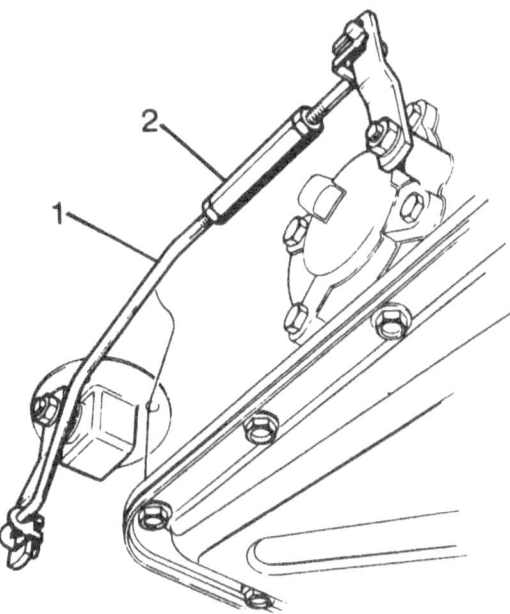

Fig. 6.29 Selector rod adjustment (Sec 31)

1 Selector rod   2 Adjuster

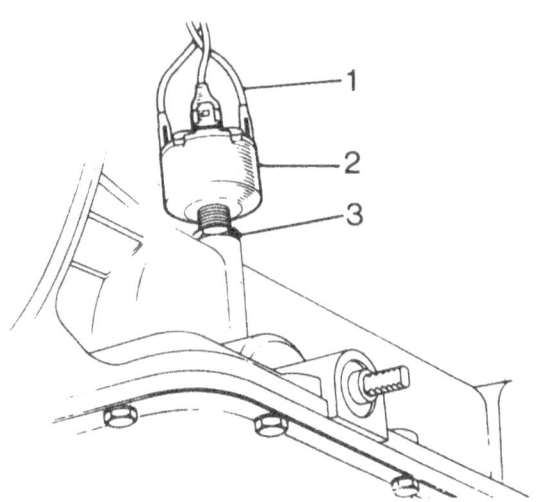

Fig. 6.30 Starter inhibitor/reverse light switch – type 35 transmission (Sec 32)

1 Electrical leads   2 Switch   3 Locknut

---

33 Fault diagnosis – automatic transmission

Stall test procedure

This test can only be satisfactorily carried out with an engine which is in good condition and capable of developing full power.

1 Run the engine until its normal operating temperature is reached.
2 Chock the wheels and apply both foot and handbrakes.
3 Select 1 or R and depress the throttle to the kick-down position for a period not exceeding 10 seconds (to avoid overheating the transmission). Note the tachometer reading which should be approximately 2200 rpm for type 65 or 2100 for type 35 transmission. If the reading is lower than 1400 rpm – type 65 or 1300 rpm – type 35, suspect the converter for stator slip; if the reading is about 1600 rpm – type 65 or 1500 rpm – type 35, the engine is not developing full power; if the reading is around 2400 rpm – type 65 or 2300 rpm – type 35, suspect brake band or clutch slip in the transmission unit.

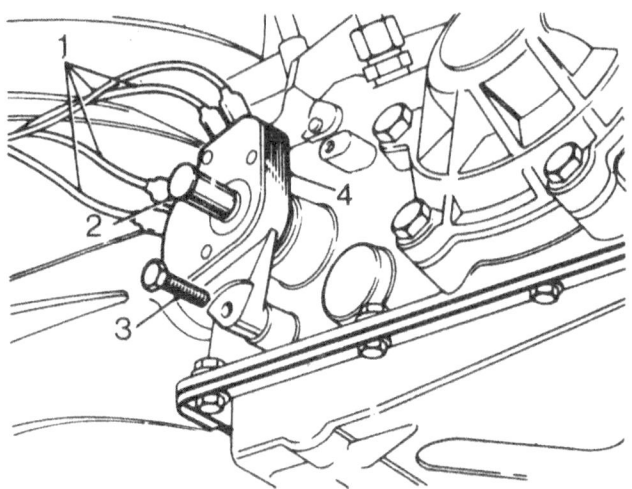

Fig. 6.31 Starter inhibitor/reverse light switch – type 65 transmission (Sec 32)

1 Electrical leads   2 Thread protector   3 Bolt   4 Switch

4 If the test is to be repeated, allow 10-15 minutes for the transmission fluid heat to dissipate.

Road test procedure

The term full throttle refers to approximately seven-eighths of the available pedal travel and kickdown is equivalent to full pedal travel.

5 Check that the starter motor operates only with the selector lever at P or N and that the reverse lights operate only at R.
6 Apply the handbrake. With the engine idling select N-D, N-2, N-R. Engagement should be positive (a cushioned 'thump' under fast idling conditions is to be expected).
7 With the transmission at the normal running temperatures, select D. Release the brakes and accelerate with minimum throttle. Check the 1-2 and 2-3 shift speeds and the smoothness of the change.
8 Stop the vehicle, select D, then re-start using 'full throttle'. Check 1-2 and 2-3 shift speeds and the smoothness of the change.
9 At 40 mph (65 km/h) apply 'full throttle'. The car should accelerate in third gear and should not downshift to second.
10 At a maximum speed of 58 mph (93 km/h) 'kick-down' fully. The transmission should downshift to second.
11 At a maximum speed of 39 mph (62 km/h) 'kick-down' fully. The transmission should downshift to first.
12 Stop the vehicle, select D, then re-start using 'kick-down'; check the 1-2 and 2-3 shift speeds.
13 At 30 mph (50 km/h), select 2 and release the throttle; check the 2-3 downshift.
14 At 34 mph (54 km/h) select 1 and release the throttle; check the 2-1 downshift.
15 With 1 still engaged, stop the vehicle and using 'kick-down' accelerate to over 40 mph (65 km/h). Check for 'slip', 'squawk', and the loss of upshifts.
16 Stop the vehicle. Select R and reverse at 'full throttle' (if possible), checking for 'slip' and 'squawk'.
17 Park the vehicle on a gradient. Apply the handbrake and select P, then release the handbrake and check the parking pawl hold. Check that the selector lever is firmly in the gate in P.

Converter diagnosis

Inability to start on steep hills, combined with poor acceleration from rest and low stall speeds (1400 rpm), indicates that the converter stator undirectional clutch is slipping. This permits the stator to rotate in an opposite direction to the impeller and turbine, and torque multiplication cannot occur. Poor acceleration in third gear above 30 mph (50 km/h) and reduced maximum speed, indicates that the stator unidirectional clutch has seized. The stator will not rotate with the turbine and impeller and the 'fluid fly-wheel' effect cannot occur. This condition will also be indicated by excessive overheating of the transmission although the stall speed will be satisfactory.

Part E – Fault diagnosis

34 Fault diagnosis – manual gearbox

Symptom	Reason/s
Weak or ineffective synchromesh	Synchronising cones worn, split or damaged Baulk ring synchromesh dogs worn, or damaged
Jumps out of gear	Broken gearchange fork rod spring Gearbox coupling dogs badly worn Selector fork rod groove badly worn Selector fork end securing screw and locknut loose
Excessive noise	Incorrect grade of oil in gearbox or oil level too low Bush or needle roller bearings worn or damaged Gearteeth excessively worn or damaged Laygear thrust washers worn allowing excessive end play
Excessive difficulty in engaging gear	Clutch pedal adjustment incorrect Clutch not fully disengaging

35 Fault diagnosis – overdrive

Symptom	Reason/s
Lack of engagement	Insufficient oil in gearbox Failure of switches or wiring (visually check solenoid operation) Control mechanism out of adjustment Check hydraulic pressure If insufficient pressure, clean and re-seal oil pump non-return valve Damaged parts within the unit requiring removal and inspection of the assembly
Will not disengage	Control mechanism out of adjustment Solenoid sticking Blocked restrictor jet in operating valve Electrical circuit earthed Sticking clutch (can sometimes be freed by tapping casing with soft mallet) Damaged parts within the unit necessitating removal and inspection of assembly
Clutch slip when overdrive selected	Insufficient oil in gearbox Solenoid lever out of adjustment Insufficient hydraulic pressure due to pump non-return valve incorrectly seating Insufficient hydraulic pressure due to worn accumulator piston Operating valve incorrectly seating Worn or glazed clutch lining
Clutch slip in reverse or free-wheeling when overdrive selected	Check solenoid setting Partially blocked restrictor jet in operating valve Worn clutch lining

Chapter 7 Propeller shaft

Contents

Specifications

Type	One piece tubular steel
Universal joint type	Hardy-Spicer

Torque wrench setting	lbf ft	kgf m
Flange securing bolts	34	4·7

1 General description

Drive from the gearbox or automatic transmission is transmitted to the differential carrier by means of a tubular propeller shaft.

At each end of the shaft a universal joint is fitted which allows for any sideways or up and down movement of the differential carrier on its rubber mountings.

Any fore and aft movement of the differential carrier is absorbed by a sliding spline at the front end of the propeller shaft.

Three different propeller shafts are used. Cars with automatic transmission have a sliding coupling with internal splines at the front and a built-in rubber coupling at the rear. Manual gearbox models have flange couplings at each end with the sliding yoke at the front. Cars fitted with overdrive have a sliding yoke at the front and a built-in rubber coupling at the rear end.

2 Propeller shaft – removal and refitting

1   Jack-up the car and support it on axle-stands or other suitable supports.
2   Undo the six nuts securing the front exhaust pipes to the exhaust manifolds. Slacken the clamp bolts securing the silencers to the rear intermediate exhaust pipes. Undo the bolts attaching the front exhaust pipes to the bracket on the gearbox mounting crossmember and remove the front pipes and silencers from under the car.
3   The propeller shaft is carefully balanced to fine limits and it is important that it is refitted in exactly the same position it was in prior to its removal. Scratch a mark on both the propeller shaft flanges and the gearbox/rear axle drive flanges to ensure accurate mating when refitting.
4   Unscrew and remove the four self-locking nuts, bolts and washers which secure each flange on the propeller shaft to the flange on the rear axle and to the flange on manual type gearboxes. On automatic transmission the front universal is splined into the gearbox (photos).
5   Remove the propeller shaft. On automatic transmission models seal the rear of the gearbox with a polythene bag to prevent the ingress of dirt.
6   Refitting the propeller shaft is the reverse of the removal procedure. Ensure that the arrows on the sliding yoke and shaft on overdrive and manual gearboxes are in alignment and that the mating marks scratched on the edges of the propeller shaft flanges line up with those on the rear axle and gearbox flanges. Always use new nylon nuts.

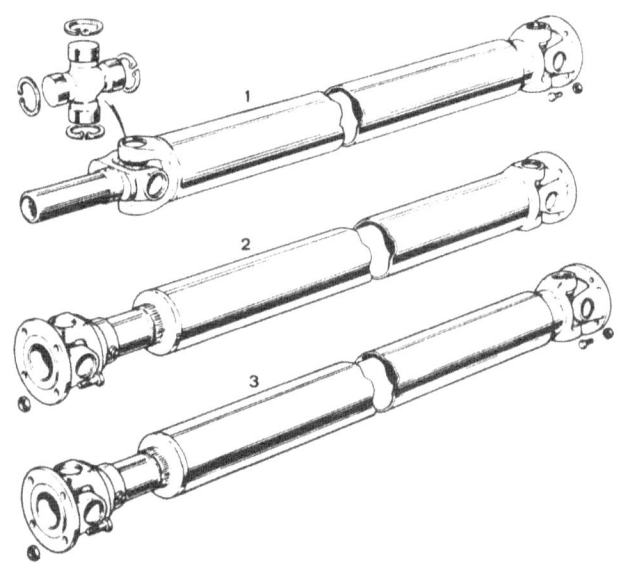

Fig. 7.1 Propeller shaft assembly (Sec 1)

1 Automatic transmission type
2 Manual gearbox type
3 Manual gearbox with overdrive type

3 Universal joints – inspection

1   Wear in the needle roller bearings is characterised by vibration in the transmission; 'clonks' on taking up the drive; and in extreme cases, through lack of lubrication, metallic squeaking; and ultimately grating and shrieking sounds as the bearings break up.
2   It is easy to check if the needle roller bearings are worn with the propeller shaft in position, by trying to turn the shafts with one hand, the other hand holding the rear axle flange when the rear universal is being checked, and the front gearbox coupling when the front universal is being checked. Any movement between the propeller shaft and the front and rear half couplings is indicative of considerable wear.

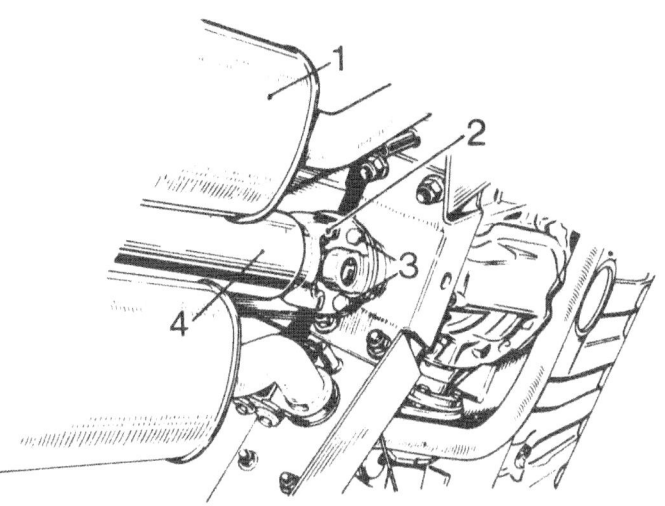

Fig. 7.2 Removing the propeller shaft (Sec 2)

1 *Silencer*   3 *Flange bolts*
2 *Rear universal joint*   4 *Propeller shaft*

2.4a Propeller shaft rear universal joint

2.4b Front universal joint (automatic transmission models)

3   If worn, the old bearings and spiders will have to be discarded and a repair kit, comprising new universal joint spiders, bearings, oil seals, and retainers, purchased. Check also by trying to lift the shaft and noticing any movement in the joints.

4   Universal joints – dismantling

1   Clean away all traces of dirt and grease from the circlips located on the ends of the bearing cups, and remove the circlips by pressing their open ends together with a pair of pliers (photo), and lever them out with a screwdriver. **Note:** *If they are difficult to remove tap the bearing cup face resting on top of the spider with a mallet which will ease the pressure on the circlip.*
2   Take off the bearing cups on the propeller shaft yoke. To do this select two sockets from a socket set, one large enough to fit completely over the bearing cup ($\frac{15}{16}$ AF) and the other smaller than the bearing cup.
3   Open the jaws of the vice and with the sockets opposite each other and the UJ in between, tighten the vice and force the narrower socket to move the opposite cup partially out of the yoke into the larger socket.
4   An alternative method of bearing cup removal is to extract the circlips and then to strike the yoke with a wooden or plastic faced mallet as shown in Fig. 7.3, until the bearing cup partially emerges. The cup can then be gripped in a vice or pliers and twisted from the yoke.

5   Universal joints – reassembly

1   Thoroughly clean out the yokes and journals. Smear jointing compound on the journal shoulders of the new spider if a retainer is used.
2   New bearings will be supplied with new seals and circlips. Make sure the needles are correctly in position and the cup $\frac{1}{3}$ full of grease.
3   Fit the spider to the propeller shaft yoke.
4   Engage the spider trunnion in the bearing cup and insert the cup into the yoke (photo).
5   Fit the opposite bearing cup to the yoke and carefully press both cups into position, ensuring that the spider trunnion engages the cups and that the needle bearings are not displaced.
6   Using a suitable socket, press the cups into the yokes until they reach the lower land of the circlip grooves. Do not press the bearing cups below this point or damage may be caused to the cups and seals (photo).
7   Fit the circlips.

4.1 Remove the circlip

5.4 Refitting a cup

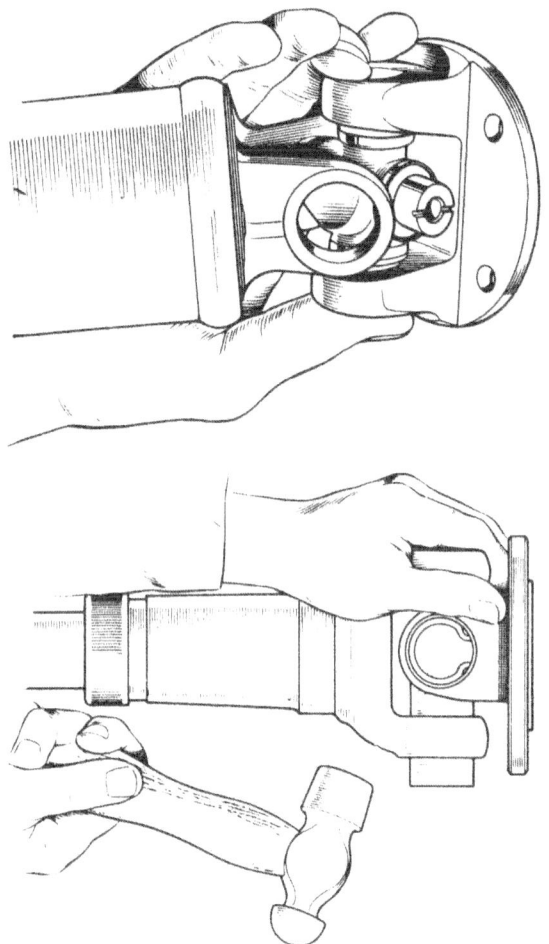

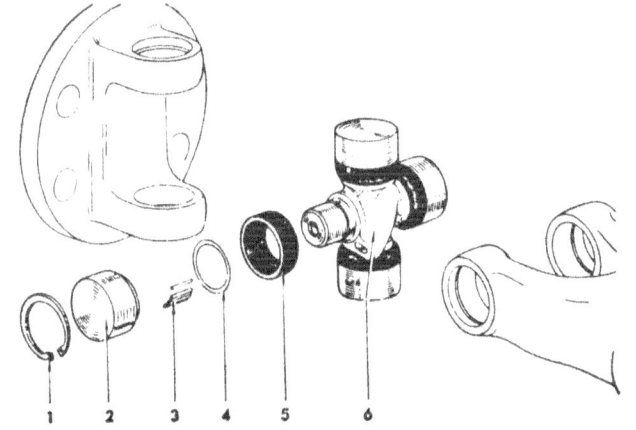

Fig. 7.3 Alternative method of dismantling a universal joint (Sec 4)

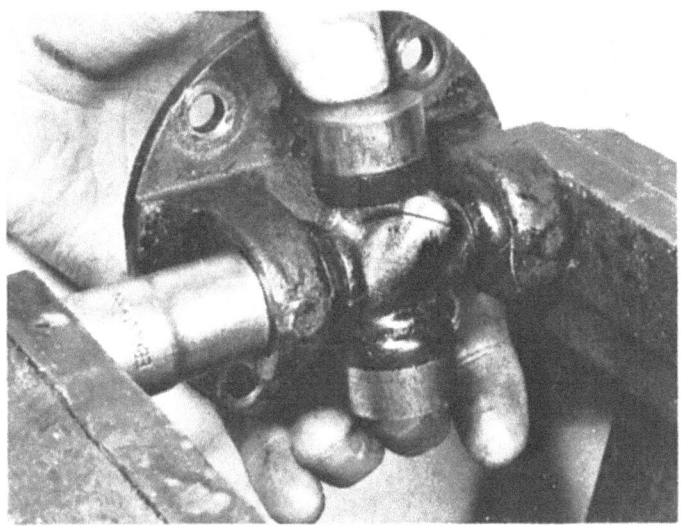

5.6 Pushing the cup in far enough to fit a circlip

Fig. 7.4 Exploded view of universal joint (Sec 5)

1 Circlip	4 Washer
2 Cup	5 Seal
3 Needle rollers	6 Spider

6   Fault diagnosis – propeller shaft

Symptom	Reason/s
Vibration	Wear in sliding sleeve splines
	Worn universal joints
	Propeller shaft out of balance
Knock when taking up drive	Worn differential drive pinion splines
	Loose drive flange connecting bolts
	Worn universal joint bearings
	Worn sliding sleeve splines

Chapter 8 Rear axle

Contents

Specifications

Type		Hypoid bevel	

Ratio		3·7 : 1	

Pinion bearing preload

		lbf in	kgf m
Earlier axles with shims		15 to 18	0·17 to 0·21
Later axles with collapsible spacer		13 to 20	0·15 to 0·23

Oil capacity		2 pints (1·13 litres)	

Torque wrench settings

	lbf ft	kgf m
Bearing caps to housing	38	5·2
Coupling flange to quill shaft	120	16·6
Rear cover to mounting plate	34	4·7
Crownwheel bolts	46	6·4
Differential carrier mounting bolts	20	2·8
Inner axleshaft bearing retainer bolts	20	2·8
Shaft inner drive flange coupling bolts	120	16·6
Rear mounting plate to body	25	3·5
Castellated pinion nut (not collapsible spacer type axle)	120	16·6
Propeller shaft flange bolts	34	4·7
Driving flange to outer axleshaft	120	16·6

1 General description

The main rear axle component is the hypoid differential unit which is fixed to the chassis at the rear of the unit by a bracket using two part rubber mountings. The front of the differential unit is mounted on a nose piece, as shown in Fig. 8.3, bolted to two subframes. Splined swing axle driveshafts, pivoting at their inner ends on universal joints attached to the differential drive flanges, carry the drive to the hub via needle roller and ball bearings mounted in independent suspension arms.

The crownwheel and pinion each run on opposed taper roller bearings, the bearing pre-load and meshing of the crownwheel and pinion being controlled by shims. Spring loaded oil seals, of the type normally found at the front of the differential nose piece, prevent loss from the differential at the pinion quill shaft and driveshaft holes.

On later axles (from axle No LD 17294) the pinion bearing preload is set by means of a collapsible spacer instead of shims as used on earlier axles.

No facility is provided for draining the differential unit on later models and it should normally only be topped-up with specified oil as described in the Routine Maintenance section at the front of this manual. Where the unit has to be drained (by removal of the rear cover) for overhaul purposes, then it should be refilled with the specified oil.

2 Rear axle differential unit – removal and refitting

1   Chock the front wheels and jack-up the rear of the car. Position the raised axle-stands under the rear jacking points and carefully lower the car until it is firmly resting on the two stands.
2   Undo the universal joint to inner axleshaft flange retaining nuts (31) (Fig. 8.3) and lift away together with the bolts (32). Repeat this operation on the other side of the differential unit.
3   Undo the four nuts securing the propeller shaft flange to the quill shaft flange (18) having first marked their relationship to each other, and carefully lower the propeller shaft to the floor. Push the free end to one side.
4   Undo the clamp bolts securing the rear intermediate exhaust pipes to the silencers and the tail pipes to the rear intermediate exhaust pipes. Release the pipes from the rubber hangers and remove the rear intermediate and tail pipes from under the car.
5   Undo the four nuts that secure the nose piece (24) (Fig. 8.3) to the subframe. Lift away the nuts, spring washers and bolts.
6   Using either a hydraulic jack or the services of an assistant take the weight of the axle casing.
7   Undo the two large nuts (61) (Fig. 8.3) and lift away the nuts followed by the backing plates (62) and lower the rubber buffers (63).
8   Carefully lower the mounting (65) ensuring that it easily frees from the studs and withdraw the axle casing and mounting from the

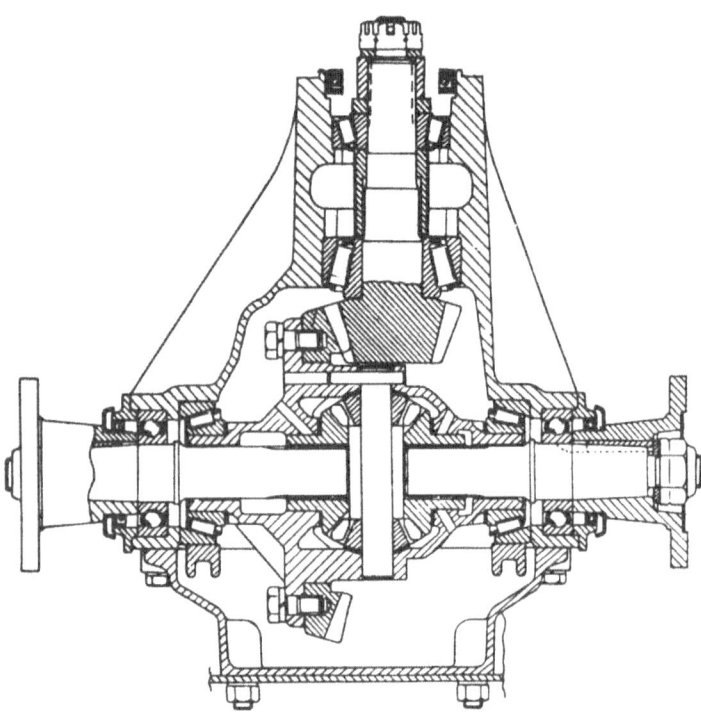

Fig. 8.1 Sectional view of axle with shimmed pinion
(Sec 1)

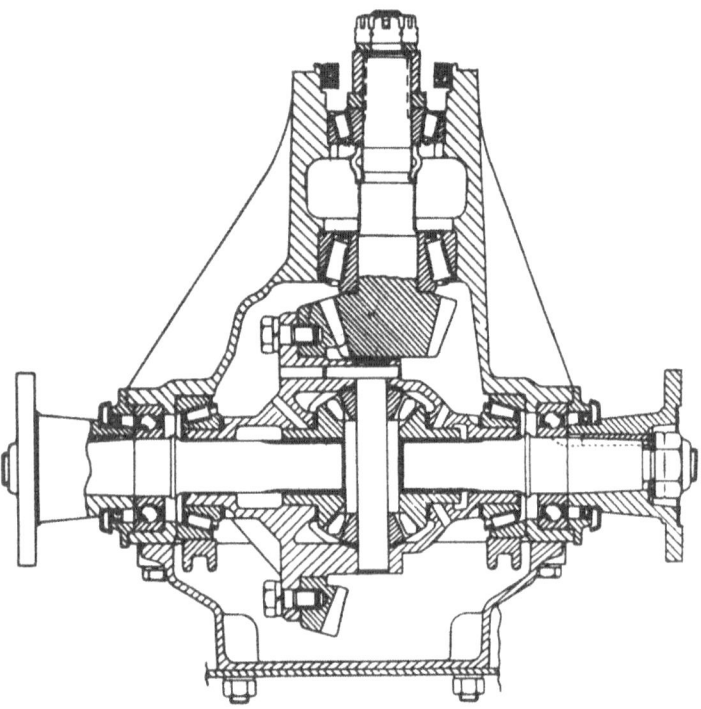

Fig. 8.2 Sectional view of axle with collapsible spacer
(Sec 1)

underside of the car, preferably on the saddle of a hydraulic jack as shown in Fig. 8.4.

9   Take the upper rubber buffers off the body studs so that they are not lost.

10   The axle casing is attached to the mounting by means of nuts (67) and studs (68). To separate the two parts, release the locking plate tabs, remove the four nuts (67) and then lift away the mounting (Fig. 8.5).

11   Refitting is the reverse of the removal procedure. Always ensure that the axle casing to mounting retaining nuts are securely locked by bending over the tabs of the locking plates. Inspect the upper and lower rubber buffers for signs of oil contamination, splitting or deterioration and renew if any of these signs are evident.

3   Axle casing and differential unit – dismantling, examination and reassembly

To dismantle the differential unit several special tools are required and without them the necessary operations cannot be carried out. They are numbered 'S4221A-10', 'S4221A-16', 'S316', 'S123A' and 'M84B'. If these can be borrowed from a local Triumph agent, well and good, but if not then we would recommend that the following work be left to the local agent.

1   Thoroughly clean the exterior of the casing and place on a clean bench.

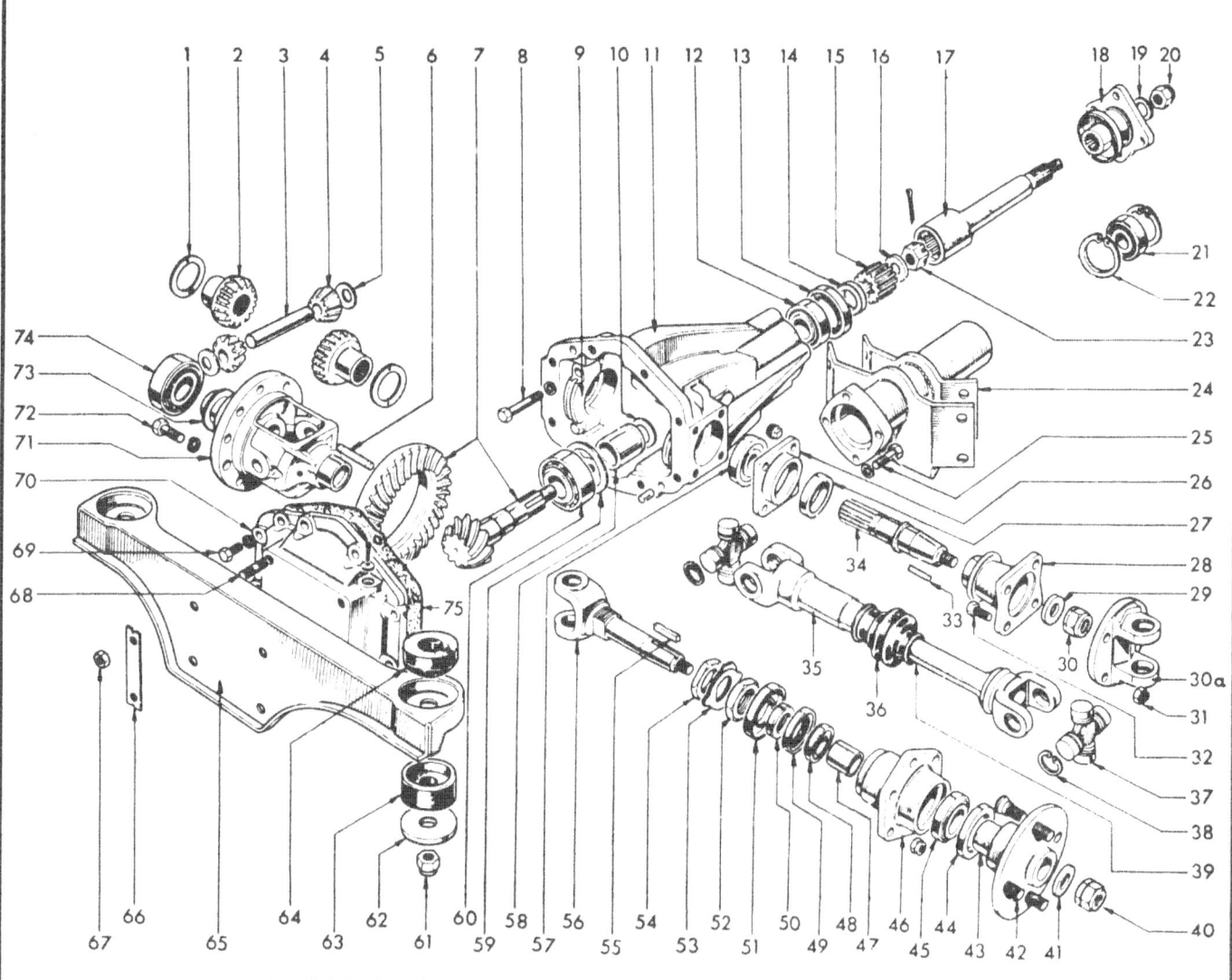

Fig. 8.3 Exploded view of rear axle – earlier type with shimmed pinion (Sec 3)

1 Thrust washer – sunwheel	27 Oil seal	51 Stone guard
2 Sunwheel	28 Flange	52 Adjusting nut
3 Cross-shaft	29 Washer	53 Tab washer
4 Planet wheel	30 Nut	54 Locknut
5 Thrust washer – planet wheel	30a Yoke	55 Key
6 Locking pin – cross-shaft	31 Nut	56 Stub shaft
7 Crownwheel and pinion	32 Bolt	57 Bearing, inner axleshaft
8 Bolt, bearing cap	33 Key	58 Spacer, pinion bearing
9 Bearing cap	34 Axleshaft, inner	59 Shim, pinion locating
10 Shim, pinion pre-loading	35 Axleshaft, fixed, outer	60 Head bearing, pinion
11 Axle casing (diff. carrier)	36 Gaiter	61 Nut
12 Tail bearing – pinion	37 Universal spider	62 Backing plate
13 Oil seal – pinion	38 Circlip	63 Buffer lower
14 Collar, centralising	39 Axleshaft, sliding, outer	64 Buffer upper
15 Coupling muff	40 Nut	65 Mounting
16 Washer	41 Washer	66 Locking plate
17 Quill shaft	42 Wheel stud	67 Nut
18 Companion flange	43 Hub	68 Stud
19 Washer	44 Oil seal	69 Bolt
20 Nut	45 Hub bearing, outer	70 Rear cover
21 Bearing, quill shaft	46 Bearing housing	71 Differential cage
22 Circlip	47 Bearing spacer, collapsible	72 Bolt
23 Castellated nut	48 Hub bearing, inner	73 Shim differential preload
24 Nose piece	49 Oil seal	74 Bearing, differential
25 Bolt	50 Bearing spacer	75 Joint, rear cover
26 Bearing retainer		

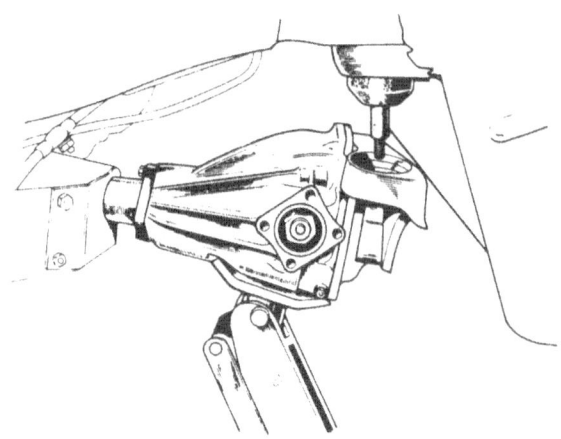

Fig. 8.4 Rear axle and mounting bracket removal (Sec 2)

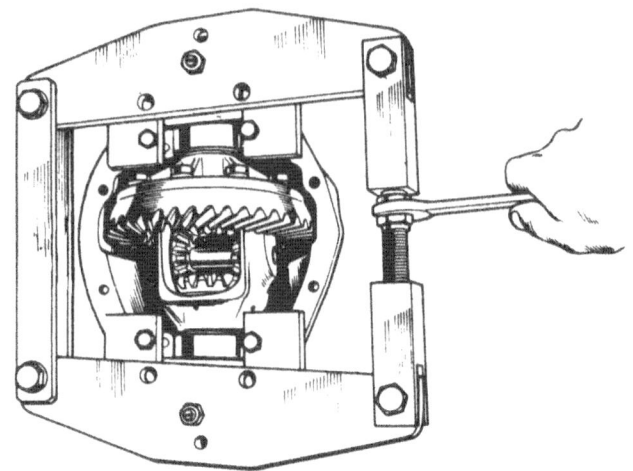

Fig. 8.7 Turn jacking screw one half turn only (Sec 3)

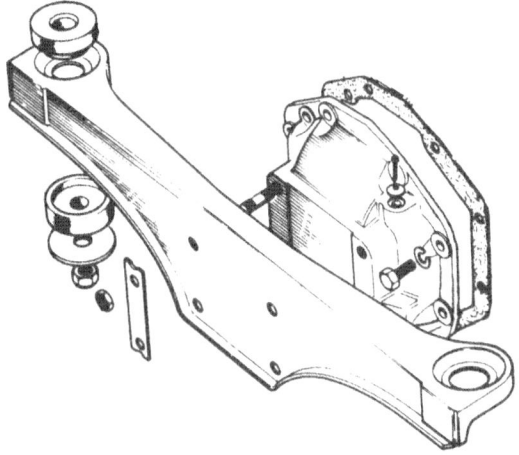

Fig. 8.5 Removing the mounting from the axle casing (Sec 2)

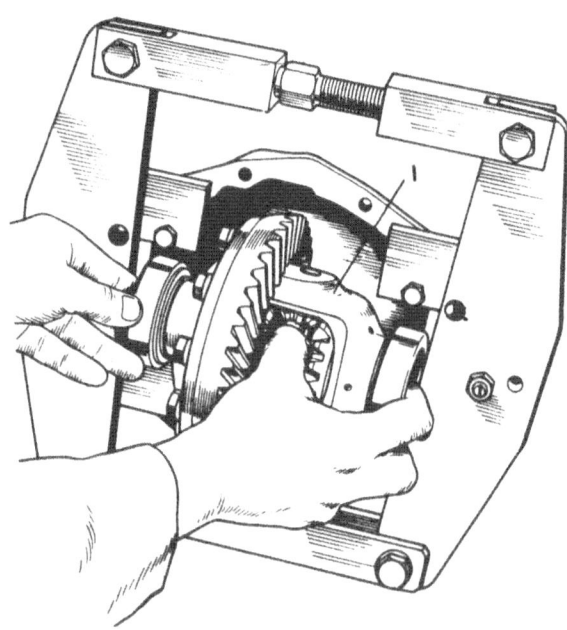

Fig. 8.8 Lifting out differential unit (1) with spreader still in position (Sec 3)

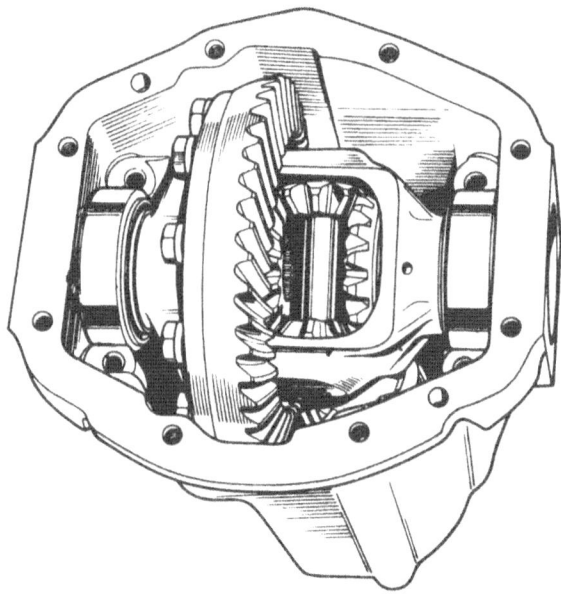

Fig. 8.6 Remove the differential bearing end caps (Sec 3)

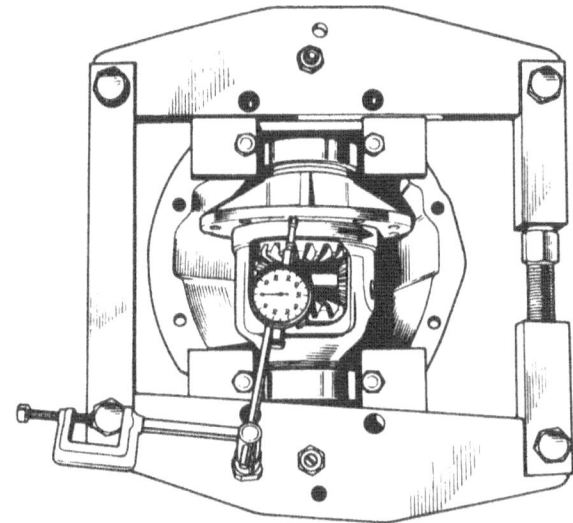

Fig. 8.9 Checking the crownwheel mounting flange for runout (Sec 3)

2   Undo the eight bolts (69) (Fig. 8.3) and lift away together with spring washers. Lift off the rear cover (70) and joint (75).
3   Undo the four bolts that hold the bearing retainer (26) to the axle casing (11) and lift away the bolts and spring washers. Ease the bearing retainers and inner axleshaft assemblies from the axle casing.
4   Remove the large nut (30) (Fig. 8.3) and washer (29) and, using a puller, separate the flange (28) from the inner axleshaft (34).
5   Next remove the key (33) followed by the bearing retainer (26) and oil seal (27).
6   Using a puller separate the bearing (57) from the inner axleshaft (34).
7   The inner axleshaft oil seal (27) may be removed from the bearing retainer (26) using a suitable diameter tubular drift. Note which way round the seal fits into the retainer to ensure correct refitting of the seal.
8   Mount the rear axle casing between the soft faces of a firm bench vice and undo the four bolts (25) (Fig. 8.3) that hold the nose piece (24) to the axle casing (11). Lift away the bolts (25) and spring washers. Withdraw the nose piece and quill shaft assembly.
9   Mark the differential bearing caps (9) and axle casing (11) to ensure correct refitting and using a socket wrench undo the four high tensile steel bolts (8). Lift away the bolts and spring washers making a note of their location for refitting in their original positions. Remove the bearing end caps (9) (see Fig. 8.6).
10 A special axle case spreader tool having a part number 'S.101' must be obtained before work can proceed further.
11 Using four $\frac{3}{8}$ x $2\frac{1}{2}$ UNF high tensile steel bolts mount the adaptor plates 'S.101-1' to the axle casing.
12 Fit the spreader tool to the adaptor plates so that the spreader pegs locate in the large holes in the adaptor plates.
13 Turn the jacking screw until it is hand tight and no more. Using an open ended spanner rotate the jacking screw *one half turn only* as this will be sufficient to spread the case to release the unit (Fig. 8.7). It is imperative that the case is not over spread otherwise irreparable damage will result.
14 Lift the differential unit, with the spreader still in position, from the axle casing as shown in Fig. 8.8.
15 Place the differential housing (7) in a vice and remove the bolts (72) and spring washers. Then remove the crownwheel (7) from its location spigot on the housing.
16 Before the differential bearings are removed from the differential housing, it is important the crownwheel mounting flange on the differential housing is checked for signs of run out. A dial indicator gauge is best used for this.
17 Thoroughly wash the differential bearings and wipe dry using a non-fluffy rag. Temporarily install the differential housing with bearings and cups in position in the axle casing.
18 Slacken the spreader jacking screw. Fit a dial indicator gauge to the axle casing with the stylus resting against the crownwheel mounting flange (Fig. 8.9).
19 Zero the dial and rotate the differential and check the runout which must not exceed 0·003 inch (0·076 mm). Should this figure be exceeded the differential bearings should be suspect and new bearings will need to be fitted.
20 Disconnect the dial indicator gauge and once again spread the axle casing and withdraw the differential unit. Release the spreader and remove the adaptor plate.
21 If the bearings show signs of wear, pitting or overheating extract them using a suitably sized puller.
22 Lift away the shims behind the bearings, and note their positions relative to the differential case to avoid the possibility of mixing up the shims.
23 Using a suitably sized pin punch carefully tap out the differential pinion shaft lock pin (6) from the differential housing (71) and withdraw the differential pinion cross-shaft (3).
24 Using the fingers, rotate the differential sunwheels (2) so that the planet wheels (4) come into line with the apertures in the differential housing. Lift out the sunwheels (2) and planet wheels (4) together with the thrust washers (5).
25 Extract the drive pinion shaft locknut split pin (early axles). Undo the castellated nut (23), or Nyloc nut and washer, using a socket wrench. The drive pinion may be locked with a mole wrench resting against the vice and clamped to the flange.
26 Using a soft metal drift carefully drive out the pinion taking care not to damage the threads. If necessary refit the nut to act as a protection for the threads.

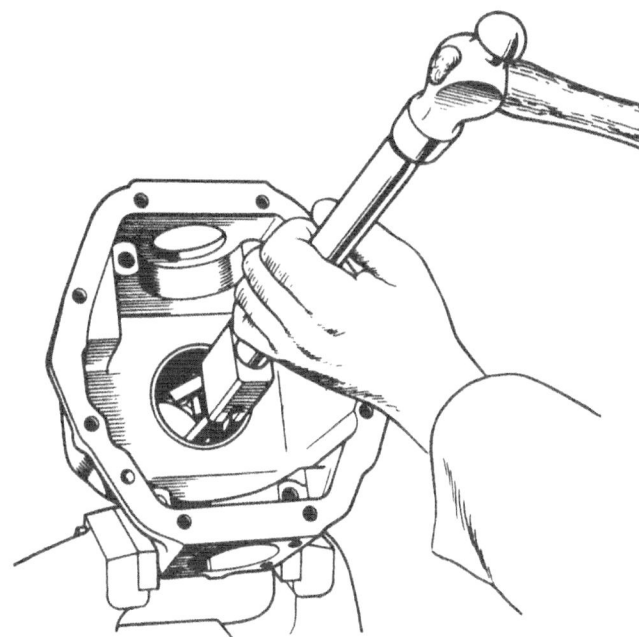

Fig. 8.10 Driving out the pinion outer track using tool 'S123A' (Sec 3)

27 Slide off the coupling muff (15), centralising collar (14), spacer (58) and any shims (59).
28 The pinion rear outer race track and seal may be removed using a soft metal drift and hammer from the inside of the axle casing.
29 The pinion head race track may be removed using a soft metal drift and hammer from the rear of the axle casing. Take care of any shims behind the race track (Fig. 8.10).
30 If necessary the pinion head race assembly (60) may be removed using a puller with the feet engaged behind the inner track.
31 Thoroughly wash all parts in paraffin and wipe dry using a non-fluffy rag. Carefully examine all parts for wear, cracks or chips. Examine the races for excessive play or loose rollers in the cages: check that the rollers are not pitted. If any part is damaged or suspect, new parts must be fitted.
32 To reassemble the final drive unit first fit the drive pinion bearing outer race track into the rear axle casing. The best method of doing this is to warm the casing in an oven and quickly drive the race outer tracks into position, less any shims that were found during dismantling. Remember to fit the tracks with the tapers the correct way round.
33 Special tools having part numbers as given in the following operations will be necessary and, if possible, these should be borrowed from the local agents, or the agents themselves be allowed to carry out the reassembly and adjustments. **Note:** *The operations described in the following paragraphs 34 to 39 do not apply to later type axles with a collapsible spacer.*
34 Refit the pinion head bearing (60) (Fig. 8.3) onto the dummy pinion shaft (tool M.84-B) and insert the assembly into the rear axle casing (11) (Fig. 8.11).
35 Refit the pinion front bearing (12), and castellated nut (23) onto the pinion shaft. The pinion bearing spacer (58) and shims (59) should be left out at this stage.
36 Tighten the castellated nut until a torque wrench setting of between 15 to 18 lbf in (0·17 to 0·21 kgf m) is required to rotate the pinion shaft. If a special preload gauge is available so much the better (see Fig. 8.12).
37 Depress the dial indicator gauge stylus against the special setting button and zero the gauge dial (tool M.84-B), as shown in Fig. 8.13.
38 Place the gauge into the axle casing so that the stylus contacts the face of the dummy pinion, as illustrated in Fig. 8.14. Put a downward pressure on the gauge body and slowly rock the gauge in the bearing bores in order to establish the point of minimum gauge reading. The minimum reading gives the thickness of shim that must be fitted under the race outer track of the rear pinion bearing.
39 Lift away the gauge dummy pinion and drive out the bearing race outer track from the final drive casing.

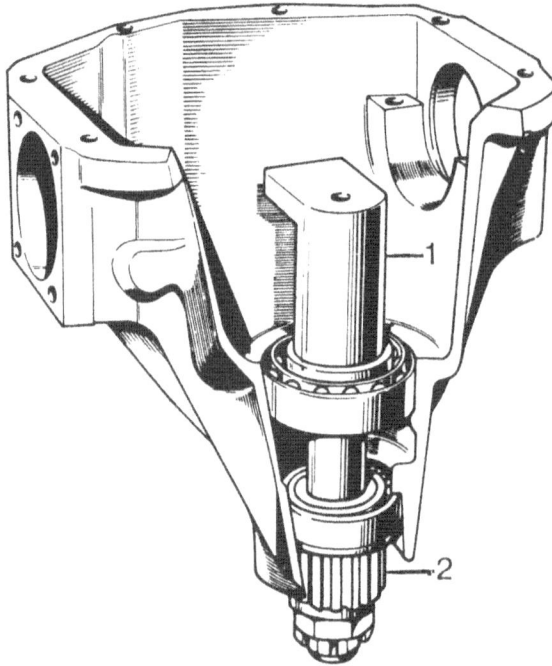

Fig. 8.11 Dummy pinion shaft fitted in casing (Sec 3)

1 Dummy pinion   2 Coupling muff

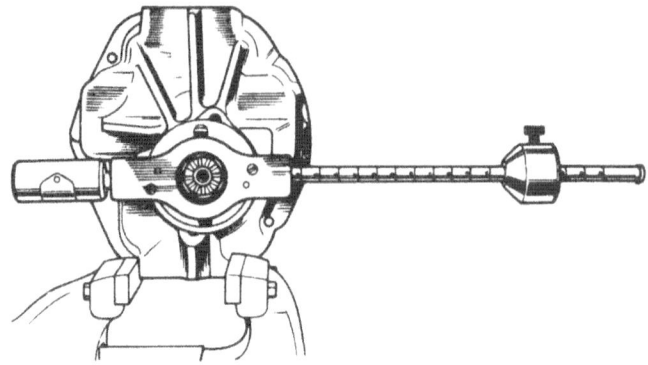

Fig. 8.12 Using special tool to determine pinion bearing preload (Sec 3)

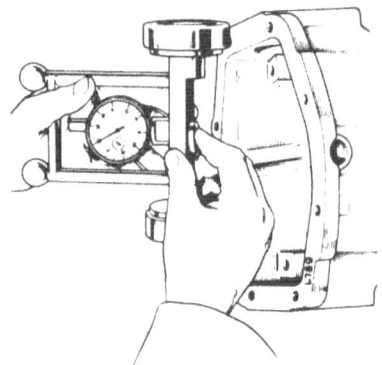

Fig. 8.13 Setting special tool 'M84B' (Sec 3)

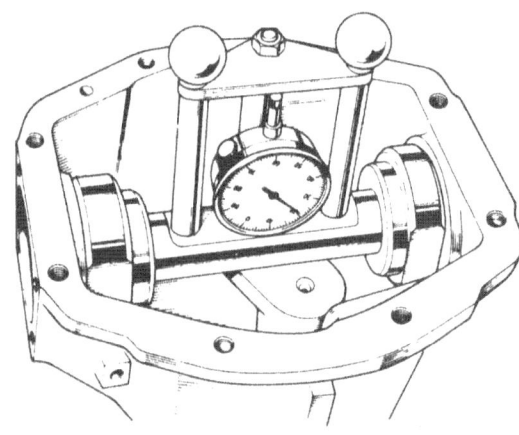

Fig. 8.14 Placement of gauge in rear axle housing. Note position of flange on end of dummy pinion (Sec 3)

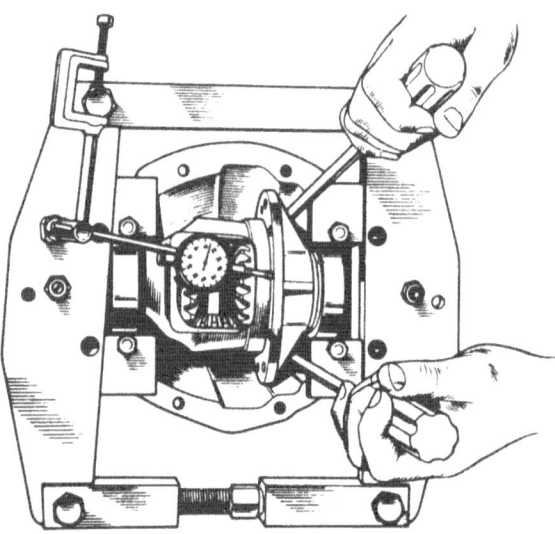

Fig. 8.15 Checking the axial movement of the crownwheel flange (Sec 3)

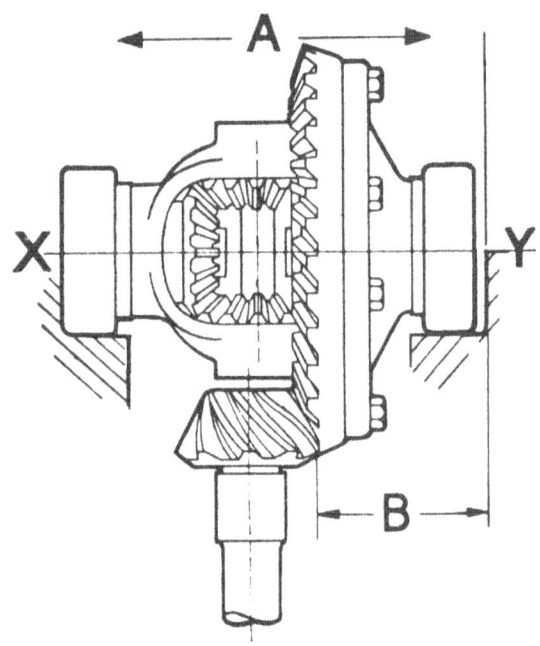

Fig. 8.16 Diagram for calculation of shim thickness (Sec 3)

A Total float   B In and out of mesh

40 Position the previously determined shims and race outer track in the axle casing by pre-heating the case and driving in the race outer track making sure that it is the right way round.
41 Fit the pinion head bearing inner track and roller cage (60) onto the pinion (7) followed by the shims (59) and the spacer (58) with its chamfered edge towards the front bearing (12) and pinion pre-load shims (10), or collapsible spacer.
42 Insert the pinion assembly into the axle casing and refit the pinion front bearing (12), centralising collar (14), coupling muff (15) and plain washer (16). Refit the pinion nut.
43 With the special holding tool (tool No. 'S316') over the coupling muff attach a preload gauge or a torque wrench to the pinion (Fig. 8.12). Carefully tighten the castellated nut. If necessary adjust the thickness of shims between the inner track of the front pinion bearing and spacer (early axles) to obtain a pinion torque of 15 to 18 lbf in (0·17 to 0·21 kgf m) when the castellated nut is tightened to 90 to 120 lbf ft (12·4 to 16·6 kgf m), or on later type axles with collapsible spacer tighten the Nyloc nut to obtain a bearing preload of 13 to 20 lbf in (0·15 to 0·23 kgf m). Take care not to overtighten the Nyloc nut or the collapsible spacer will be overstressed or even collapsed and this will necessitate dismantling and refitting a new collapsible spacer.
44 Once the correct preload has been set fit a new pinion oil seal (13), making sure that it is the correct way round with the wire spring facing inwards. Fit a new split pin to lock the castellated nut (23).
45 Place the thrust washers (1) onto the sunwheels (2) and insert these into the differential housing.
46 Smear the planet wheel thrust washers (5) with grease and attach them to the planet wheels (4). Insert the two planet wheels into the differential housing and mesh with the sunwheels. Rotate the four gears and insert the cross-shaft (3) making sure that the locking pin hole lines up with the hole in the differential cage. Check the gear backlash with feeler gauges and adjust with different thickness thrust washers.
47 Lock the cross-shaft by inserting the locking pin (6) into the differential cage using a parallel pin punch.
48 Using a suitable drift, an engineer's vice or a press, refit the differential unit bearing race inner tracks (74) onto the differential housing (71). Do not fit the adjustment shims previously noted during dismantling.
49 Fit the axle casing spreader adaptors and spreader to the axle casing.
50 Fit the bearing cage and outer track onto the inner track and place the differential unit into the axle casing.
51 Mount a dial indicator gauge onto the adaptor plate so that the gauge stylus rests on the crownwheel mounting flange of the differential housing (Fig. 8.15).
52 Carefully move the differential unit as far away as possible from the dial indicator gauge and zero the dial. Now move the differential unit as near to the indicator as possible and note the reading. Call the dimension 'A' (Fig. 8.16).
53 Remove the differential unit from the casing and refit the crownwheel (7) to the differential cage (71). Refit and tighten the bolts using

a torque wrench set to 46 lbf ft (6·4 kgf m).
54 Refit the differential unit into the axle carrier but do not install the differential bearing caps (9). Fit a dial indicator gauge onto the axle casing cover mounting flange, with the gauge stylus resting against the bolt head side of the crownwheel mounting flange on the differential housing.
55 Move the differential unit away from the indicator until the crownwheel is fully in mesh with the pinion. Zero the dial. Slide the differential unit in the opposite direction and note the reading from the dial. Call this dimension 'B'.
56 Lift out the differential unit from the axle casing and remove the differential cage bearings using a good quality three leg puller. Make sure that the bearings component parts are kept in sets.
57 Following is an example of the calculation that is now necessary to determine the correct bearing preload and meshing of the gear teeth (see Fig. 8.16).

Dimension A	0·060 in (1·524 mm)
Requisite total pre-load	0·003 in (0·076 mm)
Total shims required	0·063 in (1·600 mm)

Shim thickness required on crownwheel side bearing (Y)

Dimension B	0·025 in (0·635 mm)
Requisite backlack (mean value)	0·005 in (0·127 mm)
Subtraction gives thickness of shims on this side	0·020 in (0·508 mm)

Shim thickness on opposite crownwheel side bearing (X)

Dimension A plus pre-load	0·063 in (1·524 mm)
Shim thickness on crownwheel side	0·020 in (0·508 mm)
Subtraction gives thickness of shims on side 'X'	0·043 in (1·016 mm)

58 Fit the determined thickness shims between the bearing inner track and its abutment on the differential cage.
59 Refit the differential unit and bearing caps (9) in their previously noted original positions and tighten using a torque wrench set to 38 lbf ft (5·2 kgf m).
60 Mount the dial indicator gauge as shown in Fig. 8.17, onto the axle casing cover mounting flange with its stylus resting at 90° to the side of a crownwheel tooth. The backlash should be between 0·004 to 0·006 inch (0·102 to 0·152 mm).
61 Any corrective action may be taken by moving the shims behind the differential bearings from one side of the differential cage to the other.
62 As a final check smear a little mechanics 'blue' on several of the teeth on the crownwheel and rotate the crownwheel a few times. Compare the pattern with that given in Fig. 8.18.

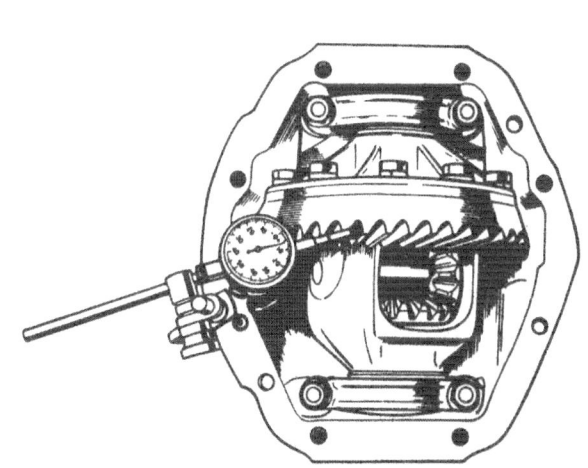
Fig. 8.17 Checking the crownwheel backlash (Sec 3)

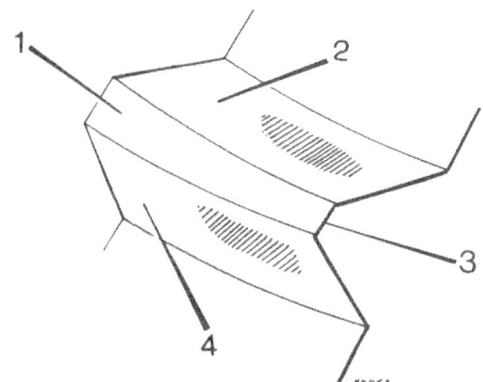
Fig. 8.18 Correct crownwheel tooth pattern (Sec 3)

1 Heel (thick end) 3 Toe (thin end)
2 Coast side (concave) 4 Driveside (convex)

4   Axleshafts and hubs – removal, dismantling and refitting

1   The axleshafts and hubs must be removed from the suspension arm, if the universal joints or hub bearings require service attention.

2   Working on one side of the car, remove the hub cap, and loosen the wheel nuts. Chock the front wheels, jack-up the rear of the car and support on stands. Take off the roadwheel.

3   Undo the two countersunk screws holding the brake drum to the hub drive flange.

4   Carefully pull off the brake drum. If it is tight, slacken off the brake adjustment, full details of which are given in Chapter 9. Using a soft faced hammer tap the flange on the circumference of the brake drum to free it from the studs.

5   Remove the six nyloc nuts, arrowed in Fig. 8.19, which hold the bearing housing to the boss on the suspension arm. There is a hole in the hub flange large enough to allow a socket to pass through.

6   Undo the four nuts and bolts holding the inboard universal coupling to the inner axleshaft flange.

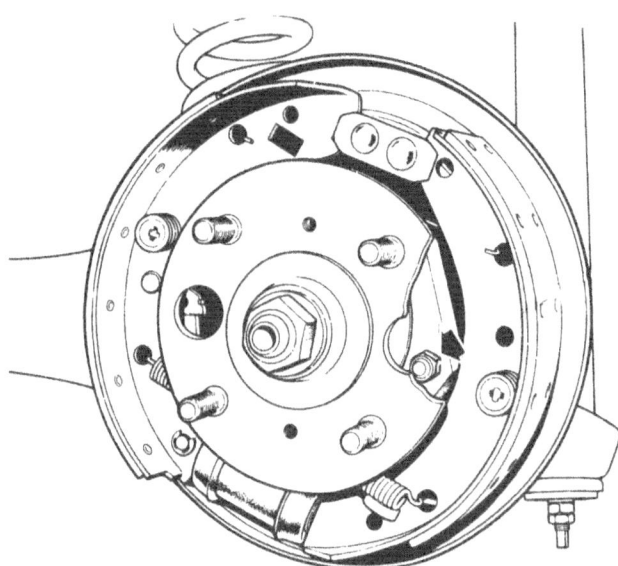

Fig. 8.19 Removing the bearing housing retaining nuts (Sec 4)

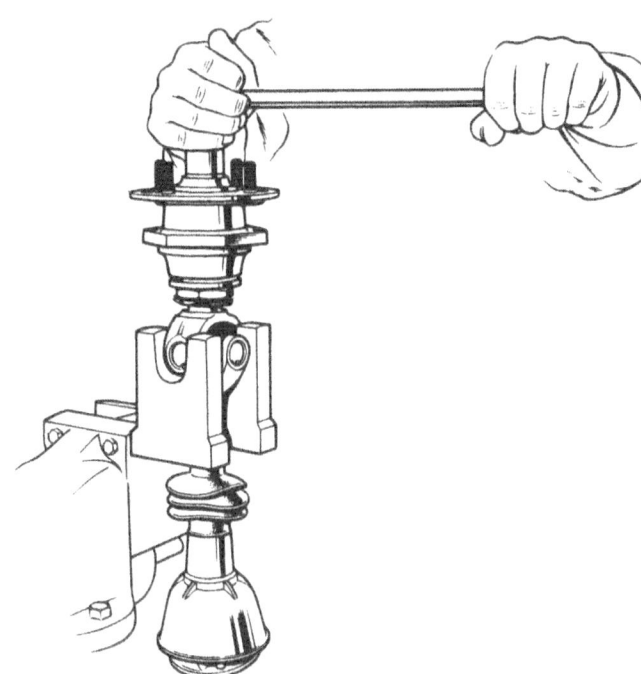

Fig. 8.20 Axleshaft mounted in vice using tool 'S318' (Sec 5)

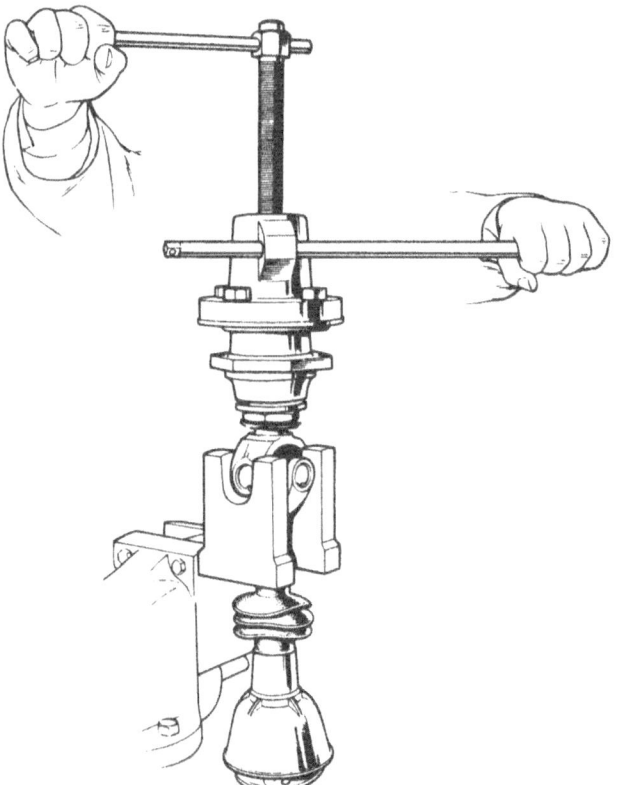

Fig. 8.21 Withdrawing the hub using tool M86C (Sec 5)

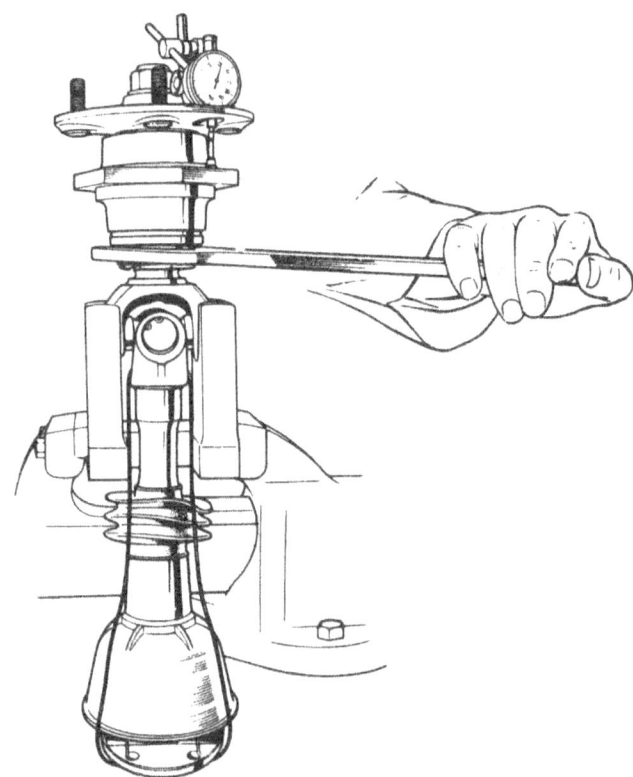

Fig. 8.22 Adjusting the hub endfloat (Sec 5)

7   Use a piece of wire threaded through the two universal joints of the axleshaft to stop the shafts from separating.

8   Carefully withdraw the axleshaft through the suspension arm boss.

9   Refitting is the reverse of the removal procedure. Do not forget to remove the wire holding the two universal joints together.

5   Stub axleshaft – dismantling and reassembly

1   To dismantle this shaft three special tools numbered 'M86C', 'S.318' and 'S.4211A16' are required as well as a torque wrench capable of being set to give a reading of 90 – 100 lb ft (12·5 – 13·8 kg/m) and a dial indicator gauge. If these can be borrowed from the local Leyland agent all well and good, but if not then we would recommend that the following work be left to the local agents:

2   Place the shaft in the holder 'S.318' as shown in Fig. 8.20, which should be mounted in a good sized vice.

3   Using the socket wrench, undo and remove the nut. Lift away the washer and with tool 'M86C' withdraw the hub. Unfortunately, there is no safe alternative method of removing the hub because of the high pressures required (see Fig. 8.21).

4   While the hub is being removed, the bearing housing will also come away with the hub.

5   Lift away the rectangular key and throw away the collapsible spacer as it must not be used again. Lift away the inner hub bearing cone followed by the bearing spacer and stone guard making sure to take note which way round it fits.

6   Undo the lockwasher tabs and turn the adjustment nut and locknut one complete revolution towards the universal joint.

7   Support the housing under its mounting face and using a soft metal drift carefully drive out the bearing outer race.

8   It will now be necessary to use tool number 'S.4221A16' to extract the outer hub bearing cone from the hub. A large puller can do this operation provided the feet are such that they can locate at the rear of the bearing inner track.

9   Thoroughly wash all dismantled components in paraffin and dry using a clean rag.

10   Inspect the bearing rollers for signs of wear, pitting or cracking which, if evident, means that the bearing must be renewed. Also inspect the stub shaft and the hub for wear or damage, especially around the inner hub bearing seat. If any part is suspect it should be renewed.

11   To reassemble, first press the outer hub bearing cone up to the shoulder on the hub. A metal tube of suitable diameter may be used to drift the bearing cone into place if a press is not available. Be careful not to tilt the cone when refitting to the hub.

12   Press the outer and inner hub bearing outer races up to the shoulder in the bearing housing. Alternatively, a soft metal drift may be used. As in the previous operation be careful not to tilt the cone when refitting the hub.

13   Refit the inner and outer oil seals.

14   Refit the stoneguard bearing spacer, the inner cone of the inner hub bearing and a new collapsible spacer onto the stubshaft and fit the rectangular key into the stubshaft. The inner end of the key should be in line with the two indentations on the shoulders of the keyway.

15   The bearing housing should be well packed with the correct grade of grease. Ensure that there is plenty of grease in the space between the two roller bearings.

16   Fit the bearing housing over the stubshaft until the inner hub bearing outer race engages with its mating cone. Special care must be taken not to damage the lip of the inner oil seal.

17   Refit the hub onto the stubshaft followed by a plain washer and nut. Using a torque wrench tighten the stubshaft nut to a torque of between 90 and 100 lbf ft (12·5 to 13·8 kgf m).

18   It will now be necessary to reset the bearing endfloat. First with the axleshaft assembled to the holding tool, as shown in Fig. 8.22, tighten the nut to the stoneguard until it is finger tight.

19   Attach a dial indicator gauge onto the hub flange with the stylus touching the bearing housing flange as shown.

20   Firmly pull the bearing housing as far as possible downwards away from the dial indicator gauge. Use a rocking motion to ensure correct contact of the bearing parts and set the dial to zero.

21   Push the bearing housing towards the dial indicator gauge once more using a rocking motion to ensure correct contact of the bearing parts and this time note the reading on the dial.

22   Slowly tighten the large nut one flat at a time. At each flat, repeat the operations in paragraphs 20 and 21 above until an endfloat reading of between 0·002 and 0·005 in (0·05 and 0·12 mm) is obtained, and lock the adjustment nut with the locknut and tab washer.

23   Should, for any reason, insufficient care have been taken and the endfloat is accidentally reduced to below 0·002 inch (0·05 mm) the collapsible spacer must be renewed yet again. It will not spring back to its original dimensions.

6   Outer axleshaft – dismantling and reassembly

1   Wash the exterior of the shaft and joints in paraffin and dry using a clean non-fluffy rag.

2   Place the assembly on a clean bench top and remove the wire that was previously threaded through the two universal joints.

3   Undo the clips holding the two ends of the rubber gaiter to the inner and outer axleshafts.

4   Carefully withdraw the outer sliding axleshaft from the fixed shaft. Lift away the gaiter and clips.

5   Inspect the gaiter for signs of cracking, splitting or hardening, especially the area around the two clips, and obtain a new gaiter if necessary.

6   Dismantling of the universal joints is identical to that for the propeller shaft universal joints, full details of which are given in Chapter 7.

7   Fault diagnosis – rear axle

Symptom	Reason/s
Vibration	Worn axleshaft bearing
	Loose axleshaft flange bolts
	Roadwheels require balancing
Noise on drive or coasting	Worn differential gears
	Worn or incorrectly adjusted crownwheel and pinion
	Lack of lubricant
'Clunk' on acceleration or deceleration	Worn driveshaft joints or loose flange bolts

Chapter 9 Braking system

Contents

Specifications

System type .... Dual circuit hydraulic, vacuum servo assisted. Mechanical-operating handbrake to the rear brakes

Front brakes
Disc diameter .... 10·625 in (270 mm)
Disc run-out (max) .... 0·007 in (0·178 mm)
Minimum pad thickness .... 0·125 in (3 mm)

Rear brakes
Type .... Drum, self adjusting, leading and trailing shoe
Drum diameter .... 9 in (228 mm)

Servo type .... Direct acting with 3 : 1 boost ratio (nominal)

Torque wrench settings

	lbf ft	kgf m
Caliper securing bolts	65	9·0
Disc to hub	34	4·7
Brake pedal bracket to bulkhead	20	2·8
Master cylinder nuts	20	2·8

1 General description

Disc brakes are fitted to the front wheels of all models with drum brakes at the rear. The mechanically operated handbrake operates on the rear wheels only.

The brakes fitted to the front two wheels are of the rotating disc and static caliper type, with one caliper per disc, each caliper containing two piston operated friction pads, which, on application of the footbrake, pinch the disc rotating between them.

Application of the footbrake creates hydraulic pressure in the master cylinder and fluid from the cylinder travels via steel and flexible pipes to the cylinders in each half of the calipers, the fluid so pushing the pistons, to which are attached the friction pads, into contact with either side of each disc.

Two rubber seals are fitted to the operating cylinders. The outer seal prevents moisture and dirt from entering the cylinder. The inner seal, which is retained in a groove inside the cylinder, prevents fluid leakage and provides a running clearance for the pad irrespective of how worn it is, by moving it back a fraction when the brake pedal is released.

As the friction pad wears so the pistons move further out of the cylinders and the level of the fluid in the hydraulic reservoir drops, thus disc pad wear is taken up automatically and eliminates the need for periodic adjustment by the owner.

The rear brakes are of the self-adjusting, single leading shoe type, with one brake cylinder per wheel for both shoes. A lever assembly is fitted between the two shoes of each brake unit and attached to this is a system of cables which in turn is connected to the handbrake lever. The handbrake also operates the automatic adjusters for the rear brakes. It is unusual to have to adjust the handbrake system as the efficiency of this system is largely dependent on the condition of the brake linings and the adjustment of the brake shoes. The handbrake can, however, be adjusted separately to the footbrake operated hydraulic system.

Connected to the brake pedal is a servo unit onto which is mounted the master cylinder. It increases the hydraulic line pressure whilst decreasing the driver's pedal effort.

A brake pressure differential warning actuator switch is mounted on the left-hand wing valance and should a loss of pressure occur in the hydraulic system a warning light on the instrument panel will light-up.

The hydraulic system is a dual circuit type with a tandem type master cylinder having two pressure outlets serving the separate independent circuits to the front and rear brakes.

2 Front disc pads – inspection and renewal

1 Apply the handbrake and loosen the front wheel nuts. Jack-up the front of the car, and remove the roadwheel.
2 Inspect the amount of friction material left on the friction pads. The pads must be renewed when the thickness of the material has worn down to $\frac{1}{8}$ in (3 mm).
3 Press down on the pad retaining spring and extract the pad retaining split pins (photo).
4 Take off the spring clips and with a slight rotational movement, remove the friction pads using a pair of sharp nosed pliers, if necessary. Lift away the anti-squeal shims (photo).
5 Carefully clean the recesses in the caliper in which the friction pad assemblies lie, and the exposed face of each piston from all traces of dirt and rust.
6 Remove the cap from the hyraulic fluid reservoir and place a large rag underneath the unit. Press the pistons in each half of the caliper right in – this will cause the fluid level in the reservoir to rise and possibly to spill over the brim onto the protective rag.
7 Fit the new friction pads into the calipers. When fitting new pads they must be renewed on both front wheels.
8 Check that the new friction pad assemblies move freely in the caliper recesses and remove any high spots on the edge of the pressure plate by carefully filing.
9 Check that the retaining spring clips show no sign of damage or loss of tension and then, if sound, refit them, press them down and insert the split pins.
10 Refit the roadwheels and remove the jacks. Press the brake pedal several times to adjust the brakes. Top-up the master cylinder as required.

3 Rear brake shoes – inspection and renewal

After a high mileage it will be necessary to fit replacement shoes with new linings. Refitting new brake linings to old shoes is not always satisfactory, but if the services of a local garage or workshop with brake lining equipment is available, then there is no reason why your own shoes should not be successfully relined.

1 Remove the hub cap, loosen off the wheel nuts, then securely jack-up the car and remove the roadwheel. Ensure the handbrake is off.
2 Refer to Fig. 9.1 and undo the two countersunk screws that hold the brake drum onto the hub.
3 Remove the brake drum. If it proves obstinate tap the rim gently with a soft headed hammer. Should this be unsatisfactory rotate the brake drum until the hole in the flange is aligned with the ratchet spring.
4 Lever the upper adjusting plate upwards so as to release the ratchet. Then lift away the drum (photo).
5 Remove the brake shoe steady pin cups and springs, and extract the brake shoe steady pins (photo).
6 Carefully ease the ends of the two brake shoes from the wheel cylinder pistons.
7 Unhook the pull off springs, making a note of their positioning to ensure correct reassembly (photo).
8 Unhook the cross lever tension spring (photo).
9 Lift the ends of the two brake shoes from the pivot plate and remove the brake shoes.
10 Thoroughly clean all traces of dust from the shoes, backplates, and brake drums with a dry paint brush. Brake dust can cause squeal and judder and it is, therefore, important to clean the brakes thoroughly.
11 Check that the pistons are free in their cylinders; that the rubber dust covers are undamaged and in position; and that there are no hydraulic fluid leaks.
12 Prior to reassembly smear a trace of white brake grease to all sliding surfaces. *Do not* lubricate the teeth on the brake shoe adjuster plates. The shoes should be free to slide on the wheel cylinder pistons and pivot plate. It is vital that no grease or oil comes into contact with the brake drums or the brake linings.
13 Refitting is a straightforward reversal of the removal procedure, but note the following points:

(a) *Do not omit to fit the steady pins and inner and outer washers if they were removed*
(b) *Ensure that the return springs are in their correct holes in the shoes and lie between them and the backplate*
(c) *Once the shoes have been refitted, lift the adjuster upper release plate and then refit the brake drum. Depress the footbrake pedal several times to bring the shoes automatically to their correct adjustment.*

4 Disc calipers – removal and refitting

1 Jack-up the front of the car and remove the roadwheel.
2 Remove the friction pads as described in Section 2.
3 Disconnect the flexible brake hose and plug the hose to prevent loss of fluid.
4 Unscrew and remove the two bolts which hold the caliper to the stub axle and then withdraw the caliper.
5 Refitting is a reversal of removal but tighten the caliper securing bolts to the specified torque and bend over the tabs of the lockplate.
6 Reconnect the flexible brake hose as described in Section 13 and finally bleed the hydraulic system as described in Section 14.

2.3 Remove the retaining split pins

2.4 Pull out the friction pads

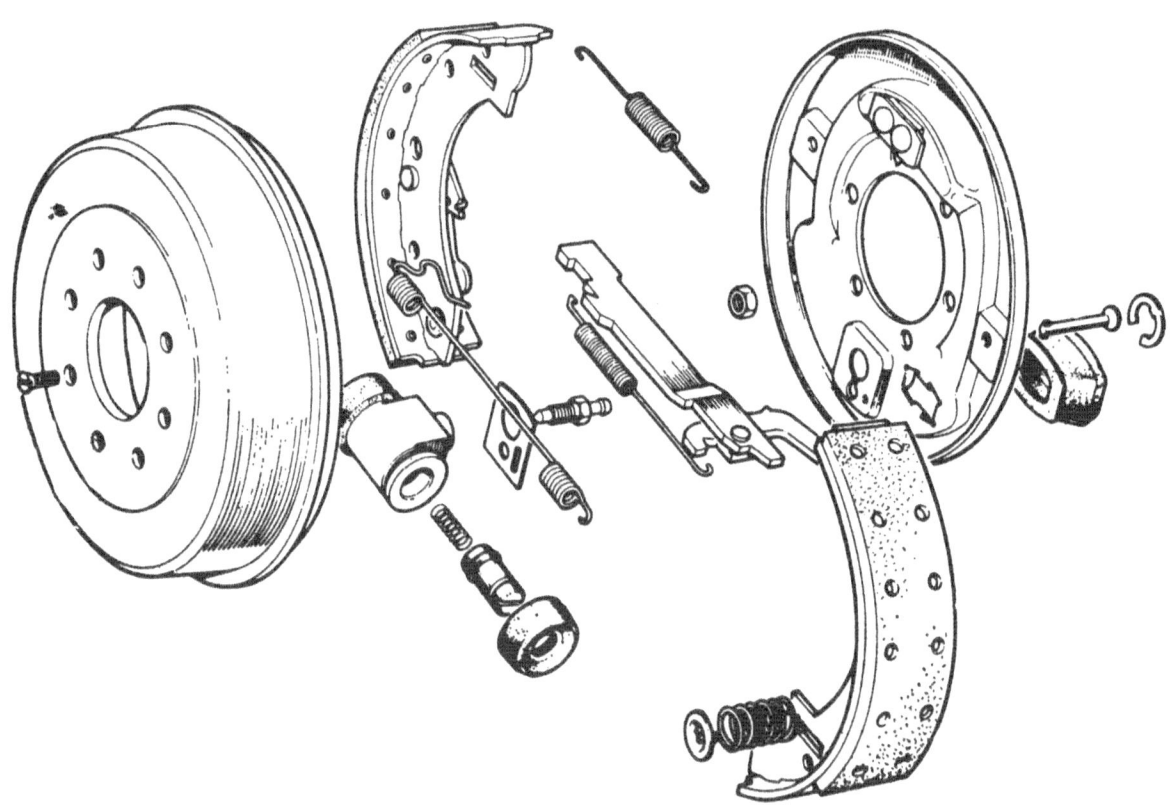

Fig. 9.1 Component parts of rear drum brake (Sec 3)

3.4 Rear brakes with drum removed

3.5 Remove the brake shoe steady pin cups and springs

3.7 Unhook the pull off spring

3.8 Unhook the cross lever tension spring

5 Disc caliper – dismantling and reassembly

1 Remove the caliper as described in the preceding Section.
2 Clean the exterior with brake fluid or methylated spirit. Do not use paraffin or petrol for this purpose as it will affect the seal between the two halves of the caliper body. *On no account unscrew the bolts which secure the two halves of the caliper together.*
3 Hold one piston in its fully depressed state and apply air pressure from a tyre pump to the fluid inlet hole in order to eject the opposite piston.
4 Extract the dust seal and its retainer and carefully prise the inner seal from its cylinder groove
5 Inspect the surfaces of the piston and cylinder for scoring or 'bright' wear areas. If these are evident, renew the entire caliper assembly.
6 If the components are in good condition, install a new inner seal which is supplied in the repair kit. Install the seal using the fingers only, having first dipped it in clean hydraulic fluid.
7 Dip the piston in clean brake fluid and insert it squarely into the cylinder so that approximately $\frac{5}{16}$ in (7·9 mm) is left protruding.
8 Install the new dust seal and retainer.
9 Hold the just installed piston in the fully depressed position and, by again applying air pressure, eject the opposite piston and repeat all the foregoing operations.

6 Brake disc – inspection, removal and refitting

1 Jack-up the front of the car and remove the roadwheel. Extract the disc pads.
2 Unbolt the caliper unit and support it on a block or tie it up with wire to prevent it from straining the flexible brake hose.
3 Check the disc for deep scoring or grooves, if evident, then the disc must be renewed. Light scoring is normal.
4 Finally, check for run-out, using either a dial gauge or a fixed block and feeler blades. The maximum run-out must not exceed that specified in the Specifications Section at the beginning of this Chapter.
5 To remove the disc, withdraw the hub as described in Chapter 11 and then unscrew and remove the four disc to hub bolts.
6 Refitting the disc is a reversal of removal, refer to Chapter 11 for method of installation and adjustment of the front hub.

7 Rear brake wheel cylinder – removal, servicing and refitting

1 Jack-up the rear of the vehicle, remove the roadwheel, brake drum and brake shoes as described in Section 3.

2 If the wheel cylinder is leaking, the seals can be renewed without withdrawing the cylinder from the brake backplate.
3 Have an assistant depress the brake pedal gently to eject the wheel cylinder pistons. Be ready to catch them and expelled fluid.
4 Examine the surfaces of the pistons and cylinder for scoring or 'bright' wear areas. If these are evident, the wheel cylinder must be renewed. To remove the cylinder, disconnect the fluid pipe union and then prise off the circlip which secures it to the backplate (Fig. 9.3).
5 If the components are in good condition, discard the old seals and install the new ones, using the fingers only to manipulate them into position. Dip the assembled pistons in clean brake fluid and insert them into the cylinder body.
6 Refit the brake shoes and drum, then bleed the system as described in Section 14.

8 Rear brake backplate – removal and refitting

1 Jack-up the car and remove the rear roadwheel and brake drum.
2 Remove the brake shoes and disconnect the handbrake cable at the backplate.
3 Disconnect the driveshaft inner flange at the differential.
4 Disconnect the brake pipe union at the rear slave cylinder.
5 Remove the six nuts securing the rear hub bearing housing and backplate to the trailing arm.
6 Withdraw the hub complete with driveshaft.
7 Remove the backplate.
8 Refitting is the reverse of the removal procedure. Bleed the hydraulic system.

9 Brake drum – inspection and renovation

1 After a high mileage, it is possible for the drum interior to have worn oval or become scored due to delayed renewal of the brake shoes after they had worn down to the rivets.
2 Test for ovality with an internal caliper at several different points. If machining the interior of the drum to correct these conditions will cause the internal diameter of the drum to exceed the original dimension (9 in [228 mm]) by more than 0·030 in (0·76 mm), then the drum should be renewed.

10 Master cylinder – removal and refitting

1 Drain the fluid from the master cylinder reservoir by attaching a rubber tube to one of the rear brake bleed screws. Unscrew the bleed screw one turn and pump the fluid out into a suitable container by

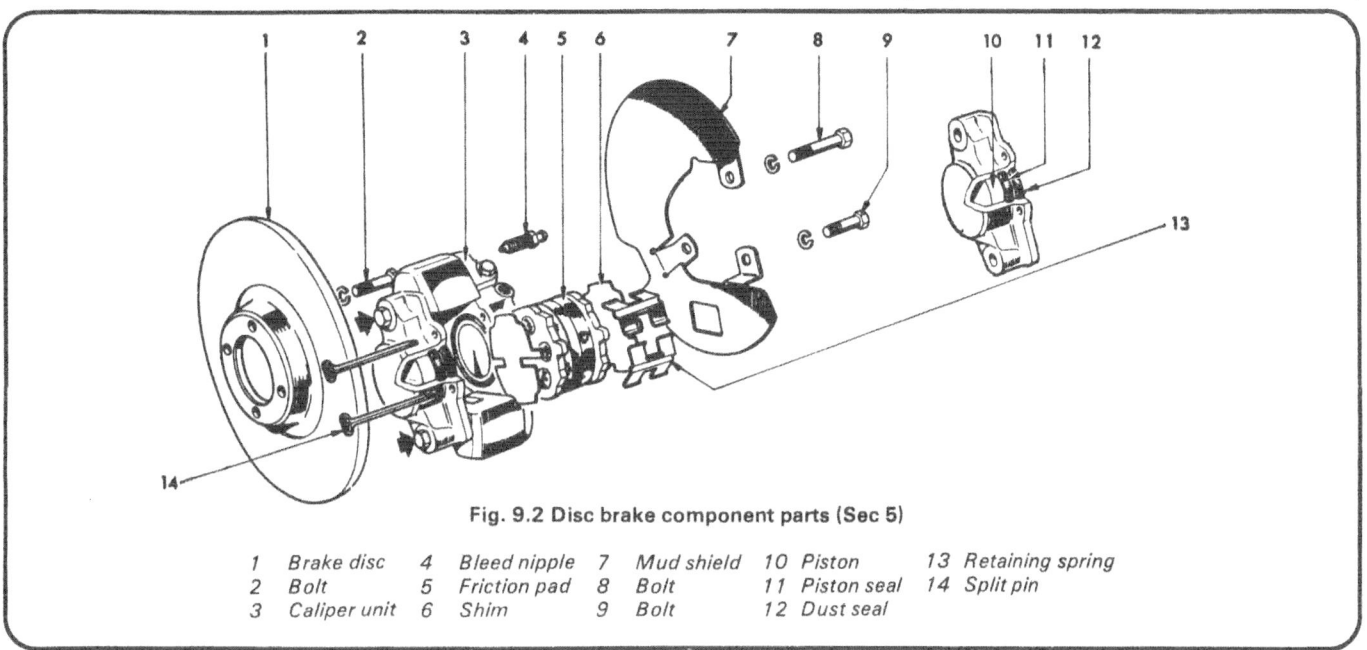

Fig. 9.2 Disc brake component parts (Sec 5)

1	Brake disc	4	Bleed nipple	7	Mud shield
2	Bolt	5	Friction pad	8	Bolt
3	Caliper unit	6	Shim	9	Bolt

10	Piston	13	Retaining spring
11	Piston seal	14	Split pin
12	Dust seal		

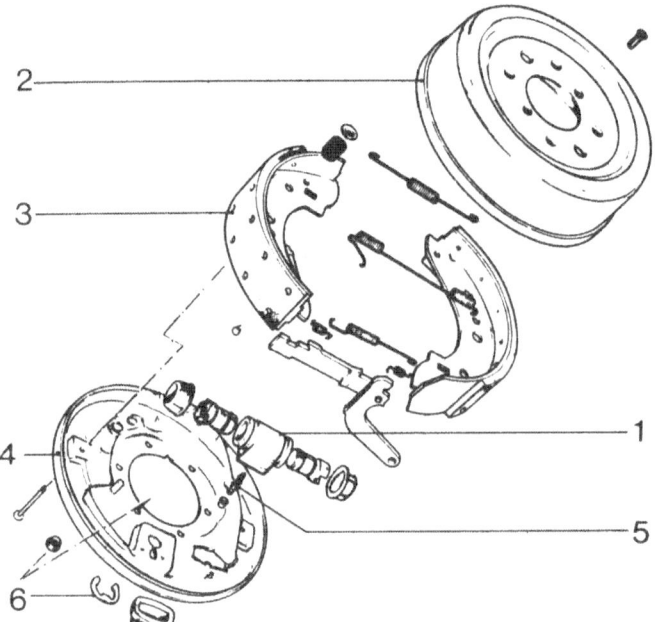

Fig. 9.3 Rear wheel brake cylinder removal (Sec 7)

1 Wheel cylinder
2 Brake drum
3 Brake shoe
4 Backplate
5 Bleed screw
6 Circlip

means of the brake pedal. Hold the pedal against the floor at the end of each stroke and tighten the bleed screw, then when the pedal returns to its normal position, loosen the bleed screw and repeat the process until the half of the master cylinder reservoir that serves the rear brakes is empty. Repeat the procedure with the rubber tube attached to one of the front caliper bleed screws to empty the front brake circuit.

2   Clean the area around the pressure pipe unions on the side of the master cylinder and disconnect the pipes. Protect the ends of the pipe to prevent the ingress of dirt.

3   Remove the vacuum servo unit and master cylinder as an assembly as described in Section 19. It is not possible to remove the master cylinder separately as the lower securing nut is inaccessible when the servo and master cylinder are fitted in position on the bulkhead.

4   Remove the nuts and spring washers securing the master cylinder to the servo unit and separate the master cylinder from the servo unit (photo).

5   Refitting is the reverse of the removal procedure.

6   Top-up the master cylinder reservoir with fresh hydraulic fluid and bleed the system as described in Section 14.

11 Master cylinder – dismantling and reassembly

1   Undo the four securing bolts and lift off the fluid reservoir.

2   Push back the retainer and springs, then remove the retaining spring clip, cup, retainer and the two springs from the master cylinder. Remove the rubber seal washer (photos).

3   Remove the circlip from the groove in the bore of the cylinder and take out the nylon spacer, rubber seal and thin washer. Remove the second circlip and the thick washer, then withdraw the pushrod, piston, spring and seals assembly (photos).

4   Pull back the return spring and using a small diameter pin punch drive out the roll pin and separate the piston assembly (photo).

5   Remove the old seals.

6   Thoroughly clean all the parts in industrial methylated spirits or hydraulic fluid. Ensure that the by-pass ports are clean (photo).

7   Examine the bore of the cylinder carefully for any signs of scoring or corrosion. If the bore is in good condition, new seals can be fitted, but if there is any doubt about the condition of the bore then a new cylinder must be fitted.

8   Assemble all the components wet by dipping them in clean brake fluid.

9   Reassembly is the reverse of the dismantling procedure. Make sure the seals are fitted the correct way round and that the circlips are located correctly in the grooves in the cylinder bore.

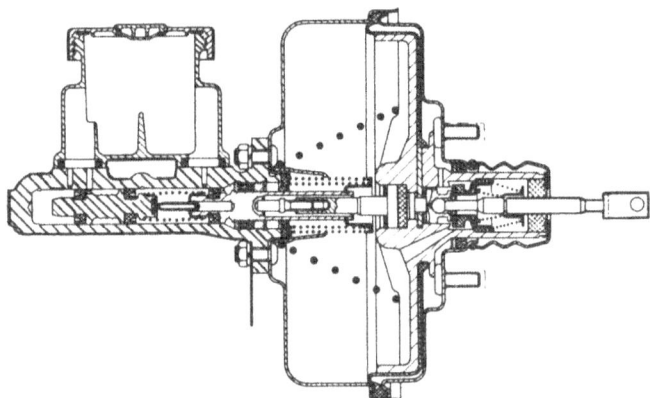

Fig. 9.4 Sectional view of master cylinder and servo unit (Sec 10)

12 Pressure differential warning actuator switch

1   This is essentially a shuttle valve in which a piston is maintained 'in balance' by the two equal pressures of the two independent hydraulic braking circuits (photo).

2   Should a leak occur in one circuit the loss of pressure will cause the piston to be displaced and it will complete an electrical circuit to illuminate a warning light on the instrument panel.

3   Should the piston of the pressure differential warning actuator have been displaced due to a leak in the hydraulic system or over enthusiastic bleeding (see Section 14) then centralise it in the following manner.

4   Fit a bleed tube to a brake bleed nipple of the hydraulic circuit which has not had a leak nor just been bled.

5   Open the bleed screw.

6   Switch on the ignition (the brake warning light will illuminate but the oil warning light will not).

7   Apply a steady pressure to the footbrake pedal until the brake warning light dims and the oil pressure light comes on. A click will be heard as the piston in the differential switch is centralised.

8   Retighten the bleed screw.

9   Should excessive pedal pressure have been applied and the piston moves to the opposite side of the valve, the centralising procedure will have to be repeated by opening a bleed nipple on the opposing hydraulic circuit.

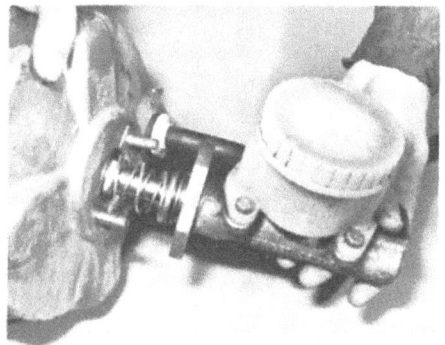

10.4 Separating the master cylinder from the servo unit

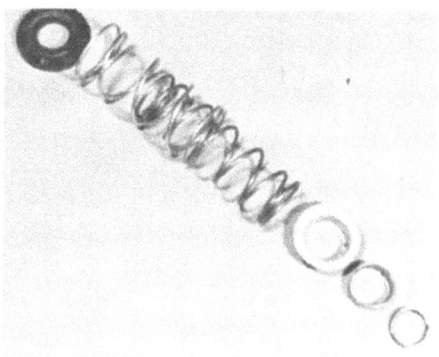

11.2a External parts of the master cylinder

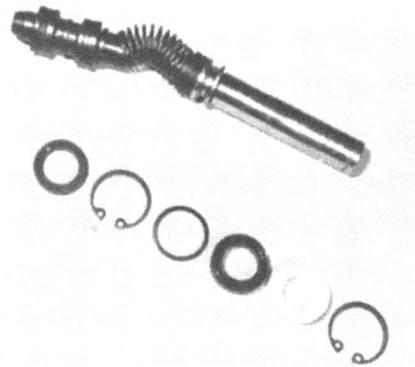

11.2b Internal parts of the master cylinder

11.3a Remove the first circlip, the nylon spacer, and rubber seal and then ...

11.3b ... the thin washer, second circlip and thick washer

11.3c Withdraw the piston assembly

11.4 Pull back the spring and remove the roll pin

11.6 Master cylinder body and fluid reservoir

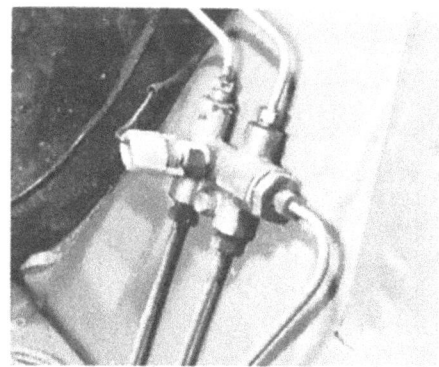

12.1 The PDWA switch is mounted on the left-hand wing valance

13 Flexible brake hoses – inspection, removal and refitting

Inspect the condition of the flexible hydraulic hoses leading from the chassis mounted metal pipes to the brake backplates. If any are swollen, damaged, cut or chafed, they must be renewed.

1   Unscrew the metal pipe union nut from its connection to the hose, and then, holding the hexagon on the base with a spanner, unscrew the attachment nut and washer.

2   The chassis end of the hose can now be pulled from the chassis mounting brackets and will be quite free.

3   Disconnect the flexible hydraulic hose at the backplate by un-screwing it from the brake cylinder. **Note**: *When releasing the hose from the backplate, the chassis end must always be freed first.*

4   Refitting is a straightforward reversal of the above procedure.

14 Brake hydraulic system – bleeding

1   Removal of all the air from the hydraulic system is essential to the correct working of the braking system, but before undertaking this examine the fluid reservoir cap to ensure that both vent holes, one on top and the second underneath but not in line, are clear; check the level of fluid and top-up if required.

2   Check all brake line unions and connections for possible seepage, and at the same time check the condition of the rubber hoses which may be perished.

3   If the condition of the wheel cylinders is in doubt, check for possible signs of fluid leakage.

4   If there is any possibility of the incorrect fluid having been put into the system, drain all the fluid out and flush through with methylated spirit. Renew all piston seals and cups since they will be affected and

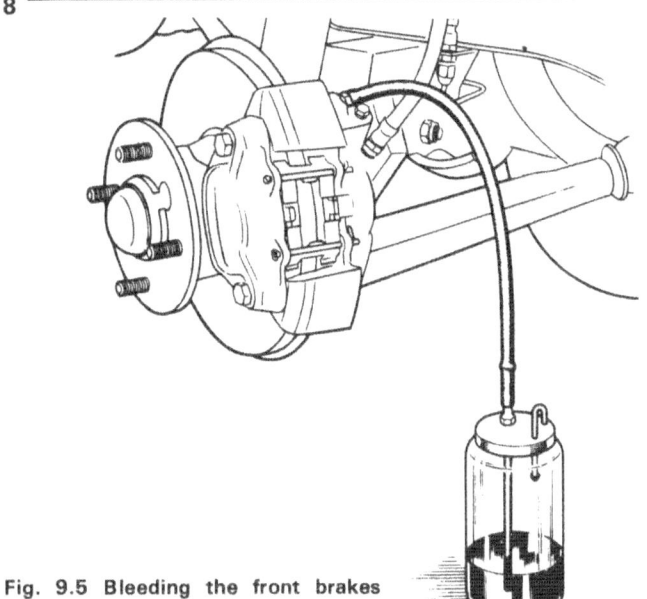

Fig. 9.5 Bleeding the front brakes
(Sec 14)

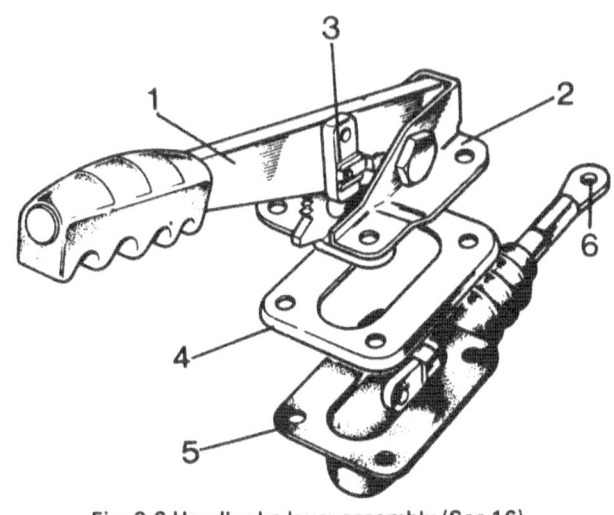

Fig. 9.6 Handbrake lever assembly (Sec 16)

1 Lever   4 Clamp plate
2 Bracket   5 Boot
3 Switch   6 Compensator link cable

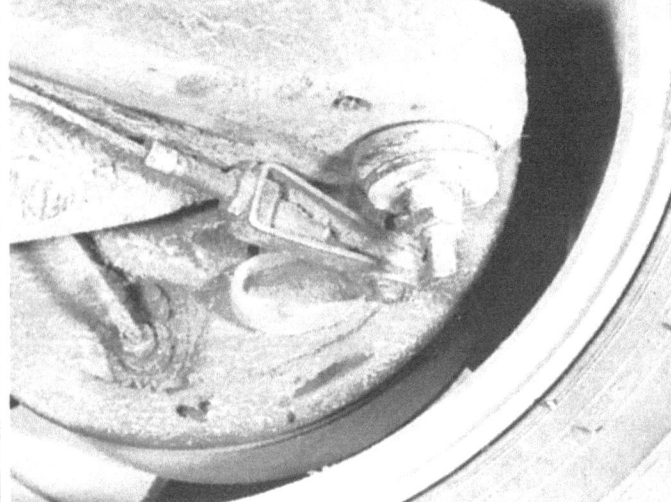

15.3 The handbrake cable is attached to the brake lever on the back-plate

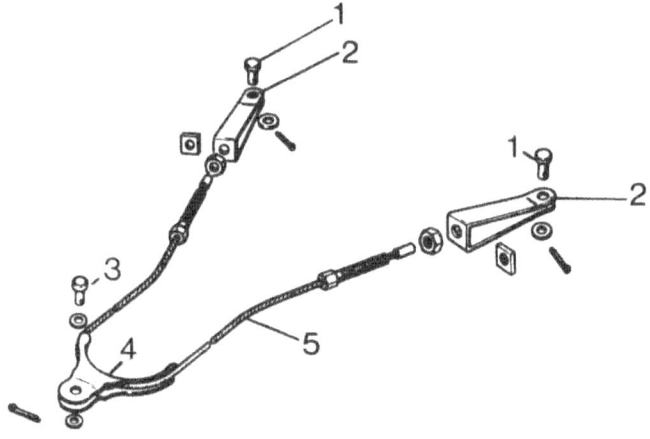

Fig. 9.7 Handbrake cable assembly (Sec 17)

1 Clevis pin   4 Compensator
2 Fork end   5 Cable
3 Clevis pin

15.5 Maintain the handbrake cable compensator in the central position

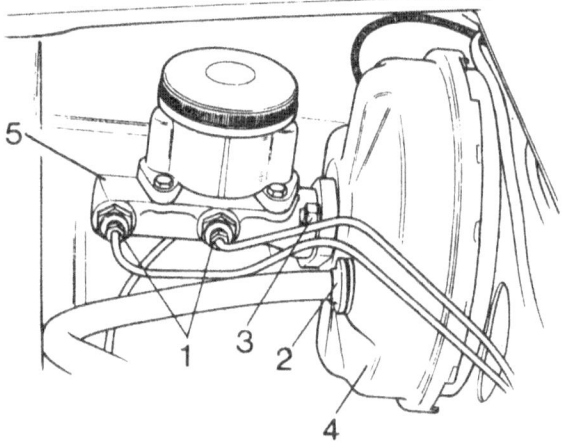

Fig. 9.8 Vacuum servo unit removal (Sec 19)

1 Brake pipe connections   4 Vacuum servo unit
2 Vacuum pipe   5 Brake master cylinder
3 Master cylinder securing bolts

could possibly fail under pressure.

5   Gather together a clean jar, a length of tubing which fits tightly over the bleed nipple, and a tin of brake fluid.

6   If both circuits are to be bled, bleed the rear brakes first but in any event always bleed the brake furthest from the master cylinder.

7   Attach a length of rubber tubing to the bleed nipple and submerge its end in a jar containing an inch or two of hydraulic fluid (Fig. 9.5).

8   If the rear brakes are being bled, fully release the handbrake.

9   Unscrew the bleed nipple one half a turn and then have an assistant depress the brake pedal *gently* until resistance is felt. Allow the pedal to return slowly.

10   Repeat the operation until no more air bubbles are ejected from the end of the tube which is below the level of the fluid in the jar.

11   Never test the pedal for sponginess midway through the bleeding process or the piston in the pressure differential switch will be displaced (see Section 12).

12   Tighten the bleed nipple when the brake pedal is in the fully depressed position.

13   Make sure that the master cylinder reservoir is kept topped-up during the bleeding process with clean brake fluid which has been kept in a sealed container and has remained unshaken for at least 24 hours.

14   Discard fluid which has been ejected from the bleed tube.

15 Handbrake – adjustment

1   The handbrake adjustment is normally taken up automatically as the rear brakes adjust themselves. However, after a very high mileage, it is possible that the cables will have stretched slightly and will, therefore require some adjustment.

2   To adjust the cables, first chock the front wheels adequately, release the handbrake then raise the rear wheels. Support the rear of the car on firmly based axle stands.

3   Now remove the clevis pins from the fork ends behind the rear backplates (photo).

4   Operate the handbrake lever on the rear backplates to ensure that minimum shoe/drum clearance exists.

5   Whilst maintaining the handbrake cable compensator in the central position, adjust the cable forks so that the clevis pins can be entered without straining the cables at all (photo).

6   Now fit the clevis pins and new split pins. The head of the clevis pin should be to the top of the fork. Lock the fork ends by tightening the locknuts.

7   Remove the axle-stands and lower the car. Check the operation of the handbrake.

16 Handbrake lever – removal and refitting

1   Chock the front wheels, release the handbrake, jack-up the rear of the car and support on firmly based stands.

2   Working under the car, extract the split pin securing the compensator clevis pin. Lift away the plain washer and withdraw the clevis pin noting that the head is uppermost.

3   Now working inside the car, take out the two bolts securing each front seat slide to the floor panels and lift away the two front seats.

4   Release the two front seat safety belts from the buckle clamps.

5   Lift out the rear ashtray container, undo the securing screws and remove the ashtray casing. Remove the ashtray console securing bolt, lift out the console and then undo the seat belt buckle clamp securing bolts and remove the buckle clamp.

6   Remove the two screws located under the console panel in front of the gear lever after prising off the panel. Pull back the carpet to gain access to the handbrake lever bracket attaching bolts.

7   Disconnect the electrical lead from the handbrake switch located under the handbrake lever gaiter.

8   Remove the handbrake bracket to floor securing bolts and lift out the handbrake lever assembly.

9   Refitting the handbrake lever is the reverse of the removal procedure. Do not forget to connect the wiring to the handbrake warning light switch.

17 Handbrake cable – renewal

1   Chock the front wheels, raise the rear of the car and support it on

firmly based stands. Release the handbrake.

2   Withdraw the split pin from the clevis pin securing the handbrake lever cable to the compensator and remove the washers and the clevis pin.

3   Disconnect the handbrake lever from the handbrake operating levers at the back of each rear wheel by removing the clevis pins. Note that the head of the clevis pin is to the top of the fork.

4   Slacken the locknuts and remove the fork ends and locknuts from the cable.

5   Refitting the handbrake cable is the reverse of the removal procedure. Adjust the handbrake cable as described in Section 15.

18 Vacuum servo unit – general description

The vacuum servo unit is fitted into the braking system of a car to make braking easier by reducing the physical effort required by the driver to depress the brake pedal and so bring the car to a halt or slow down from high speed.

The servo unit and hydraulic master cylinder are connected together so that the servo unit piston rod acts as the master cylinder pushrod. The driver's braking effort is transmitted through another pushrod to the servo unit piston and its built-in control system. The servo unit piston does not fit tightly into the cylinder but has a strong diaphragm to keep its edges in constant contact with the cylinder walls so ensuring an airtight seal between the two parts. The forward chamber is held under vacuum conditions created in the inlet manifold of the engine and, during periods when the brake pedal is not in use, the controls open a passage to the rear chamber so placing it under vacuum conditions as well. When the brake pedal is depressed the vacuum passage to the rear chamber is cut off and the chamber opened to atmospheric pressure. The consequent rush of air pushes the servo piston forward in the vacuum chamber and operates the main pushrod to the master cylinder.

The controls are designed so that assistance is given under all conditions and when the brakes are not required vacuum in the rear chamber is established when the brake pedal is released. All air from the atmosphere entering the rear chamber is passed through a small air filter.

19 Vacuum servo unit – removal and refitting

1   Drain the brake fluid from the master cylinder reservoir and disconnect the brake pipes as described in Section 10.

2   Disconnect the vacuum hose from the servo unit.

3   Working inside the car withdraw the split pin from the clevis pin connecting the pushrod fork to the brake pedal and remove the washer and clevis pin.

4   Undo the four nuts attaching the servo unit to the brake pedal bracket and remove the spring washers.

5   Remove the servo unit (complete with master cylinder) from the engine compartment. Undo the two attaching bolts and remove the master cylinder.

6   Refitting is the reverse of the removal procedure. Do not forget to reconnect the vacuum pipe (photo).

7   Bleed the hydraulic system as described in Section 14.

20 Vacuum servo unit – servicing

If the brake servo unit is faulty and requires overhaul it is recommended that a service exchange unit is obtained rather than try to repair it. Under normal driving conditions the servo will not require attention, however it is recommended that the filter element is renewed every 36 000 miles (60 000 km).

1   To remove the filter, first remove the servo unit as described in Section 19.

2   Slide the rubber boot and end cap along the pushrod and withdraw the old filter from the neck of the diaphragm housing.

3   Press a new filter into position then fit the end cap and rubber boot.

4   Refit the servo unit.

5   The brake servo non-return valve can be renewed by disconnecting the vacuum pipe from the servo unit and unscrewing the valve

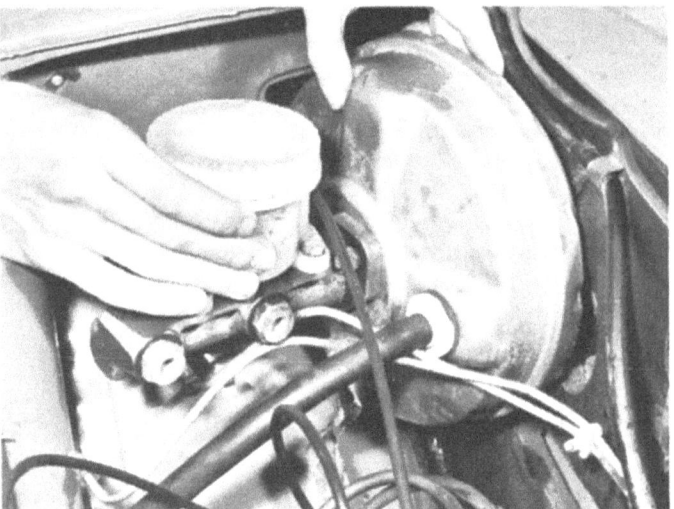

19.6 Refitting the vacuum servo and master cylinder assembly

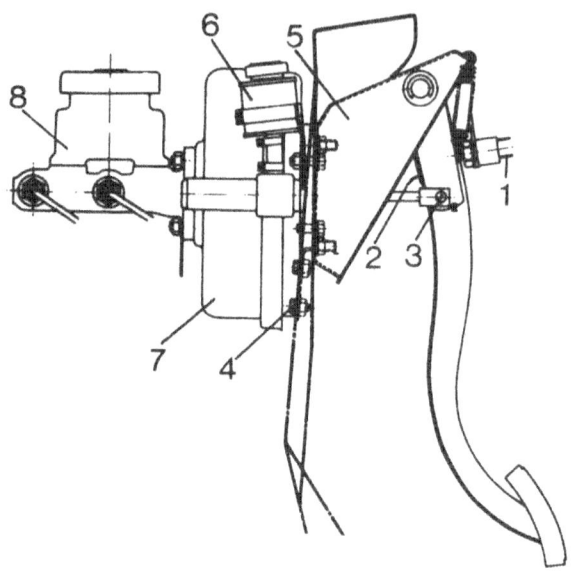

Fig. 9.9 Removing the pedal assembly (Sec 21)

1 Brake switch	5 Support bracket
2 Brake pedal	6 Clutch master cylinder
3 Clevis pin	7 Servo unit
4 Bolts and nuts	8 Brake master cylinder

from the front shell. When fitting the non-return valve always use a new O-ring seal.

21 Brake and clutch pedal assembly – removal and refitting

1   It is unusual for either the brake or clutch pedal to require repair except for the possibility of a worn pivot shaft or pedal bushes.
2   Working from inside the car with the front seats well back, first disconnect the two cable terminals from the brake light switch.
3   Withdraw the split pins from the clevis pins which secure the brake pedal to the servo unit pushrod and the clutch pedal (manual gearbox) to the clutch master cylinder.
4   Undo the six support bracket mounting bolts and the four nuts.
5   Using string or wire support the weight of the servo unit and master cylinder assembly and then lift out the support bracket and pedal assembly.

6   Carefully unhook the return springs and remove the circlips from the ends of the pedal shaft using a thin screwdriver.
7   Using a drift of suitable diameter carefully drive out the pivot shaft. Collect the two large spring washers.
8   If the bushes in the pedal bosses require renewing, drive out the old bushes with a drift. Renewal of the bushes can be easily performed by carefully tightening the jaws of a vice, so pushing the bushes into position.
9   Reassembly and refitting of the bracket and pedal assembly is the reverse sequence to the dismantling and removal procedure. Grease the pedal bushes before refitting the pivot shaft.

22 Fault diagnosis – braking system

Symptom	Reason
Pedal travels almost to floor before brakes operate	Brake fluid level too low Caliper leaking or wheel cylinder leaking Master cylinder leaking (bubbles in master cylinder fluid) Brake flexible hose leaking Brake line fractured Brake system unions loose Pad or shoe linings over 75% worn Rear brakes badly out of adjustment
Brake pedal feels springy	New linings not yet bedded-in Brake discs or drums badly worn or cracked Master cylinder securing nuts loose
Brake pedal feels 'spongy' and 'soggy'	Caliper or wheel cylinder leaking Master cylinder leaking (bubbles in master cylinder reservoir) Brake pipe line or flexible hose leaking Unions in brake system loose
Excessive effort required to brake car	Pad or shoe linings badly worn New pads or shoes recently fitted – not yet bedded in Harder linings fitted than standard causing increase in pedal pressure Linings and brake drums contaminated with oil, grease or hydraulic fluid

Symptom	Reason/s
Brakes uneven and pulling to one side	Linings and discs or drums contaminated with oil, grease or hydraulic fluid Tyre pressures unequal Brake caliper loose Brake pads or shoes fitted incorrectly Different type of linings fitted at each wheel Anchorages for front suspension or rear suspension loose Brake discs or drums badly worn, cracked or distorted
Brakes tend to bind, drag or lock-on	Rear brakes overadjusted (release automatic adjuster) Air in system

Chapter 10 Electrical system

Contents

Specifications

Battery

Type	12 volt, lead acid
Capacity	56 amp/hour at 20-hour rate
Polarity	Negative earth

Alternator

	11AC	18ACR
Make	Lucas	
Type	**11AC**	**18ACR**
Polarity	Negative earth	Negative earth
Minimum brush length	0.20 in (5.0 mm) protrudes from brush box when free	0.20 in (5.0 mm) protrudes from brush box when free
Nominal output	43 amps	45 amps
Relay type	Lucas 16RA	
Cut-in voltage	2.5 to 3.5 volts	
Drop-off voltage	0.5 to 2.0 volts	
Control unit	Lucas 4TR	

Starter motor

Type	Lucas M418G, pre-engaged
Minimum brush length	0.312 in (7.94 mm)
Brush spring tension	36 oz (1000 g)

Windscreen wiper motor

Type	Lucas 16W, two speed
Drive to wheelboxes	Rack and cable
Armature endfloat	0.002 to 0.008 in (0.05 to 0.20 mm)
Running current (after 60 seconds)	1.5 to 2.0 amps
Wiper speed	
1st speed	46 to 52 rpm
2nd speed	60 to 70 rpm
Minimum brush length	
1st speed	0.180 in (4.76 mm)
2nd speed	0.280 in (7.11 mm)
Earth	0.180 in (4.76 mm)
Brush spring tension	5 to 7 oz (140 to 200 g)

Fuse system

Number of fuses .... 12 in fuse block and two line fuses

Circuit protected:

Fuses No	Circuit	Amps
1-2	Horn, cigarette lighter, puddle lamps, B post lamp, console lamps, glovebox, clock and headlamp flasher	35
3-4	Fuel gauge, temperature gauge, tachometer, windscreen washer, stop lamps, reverse lamps, and turn indicators	35
5-6	Front and tail parking lights	5
7-8	Front side lamp, tail lamp, night dimming relay, number plate lamp, cigarette lighter illumination, automatic transmission selector light and instrument illumination	10
9-10	Not used	
11-12	Headlamp main beam 1	25
13-14	Headlamp main beam 2	25
15-16	Headlamp dip beam RH	10
17-18	Headlamp dip beam LH	10
19-20	Windscreen wiper motor	15
21-22	Heater motor	25
23-24	Overdrive	10
Line fuse	Radio (if fitted)	5
Line fuse	Fog lamp (if fitted)	10

Bulbs

	Wattage
Headlamp LH dip outer *	55
Headlamp LH dip inner *	55
Headlamp RH dip outer *	45/40
Headlamp RH dip inner *	45/40
Front parking lamps	6
Front flasher lamps	21
Flasher repeater lamps	5
Rear flasher lamps	21
Tail/stop lamps	6/21
Reverse lamps	21
Number plate lamp	5
Luggage boot lamp	5
Console lamp	3
Glovebox lamp	
Early models	6
Later models	3
Puddle lamps	5
B post lamps	6
Clock illumination	2
Instrument illumination	2.2
Brake line warning light	2.2
Hazard warning light	2.2
Warning light cluster	1.5
Cigarette lighter illumination	2.2
Heater rear window warning light	2.2
Selector panel light (automatic transmission)	3

These ratings may vary in certain overseas territories

1 General description

The electrical system is of the 12 volt type and the major components comprise a 12 volt battery of which the negative terminal is earthed, a Lucas alternator, which is fitted to the right-hand side of the engine and is belt driven from the pulley on the front of the crankshaft, and a starter motor mounted on the rear left-hand side of the engine.

The battery supplies current for the ignition, lighting and other electrical circuits, and provides a reserve of electricity when the current consumed by the electrical equipment exceeds that being produced by the alternator. Normally the alternator is able to meet any demand placed upon it.

The battery is charged by a Lucas 11AC alternator on early cars, later cars are equipped with an 18ACR type alternator.

When fitting electrical accessories to cars with a negative earth system it is important, if they contain silicone diodes or transistors, that they are connected correctly, otherwise serious damage may result to the component concerned. Items such as radios, tape players, electronic tachometers, automatic dipping, parking lamps and anti-dazzle mirrors should all be checked for correct polarity.

It is important that the battery positive earth lead is always disconnected if the battery is to be boost charged or if any body or mechanical repairs are to be carried out, using electric arc welding equipment, otherwise serious damage can be caused to the more delicate instruments, especially those containing semi-conductors.

2 Battery – removal and refitting

1 The battery is mounted on a carrier located on the right-hand of the engine compartment at the front. It should be removed at three monthly intervals for cleaning and testing.

2 Disconnect the negative and then the positive leads from the battery terminals by removing the battery retaining clamp bolts.

3 Lift the windscreen washer reservoir off its bracket and place to one side. On cars from North America remove the absorption canister by pulling it off its mounting bracket.

4 Loosen the steering pump mounting bolts, push the pump downwards and take the drivebelt off the pump pulley.

5 Remove the pivot bolt and adjustment bolts then lift the pump onto the wiring valance. Do not disconnect the power steering hydraulic pipes.

6 Unscrew the battery clamp bar retaining wing nuts and lower the clamp bar.

7 Carefully lift the battery out with the strap carrier fitted on the battery. Hold the battery upright to prevent spillage of the electrolyte.

8 Refitting the battery is the reverse of the removal procedure. Smear the terminals with petroleum jelly to prevent corrosion. Adjust the tension of the steering pump drivebelt as described in Chapter 11.

3 Battery – maintenance and inspection

1 Normal weekly battery maintenance consists of checking the electrolyte level of each cell to ensure that the separators are covered by $\frac{1}{4}$ inch (6.35 mm) of electrolyte. If the level has fallen, top-up the battery using distilled water only. Do not overfill. If a battery is over-filled or any electrolyte spilt, immediately wipe away the excess as electrolyte attacks and corrodes any metal it comes into contact with very rapidly.

2 As well as keeping the terminals clean and covered with petroleum jelly, the top of the battery, and especially the top of the cells, should be kept clean and dry. This helps prevent corrosion and ensures that the battery does not become partially discharged by leakage through dampness and dirt.

3 Once every three months remove the battery and inspect the battery securing bolts, the battery clamp plate, tray, and battery leads for corrosion (ie white fluffy deposits on the metal which are brittle to touch). If any corrosion is found, clean off the deposits with ammonia and paint over the clean metal with an anti-rust/anti-acid paint.

4 At the same time inspect the battery case for cracks. If a crack is found, clean and plug it with one of the proprietary compounds marketed for this purpose. If leakage through the crack has been excessive then it will be necessary to refill the appropriate cell with

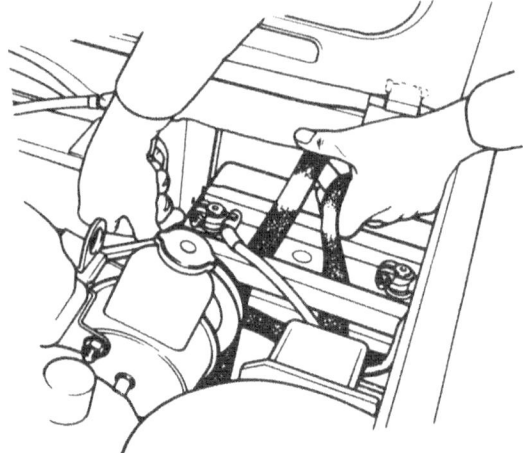

Fig. 10.1 Removing the battery (Sec 2)

fresh electrolyte as detailed later. Cracks are frequently caused to the top of the battery cases by pouring in distilled water, in the middle of winter, *after* instead of *before* a run. This gives the water no chance to mix with the electrolyte and so the former freezes and splits the battery case.

5 If topping up the battery becomes excessive and the case has been inspected for cracks that could cause leakage, but none are found, the battery is being overcharged and the voltage regulator will have to be checked and reset.

6 With the battery on the bench at the three monthly interval check, measure its specific gravity with a hydrometer to determine the state of charge and condition of the electrolyte. There should be very little variation between the different cells and if a variation in excess of 0.025 is present it will be due to either:

(a) *Loss of electrolyte from the battery sometimes caused by spillage or a leak, resulting in a drop in the specific gravity of the electrolyte when the deficiency was replenished with distilled water instead of fresh electrolyte*

(b) *An internal short circuit caused by buckling of the plates or a similar malady pointing to the likelihood of total battery failure in the near future*

7 The specific gravity of the electrolyte for fully charged conditions at the electrolyte temperature indicated, is listed in Table A. The specific gravity of a fully discharged battery at different temperatures of the electrolyte is given in Table B.

8 Specific gravity is measured by drawing up into the body of a hydrometer sufficient electrolyte to allow the indicator to float freely. The level at which the indicator floats indicates the specific gravity.

Table A – Specific gravity – battery fully charged
1.268 at	100°F or 38°C	electrolyte temperature
1.272 at	90°F or 32°C	electrolyte temperature
1.276 at	80°F or 27°C	electrolyte temperature
1.280 at	70°F or 21°C	electrolyte temperature
1.284 at	60°F or 16°C	electrolyte temperature
1.288 at	50°F or 10°C	electrolyte temperature
1.292 at	40°F or 4°C	electrolyte temperature
1.296 at	30°F or −1.5°C	electrolyte temperature

Table B – Specific gravity – battery fully discharged
1.098 at	100°F or 38°C	electrolyte temperature
1.102 at	90°F or 32°C	electrolyte temperature
1.106 at	80°F or 27°C	electrolyte temperature
1.110 at	70°F or 21°C	electrolyte temperature
1.114 at	60°F or 16°C	electrolyte temperature
1.118 at	50°F or 10°C	electrolyte temperature
1.122 at	40°F or 4°C	electrolyte temperature
1.126 at	30°F or −1.5°C	electrolyte temperature

4 Electrolyte – replenishment

1 If the battery is in a fully charged state and one of the cells maintains a specific gravity reading which is 0.025 or more lower than the others, and a check of each cell has been made with a voltage

meter to check for short circuits (a four to seven second test should give a steady reading of between 1.2 to 1.8 volts), then it is likely that electrolyte has been lost from the cell with the low reading at some time.

2   Top-up the cell with a solution of 1 part sulphuric acid to 2.5 parts of water. If the cell is already fully topped-up draw some electrolyte out of it with an old hydrometer. The total capacity of each cell is ¾ pint.

3   When mixing the sulphuric acid and water *never add water to sulphuric acid* – always pour the acid slowly onto the water in a glass container. *If water is added to sulphuric acid it will explode.*

4   Continue to top up the cell with the freshly made electrolyte and then recharge the battery and check the hydrometer readings.

5   Battery – charging

1   In winter time when heavy demand is placed upon the battery, such as when starting from cold, and when much electrical equipment is continually being used, it is a good idea to occasionally have the battery fully charged from an external source at the rate of 3.5 to 4 amps.

2   Continue to charge the battery at this rate until no further rise in specific gravity is noted over a four hour period.

3   Alternatively, a trickle charger, charging at the rate of 1.5 amps can be safely used overnight.

4   Specially rapid 'boost' charges which are claimed to restore the power of the battery in 1 to 2 hours are not recommended as they can cause serious damage to the battery plates through over-heating.

5   While charging the battery note that the temperature of the electrolyte should never exceed 100°F.

6   Alternator – general description

The main advantage of an alternator lies in its ability to provide a high charge at low engine speeds. Even when driving slowly in heavy traffic with the windscreen wipers, heater, lights and perhaps radio, switched on the alternator will ensure a charge reaches the battery.

The two types of alternator used generate alternating current (ac) which is changed to direct current (dc) by an internal diode system.

They each have a regulator which regulates the output at 14.0 to 14.4 volts on 18ACR alternators and 13.9 to 14.3 volts on 11AC alternators. The regulator is mounted internally on the 18ACR alternator and mounted on the right-hand inner wing for type 11AC alternators. A warning lamp illuminates if the alternator fails to operate.

The alternator assembly basically consists of a fixed coil winding (stator) in an aluminium housing, which incorporates the mounting lugs. Inside this stator, rotates a shaft wound coil (stator). The shaft is supported at each end by ball race bearings which are lubricated for life.

Slip rings are used to conduct current to and from the rotor field coils via two carbon brushes which bear against them.

The rotor is belt driven from the engine through a pulley keyed to the rotor shaft. A pressed steel fan adjacent to the pulley draws cooling air through the machine. This fan forms an integral part of the alternator specification. It has been designed to provide adequate air flow with a minimum of noise, and to withstand the high stresses associated with the maximum speed. Rotation is clockwise viewed on the drive end.

The brush gear is housed in a moulding, screwed to the outside of the slip ring end bracket. This moulding thus encloses the slip ring and brush gear assembly, and together with the shielded bearing, protects the assembly against the entry of dust and moisture.

The regulator is set during manufacture and requires no further attention.

Electrical connections to external circuits are by two Lucar connector blades and a multi-socket connector which ensure correct connection of the wiring.

7   Alternator – routine maintenance

1   The equipment has been designed for the minimum amount of maintenance in service, the only items subject to wear being the brushes and bearings.

2   Brushes should be examined after about 75 000 miles (120 000 km) and renewed if necessary. The bearings are pre-packed with grease for life, and should not require further attention.

3   Check the drivebelt tension every 3000 miles (5000 km) for correct adjustment which should be 0.50 to 0.75 in (12 to 20 mm) at the centre of the run between the alternator and crankshaft pulleys. Adjust, if necessary, as described in Section 10.

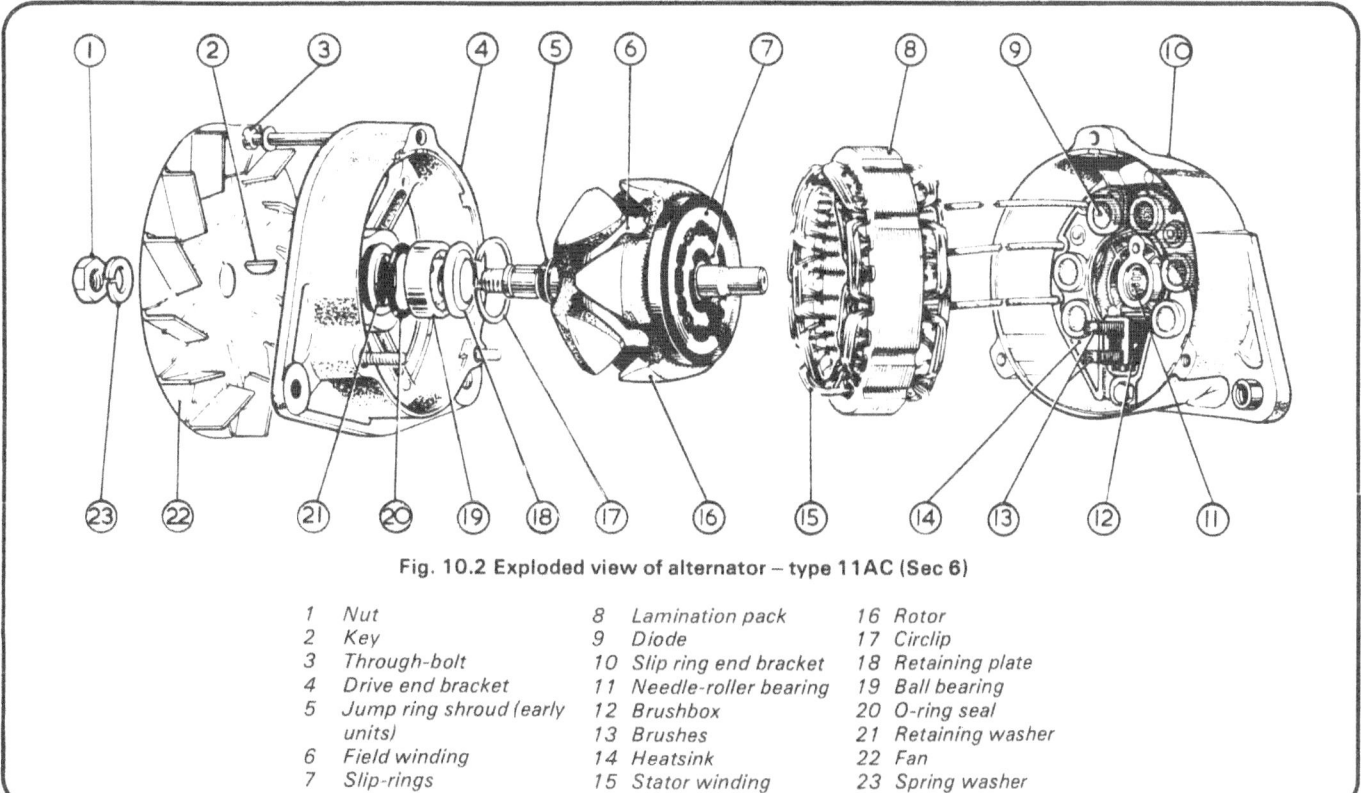

Fig. 10.2 Exploded view of alternator – type 11AC (Sec 6)

1	Nut	8	Lamination pack	16	Rotor
2	Key	9	Diode	17	Circlip
3	Through-bolt	10	Slip ring end bracket	18	Retaining plate
4	Drive end bracket	11	Needle-roller bearing	19	Ball bearing
5	Jump ring shroud (early units)	12	Brushbox	20	O-ring seal
6	Field winding	13	Brushes	21	Retaining washer
7	Slip-rings	14	Heatsink	22	Fan
		15	Stator winding	23	Spring washer

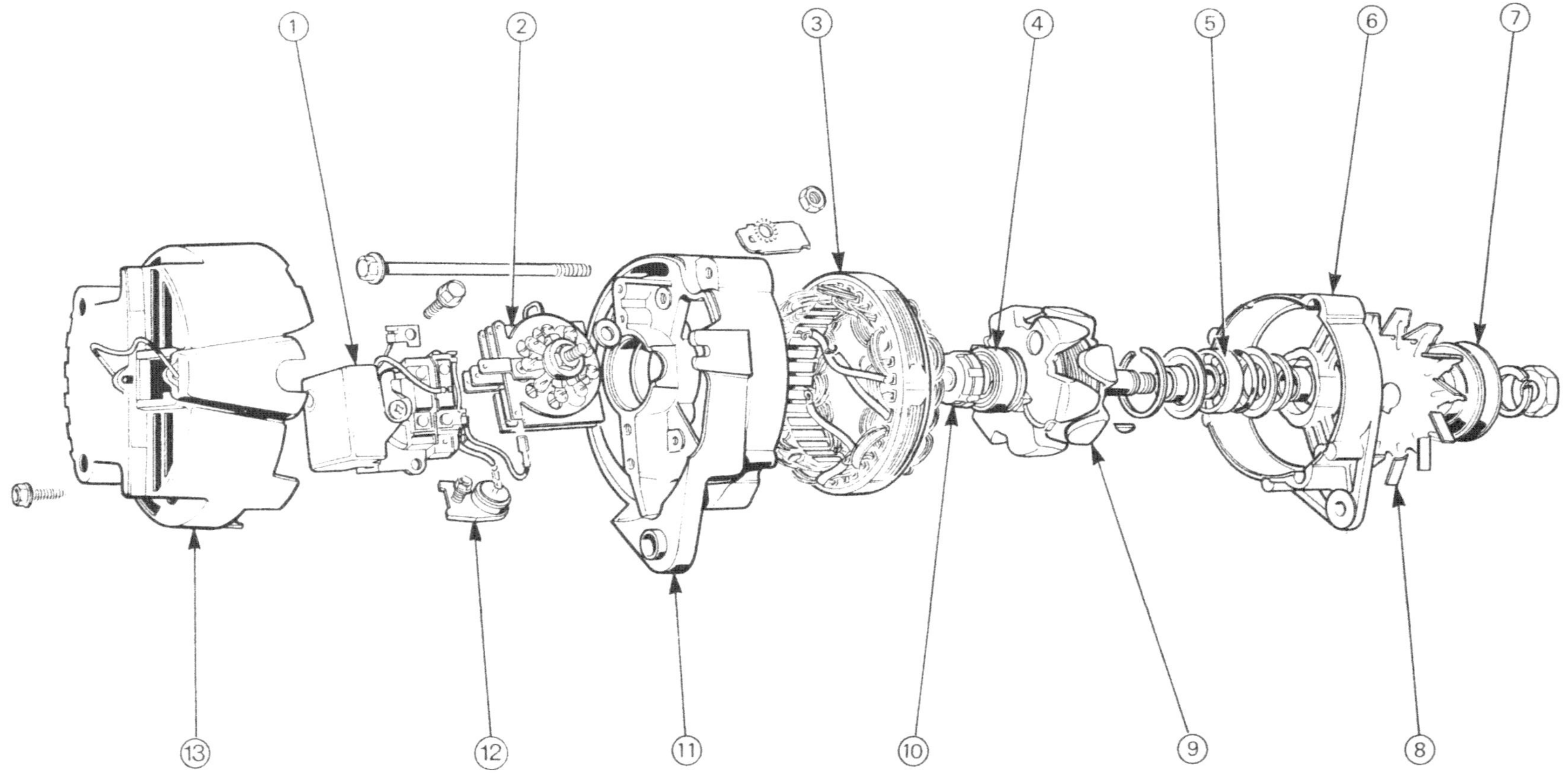

Fig. 10.3 Exploded view of alternator – type 18ACR (Sec 6)

1 Regulator
2 Rectifier (diode) pack
3 Stator
4 Slip ring end bearing
5 Drive end bearing
6 Drive end housing
7 Pulley
8 Fan
9 Rotor
10 Slip ring
11 Slip ring end housing
12 Surge protection diode
13 End cover

8 Alternator – special procedures

Whenever the electrical system of the car is being attended to, or external means of starting the engine are used, there are certain precautions that must be taken otherwise serious and expensive damage can result.

1   Always make sure that the negative terminal of the battery is earthed. If the terminal connections are accidentally reversed or if the battery has been reverse charged the alternator diodes will burn out.

2   The output terminal on the alternator marked 'BAT' or B+ must never be earthed but should always be connected directly to the positive terminal of the battery.

3   Whenever the alternator is to be removed or when disconnecting the terminals of the alternator circuit always disconnect the battery earth terminal first.

4   The alternator must never be operated without the battery to alternator cable connected.

5   Should it be necessary to use a booster charge or booster battery to start the engine always double check that the negative cable is connected to negative terminal and the positive cable to positive terminal.

9 Alternator – removal and refitting

1   Apply the handbrake, chock the rear wheels, jack-up the front of the car and support it on axle-stands.

2   Undo the four nuts that attach the anti-roll bar U-bolts to the body and pull the anti-roll bar downwards to give clearance for the removal of the alternator (Fig. 10.4).

3   Disconnect the battery.

4   Disconnect the wiring from the alternator by removing the multi-socket connector and disconnecting the two Lucar connectors (photo).

5   Slacken the pivot bolt and the three bolts securing the mounting bracket to the engine, then push the alternator inwards towards the engine and take the drivebelt off the alternator pulley (Fig. 10.5).

6   Remove the bottom bolt from the mounting bracket and taking the weight of the alternator remove the pivot bolt and withdraw the alternator from under the car.

7   Refitting is the reverse of the removal procedure. Make sure the pivot bolt is fitted with the washers in position as shown in Fig. 10.6 so that no strain is put on the two mounting lugs of the alternator. Adjust the drivebelt tension as described in Section 10.

9.4 Disconnect the wiring from the rear of the alternator

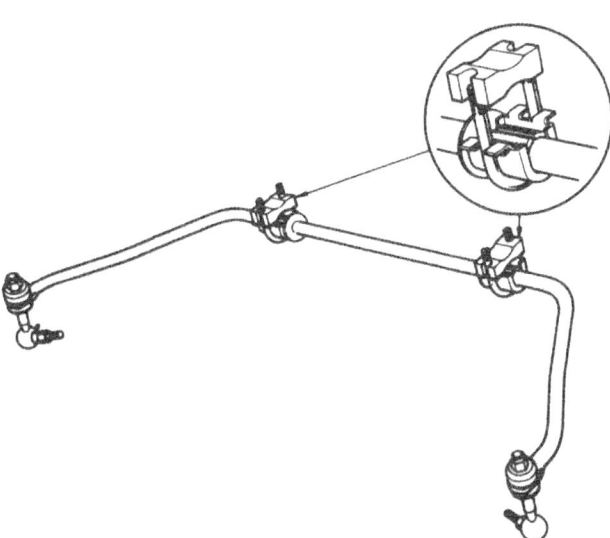

Fig. 10.4 Anti-roll bar clamps removal (Sec 9)

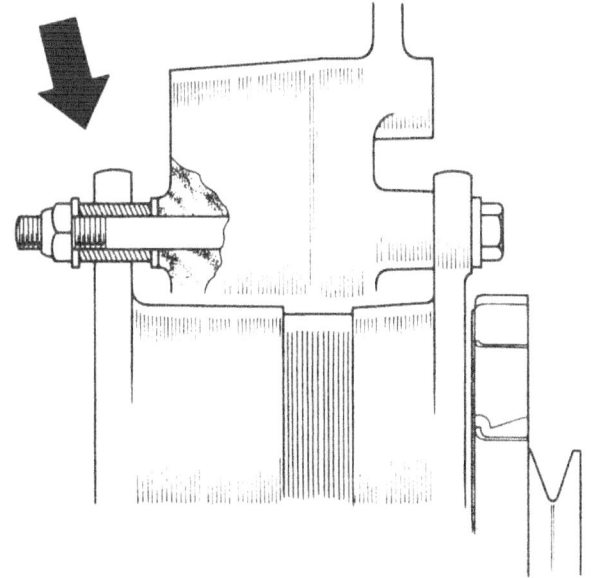

Fig. 10.6 Fitting the alternator pivot bolt (Sec 9)

Fig. 10.5 Alternator attaching bolts (Sec 9)

10 Alternator drivebelt – adjustment

1   Loosen the alternator pivot bolt and the three bolts securing the mounting bracket to the engine.
2   Move the alternator out from the engine, a wooden lever can be used if applied to the alternator drive end bracket (do not lever any other part of the alternator), and tighten the pivot bolt and bracket bolts. The drivebelt tension is correct when there is 0.5 to 0.75 in (12 to 20 mm) lateral movement at the mid-point position of the belt between the alternator pulley and crankshaft pulley. Make sure the belt is within the specified limits. If the belt is loose it will slip, wear rapidly and cause the alternator to malfunction, if it is too tight the alternator bearings will wear rapidly resulting in premature failure of the alternator.

11 Alternator – fault finding and repair

Due to the specialist knowledge and equipment required to test or service an alternator it is recommended that if the performance is suspect, the car be taken to an automobile electrician who will have the facilities for such work.

12 Alternator brushes – removal, inspection and refitting

1   *11 AC alternator:* Remove the two nuts, two washers, Lucar terminal and red plastic strap at the output terminal. Undo the two securing screws and remove the brush box assembly.
2   *18 ACR alternator:* Undo and remove the two screws that secure

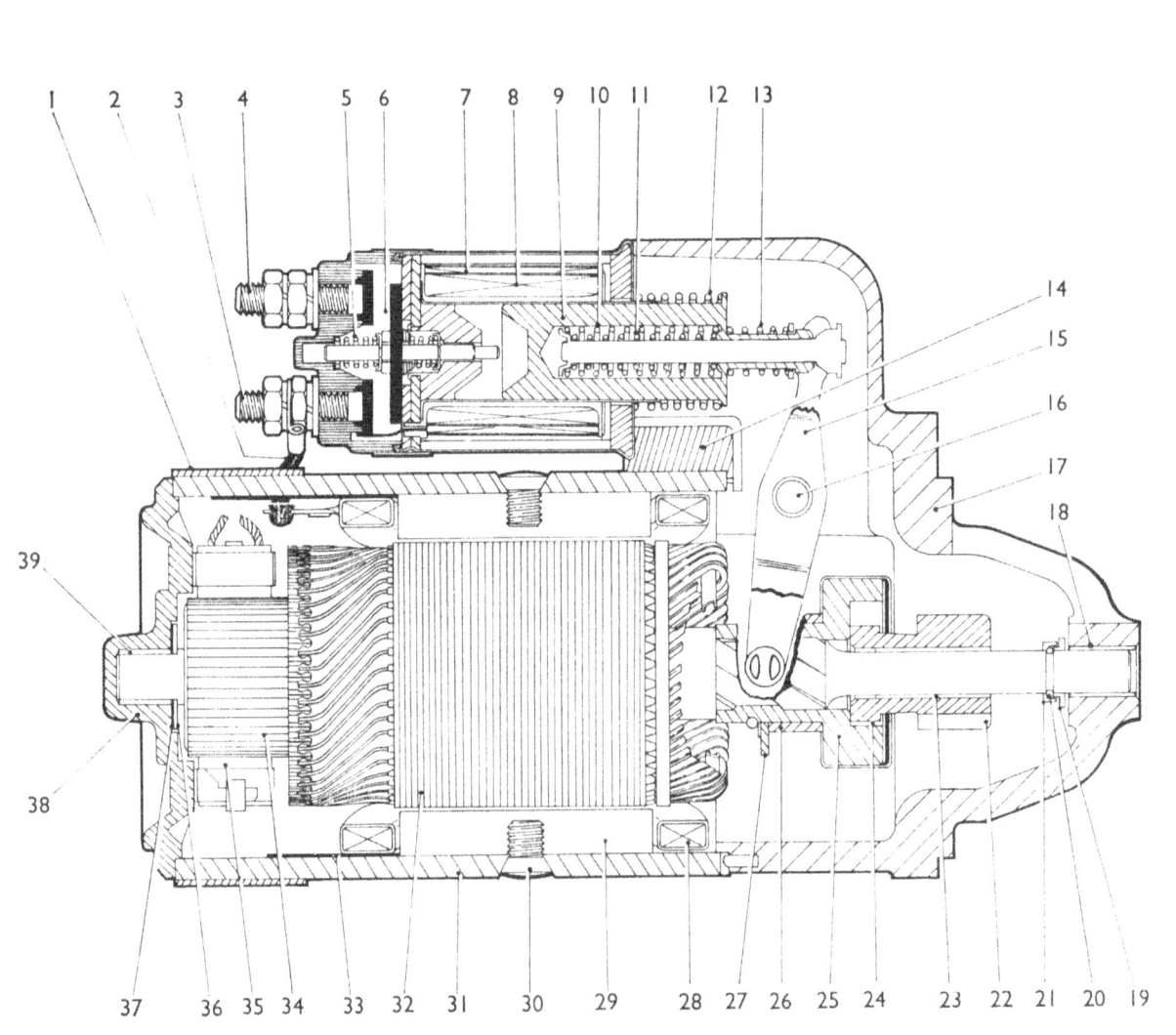

Fig. 10.7 Sectional view of starter motor (Sec 13)

1	*Cover band*	*11*	*Inner engaging spring*
2	*Motor lead*	*12*	*Return spring*
3	*'STA' terminal*	*13*	*Lost motion spring*
4	*Solenoid battery terminal*	*14*	*Rubber moulding*
5	*Contact assembly spring*	*15*	*Engaging lever*
6	*Contact assembly*	*16*	*Eccentric pin*
7	*Hold-in winding*	*17*	*Fixing bracket*
8	*Pull-in winding*	*18*	*Fixing bracket bearing bush*
9	*Plunger*	*19*	*Thrust washer*
10	*Outer engaging spring*	*20*	*Jump ring*

21	*Thrust collar starter drive*	*31*	*Yoke*
22	*Pinion*	*32*	*Armature*
23	*Pinion bearing*	*33*	*Insulation strip*
24	*Roller clutch action*	*34*	*Commutator*
25	*Drive sleeve*	*35*	*Brush*
26	*Distance piece*	*36*	*Steel thrust washer*
27	*Drive operating plate*	*37*	*Fabric thrust washer*
28	*Field winding*	*38*	*Commutator end bracket*
29	*Pole shoe*	*39*	*Commutator end bracket*
30	*Pole shoe screw*		*bearing bush*

the moulded end cover. Lift off the cover. Remove the brush retaining screws and withdraw the brushes from the brush box.

3   Measure the length of the brushes and if they have worn down to 0.2 in (5 mm) or less, they must be renewed.

4   Insert the new brushes and check to make sure that they are free to move in their guides. If they bind, lightly polish them with a very fine file.

5   Reassemble in the reverse order of dismantling. Make sure that leads which may have been connected to any of the screws are reconnected correctly.

13   Starter motor – general description

The starter motor is mounted on the left-hand side of the engine at the rear. The motor is of the four field coil, four pole piece type and has four spring loaded commutator brushes. Two of these brushes are earthed and the other two are insulated and attached to the field coils.

The solenoid is fitted to the top of the motor. The plunger inside the solenoid is connected to a centre pivoting lever the other end of which is in contact with the drive sleeve and drivegear. When the starter motor switch is operated the solenoid is energized causing the plunger to move into the solenoid and the pinion to move into mesh with the starter ring gear. Upon the pinion being in full mesh with the ring gear, heavy duty contacts in the rear of the solenoid are closed and current is supplied to the motor so rotating the pinion and ring gear.

Once the engine has started the starter switch is released and under spring action the plunger is moved from the centre of the solenoid and by means of the pivoting lever the pinion is moved out of mesh with the ring gear.

14   Starter motor – testing on the car

1   If the starter motor fails to operate then check the condition of the battery by turning on the headlamps. If they glow brightly for several seconds and then gradually dim, the battery is in an uncharged condition.

2   If the headlamps continue to glow brightly and it is obvious that the battery is in good condition, then check the tightness of the earth lead from the battery terminal to its connection on the body frame particularly, and other battery wiring. Check the tightness of the connections at the rear of the solenoid. Check the wiring with a voltmeter for breaks or short circuits.

3   If the wiring is in order check the starter motor for continuity using a voltmeter.

4   If the battery is fully charged, the wiring in order, and the motor electrical circuit checked for continuity, and it still fails to operate, then it will have to be removed from the car for examination. Before this is done, however, ensure that the pinion gear has not jammed in mesh with the flywheel due to a broken solenoid spring or dirty pinion gear splines. To release the pinion, engage a low gear and with the ignition switched off, rock the car backwards and forwards which should release the pinion from mesh with the ring gear (manual gearbox only). If the pinion still remains jammed the starter motor must be removed for further examination.

15   Starter motor – removal and refitting

1   Disconnect the earth lead from the battery negative terminal.

2   Chock the rear wheels then raise the front of the car and support it on axle-stands or other suitable supports.

3   Remove the three nuts securing the left-hand front exhaust pipe to the exhaust manifold. Slacken the clamp at the front of the left-hand silencer and remove the front left-hand exhaust pipe.

4   Disconnect the heavy duty cable from the battery at the solenoid and also the two Lucar terminals.

5   Working from the engine compartment and using a socket with a long extension undo the starter motor top securing bolt. The extension must be long enough so that a ratchet handle can be used near the cooling fan. If necessary hold the nut at the rear with an open spanner.

6   Working underneath the car remove the starter motor bottom mounting bolt and then withdraw the starter motor downwards and out from under the car.

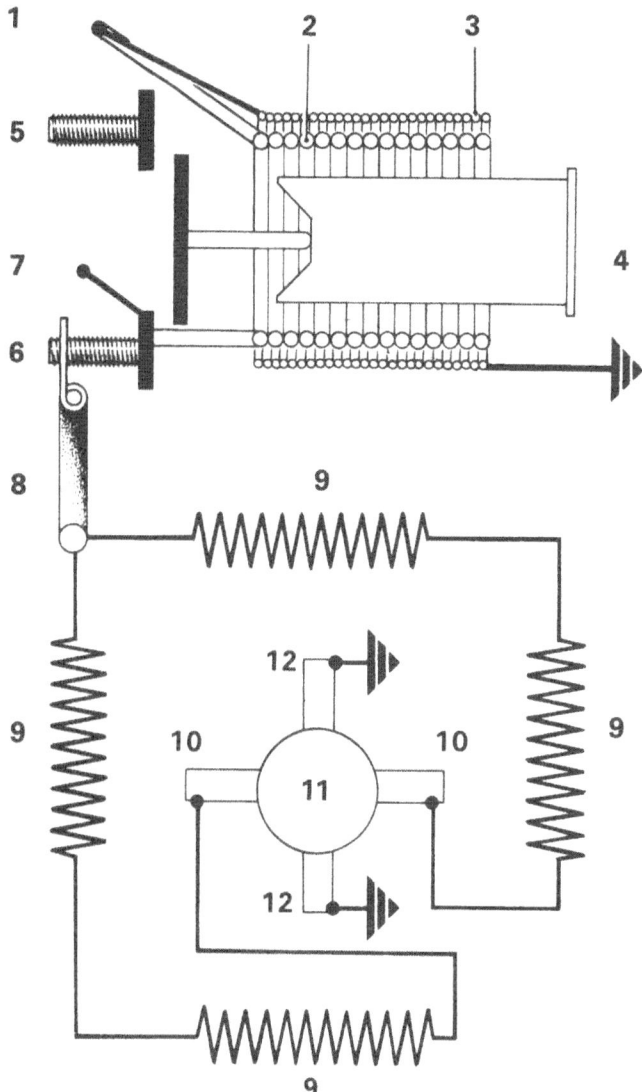

Fig. 10.8 Starter motor internal circiut (Sec 13)

1 Unmarked 'WR wire' connector	7 'IGN' connector
2 Pull-in winding	8 Motor lead
3 Hold-in winding	9 Field windings
4 Plunger	10 Field winding brushes
5 Solenoid battery terminal	11 Commutator
6 'STA' terminal	12 Earth brushes

7   Refitting the starter motor is the reverse of the removal procedure. Check that all connections are secure.

16   Starter motor – dismantling and overhaul

1   With the starter motor on the bench, loosen the screw on the cover band and slip the cover band off with a piece of wire bent into the shape of a hook. Lift back each of the brush springs in turn and check the movement of the brushes in their holders by pulling on the flexible connectors. If the brushes are so worn that their faces do not rest against the commutator or if the ends of the brush leads are exposed on their working faces they must be renewed.

2   If any of the brushes tend to stick in their holders then wash them with a petrol moistened cloth and, if necessary, lightly polish the sides of the brushes with a very fine file, until the brushes move quite freely in their holders.

3   Undo the large nut holding the heavy duty cable to the lower solenoid terminal (marked STA). Remove the nut, spring washer and cable connector.

4   Undo the two nuts securing the solenoid to the front fixing bracket. Remove the nuts and spring washers and carefully withdraw the solenoid from its mounting. It will be observed that the plunger will be left attached to the engagement lever.

5   Lift the plunger return spring away from the plunger and put in a safe place. Disengage the end of the plunger from the top of the engagement lever.

6   Undo the locknut securing the eccentric pin to the starter motor body. This will be found at the front towards the top of the motor on the right-hand side. Unscrew the eccentric pin.

7   Unscrew the two through bolts from the rear of the starter motor body which will release the yoke from the fixing bracket. To separate the two parts, using a soft faced hammer, tap the fixing bracket mounting lugs whilst holding the yoke. This will release the locating dowels in the end of the fixing bracket.

8   Pull the commutator end bracket off the rear of the yoke. Lift off the steel thrust washer and fibre thrust washer from the spigot on the end of the commutator. Also lift away the rubber moulding located at the top of the yoke and the fixing bracket.

9   Carefully withdraw the armature with the drive pinion assembly and engagement lever from the fixing bracket. It should be noted that there is a small thrust washer at the pinion end of the armature shaft which is next removed.

10 If it is necessary to dismantle the starter pinion drive obtain a $\frac{5}{8}$ inch (15.9 mm) internal diameter tube, position the tube over the end of the shaft and force the thrust collar from the jump ring towards the starter drive. Using a screwdriver carefully prise the ring from the shaft groove.

11 Lift away the thrust collar and slide off the starter pinion drive assembly.

12 At this stage if the brushes are to be renewed, their flexible connectors must be unsoldered and the connectors of new brushes soldered in their place. Check that the new brushes move freely in their holders as detailed above. If cleaning the commutator with petrol fails to remove all the burnt areas and spots, then wrap a piece of glass paper round the commutator and rotate the armature.

13 If the commutator is very badly worn, remove the drivegear as described in paragraph 10, then mount the armature in a lathe and with the lathe turning at high speed, take a very fine cut and finish the surface by polishing with glass paper. Do not undercut the mica insulators between the commutator segments.

14 With the starter motor dismantled, test the four field coils for an open circuit. Connect a 12 volt battery with a 12 volt bulb in one of the leads between the field terminal post and the tapping point of the field coils to which the brushes are connected. An open circuit is proved by the bulb not lighting.

15 If the bulb lights, it does not necessarily mean that the field coils are in order, as there is a possibility that one of the coils will be earthed to the starter yoke or pole shoes. To check this, remove the lead from the brush connector and place it against a clean portion of the starter yoke. If the bulb lights the field coils are earthing. Renewal of the field coil calls for the use of a wheel operated screwdriver, a soldering iron, caulking and riveting operations, and is normally beyond the scope of the majority of owners. The starter yoke should be taken to a reputable electrical engineering works for new field coils to be fitted. Alternatively, purchase an exchange Lucas starter motor.

16 If the armature is damaged this will be evident after visual inspection. Look for signs of burning, discolouration and for conductors that have lifted away from the commutator.

17 With the starter motor stripped down check the condition of the bushes. They should be renewed when they are sufficiently worn to allow visible side movement of the armature shaft.

18 The old bushes are simply driven out with a suitable drift and the new bushes inserted by the same method. As the bearings are of the phosphor bronze type it is essential that they are allowed to stand in engine oil for at least 24 hours before fitment.

19 Reassembly is the reverse sequence to dismantling but it will be necessary to adjust the pinion movement.

20 Once the starter motor has been completely reassembled and tested for correct operation by securing it in a vice and connecting a heavy gauge cable between the starter motor solenoid lower terminal and a 12 volt battery, connect the cable from the other battery terminal to earth on the starter motor body. If the motor turns at high

speed it is in good order.

21 Disconnect the heavy duty cable from the lower terminal marked 'STA' and by referring to Fig. 10.8, connect a 6 volt battery to the starter motor as shown. Do not make the final battery connection yet.

22 Undo but do not remove the eccentric pin locknut on the side of the fixing bracket. Then screw the eccentric pin in fully.

23 Connect the final battery connection so energizing the solenoid, pull-in winding and hold-in winding which will, via the engaging lever, move the pinion to its engagement position.

24 Refer to Fig. 10.7 and locate a feeler gauge between the pinion and thrust washer. With the fingers, gently press the pinion towards the motor, so that any lost motion in the linkage may be taken up.

25 Using a screwdriver rotate the eccentric pin until the gap is between 0.005 to 0.015 inch (0.127 to 0.38 mm). Finally tighten the eccentric pin locknuts.

17 Flasher circuit – fault tracing and rectification

1   The turn signal flasher unit and the hazard flasher unit are located behind the parcel shelf.

2   If the flasher unit works twice as fast as usual when indicating either right or left, this is a sure sign of a broken filament in the front or rear indicator bulb on the side operating too quickly.

3   If the external flashers are working but the internal flasher warning light has ceased to function, check the filament of the warning bulb and renew if necessary.

4   With the aid of the wiring diagram check all the flasher circuit connections if a flasher bulb is sound but does not work.

5   With the ignition turned on check that current is reaching the flasher unit by connecting a voltmeter between the 'plus' or 'B' terminal and earth. If this test is positive connect the 'plus' or 'B' terminal and the 'L' terminal and operate the flasher switch. If the flasher bulb lights up the flasher unit itself is defective and must be renewed as it is not possible to dismantle and repair it.

6   To renew the turn signal flasher pull the unit from its clips and disconnect the Lucar connections. Make a note of the connections so that they can be connected correctly. The hazard flasher unit is removed by simply pulling it from its socket.

18 Windscreen wiper mechanism – maintenance

1   Renew the windscreen wiper blades at intervals of 12 000 miles (19 000 km) or more frequently if necessary.

2   The cable which drives the wiper blades from the gearbox attached to the windscreen wiper motor is pre-packed with grease and requires no maintenance. The washer round the wheelbox spindle can be lubricated with several drops of glycerine every 6000 miles (9600 km).

19 Windscreen wiper blades – removal and refitting

Passenger side

1   Before removing the wiper blade pull the arm away from the windscreen, then lift clip A and at the same time tilt the cage B (Fig. 10.9) and slide the blade from the arm.

2   Refit the blade by pushing it on to the arm to engage with the raised pip.

Driver side

3   Position the windscreen wiper in a vertical position. To do this wet the windscreen and switch on the ignition and the wipers, then switch off the ignition when the wipers are at the required position.

4   Lift the wiper arm away from the windscreen and pull out the bottom end of the pantograph arm to free the ball socket.

5   Position the pantograph arm and blade as shown in Fig. 10.10, free the blade pin from the retaining plate and withdraw the wiper blade.

6   Refitting is the reverse of the removal procedure.

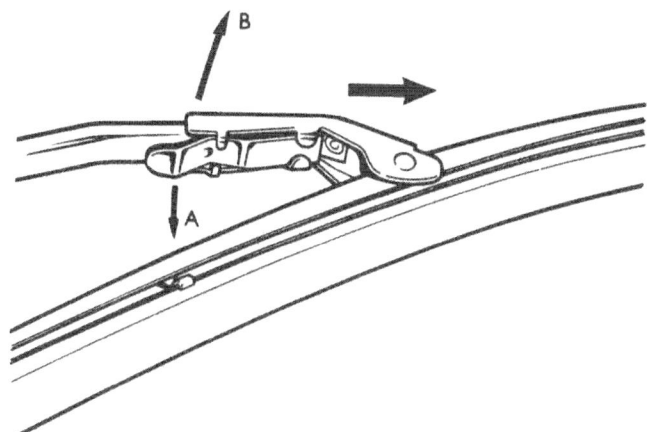

Fig. 10.9 Removing wiper blade – passenger side (Sec 19)

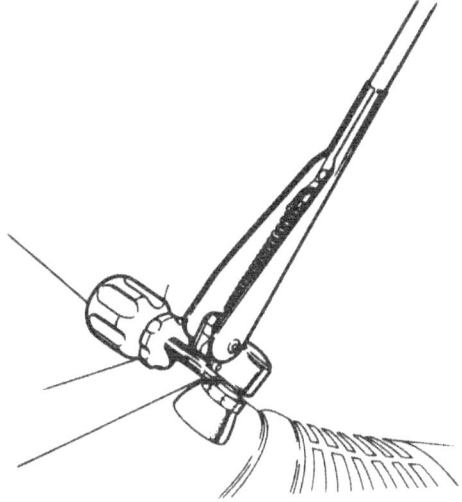

Fig. 10.11 Using a screwdriver to remove the windscreen wiper arm (Sec 20)

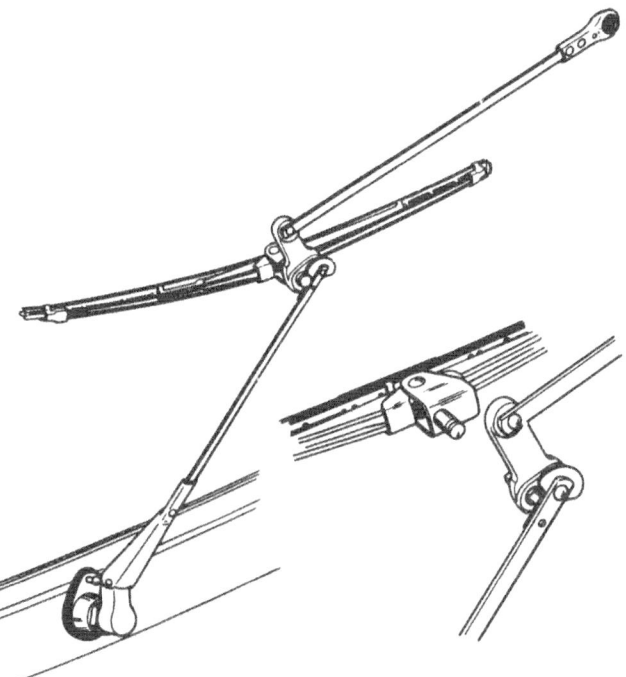

Fig. 10.10 Removing wiper blade – driver side (Sec 19)

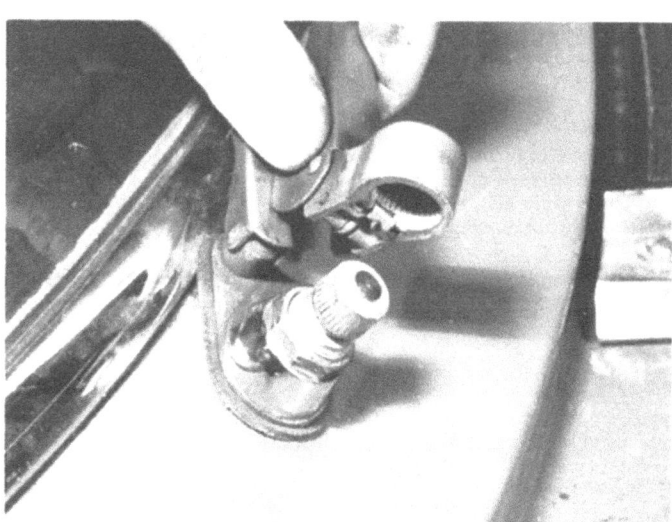

20.6 Refitting the wiper arm on the spindle

20 Windscreen wiper arms – removal and refitting

Passenger side

1   Before removing the wiper arm, turn the windscreen wiper switch on and off to ensure that the arm is in its normal parked position parallel with the bottom of the windscreen.

2   To remove the arm, pivot the arm away from the windscreen and pull the wiper arm off the spindle. It may be necessary to use a screwdriver as shown in Fig. 10.11 to free the retaining clip from the spindle groove.

3   When refitting the arm, position it in the correct relative parked position and then press the arm on to engage the clip in the spindle groove.

Driver side

4   With the wipers in the parked position lift the wiper arm away from the windscreen and at the same time pull out the bottom end of the pantograph arm to free the ball socket.

5   The arm can now be pulled from the spindle, use a screwdriver, if necessary, to free the retaining clip from the spindle groove.

6   When refitting the arm ensure the wiper spindles are in the parked position, then position the wiper arm to the park position and push it

onto the spindle (photo).

7   Move the wiper arm towards the windscreen and at the same time engage the bottom end of the pantograph arm on the ball end.

21 Windscreen wiper mechanism – fault diagnosis and rectification

Should the windscreen wipers fail, or work very slowly, then check the terminals for loose connections, and make sure the insulation of the external wiring is not broken or cracked. If this is in order then check the current the motor is taking by connecting a 1-20 volt voltmeter in the circuit and turning on the wiper switch. Consumption should be 1.5 amps on the low speed setting and 2.0 amps on the high speed setting.

If no current is passing through check the 19-20 fuse. If the fuse has blown renew it after having checked the wiring of the motor and other electrical circuits serviced by this fuse for the short circuit. If the fuse is in good condition check the wiper switch.

If the wiper takes a very high current check the wiper blades for freedom of movement. If this is satisfactory check the gearbox cover and gear assembly for damage and measure the armature endfloat which should be between 0.009 to 0.012 inch (0.20 to 0.30 mm). The endfloat is set by the adjusting screw. Check that excessive friction in the cable connecting tubes caused by too small a curvature is not the cause of the high current consumption.

If the motor takes a very low current ensure that the battery is fully charged. Check the brush gear after removing the commutator end bracket and ensure that the brushes are free to move and, if necessary, renew the tension spring. If the brushes are very worn they should be replaced with new ones. The brush levers should be quite free on their pivots. If stiff, loosen them by moving them backwards and forwards by hand and by applying a little thin machine oil. Check the armature by substitution if this unit is suspected.

22 Windscreen wiper motor – removal and refitting

1   Disconnect the electrical wiring from the motor by disconnecting the plug from the limit switch.
2   Unscrew the securing screws and remove the gearbox cover. Slide off the crankpin circlip and collect the washer (Fig. 10.12).
3   The connecting rod can now be withdrawn. Collect the second washer.
4   Undo the two bolts securing the motor mounting strap and lift off the strap.
5   Carefully remove the motor from its mounting while freeing the cross-head, rack and tube assembly.
6   Refitting is the reverse of the removal procedure. Lubricate the final gear crankpin with Shell Turbo 41 oil and the cross-head end of the connecting rod with Ragosene Listate grease.

23 Windscreen wiper motor – dismantling, inspection and reassembly

1   Remove the five gearbox cover retaining screws and lift away the cover. Remove the circlip and flat washer securing the connecting rod to the crankpin on the shaft and gear. Lift away the connecting rod followed by the second washer. Lift out the cross-head.
2   Remove the slider block taking note of the cam slope direction.

3   Remove the spring clip and washer securing the shaft and gear to the gearbox body.
4   Ensure that there are no burrs on the drive end of the shaft, then withdraw it and remove the dished washer.
5   Remove the thrust screw complete with locknut.
6   Remove the cover through-bolts, carefully withdraw the cover about 0.2 in (5 mm) then continue withdrawing, allowing the brushes to drop clear of the commutator.
7   Pull the armature out of the cover then remove the brush and limit switch assembly (five screws). Mark the position of the limit switch on the gearbox with a pencil.
8   Examine the armature worm and gear for excessive wear on the teeth, renewing the parts as necessary. In view of the expense of renewing an armature for wear alone, a certain amount of wear can be tolerated. Also, if the armature requires repair for any reason it is worthwhile considering a new wiper motor.
9   Remove any dust with a brush or compressed air jet. Do not allow any liquid cleaner into contact with the field coils.
10 Inspect the commutator for signs of burning or pitting, and if evident, clean with a little fine glass paper. Wash away any dust with petrol.
11 Examine the brushes for wear and general condition, renewing as necessary. The minimum permissible brush length is given in the Specifications.
12 Check for wear in the bearings and renew if necessary.
Note: *Shell Turbo 41 oil and Regosene Listate grease will be needed during reassembly.*
13 Fit the brush and limit switch assembly and secure with five screws. Slacken the two limit screws and align the pencil marks made at dismantling, then tighten the screws.
14 Lubricate the cover bearing, and saturate the felt washer with Shell Turbo 41 oil.
15 Fit the armature into the cover against the permanent magnetic pull.
16 Lubricate the self aligning bearing with Shell Turbo 41 oil then fit the armature through the brush plate and cover. Take care to lift the brushes on the commutator, and ensure that they are not contaminated with oil.

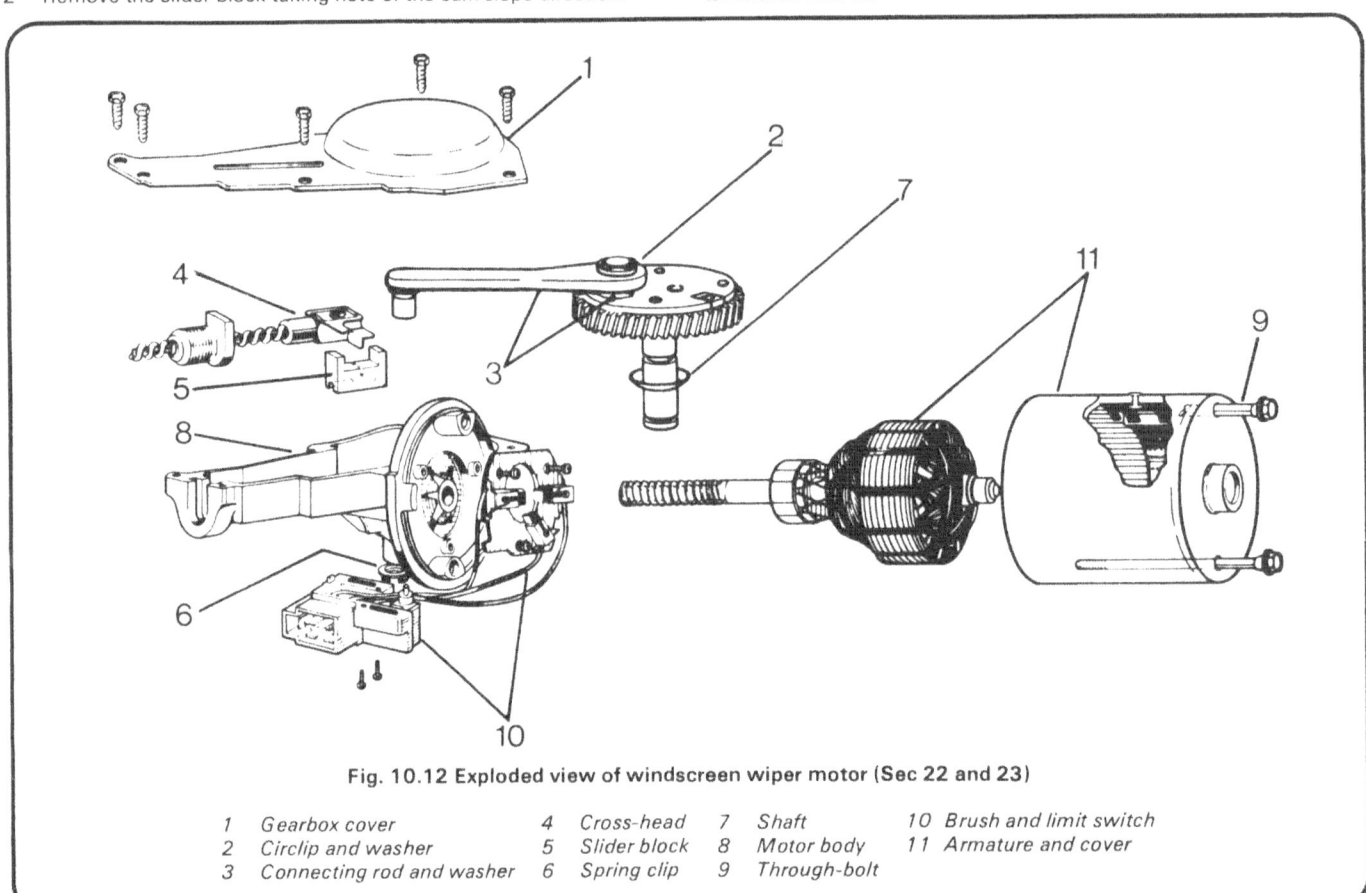

Fig. 10.12 Exploded view of windscreen wiper motor (Sec 22 and 23)

1 Gearbox cover	4 Cross-head	7 Shaft	10 Brush and limit switch
2 Circlip and washer	5 Slider block	8 Motor body	11 Armature and cover
3 Connecting rod and washer	6 Spring clip	9 Through-bolt	

17 Turn the cover to align the two markings then fit the through-bolts (Fig. 10.13).
18 Fit the thrust screw and locknut.
19 Adjust the armature endfloat by turning the thrust screw inwards until resistance is felt then screwing it out again $\frac{1}{4}$ turn. Tighten the locknut.
20 Lubricate the gearbox bushes with Shell Turbo 41 oil.
21 Fit the dished washer with the concave surface towards the final gear then insert the shaft. Fit the retaining washer and the spring clip.
22 Lubricate the slider block cam slope, block sides and guide channel with Ragosine Listate grease. Fit the slider block with the cam slope as shown in Fig. 10.14.
23 Fit the washer that is located under the connecting rod. Lubricate the cross-head end of the connecting rod with Ragosine Listate grease then insert the connecting rod. Fit the retaining washer and circlip.
24 Refit the gearbox cover (five screws).

---

24 Windscreen wiper rack – removal and refitting

1 Remove the wiper arms as described in Section 20.
2 Remove the windscreen wiper motor, refer to Section 22.
3 Withdraw the windscreen wiper rack by pulling the cross-head.
4 Refitting is the reverse of the removal procedure. While inserting the rack turn each wheelbox spindle slightly to permit engagement of the rack.

---

25 Windscreen wiper wheelboxes – removal and refitting

1 Disconnect the earth strap from the negative terminal of the battery.
2 Remove the rack as described in Section 24.

Driver side
3 Remove the instrument panel as described in Section 46.
4 Undo the two securing nuts and remove the wheelbox rear plate. Position the tube ends to the side.
5 Undo the spindle nut and remove the wheelbox.

Passenger side
6 Remove the glove box and the passenger's demister duct.
7 Undo the two securing nuts and remove the wheelbox rear plate. Position the tube ends to the side then remove the spindle nut and lift out the wheelbox.
8 Refitting the wheelboxes is the reverse of the removal procedure.

---

26 Windscreen washer – description and servicing

1 The combined washer motor/pump and fluid reservoir is located on the left-hand side of the engine compartment.
2 Always maintain a good level of fluid in the reservoir and never operate the washer switch if the reservoir is empty or at any time for periods in excess of 10 seconds.
3 In winter one part of methylated spirit should be mixed with two parts of water to prevent freezing of the washer fluid.
4 Failure of the washer/pump unit may be due to corroded or loose connecting leads or a blown fuse. If these are in order, then the unit will have to be renewed as it is not repairable.
5 To remove the washer unit, disconnect the Lucar connectors and fluid outlet pipe.
6 Remove the unit by pulling it upwards to free it from the mounting bracket.
7 When refitting early type units the green wire is connected to the positive terminal, marked 12V DC +, and the green/black wire to the negative terminal. Later units have Lucar terminals of different sizes and cannot be wrongly connected.

---

27 Horns – fault tracing and rectification

1 If a horn works badly or fails completely, first check the wiring leading to it for short circuits and loose connections. Also check that the horn is firmly secured and that there is nothing lying on the horn body.
2 The horn should never be dismantled but it is possible to adjust it.

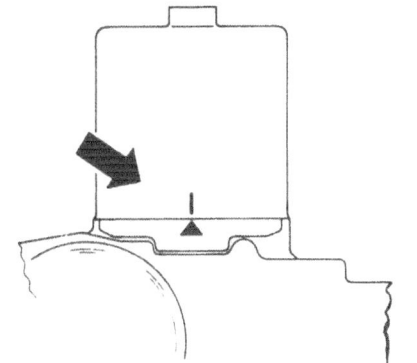

Fig. 10.13 Armature cover to gearbox alignment marks (Sec 23)

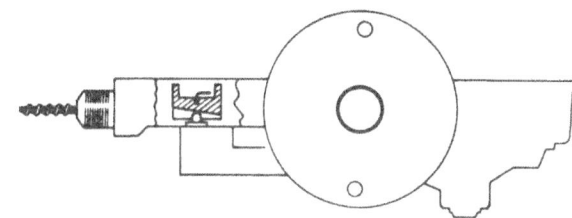

Fig. 10.14 Fitting the slider block (Sec 23)

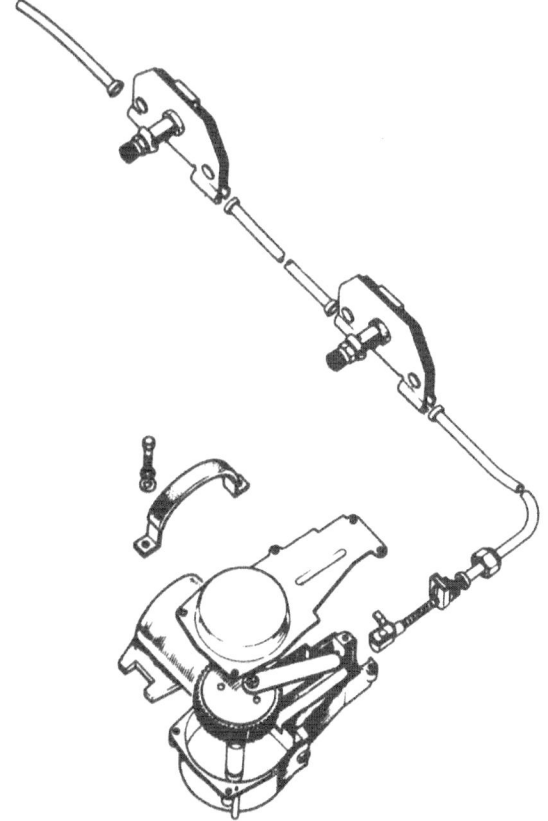

Fig. 10.15 Windscreen wiper motor, rack and wheelboxes (Sec 24 and 25)

This adjustment is to compensate for wear only and will not affect the tone. At the rear of the horn is a small adjusting screw on the broad rim, nearly opposite the two terminals. Do not confuse this with the large screw in the centre.

3   Turn the adjustment screw anti-clockwise until the horn just fails to sound. Then turn the screw a quarter of a turn clockwise, which is the optimum setting.

4   It is recommended that if the horn is to be reset in the car the fuse should be removed and replaced with a piece of wire otherwise the fuse will continually blow due to the continuous high current required for the horn in continual operation.

28 Window lift motor – removal and refitting

The window lift motor must not be separated from the regulator while in-situ as the lever spring will fly out and may cause personal injury.

1   Remove the window regulator and motor assembly as a complete unit, refer to Chapter 12.

2   Mount the assembly in a vice. Connect a battery to the motor and align the large hole in the segment with the hole on the centre line of

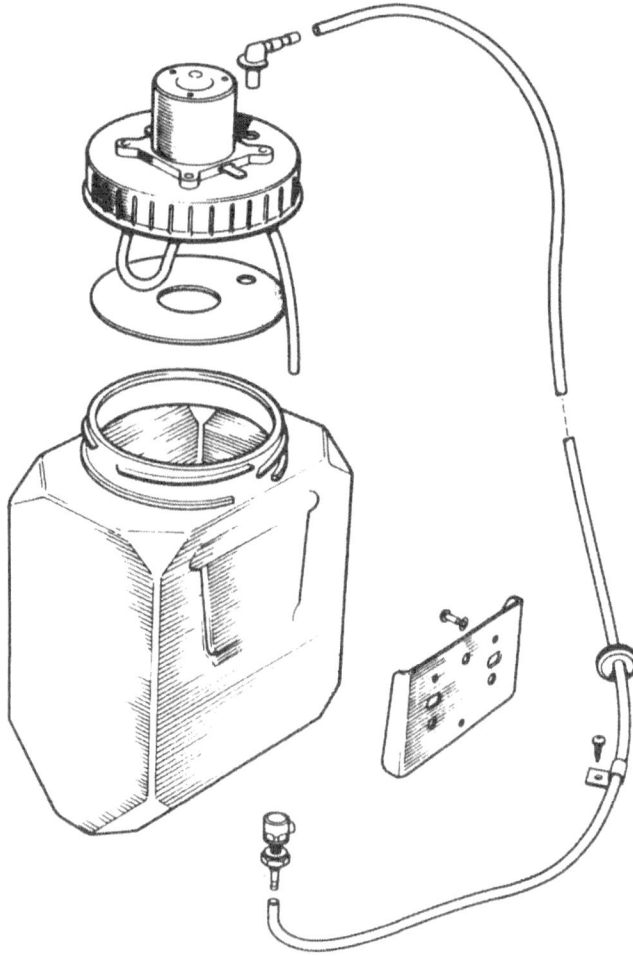

Fig. 10.16 Windscreen washer pump and reservoir assembly (Sec 26)

Fig. 10.17 Location of window lift motor circuit breaker (Sec 29)

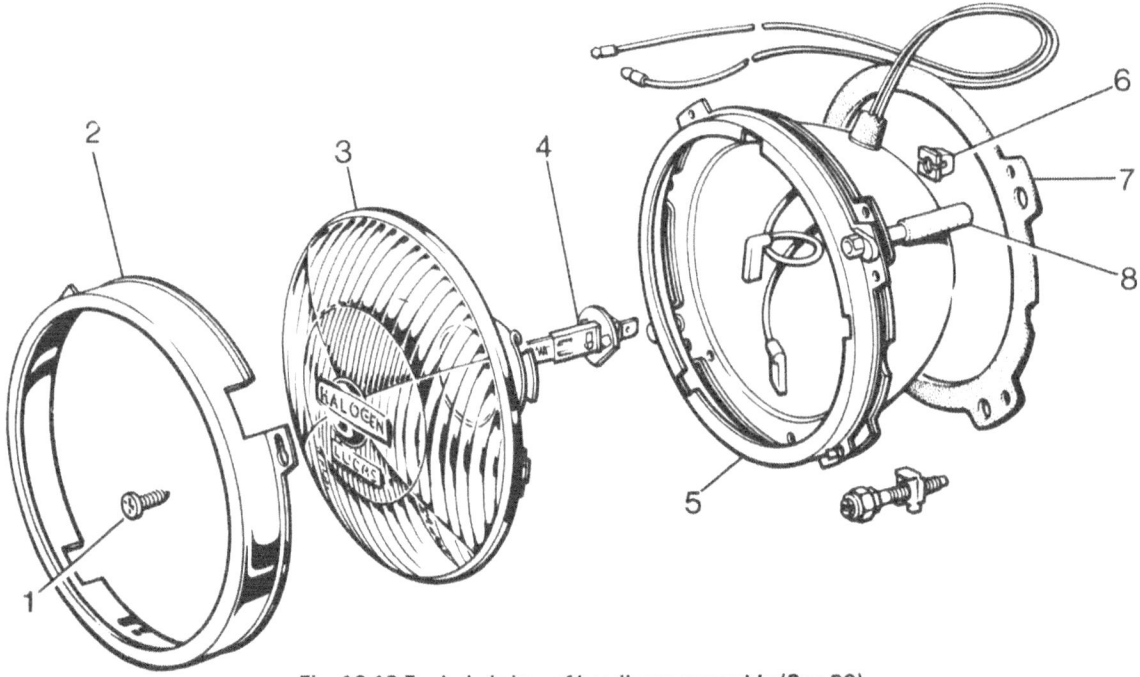

Fig. 10.18 Exploded view of headlamp assembly (Sec 30)

1 Securing screw	3 Light unit	5 Base assembly	7 Gasket
2 Rim	4 Bulb	6 Locknut	8 Sleeve

the regulator plate.

3   Fit a bolt through the hole then remove the three retaining bolts and lift the motor from the regulator plate.

4   Refitting is the reverse of the removal procedure.

29 Window lift motor circuit breaker – removal and refitting

If the movement of the window is obstructed the motor draws excess current and this actuates the circuit breaker. The circuit breaker is self-resetting with a quick recovery time. It is located on the component mounting panel.

1   To remove the circuit breaker remove the parcel shelf, then disconnect the two Lucar connectors and lift the circuit breaker (arrowed in Fig. 10.17) from the component mounting panel.

2   Refitting is the reverse of the removal procedure.

30 Headlamp – removal and refitting

1   Remove the relevant grille section according to which lamp is to be removed. The centre section is secured with four screws and the outer and intermediate sections each have two securing screws.

2   Slacken the three headlamp securing screws, turn the retaining rim anti-clockwise and pull the lamp forward (photo). Do not disturb the beam adjustment screws (Fig. 10.20) otherwise the light units will have to be reset.

3   *Sealed beam units:* Pull the connector from the lamp.

4   *Lamps fitted with renewable bulbs:* Disconnect the plug or Lucar connectors then disengage the retaining clip and remove the bulb. Do not touch the bulb glass. If it is touched wash it with methylated spirit (photos).

5   Undo the three securing screws and remove the lamp base assembly and gasket.

6   Refitting is the reverse of the removal procedure.

7   Should the beam alignment need to be reset it is recommended that this be left to the local agent who will have the necessary equipment to check the alignment accurately.

31 Front parking and flasher lamps – bulb renewal

1   The bulbs in these lamps are accessible after removing the lens securing screws and then the lens (photo).

2   To remove the bulb push it in and turn it anti-clockwise.

3   Refitting is the reverse of the removal procedure.

32 Front and rear marker lamps – bulb renewal

1   The bulbs in these lamps are accessible after removing the single lens securing screw and then pulling the front edge of the lens to release the rear lug.

2   To remove the bulb push it in and turn it anti-clockwise.

3   Refitting is the reverse of the removal procedure.

33 Rear lamp cluster – bulb renewal

1   Pull back the carpet in the luggage boot, remove the two securing screws and lift off the lamp cover.

2   Pull the relevant bulb holder out of the lamp unit and then remove the bulb by pushing it in and turning it anti-clockwise (photo).

3   Refitting is the reverse of the removal procedure.

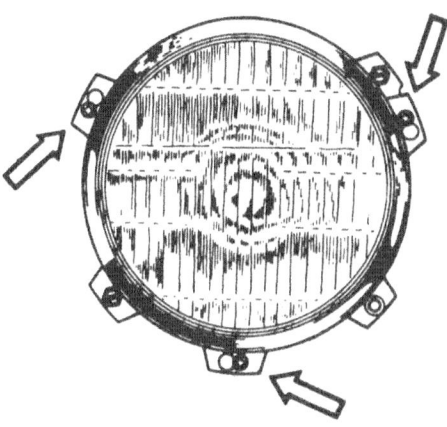

Fig. 10.19 Headlamp securing screws (Sec 30)

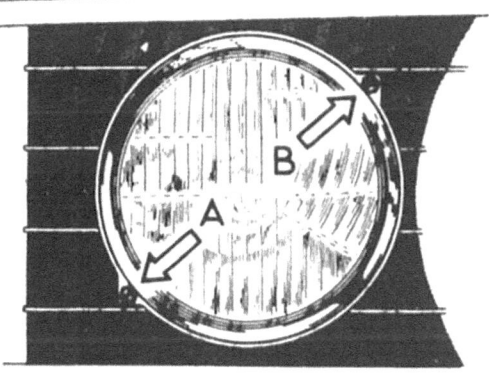

Fig. 10.20 Beam adjusting screws (Sec 30)

A *Beam horizontal adjusting screw*
B *Beam height adjusting screw*

30.2 Removing the headlamp unit

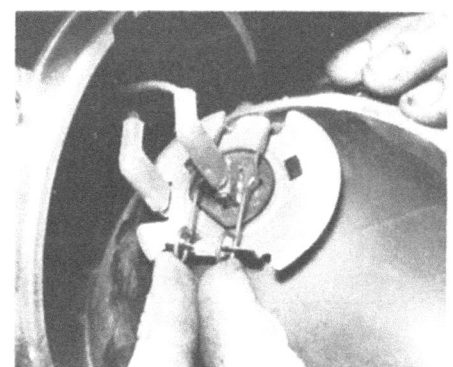

30.4a Release the retaining clip ...

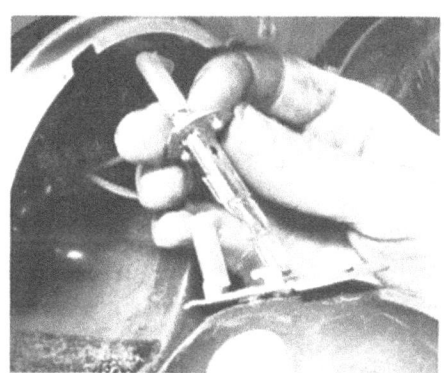

30.4b ... and then withdraw the bulb

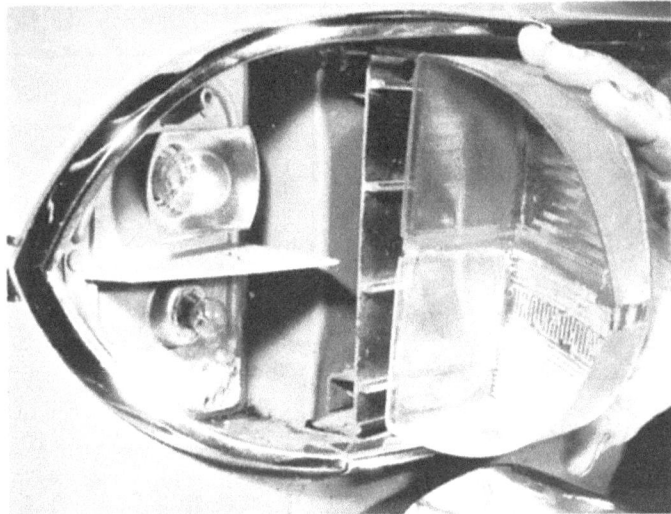

31.1 Removing the front parking and flasher lamp lens

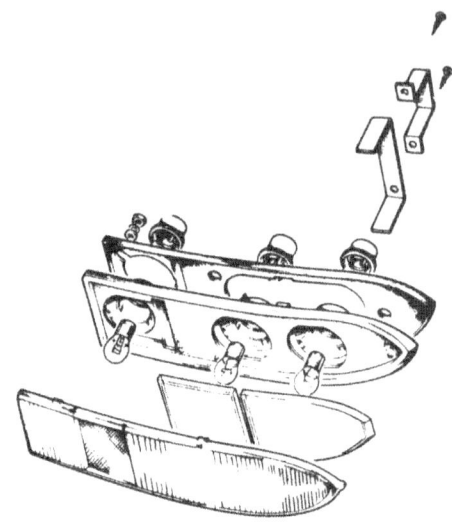

Fig. 10.21 Rear lamp cluster (Sec 33)

33.2 Removing a bulb in the rear lamp cluster

Fig. 10.22 Rear number plate lamp – early models (Sec 34)

34 Rear number plate lamp – bulb renewal

Early models – bumper mounted

1 Undo the two retaining screws and remove the chrome cover.
2 Remove the lens by disengaging the retaining lugs from the rubber base and then remove the two bulbs.
3 Refitting is the reverse of the removal procedure.

Later models – boot lid mounted

4 To gain access to the bulbs undo the two screws securing the cover and remove the cover and then remove the bulbs.
5 Refitting is the reverse of the removal procedure.

35 Puddle lamp – bulb renewal

1 Remove the single screw securing the lens and slide the lens to the rear until it is free of the channels, then remove the bulb (photo).
2 Refitting is a reverse of the removal procedure.

36 Luggage boot lamp – bulb renewal

1 Carefully prise the chrome ring from the lamp body.
2 Withdraw the lens and remove the bulb (photo).
3 Refitting is a reverse of the removal procedure.

37 Interior lamp – bulb renewal

1 The festoon type bulb in the interior lamp is accessible after removing the two securing screws and taking off the lens (photo). The bulb is then pulled out.
2 Refitting is the reverse of the removal procedure.

38 Instrument panel – bulb renewal

1 These bulbs can only be renewed after the instrument panel has been released and pulled forward to gain access to the bulb holders.
2 Instrument panel removal is described in Section 46.

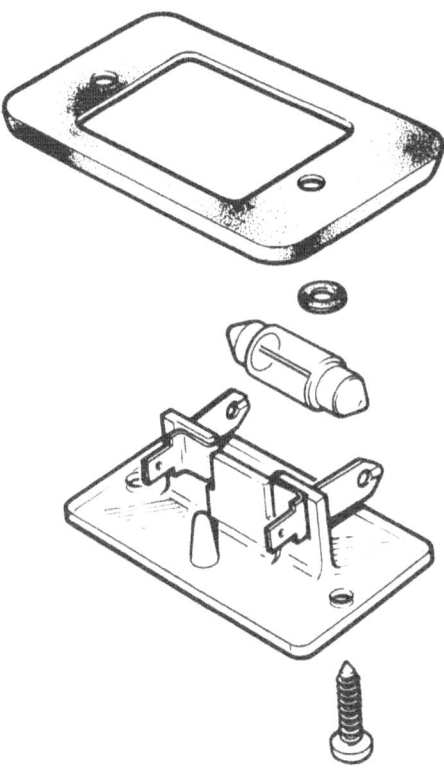

Fig. 10.23 Rear number plate lamp – later models (Sec 34)

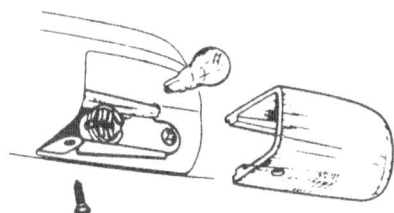

Fig. 10.24 Puddle lamp (Sec 35)

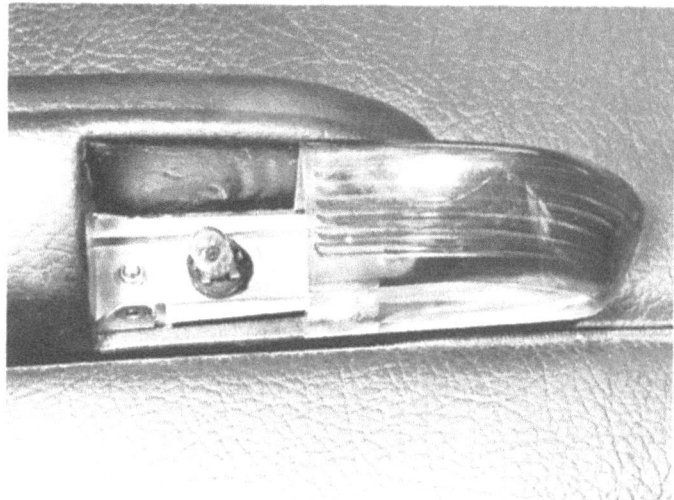

35.1 Slide the puddle lamp lens to the rear

36.2 Removing the luggage boot lamp lens

39 Warning light cluster – bulb renewal

1   Release the instrument panel and pull it forward, refer to Section 46, to rest on the steering column.
2   Pull the plug connector from the unit.
3   Remove the retaining screw, spring washer and plain washer and withdraw the base plate.
4   Renew the appropriate bulb/s.
5   Refitting is the reverse of the removal procedure.

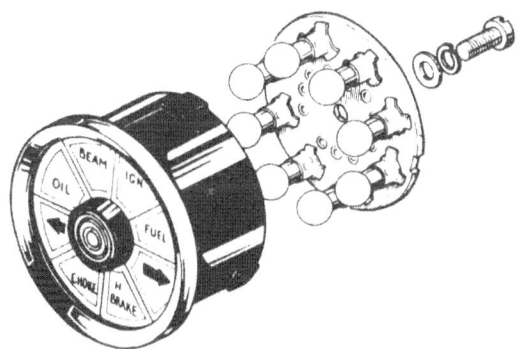

Fig. 10.25 Warning light cluster (Sec 39)

37.1 Renewing the interior lamp festoon bulb

40 Night dimming relay (early models only) – general description

1   The night dimming relay dims stop lamps and rear flasher lamps when the parking lamps are illuminated. At night minimum discomfort to other road users is ensured but in daylight the safety of full intensity is provided.

2   The relay winding, controlled by the parking lamp circuit, comprises three sets of normally closed contacts with associated resistors permanently in parallel. The stop lamps, the left-hand rear flasher lamp and the right-hand flasher lamp are each associated with one contact/resistor set (Fig. 10.26).

3   When the relay is de-energized the contacts are closed and the lamps operate at full intensity; when the relay is energized the contacts are open. The resistors are positioned in series with the lamps which then operate at a reduced voltage.

4   To maintain the correct frequency of operation of the indicator flasher unit the current must be kept constant, so to provide current compensation for either flasher circuit a fourth resistor is used. This resistor is brought into circuit by the double contact set between terminals 2 and 5. The switching is such that when either flasher circuit is energized, a parallel path exists through R3, the resistor of the unselected flasher circuit and across the filament of the unselected rear flasher lamp to earth. While providing compensation, this current is not large enough to illuminate the unselected flasher lamp.

41 Night dimming relay (early models only) – removal and refitting

1   Disconnect the battery negative terminal.

2   Remove the carpet from the luggage boot, the left-hand floor panel and the left-hand side trim panel.

3   Undo the two securing screws and withdraw the relay.

4   Make a note of the wiring connections then disconnect the two Lucar connections and the two multi-socket connectors.

5   Refitting is the reverse of the removal procedure.

42 Ignition/starter switch – removal and refitting

1   Disconnect the battery negative terminal.

2   Remove the steering column as described in Chapter 11.

3   Undo the two screws securing the upper half of the steering column shroud, raise it enough to permit access to disconnect the three Lucar connectors from the master light switch, then lift the upper shroud away.

4   Remove the lower half of the shroud (one screw).

5   Remove the harness cover clip securing screw, washers and nut, then slide the sleeve downwards and lift it away.

6   Remove the harness cover (two screws).

7   Using a Posidriv screwdriver undo the switch securing screws (two) and withdraw the ignition/starter switch from the steering lock assembly.

8   Refitting the switch is the reverse of the removal procedure. Connect the Lucar connectors to the master light switch, brown wire to terminal 4, red wire to terminal 1 and blue wire to terminal 8.

43 Master lighting switch – removal and refitting

1   Refer to Section 42 and carry out operations 1 to 3.

2   Depress the spring plunger in the switch, by inserting a suitable probe in the hole in the knob, and pull the knob off the spindle.

3   Undo the securing nut and withdraw the switch.

4   Refitting is the reverse of the removal procedure. When reconnecting the Lucar connectors refer to Section 42, paragraph 8.

44 Combination switch – removal and refitting

1   Refer to Section 42 and carry out the operations described in paragraphs 1-6.

2   Undo the two securing screws and withdraw the windscreen washer/wiper switch.

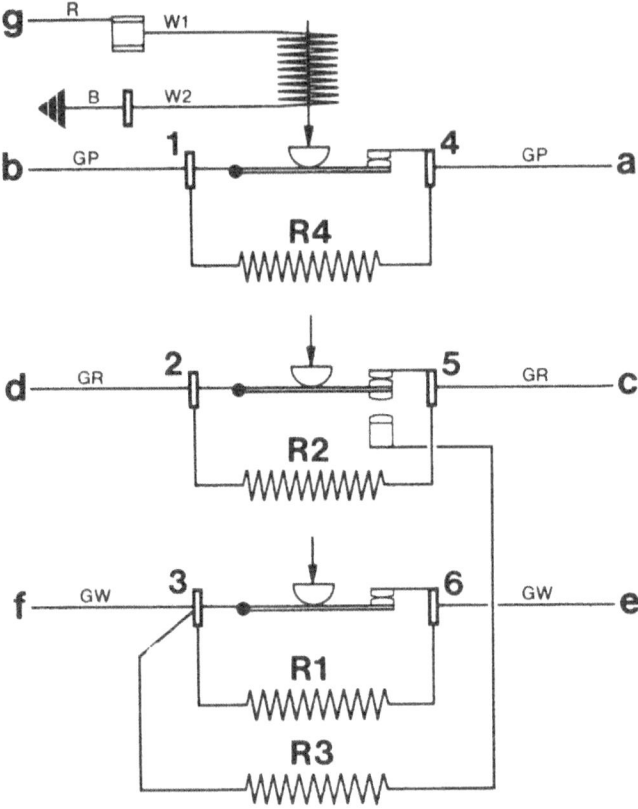

Fig. 10.26 Night dimming relay wiring circuit (Sec 40)

a From stop lamp switch
b To both stop lamps
c From turn signal switch
d To LH rear flasher lamp
e From turn signal switch
f To RH rear flasher lamp
g From master light switch

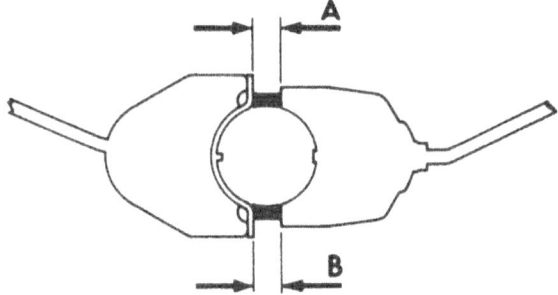

Fig. 10.27 Positioning the combination switch (Sec 44)

3   Refer to Fig. 10.27 and note the dimensions A and B.

4   Undo the two securing screws and withdraw the switch and clamp.

5   Refitting is the reverse of the removal procedure. When tightening the switch securing screws ensure that dimensions A and B are maintained as noted at removal so that the switch stalk will be centralised in the shroud aperture.

45 Fuses

1   The fuse block is mounted on the bulkhead under a protective cover. The cover has locating lugs and can only be fitted one way (photo).

2   The fuse block has twelve fuse positions and the circuits protected are shown in Specifications at the beginning of this Chapter. The fuse

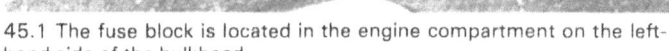

45.1 The fuse block is located in the engine compartment on the left-hand side of the bulkhead

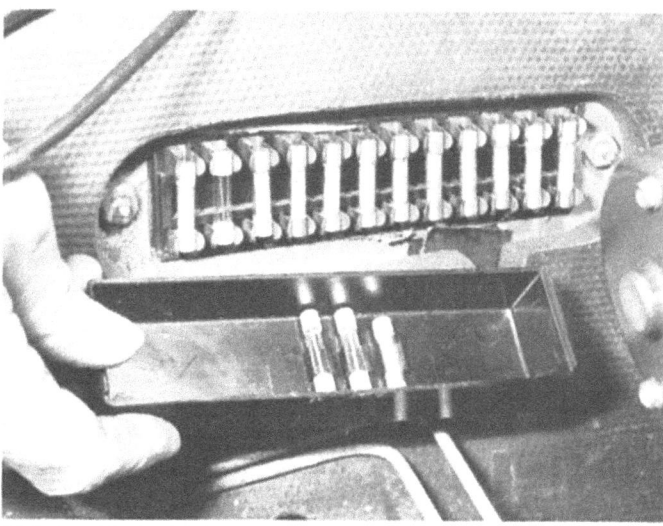

45.2 Fuse block with the cover removed

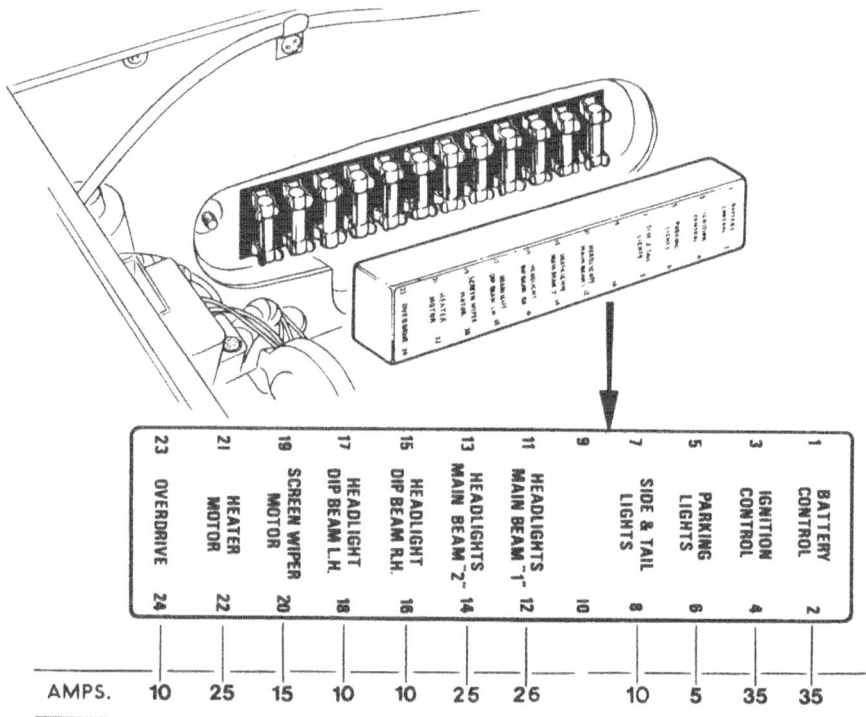

23	21	19	17	15	13	11	9	7	5	3	1
OVERDRIVE	HEATER MOTOR	SCREEN WIPER MOTOR	HEADLIGHT DIP BEAM L.H.	HEADLIGHT DIP BEAM R.H.	HEADLIGHTS MAIN BEAM "2"	HEADLIGHTS MAIN BEAM "1"		SIDE & TAIL LIGHTS	PARKING LIGHTS	IGNITION CONTROL	BATTERY CONTROL
24	22	20	18	16	14	12	10	8	6	4	2
AMPS. 10	25	15	10	10	25	26		10	5	35	35

Fig. 10.28 The fuse block and cover (Sec 45)

block cover houses three spare fuses (photo).

3 Two line fuses are also used. They are located near the component mounting plate mounted on the bulkhead, behind the parcel shelf which must be removed to gain access to the fuse holders (Fig. 10.29).

4 Before renewing a blown fuse, it is important to find the cause of the trouble and for it to be rectified, as the fuse acts as a safety device and protects the electrical system against expensive damage should a fault occur.

5 Always renew a blown fuse with a fuse of the same amperage, do not use anything else to complete the circuit.

46 Instrument panel – removal and refitting

1 Disconnect the earth strap from the negative terminal on the battery.

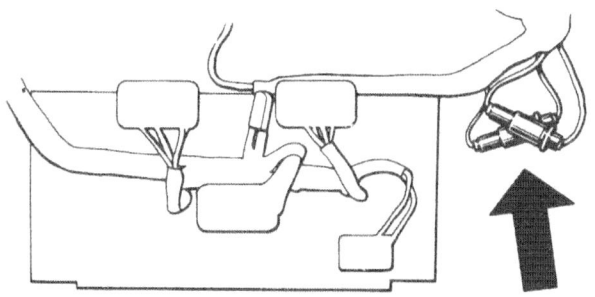

Fig. 10.29 Location of the two line fuses (Sec 45)

2   Move the steering column to its lowest position.
3   Disconnect the vent hose from the heater outlet duct on the driver's side. Remove the panel rheostat knob.
4   Undo the four screws securing the instrument panel and pull the panel forward far enough to permit the speedometer cable and clock reset cable to be disconnected by unscrewing the retaining knurled nuts.
5   Now withdraw the panel and rest it on the steering column as shown in Fig. 10.30.
6   Remove the glove box and lid assembly.
7   Disconnect the two Lucar connectors from the rheostat and the three harness plugs.
8   Remove the trip reset knurled nut (early models) and then lift out the instrument panel.
9   Refitting is the reverse of the removal procedure.

47 Instruments – removal and refitting

1   To renew a warning or indicator lamp bulb or to remove an instrument, refer to Section 46 and carry out the procedure described in paragraphs 1 to 5.
2   With the panel in this position the various instruments can be removed by disconnecting the Lucar connectors and undoing the securing screws and clamp as appropriate.
3   When refitting the tachometer it is most important that the leads are connected as shown in Fig. 10.31 as it contains polarity-sensitive components and irreparable damage may be caused if incorrectly connected.

48 Inner speedometer cable – removal and refitting

1   Refer to Section 46 and carry out the procedure described in paragraphs 1 to 5.
2   Carefully withdraw the inner cable.
3   When refitting the inner cable, smear it lightly with grease (not oil) and feed it into the outer cable. Turning the cable as it is pushed in will help it to slide through the outer cable.
4   Now pull the cable out approximately 8 in (200 mm) and wipe off any surplus grease, then push the cable in again and rotate it to ensure that the squared end of the cable is located in the drivegear at the gearbox.
5   Reverse the operations described in Section 46, paragraphs 1 to 5.

49 Radios and tape players – installation

A radio or tape player is an expensive item to buy; and will only give its best performance if fitted properly. It is useless to expect concert hall performance from a unit that is suspended from the dashpanel by string with its speaker resting on the back seat or parcel shelf! If you do not wish to do the installation yourself there are many in-car entertainment specialists who can do the fitting for you.

Make sure the unit purchased is of the same polarity as the vehicle. Ensure that units with adjustable polarity are correctly set before commencing installation.

It is difficult to give specific information with regard to fitting, as final positioning of the radio/tape player, speakers and aerial is entirely a matter of personal preference. However, the following paragraphs give guidelines to follow, which are relevant to all installations.

Radios
Most radios are a standardised size of 7 inches wide, by 2 inches deep – this ensures that they will fit into the radio aperture provided in most cars. If your car does not have such an aperture, then the radio must be fitted in a suitable position either in, or beneath, the dashpanel. Alternatively, a special console can be purchased which will fit between the dashpanel and the floor, or on the transmission tunnel. These consoles can also be used for additional switches and instrumentation if required. Where no radio aperture is provided, the following points should be borne in mind before deciding exactly where to fit the unit.

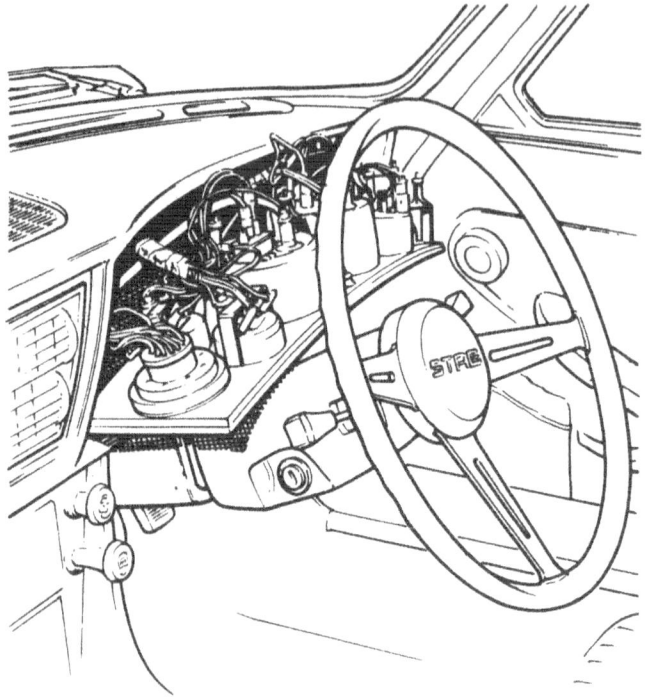

Fig. 10.30 Removing the instrument panel (Sec 46)

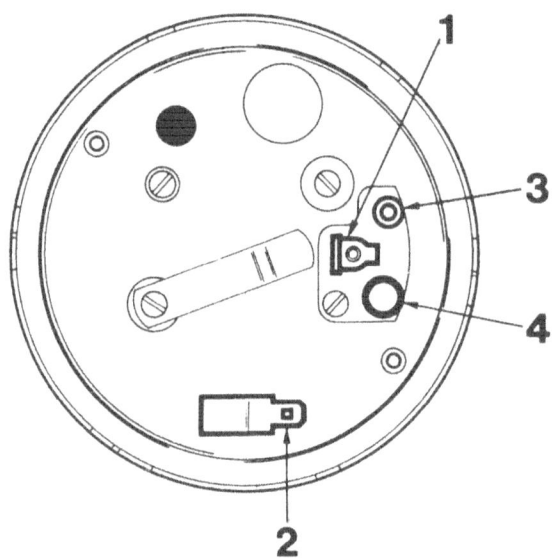

Fig. 10.31 Tachometer electrical connections (Sec 47)

1 *Green wire*   3 *White wire*
2 *Black wire*   4 *White/slate wire*

(a) *The unit must be within easy reach of the driver wearing a seat belt*
(b) *The unit must not be mounted in close proximity to an electric tachometer, the ignition switch and its wiring, or the flasher unit and associated wiring*
(c) *The unit must be mounted within reach of the aerial lead, and in such a place that the aerial lead will not have to be routed near the components detailed in the preceding paragraph 'b'*
(d) *The unit should not be positioned in a place where it might cause injury to the car occupants in an accident; for instance, under the dashpanel above the driver's or passenger's legs*
(e) *The unit must be fitted really securely*

Some radios will have mounting brackets provided together with instructions: others will need to be fitted using drilled and slotted metal strips, bent to form mounting brackets – these strips are available from most accessory stores. The unit must be properly earthed, by fitting a separate earth lead between the casing of the radio and the vehicle frame.

Use the radio manufacturer's instructions when wiring the radio into the vehicle's electrical system. If no instructions are available refer to the relevant wiring diagram to find the location of the radio 'feed' connection in the vehicle's wiring circuit. A 1-2 amp 'in-line' fuse must be fitted in the radio's 'feed' wire – a choke may also be necessary (see next Section).

The type of aerial used, and its fitted position, is a matter of personal preference. In general the taller the aerial, the better the reception. It is best to fit a fully retractable aerial – especially, if a mechanical car-wash is used or if you live in an area where cars tend to be vandalised. In this respect electric aerials which are raised and lowered automatically when switching the radio on or off are convenient, but are more likely to give trouble than the manual type.

When choosing a site for the aerial the following points should be considered:

(a) *The aerial lead should be as short as possible, this means that the aerial should be mounted at the front of the vehicle*

(b) *The aerial must be mounted as far away from the distributor and HT leads as possible*

(c) *The part of the aerial which protrudes beneath the mounting point must not foul the roadwheels, or anything else*

(d) *If possible the aerial should be positioned so that the coaxial lead does not have to be routed through the engine compartment*

(e) *The plane of the panel on which the aerial is mounted should not be so steeply angled that the aerial cannot be mounted vertically (in relation to the 'end-on' aspect of the vehicle). Most aerials have a small amount of adjustment available*

Having decided on a mounting position, a relatively large hole will have to be made in the panel. The exact size of the hole will depend upon the specific aerial being fitted, although, generally, the hole required is of $\frac{3}{4}$ inch diameter. On metal bodied cars, a 'tank-cutter' of the relevant diameter is the best tool to be used for making the hole. This tools needs a small diameter pilot hole drilled through the panel, through which the tool clamping bolt is inserted. On GRP bodied cars, a 'hole-saw' is the best tool to use. Again, this tool will require the drilling of a small pilot hole. When the hole has been made the raw edges should be de-burred with a file and then painted, to prevent corrosion.

Fit the aerial according to the manufacturer's instructions. If the aerial is very tall, or if it protrudes beneath the mounting panel for a considerable distance it is a good idea to fit a stay between the aerial and the vehicle frame. This stay can be manufactured from the slotted and drilled metal strips previously mentioned. The stay should be securely screwed or bolted in place. For best reception it is advisable to fit an earth lead between the aerial body and the vehicle frame – this is essential on fibre glass bodied vehicles.

It will probably be necessary to drill one, or two holes through bodywork panels in order to feed the aerial lead into the interior of the car. Where this is the case ensure that the holes are fitted with rubber grommets to protect the cable and to stop possible entry of water.

Positioning and fitting of the speaker depends mainly on its type. Generally, the speaker is designed to fit direcly into the aperture already provided in the car (usually in the shelf behind the rear seats, or in the top of the dashpanel). Where this is the case, fitting the speaker is just a matter of removing the protective grille from the aperture and screwing or bolting the speaker in place. Take great care not to damage the speaker diaphragm whilst doing this. It is a good idea to fit a 'gasket' between the speaker frame and the mounting panel in order to prevent vibration – some speakers will already have such a gasket fitted.

If a 'pod' type speaker was supplied with the radio, the best acoustic results will normally be obtained by mounting it on the shelf behind the rear seat. The pod can be secured to the mounting panel with self-tapping screws.

When connecting a rear mounted speaker to the radio, the wires should be routed through the vehicle beneath the carpets or floor mats – preferably through the middle, or along the side of the floorpan, where they will not be trodden on by passengers. Make the relevant connections as directed by the radio manufacturer.

By now you will have several yards of additional wiring in the car; use PVC tape to secure this wiring out of harm's way. Do not leave electrical leads dangling. Ensure that all new electrical connections are properly made (wires twisted together will not do) and completely secure.

The radio should now be working, but before you pack away your tools it will be necessary to 'trim' the radio to the aerial. Follow the radio manufacturer's instructions regarding this adjustment.

Tape players

Fitting instructions for both cartridge and cassette stereo tape players are the same and in general the same rules apply as when fitting a radio. Tape players are not usually prone to electrical interference like radios – although it can occur – so positioning is not so critical. If possible the player should be mounted on an 'even-keel'. Also, it must be possible for a driver wearing a seat belt to reach the unit in order to change, or turn over, tapes.

For the best results from speakers designed to be recessed into a panel, mount them so that the back of the speaker protrudes into an enclosed chamber within the vehicle (eg; door interiors or the boot cavity).

To fit recessed type speakers in the front doors first check that there is sufficient room to mount the speaker in each door without it fouling the latch or window winding mechanism. Hold the speaker against the skin of the door, and draw a line around the periphery of the speaker. With the speaker removed draw a second 'cutting' line, within the first, to allow enough room for the entry of the speaker back, but at the same time providing a broad seat for the speaker flange. When you are sure that the 'cutting-line' is correct, drill a series of holes around its periphery. Pass a hacksaw blade through one of the holes and then cut through the metal between the holes until the centre section of the panel falls out.

De-burr the edges of the hole and then paint the raw metal to prevent corrosion. Cut a corresponding hole in the door trim panel – ensuring that it will be completely covered by the speaker grille. Now drill a hole in the door edge and a corresponding hole in the door surround. These holes are to feed the speaker leads through – so fit grommets. Pass the speaker leads through the door trim, door skin and out through the holes in the side of the door and door surround. Refit the door trim panel and then secure the speaker to the door using self-tapping screws. **Note:** *If the speaker is fitted with a shield to prevent water dripping on it, ensure that this shield is at the top.*

'Pod' type speakers can be fastened to the shelf behind the rear seat, or anywhere else offering a corresponding mounting point on each side of the car. If the 'pod' speakers are mounted on each side of the shelf behind the rear seat, it is a good idea to drill several large diameter holes through to the trunk cavity beneath each speaker – this will improve the sound reproduction. 'Pod' speakers sometimes offer a better reproduction quality if they face the rear window – which then acts as a reflector – so it is worthwhile experimenting before finally fixing the speakers.

50 Radios and tape players – suppression of interference (general)

To eliminate buzzes, and other unwanted noises, costs very little and is not as difficult as sometimes thought. With a modicum of common sense and patience and following the instructions in the following paragraphs, interference can be virtually eliminated.

The first cause for concern is the generator. The noise this makes over the radio is like an electric mixer and the noise speeds up when you rev up the engine (if you wish to prove the point, you can remove the fanbelt and try it). The remedy for this is simple; connect a 1.0 mf-3.0 mf capacitor between earth, probably the bolt that holds down the generator base, and the *large* terminal on the generator. This is most important, for if you connect it to a small terminal, you will probably damage the generator permanently (see Fig. 10.32).

A second common cause of electrical interference is the ignition system. Here a 1.0 mf capacitor must be connected between earth and the SW or + terminal on the coil (see Fig. 10.33). This may stop the tick-tick-tick sound that comes over the speaker. Next comes the spark itself.

There are several ways of curing interference from the ignition HT system. One is the use of carbon-cored HT leads as original equipment. Where copper cable is substituted then you must use resistive

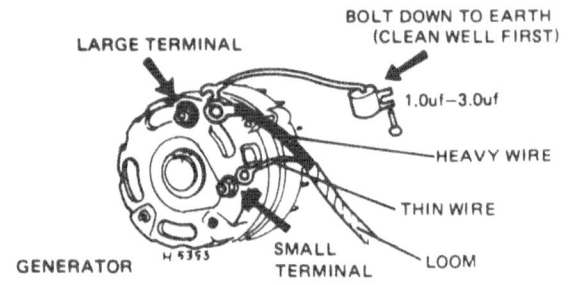

Fig. 10.32 The correct way to connect a capacitor to the generator (Sec 50)

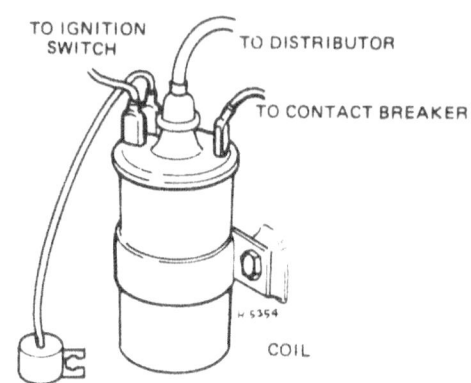

Fig. 10.33 The capacitor must be connected to the ignition switch side of the coil (Sec 50)

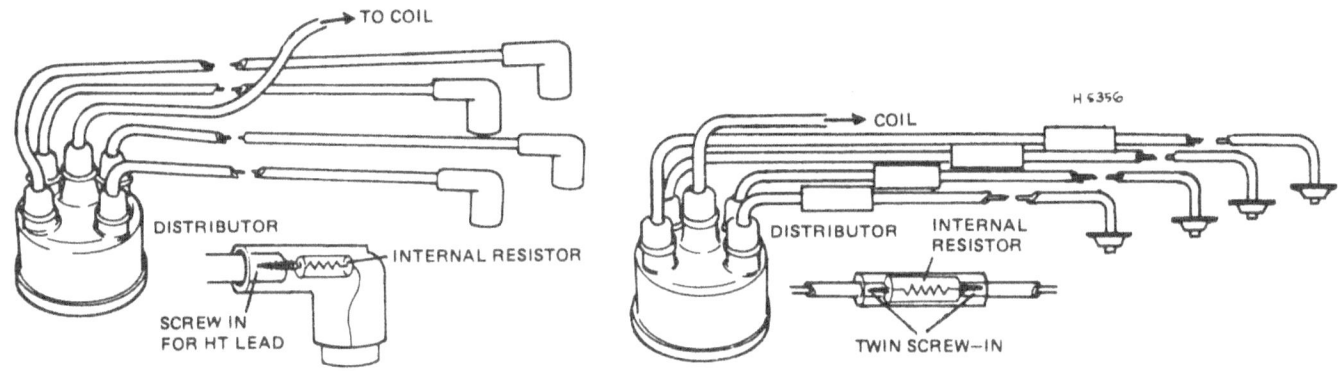

Fig. 10.34 Ignition HT lead suppressors (Sec 50)
Resistive spark plug caps (left) 'In-line' suppressors (right)

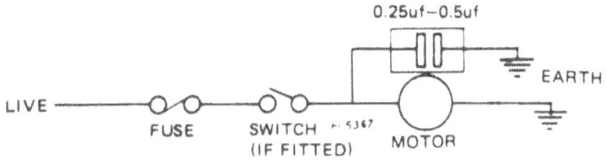

Fig. 10.35 Correct method of suppressing electric motors (Sec 50)

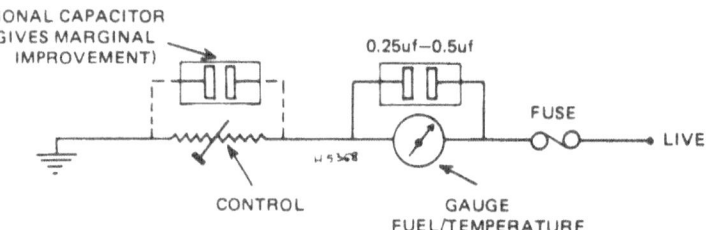

Fig. 10.36 Method of suppressing gauges and their control units (Sec 50)

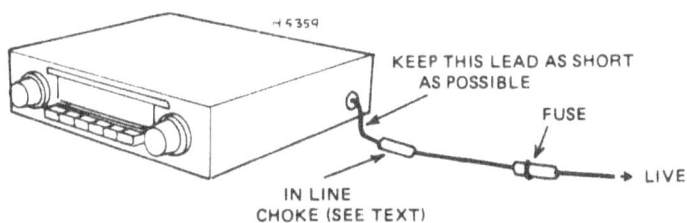

Fig. 10.37 An 'in-line' choke should be fitted into the live supply load as close to the unit as possible (Sec 50)

spark plug caps (see Fig. 10.34) of about 10,000 ohm to 15,000 ohm resistance. If, due to lack of room, these cannot be used, an alternative is to use in-line suppressors – if the interference is not too bad, you may get away with only one suppressor in the coil to distributor line. If the interference does continue (a 'clacking' noise) then modify all HT leads.

At this stage it is advisable to check that the radio is well earthed, also the aerial and to see that the aerial plug is pushed well into the set and that the radio is properly trimmed (see preceding Section). In addition, check that the wire which supplies the power to the set is as short as possible and does not wander all over the car. At this stage it is a good idea to check that the fuse is of the correct rating. For most sets this will be about 1 to 2 amps.

At this point the more usual causes of interference have been suppressed. If the problem still exists, a look at the causes of interference may help to pinpoint the component generating the stray electrical discharges.

The radio picks up electromagnetic waves in the air; now some are made by regular broadcasters, and some, which we do not want, are made by the car itself. The home made signals are produced by stray electrical discharges floating around in the car. Common producers of these signals are electric motors, ie, the windscreen wipers, electric screen washers, electric window winders, heater fan or an electric aerial if fitted. Other sources of interference are flashing turn signal and instruments. The remedy for these cases is shown in Fig. 10.35 for an electric motor whose interference is not too bad and Fig. 10.36 for instrument suppression. Turn signals are not normally suppressed. In recent years, radio manufacturers have included in the line (live) of the radio, in addition to the fuse, an 'in-line' choke. If your circuit lacks one of these, put one in as shown in Fig. 10.37.

All the foregoing components are available from radio stores or accessory stores. If you have an electric clock fitted this should be suppressed by connecting a 0.5 mf capacitor directly across it as shown for a motor in Fig. 10.35.

If after all this, you are still experiencing radio interference, first assess how bad it is, for the human ear can filter out unobtrusive unwanted noises quite easily. But if you are still adamant about eradicating the noise, then continue.

As a first step, a few 'experts' seem to favour a screen between the radio and the engine. This is OK as far as it goes – literally! – for the whole set is screened anyway and if interference can get past that then a small piece of aluminium is not going to stop it.

A more sensible way of screening is to discover if interference is coming down the wires. First, take the live lead; interference can get between the set and the choke (hence the reason for keeping the wires short). One remedy here is to screen the wire and this is done by buying screened wire and fitting that. The loudspeaker lead could be screened also to prevent 'pick-up' getting back to the radio although this is unlikely.

Without doubt, the worst source of radio interference comes from the ignition HT leads, even if they have been suppressed. The ideal way of suppressing these is to slide screening tubes over the leads themselves. As this is impractical, we can place an aluminium shield over the majority of the lead areas. In a vee- or twin-cam engine this is relatively easy; for a straight engine, the results are not particularly good.

Now for the really impossible cases, here are a few tips to try out. Where metal comes into contact with metal, an electrical disturbance is caused which is why good clean connections are essential. To remove interference due to overlapping or butting panels you must bridge the join with a wide braided earth strap (like that from the frame to the engine/transmission). The most common moving parts that could create noise and should be strapped are, in order of importance:

(a) Silencer to frame
(b) Exhaust pipe to engine block and frame
(c) Air cleaner to frame
(d) Front and rear bumpers to frame
(e) Steering column to frame
(f) Bonnet and boot lids to frame
(g) Hood frame to bodyframe on soft tops

These faults are most pronounced when (1) the engine is idling, (2) labouring under load. Although the moving parts are already connected with nuts, bolts, etc, these do tend to rust and corrode, thus creating a high resistance interference source.

If you have a 'ragged' sounding pulse when mobile, this could be wheel or tyre static. This can be cured by buying some anti-static powder and sprinkling it liberally inside the tyres.

If the interference takes the shape of a high pitched screeching noise that changes its note when the car is in motion and only comes now and then, this could be related to the aerial, especially if it is of the telescopic or whip type. This source can be cured quite simply by pushing a small rubber ball on top of the aerial as this breaks the electric field before it can form; but it would be much better to buy yourself a new aerial of a reputable brand. If, on the other hand, you are getting a loud rushing sound every time you brake, then this is brake static. This effect is most prominent on hot dry days and is cured only by fitting a special kit, which is quite expensive.

In conclusion, it is pointed out that it is relatively easy, and therefore cheap, to eliminate 95 per cent of all noise, but to eliminate the final 5 per cent is time and money consuming. It is up to the individual to decide if it is worth it. Please remember also, that you cannot get a concert hall performance out of a cheap radio.

Finally, players and eight track players are not usually affected by car noise but in a very bad case, the best remedies are the first three suggestions plus using a 3-5 amp choke in the 'live' line and in incurable cases screen the live and speaker wires.

Note: *If you car is fitted with electronic ignition, then it is not recommended that either the spark plug resistors or the ignition coil capacitor be fitted as these may damage the system. Most electronic ignition units have built-in suppression and should, therefore, not cause interference.*

51 Fault diagnosis – electrical system

Symptom	Reason/s
Starter motor fails to turn engine	Battery discharged
	Battery defective internally
	Battery terminal leads loose or earth lead not securely attached to body
	Loose or broken connections in starter motor circuit
	Starter motor switch or solenoid faulty
	Starter motor pinion jammed in mesh with flywheel gear ring
	Starter brushes badly worn, sticking or brush wires loose
	Commutator dirty, worn or burnt
	Starter motor armature faulty
	Field coils earthed
Starter motor turns engine very slowly	Battery in discharged condition
	Starter brushes badly worn, sticking or brush wires loose
	Loose wires in starter motor circuit

Symptom	Reason/s
Starter motor operates without turning engine	Starter motor pinion sticking on the screwed sleeve Pinion or flywheel gear teeth broken or worn
Starter motor noisy or engagement excessively rough	Pinion or flywheel teeth broken or worn Starter motor retaining bolts loose
Starter motor remains in operation after ignition key released	Faulty ignition switch Faulty solenoid
Charging system indicator on with ignition switch off	Faulty alternator diode
Charging system indicator light on – engine speed above idling	Loose or broken drivebelt Shorted negative diode or faulty voltage regulator No output from alternator
Charge indicator light not on when ignition switched on but engine not running	Burned out bulb Field circuit open Lamp circuit open
Battery will not hold charge for more than a few days	Battery defective internally Electrolyte level too weak or too low Battery plates heavily sulphated
Horns will not operate intermittently	Loose connections Defective switch Defective relay Defective horns
Horns blow continually	Faulty relay Relay wiring grounded Horn button stuck (grounded)
Lights do not come on	If engine not running, battery discharged Light bulb filament burnt out or bulbs broken Wire connections loose, disconnected or broken Light switch shorting or otherwise faulty
Lights come on but fade out	If engine not running battery discharged
Lights give very poor illumination	Lamp glasses dirty Lamps badly out of adjustment
Lights work erratically – flashing on and off, especially over rough surface	Battery terminals or earth connection loose Lights not earthing properly Contacts in light switch faulty
Wiper motor fails to work	Blown fuse Wire connections loose, disconnected, or broken Brushes badly worn Armature worn or faulty Field coils faulty
Wiper motor works very slowly and takes excessive current	Commutator dirty, greasy or burnt Armature bearings dirty or unaligned Armature badly worn or faulty
Wiper motor works slowly and takes little current	Brushes badly worn Commutator dirty, greasy or burnt Armature badly worn or faulty
Wiper motor works but wiper blades remain static	Wiper motor gearbox parts badly worn or teeth stripped

Wiring diagrams
(pages 146–173)

Fig. 10.38 Wiring diagram – RH steering with heater (Up to Commission No LD 2000)

1 Alternator
2 Charging system relay
3 Alternator control unit
4 Ignition warning light
5 Battery
6 Battery condition indicator
7 Ignition/starter switch
8 Radio supply
9 Inertia cut-out
10 Petrol pump
11 Inhibitor switch – Borg-Warner automatic only
12 Starter motor
13 Ballast resistor
14 Ignition coil – 6 volt
15 Ignition distributor
16 Master light switch
17 Fog lamp supply
18 RH tail lamp
19 RH front parking lamp
20 LH tail lamp
21 LH front parking lamp
22 Night dimming relay
23 Plate illumination lamp
24 Panel rheostat
25 Cigarette lighter illumination
26 Selector panel illumination – Borg-Warner automatic only
27 Instrument illumination
28 Dip and main beam

29 Main/dip/flash switch
30 Main beam
31 Main beam warning light
32 Horn relay
33 Horn-push
34 Horn
35 Cigarette lighter
36 Luggage boot lamp
37 Luggage boot lamp switch
38 RH door switch
39 RH puddle lamp
40 Interior lamp switch
41 RH 'B post' lamp
42 RH console lamp
43 LH door switch
44 LH puddle lamp
45 LH 'B post' lamp
46 LH console lamp
47 Glovebox/map lamp
48 Glovebox/map lamp switch
49 Clock
50 Windscreen wiper switch
51 Windscreen wiper motor
52 Tachometer
53 Voltage stabilizer
54 Fuel indicator
55 Fuel tank unit
56 Fuel warning light

57 Temperature indicator
58 Temperature transmitter
59 Windscreen washer pump
60 Windscreen washer switch
61 Reverse lamp
62 Reverse lamp switch
63 Stop lamp switch
64 Stop lamp
65 Turn signal flasher unit
66 Turn signal switch
67 LH front flasher lamp
68 LH flasher repeater lamp
69 LH rear flasher lamp
70 RH front flasher lamp
71 RH flasher repeater lamp
72 RH rear flasher lamp
73 Turn signal warning light
74 Handbrake warning light
75 Handbrake switch
76 Temperature warning light
77 Temperature switch
78 Choke warning light
79 Choke switch
80 Brake line failure warning light
81 Brake line failure switch
82 Oil pressure warning light
83 Oil pressure switch
84 Ignition controlled relay

85 Overdrive gear lever switch – optional extra
86 Overdrive gearbox switch – optional extra
87 Overdrive solenoid – optional extra
88 Window lift circuit breaker
89 LH window lift switch
90 LH window lift motor
91 RH window lift switch
92 RH window lift motor
93 Ignition controlled relay
94 Heated backlight switch
95 Heated backlight
96 Heated backlight warning light
97 Heater switch
98 Heater rheostat
99 Heater motor

Colour code
N Brown
U Blue
R Red
P Purple
K Pink
S Slate
LG Light green
G Green
W White
Y Yellow
B Black

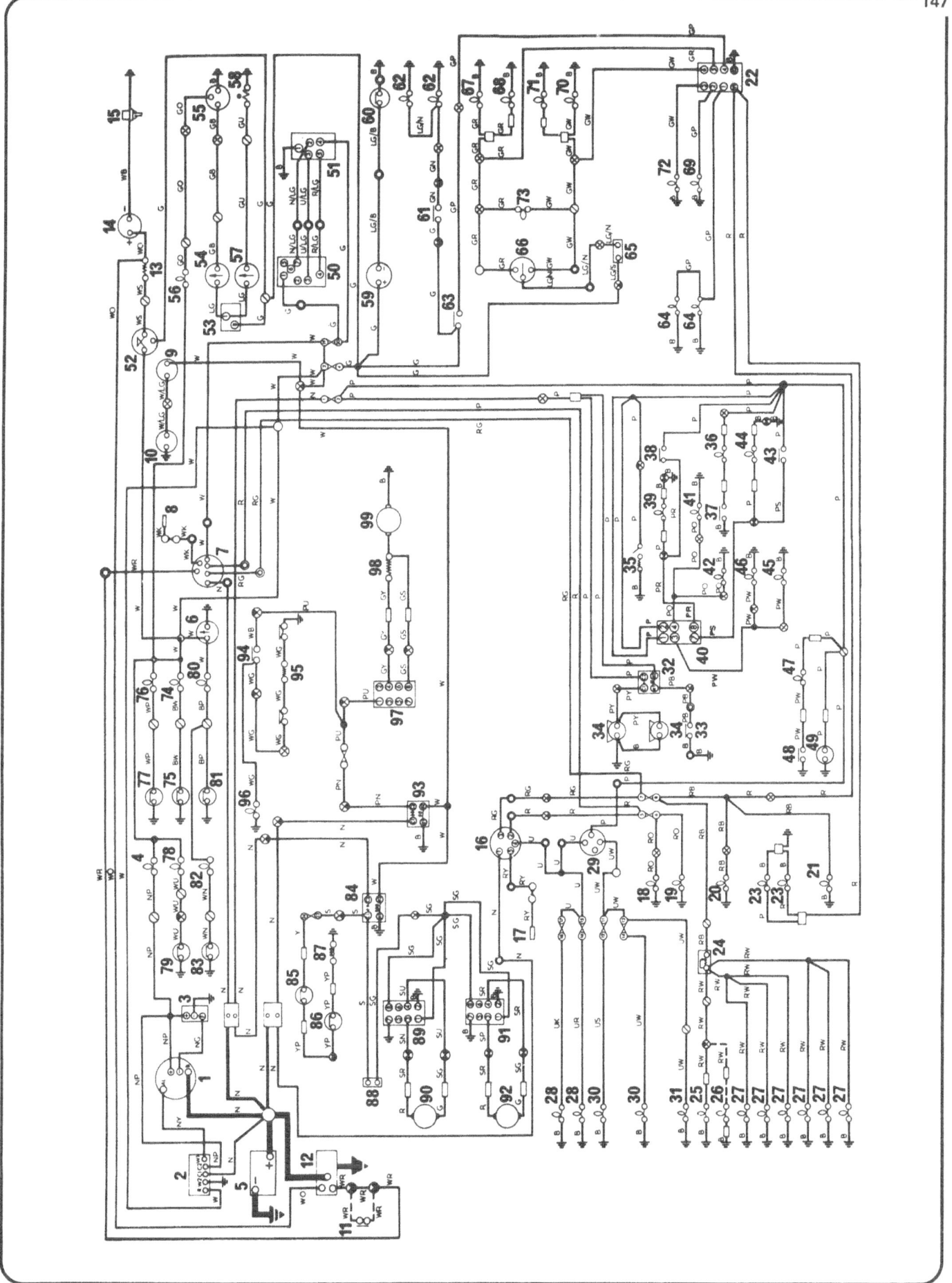

148

Fig. 10.39 Wiring diagram — RH steering with air conditioning (Up to Commission No LD 2000)

1 Alternator
2 Charging system relay
3 Alternator control unit
4 Ignition warning light
5 Battery
6 Battery condition indicator
7 Ignition/starter switch
8 Radio supply
9 Inertia cut-out
10 Petrol pump
11 Inhibitor switch – Borg-Warner automatic only
12 Starter motor
13 Ballast resistor
14 Ignition coil – 6 volt
15 Ignition distributor
16 Master light switch
17 Fog lamp supply
18 RH tail lamp
19 RH front parking lamp
20 LH tail lamp
21 LH front parking lamp
22 Night dimming relay
23 Plate illumination lamp
24 Panel rheostat
25 Cigarette lighter illumination
26 Selector panel illumination – Borg-Warner automatic only
27 Instrument illumination
28 Dip and main beam
29 Main/dip/flash switch
30 Main beam
31 Main beam warning light
32 Horn relay
33 Horn-push
34 Horn
35 Cigarette lighter
36 Luggage boot lamp
37 Luggage boot lamp switch
38 RH door switch
39 RH puddle lamp

40 Interior lamp switch
41 RH 'B post' lamp
42 RH console lamp
43 LH door switch
44 LH puddle lamp
45 LH 'B post' lamp
46 LH console lamp
47 Glovebox/map lamp
48 Glovebox/map lamp switch
49 Clock
50 Windscreen wiper switch
51 Windscreen wiper motor
52 Tachometer
53 Voltage stabilizer
54 Fuel indicator
55 Fuel tank unit
56 Fuel warning light
57 Temperature indicator
58 Temperature transmitter
59 Windscreen washer pump
60 Windscreen washer switch
61 Reverse lamp switch
62 Reverse lamp
63 Stop lamp switch
64 Stop lamp
65 Turn signal flasher unit
66 Turn signal switch
67 LH front flasher lamp
68 LH flasher repeater lamp
69 LH rear flasher lamp
70 RH front flasher lamp
71 RH flasher repeater lamp
72 RH rear flasher lamp
73 Turn signal warning light
74 Handbrake warning light
75 Handbrake switch
76 Temperature warning light
77 Temperature switch
78 Choke warning light
79 Choke switch

80 Brake line failure warning light
81 Brake line failure switch
82 Oil pressure warning light
83 Oil pressure switch
84 Ignition controlled relay
85 Overdrive gear lever switch – optional extra
86 Overdrive gearbox switch – optional extra
87 Overdrive solenoid – optional extra
88 Window lift circuit breaker
89 LH window lift switch
90 LH window lift motor
91 RH window lift switch
92 RH window lift motor
93 Ignition controlled relay
94 Heated back-light switch
95 Heated back-light
96 Heated back-light warning light
97 Heater switch
98 Condenser motor, compressor clutch and rear screen relay
99 Condenser cooling motors
100 High pressure cut-out
101 Thermostat
102 LH blower motor
103 RH blower motor
104 Micro-switch
105 Blower motor change speed relay
106 Compressor clutch

Colour code
N Brown
U Blue
R Red
P Purple
K Pink
S Slate
LG Light green
G Green
W White
Y Yellow
B Black

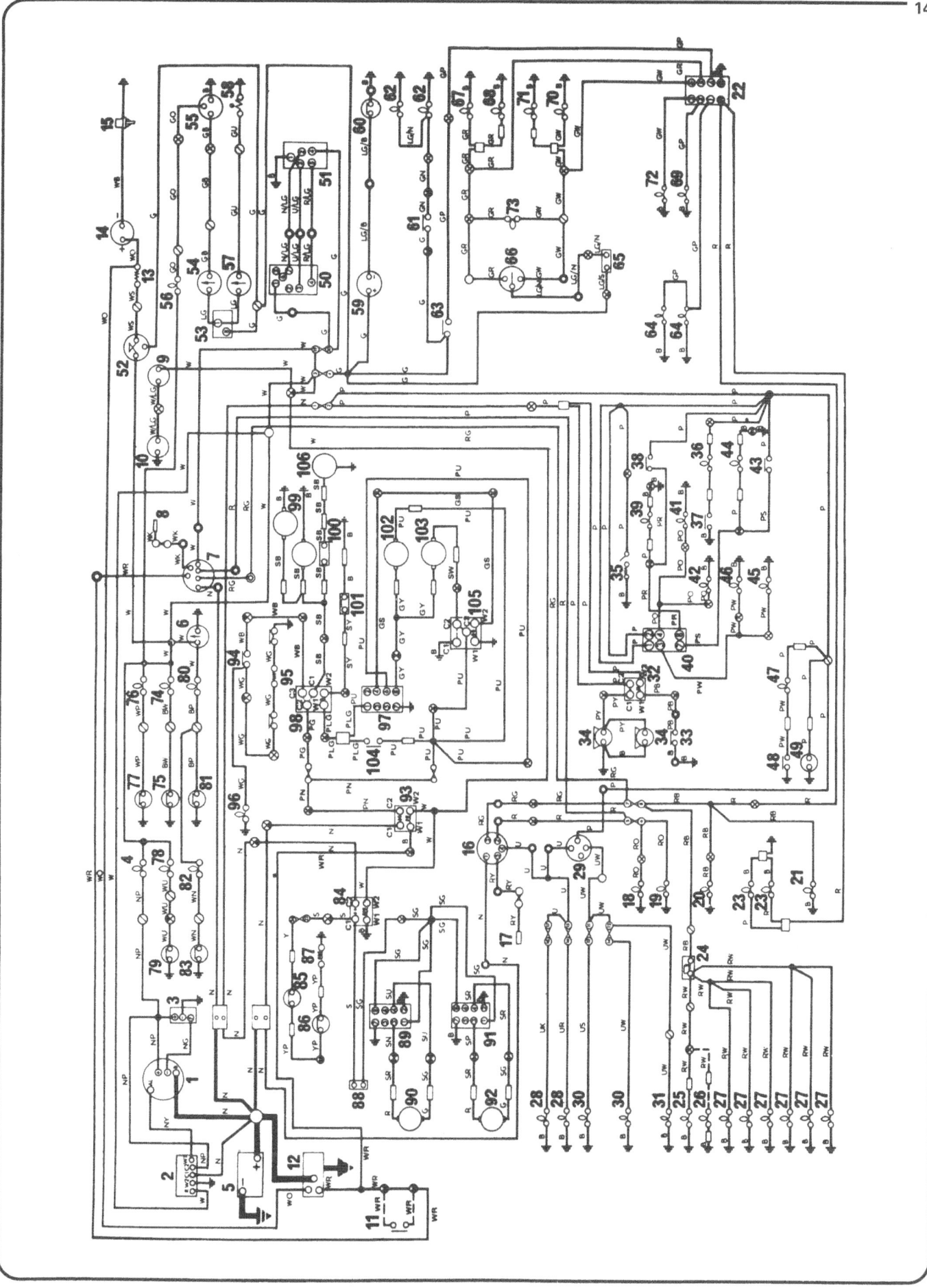

Fig. 10.40 Wiring diagram – RH steering with heater (From Commission No LD 2001)

1 Alternator
2 Ignition warning light
3 Battery
4 Battery condition indicator
5 Ignition/starter switch
6 Radio supply
7 Inertia switch
8 Fuel pump
9 Inhibitor switch – Borg-Warner automatic only
10 Starter motor
11 Ballast resistance wire
12 Ignition coil – 6 volt
13 Ignition distributor
14 Master light switch
15 RH side lamp
16 RH tail lamp
16 LH tail lamp
17 LH tail lamp
19 Number-plate illumination lamp
20 Night dimming relay – windings*
21 Panel rheostat
22 Main/dip/flash switch
23 LH outer headlamp
24 RH outer headlamp
25 RH inner headlamp – main
26 LH inner headlamp – main
27 Main beam warning light
28 Selector panel illumination – Borg-Warner automatic only
29 Cigarette lighter illumination
28 Instrument illumination
31 Horn
32 Horn relay
33 Horn-push
34 Clock
35 Glovebox lamp switch
36 Glovebox lamp
37 Cigarette lighter
38 Courtesy lamp switch
39 RH footwell lamp
40 Courtesy lamp
41 RH door switch
42 RH puddle lamp

43 LH puddle lamp
44 LH door switch
45 LH footwell switch
46 Courtesy lamp
47 Boot lamp switch
48 Boot lamp
49 Tachometer
50 Fuel warning light
51 Tank unit
52 Fuel gauge
53 10V stabilizer
54 Temperature gauge
55 Temperature transmitter
56 Wiper switch
57 Wiper motor
58 Thermal delay unit
59 Windscreen washer switch
60 Windscreen washer pump
61 Flasher unit
62 Turn signal switch
63 RH flasher warning light
64 RH front flasher lamp
65 Night dimming relay – contacts*
66 LH rear flasher lamp
67 LH flasher warning light
68 LH front flasher lamp
69 Night dimming relay – contacts*
70 LH rear flasher lamp
71 RH flasher repeater lamp
72 LH flasher repeater lamp
73 Reverse lamp switch
74 LH reverse lamp
75 RH reverse lamp
76 Stop lamp switch
77 Dimming relay – contacts*
78 LH stop lamp
79 RH stop lamp
80 Handbrake warning light switch
81 Handbrake warning light
82 Oil pressure switch

83 Oil warning light
84 Dual brake warning switch
85 Dual brake warning light
86 Choke switch
87 Choke warning switch
88 Overdrive switch – optional extra
89 Gearbox switch – optional extra
90 Overdrive solenoid – optional extra
91 Heated backlight warning light
92 Heated backlight
93 Heated backlight switch
94 Ignition controlled relays
95 Window lift circuit breaker
96 LH window lift switch
97 RH window lift switch
98 LH window lift motor
99 RH window lift motor
100 Heater switch
101 Heater rheostat
102 Heater motor

Colour code
N Brown
U Blue
R Red
P Purple
K Pink
S Slate
LG Light green
G Green
W White
Y Yellow
B Black

——————— Printed circuit

— — — — — Optional equipment

* A night dimming relay was fitted to selected markets – earlier models only – in this commission number range

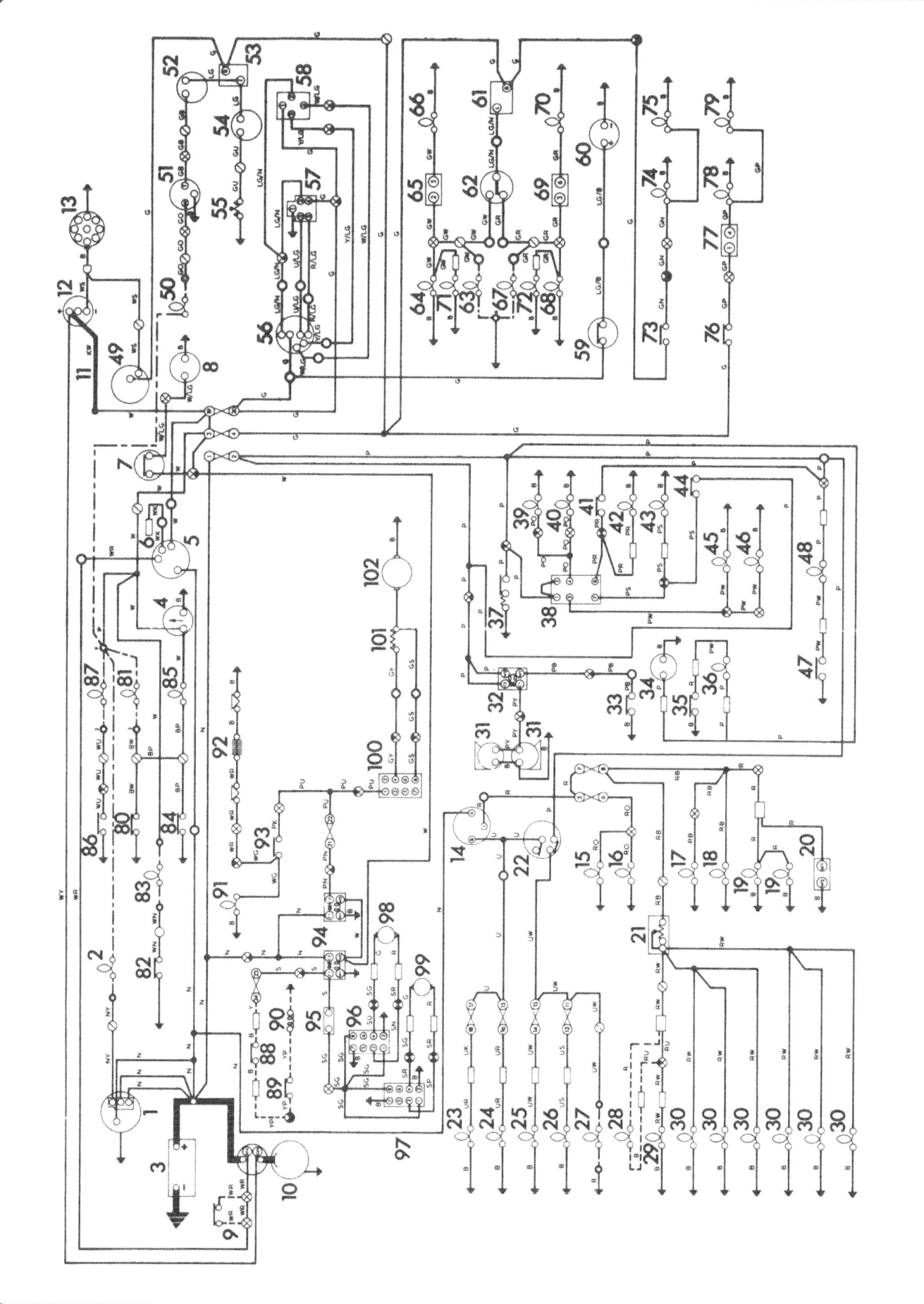

Fig. 10.41 Wiring diagram – RH steering with air conditioning (From Commission No LD 2001)

1 Alternator
2 Ignition warning light
3 Battery
4 Battery condition indicator
5 Ignition/starter switch
6 Radio supply
7 Inertia switch
8 Fuel pump
9 Inhibitor switch – Borg-Warner automatic only
10 Starter motor
11 Ballast resistance wire
12 Ignition coil – 6 volt
13 Ignition distributor
14 Master light switch
15 RH side lamp
16 RH tail lamp
17 LH tail lamp
18 LH side lamp
19 Number-plate illumination lamp
20 Night dimming relay – windings
21 Panel rheostat
22 Main/dip/flash switch
23 LH outer headlamp
24 RH outer headlamp
25 RH inner headlamp – main
26 LH inner headlamp – main
27 Main beam warning light
28 Selector panel illumination – Borg-Warner automatic only
29 Cigarette lighter illumination
30 Instrument illumination
31 Horn
32 Horn relay
33 Horn-push
34 Clock
35 Glove-box lamp switch
36 Glove-box lamp
37 Cigarette lighter
38 Courtesy lamp switch
39 RH footwell lamp
40 Courtesy lamp
41 RH door switch
42 RH puddle lamp

43 LH puddle lamp
44 LH door switch
45 LH footwell lamp
46 Courtesy lamp
47 Boot lamp switch
48 Boot lamp
49 Tachometer
50 Fuel warning light
51 Tank unit
52 Fuel gauge
53 10V stabiliser
54 Temperature gauge
55 Temperature transmitter
56 Wiper switch
57 Wiper motor
58 Thermal delay unit
59 Windscreen washer switch
60 Windscreen washer pump
61 Flasher unit
62 Turn signal switch
63 RH flasher warning light
64 RH front flasher lamp
65 Night dimming relay – contacts*
66 LH rear flasher lamp
67 LH flasher warning light
68 LH front flasher lamp
69 Night dimming relay – contacts*
70 LH rear flasher lamp
71 Air conditioning relay
72 Condenser cooling motors
73 Reverse lamp switch
74 LH reverse lamp
75 RH reverse lamp
76 Stop lamp switch
77 Dimming relay – contacts*
78 LH stop lamp
79 RH stop lamp
80 Handbrake warning light switch
81 Handbrake warning light
82 Oil pressure switch
83 Oil warning light
84 Dual brake warning switch

85 Dual brake warning light
86 Choke switch
87 Choke warning light
88 Overdrive switch – optional extra
89 Gearbox switch – optional extra
90 Overdrive solenoid – optional extra
91 Heated back-light warning light
92 Heated back-light
93 Heated back-light switch
94 Ignition controlled relays
95 Window lift circuit breaker
96 LH window lift switch
97 RL window lift switch
98 LH window lift motor
99 RH window lift motor
100 Blower switch
101 Thermostat
102 High pressure cut-out
103 Compressor clutch
104 RH blower motor
105 LH blower motor
106 Blower motors change-over relay

Colour code
N Brown
U Blue
R Red
P Purple
K Pink
S Slate
LG Light green
G Green
W White
Y Yellow
B Black

——————————— Printed circuit

——————————— Optional equipment

A night dimming relay was fitted to selected markets – earlier models only – in this commission number range

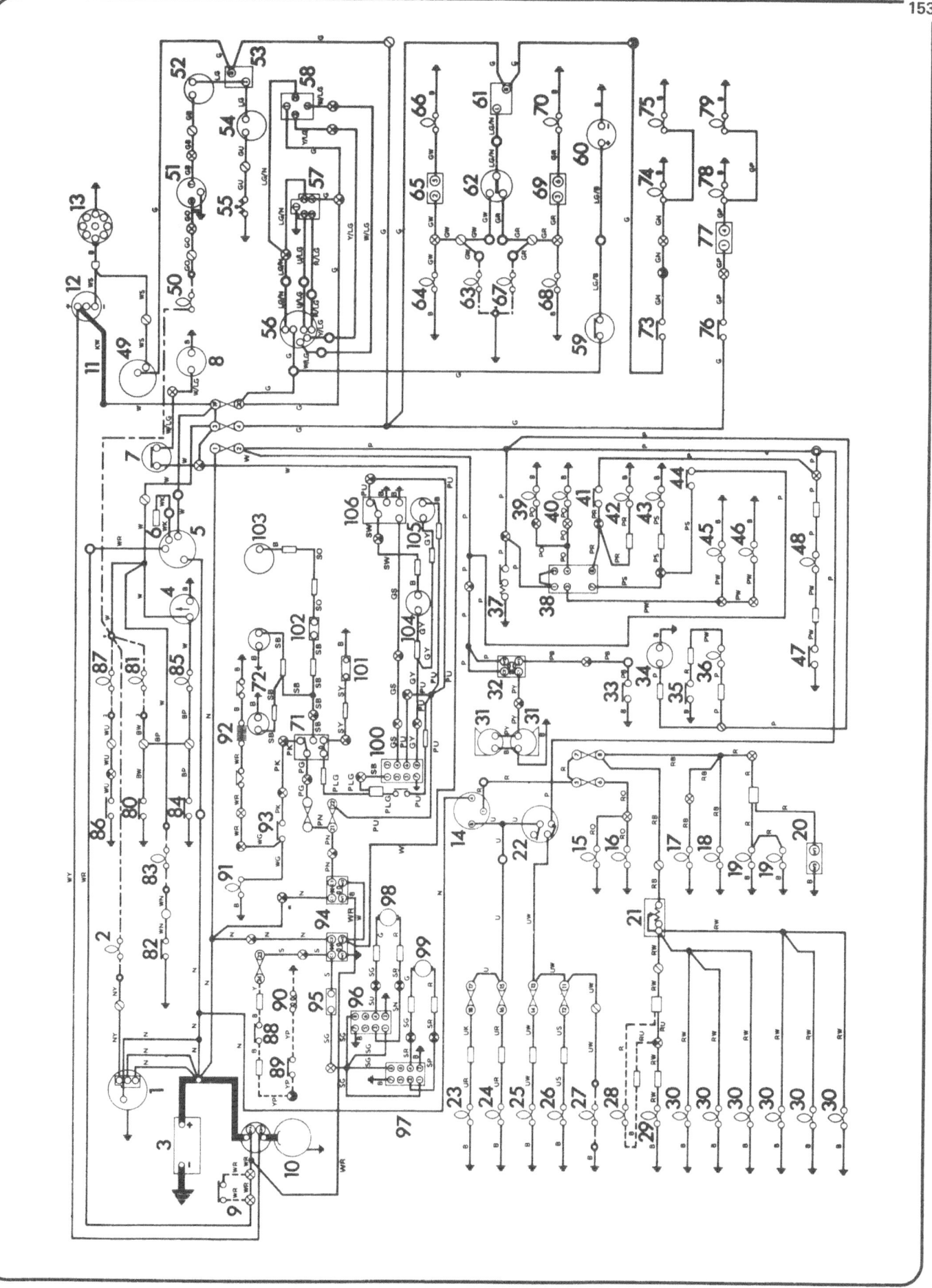

Fig. 10.42 Wiring diagram – LH steering with heater (Up to Commission No LD 2000)

1 Alternator
2 Charging system relay
3 Alternator control unit
4 Ignition warning light
5 Battery
6 Battery condition indicator
7 Ignition/starter switch
8 Radio supply
9 Inertia cut-out
10 Petrol pump
11 Inhibitor switch – Borg-Warner automatic only
12 Starter motor
13 Ballast resistor
14 Ignition coil – 6 volt
15 Ignition distributor
16 Master light switch
17 Fog lamp supply
18 LH tail lamp
19 LH front parking lamp
20 RH tail lamp
21 RH front parking lamp
22 Night dimming relay
23 Plate illumination lamp
24 Panel rheostat
25 Cigarette lighter illumination
26 Selector panel illumination – Borg-Warner automatic only
27 Instrument illumination
28 Main/dip/flash switch
29 Dip beam
30 Main beam
31 Main beam warning light
32 Horn relay
33 Horn-push
34 Horn
35 Hazard flasher unit
36 Hazard switch
37 Hazard warning light
38 Cigarette lighter

39 Luggage boot lamp
40 Luggage boot lamp switch
41 RH door switch
42 RH puddle lamp
43 Interior lamp switch
44 RH 'B post' lamp
45 RH console lamp
46 LH door switch
47 LH puddle lamp
48 LH 'B post' lamp
49 LH console lamp
50 Glovebox/map lamp
51 Glovebox/map lamp switch
52 Clock
53 Windscreen wiper switch
54 Windscreen wiper motor
55 Tachometer
56 Voltage stabilizer
57 Fuel indicator
58 Fuel tank unit
59 Fuel warning light
60 Temperature indicator
61 Temperature transmitter
62 Windscreen washer pump
63 Windscreen washer switch
64 Reverse lamp switch
65 Reverse lamp
66 Stop lamp switch
67 Stop lamp
68 Turn signal flasher unit
69 Turn signal switch
70 LH front flasher lamp
71 LH flasher repeater lamp
72 LH rear flasher lamp
73 RH front flasher lamp
74 RH flasher repeater lamp
75 RH rear flasher lamp
76 Turn signal warning light
77 Handbrake warning light

78 Handbrake switch
79 Temperature warning light
80 Temperature switch
81 Choke warning light
82 Choke switch
83 Brake line failure warning light
84 Brake line failure switch
85 Oil pressure warning light
86 Oil pressure switch
87 Ignition controlled relay
88 Overdrive gear lever switch – optional extra
89 Overdrive gearbox switch – optional extra
90 Overdrive solenoid – optional extra
91 Window lift circuit breaker
92 LH window lift switch
93 LH window lift motor
94 RH window lift switch
95 RH window lift motor
96 Ignition controlled relay
97 Heated back-light switch
98 Heated back-light
99 Heated back-light warning light
100 Heater switch
101 Heater rheostat
102 Heater motor

Colour code
N Brown
U Blue
R Red
P Purple
K Pink
S Slate
LG Light green
G Green
W White
Y Yellow
B Black

155

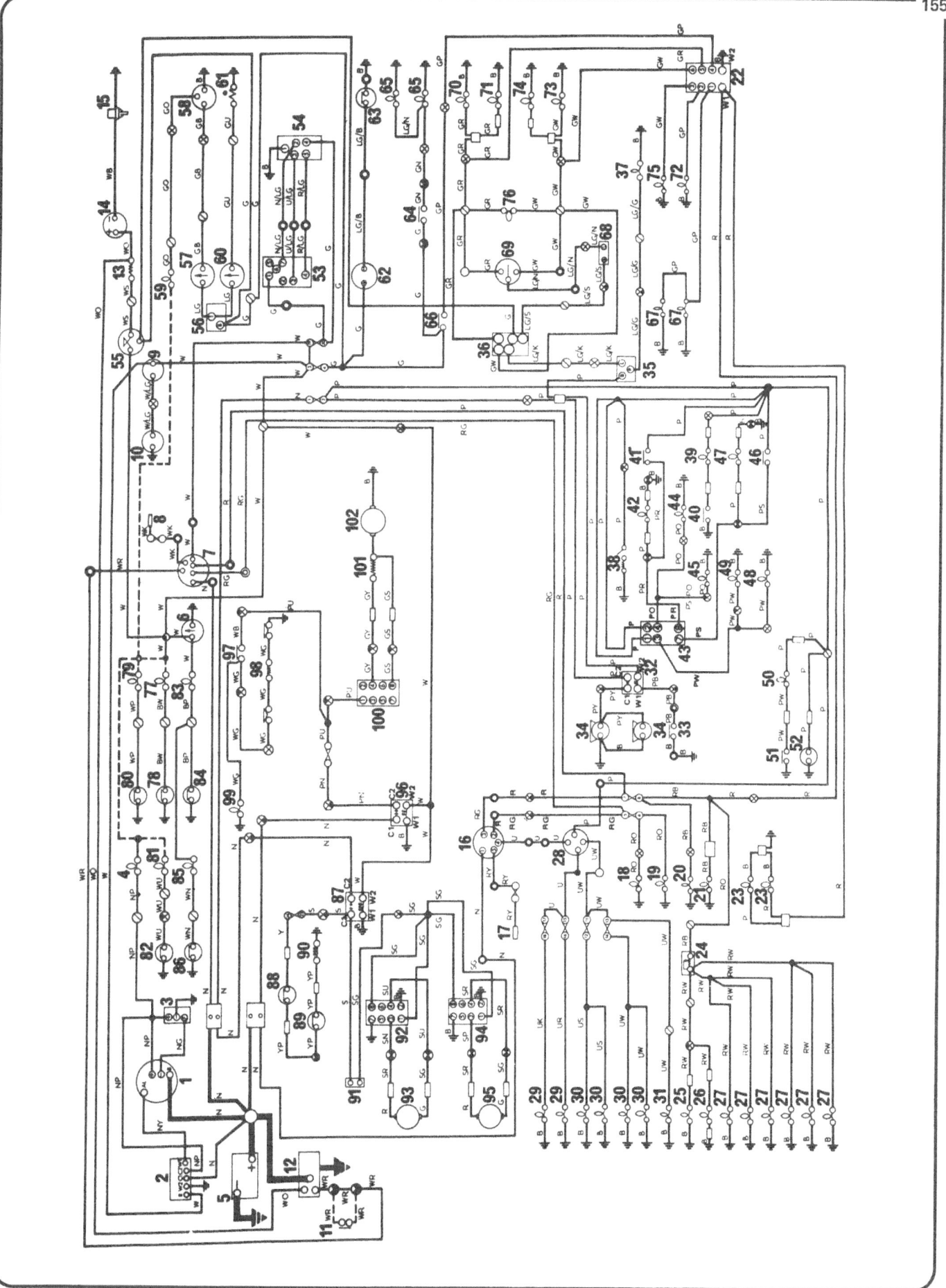

Fig. 10.43 Wiring diagram – LH steering with air conditioning (Up to Commission No LD 2000)

1	Alternator
2	Charging system relay
3	Alternator control unit
4	Ignition warning light
5	Battery
6	Battery condition indicator
7	Ignition/starter switch
8	Radio supply
9	Inertia cut-out
10	Petrol pump
11	Inhibitor switch – Borg-Warner automatic only
12	Starter motor
13	Ballast resistor
14	Ignition coil – 6 volt
15	Ignition distributor
16	Master light switch
17	Fog lamp supply
18	LH tail lamp
19	LH front parking lamp
20	RH tail lamp
21	RH front parking lamp
22	Night dimming relay
23	Plate illumination lamp
24	Panel rheostat
25	Cigarette lighter illumination
26	Selector panel illumination – Borg-Warner automatic only
27	Instrument illumination
28	Main/dip/flash switch
29	Dip beam
30	Main beam
31	Main beam warning light
32	Horn relay
33	Horn-push
34	Horn
35	Hazard flasher unit
36	Hazard switch
37	Hazard warning light
38	Cigarette lighter
39	Luggage boot lamp
40	Luggage boot lamp switch
41	RH door switch
42	RH puddle lamp
43	Interior lamp switch
44	RH 'B post' lamp
45	RH console lamp
46	LH door switch
47	LH puddle lamp
48	LH 'B post' lamp
49	LH console lamp
50	Glovebox/map lamp
51	Glovebox/map lamp switch
52	Clock
53	Windscreen wiper switch
54	Windscreen wiper motor
55	Tachometer
56	Voltage stabilizer
57	Fuel indicator
58	Fuel tank unit
59	Fuel warning light
60	Temperature indicator
61	Temperature transmitter
62	Windscreen washer pump
63	Windscreen washer switch
64	Reverse lamp switch
65	Reverse lamp
66	Stop lamp switch
67	Stop lamp
68	Turn signal flasher unit
69	Turn signal switch
70	LH front flasher lamp
71	LH flasher repeater lamp
72	LH rear flasher lamp
73	RH front flasher lamp
74	RH flasher repeater lamp
75	RH rear flasher lamp
76	Turn signal warning light
77	Handbrake warning light
78	Handbrake switch
79	Temperature warning light
80	Temperature switch
81	Choke warning light
82	Choke switch
83	Brake line failure warning light
84	Brake line failure switch
85	Oil pressure warning light
86	Oil pressure switch
87	Ignition controlled relay
88	Overdrive gear lever switch – optional extra
89	Overdrive gearbox switch – optional extra
90	Overdrive solenoid – optional extra
91	Window lift circuit breaker
92	LH window lift switch
93	LH window lift motor
94	RH window lift switch
95	RH window lift motor
96	Ignition controlled relay
97	Heated back-light switch
98	Heated back-light
99	Heated back-light warning light
100	Micro-switch
101	Clutch relay
102	Thermostat
103	Condenser cooling motors
104	High pressure cut-out
105	Compressor clutch
106	Blower switch
107	Blower motors change speed relay
108	LH blower motor
109	RH blower motor

Colour code

N	Brown
U	Blue
R	Red
P	Purple
K	Pink
S	Slate
LG	Light green
G	Green
W	White
Y	Yellow
B	Black

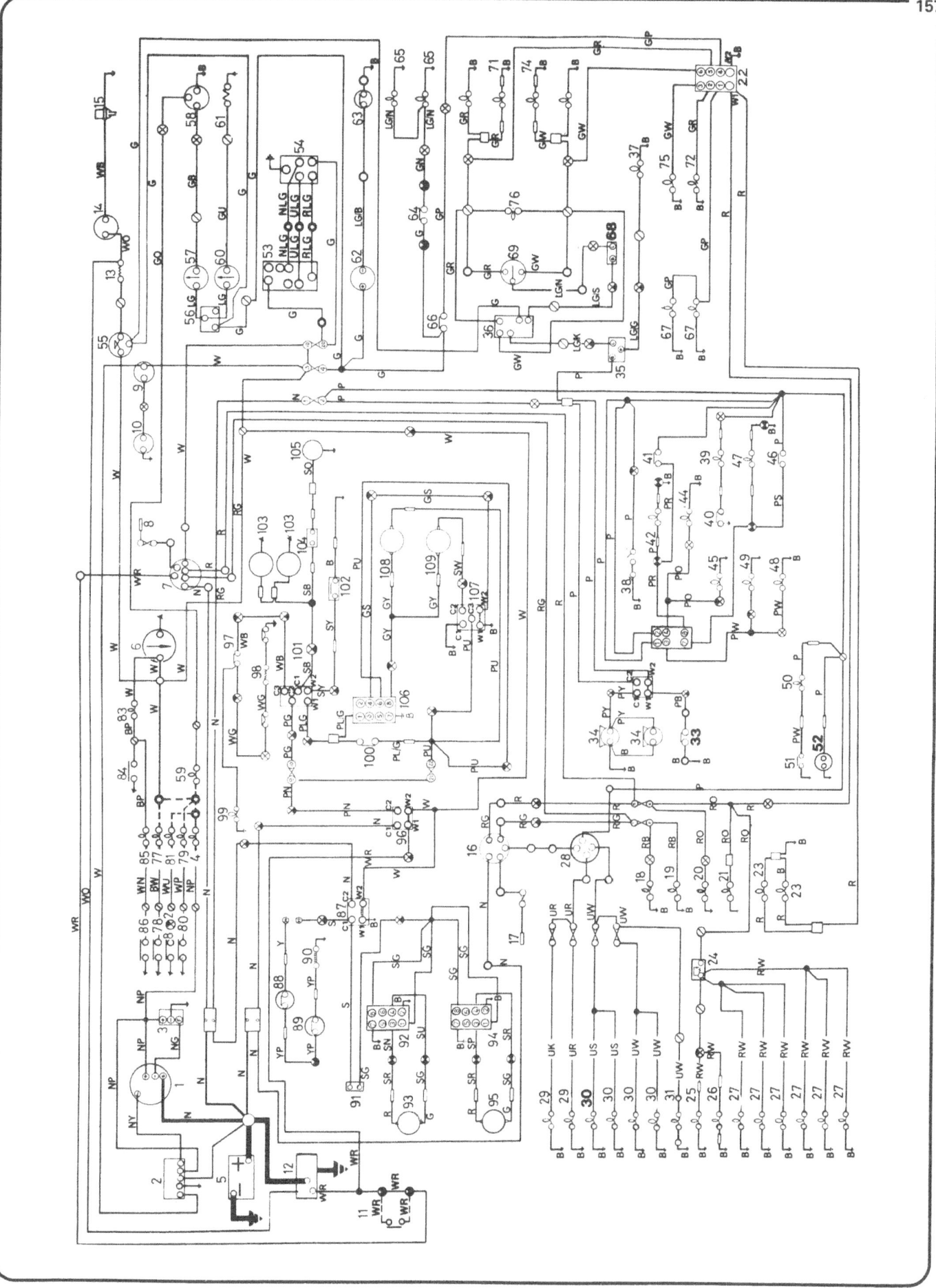

Fig. 10.44 Wiring diagram – LH steering with heater (From Commission No LD 2001)

1 Alternator
2 Dimmer relay*
3 Dimmer relay*
4 Ignition warning light
5 Battery
6 Battery condition indicator
7 Ignition/starter switch
8 Radio supply
9 Inertia cut-out
10 Petrol pump
11 Inhibitor switch – Borg-Warner automatic only
12 Starter motor
13 Roof connector
14 Ignition coil – 6 volt
15 Ignition distributor
16 Master light switch
17 Fog lamp supply (earlier models only)
18 LH tail lamp
19 LH front parking lamp
20 RH tail lamp
21 RH front parking lamp
22 Dimmer relay*
23 Plate illumination lamp
24 Panel rheostat
25 Cigarette lighter illumination
26 Selector panel illumination – Borg-Warner automatic only
27 Instrument illumination
28 Main/dip/flash switch
29 Dip beam
30 Main beam
31 Main beam warning light
32 Horn relay
33 Horn-push
34 Horn
35 Hazard flasher unit
36 Hazard switch
37 Wiper delay unit
38 Cigarette lighter
39 Luggage boot lamp

40 Luggage boot lamp switch
41 RH door switch
42 RH puddle lamp
43 Interior lamp switch
44 RH 'B post' lamp
45 RH console lamp
46 LH door switch
47 LH puddle lamp
48 LH 'B post' lamp
49 LH console lamp
50 Glovebox/map lamp
51 Glovebox/map lamp switch
52 Clock
53 Windscreen wiper switch
54 Windscreen wiper motor
55 Tachometer
56 Voltage stabilizer
57 Fuel indicator
58 Fuel tank unit
59 Fuel warning light
60 Temperature indicator
61 Temperature transmitter
62 Windscreen washer pump
63 Windscreen washer switch
64 Reverse lamp switch
65 Reverse lamp
66 Stop lamp switch
67 Stop lamp
68 Turn signal flasher unit
69 Turn signal switch
70 LH front flasher lamp
71 LH flasher repeater lamp
72 LH rear flasher lamp
73 RH front flasher lamp
74 RH flasher repeater lamp
75 RH rear flasher lamp
76 Dimmer relay*
77 Handbrake warning light
78 Handbrake switch
79 LH flasher warning light

80 RH flasher warning switch
81 Choke warning light
82 Choke switch
83 Brake line failure warning light
84 Brake line failure switch
85 Oil pressure warning light
86 Oil pressure switch
87 Ignition controlled relay
88 Overdrive gear lever switch – optional extra
89 Overdrive gearbox switch – optional extra
90 Overdrive solenoid – optional extra
91 Window lift circuit breaker
92 LH window lift switch
93 LH window lift motor
94 RH window lift switch
95 RH window lift motor
96 Ignition controlled relay
97 Heated back-light switch
98 Heated back-light
99 Heated back-light warning light
100 Heater switch
101 Heater rheostat
102 Heater motor

Colour code
N Brown
U Blue
R Red
P Purple
K Pink
S Slate
LG Light green
G Green
W White
Y Yellow
B Black

*A night dimmer relay was fitted to selected markets – earlier models only – in this commission number range

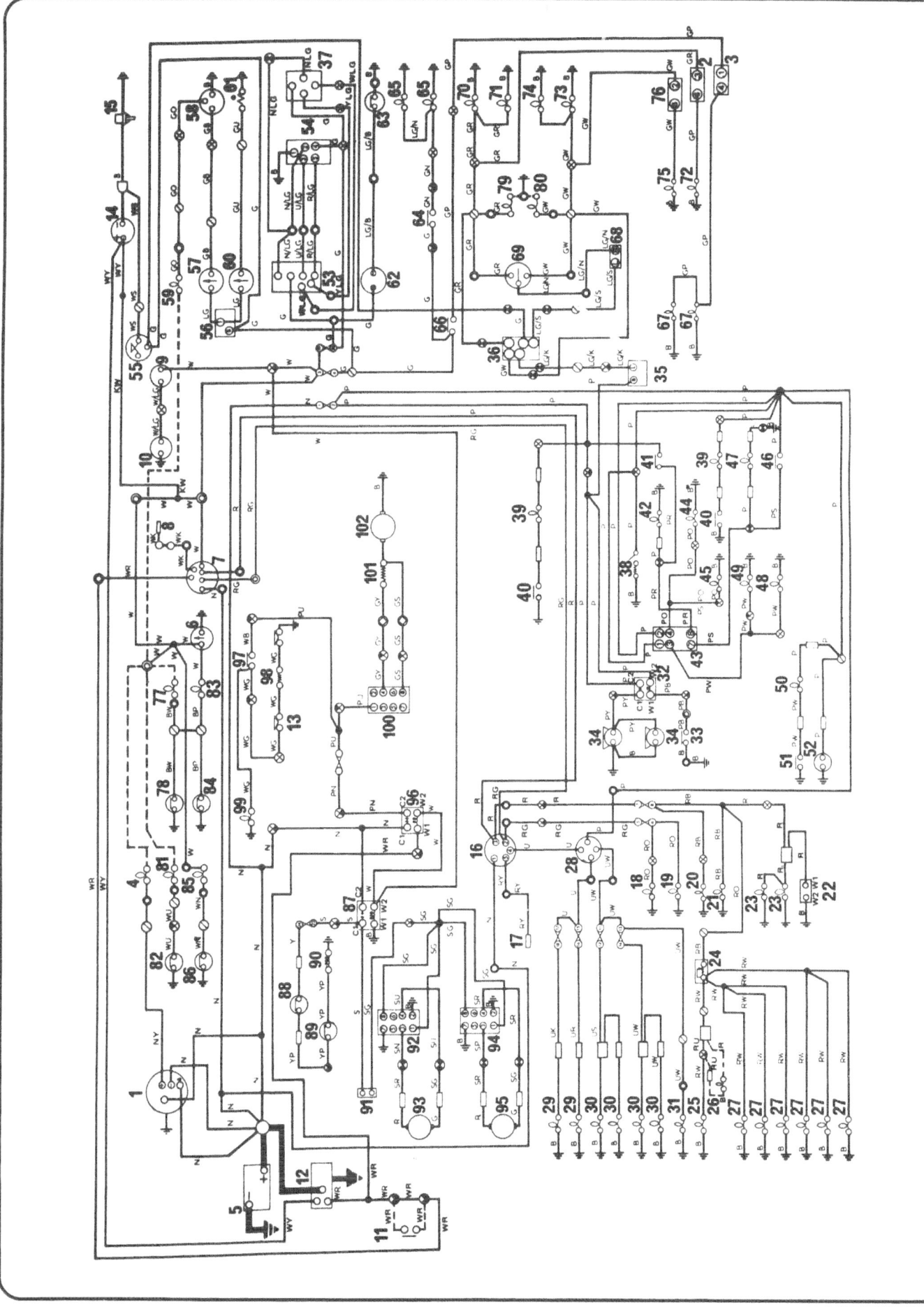

159

Fig. 10.45 Wiring diagram – LH steering with air conditioning (From Commission No LD 2001)

1 Alternator
2 Dimmer relay*
3 Dimmer relay*
4 Ignition warning light
5 Battery
6 Battery condition indicator
7 Ignition/starter switch
8 Radio supply
9 Inertia cut-out
10 Petrol pump
11 Inhibitor switch – Borg-Warner automatic only
12 Starter motor
13 Roof connector
14 Ignition coil – 6 volt
15 Ignition distributor
16 Master light switch
17 Fog lamp supply (earlier models only)
18 LH tail lamp
19 LH front parking lamp
20 RH tail lamp
21 RH front parking lamp
22 Dimmer relay*
23 Plate illumination lamp
24 Panel rheostat
25 Cigarette lighter illumination
26 Selector panel illumination – Borg-Warner automatic only
27 Instrument illumination
28 Main/dip/flash switch
29 Dip beam
30 Main beam
31 Main beam warning light
32 Horn relay
33 Horn-push
34 Horn
35 Hazard flasher unit
36 Hazard switch
37 Wiper delay unit
38 Cigarette lighter
39 Luggage boot lamp
40 Luggage boot lamp switch
41 RH door switch

42 RH puddle lamp
43 Interior lamp switch
44 RH 'B post' lamp
45 RH console lamp
46 LH door switch
47 LH puddle lamp
48 LH 'B post' lamp
49 LH console lamp
50 Glovebox/map lamp
51 Glovebox/map lamp switch
52 Clock
53 Windscreen wiper switch
54 Windscreen wiper motor
55 Tachometer
56 Voltage stabilizer
57 Fuel indicator
58 Fuel tank unit
59 Fuel warning light
60 Temperature indicator
61 Temperature transmitter
62 Windscreen washer pump
63 Windscreen washer switch
64 Reverse lamp switch
65 Reverse lamp
66 Stop lamp switch
67 Stop lamp
68 Turn signal flasher unit
69 Turn signal switch
70 LH front flasher lamp
71 LH flasher repeater lamp
72 LH rear flasher lamp
73 RH front flasher lamp
74 RH flasher repeater lamp
75 RH rear flasher lamp
76 Dimmer relay*
77 Handbrake warning light
78 Handbrake switch
79 LH flasher warning light
80 RH flasher warning light
81 Choke warning light
82 Choke switch
83 Brake line failure warning light

84 Brake line failure switch
85 Oil pressure warning light
86 Oil pressure switch
87 Ignition controlled relay
88 Overdrive gear lever switch – optional extra
89 Overdrive gearbox switch – optional extra
90 Overdrive solenoid – optional extra
91 Window lift circuit breaker
92 LH window lift switch
93 LH window lift motor
94 RH window lift switch
95 RH window lift motor
96 Ignition controlled relay
97 Heated back-light switch
98 Heated back-light
99 Heated back-light warning light
100 Micro-switch
101 Air conditioning relay
102 Thermostat
103 Condenser cooling motors
104 High pressure cut-out
105 Compressor clutch
106 Blower switch
107 Blower motor change speed relay
108 LH blower motor
109 RH blower motor

Colour code

N Brown
U Blue
R Red
P Purple
K Pink
S Slate
LG Light green
G Green
W White
Y Yellow
B Black

* A night dimming relay was fitted to selected markets – earlier models only – in this commission number range

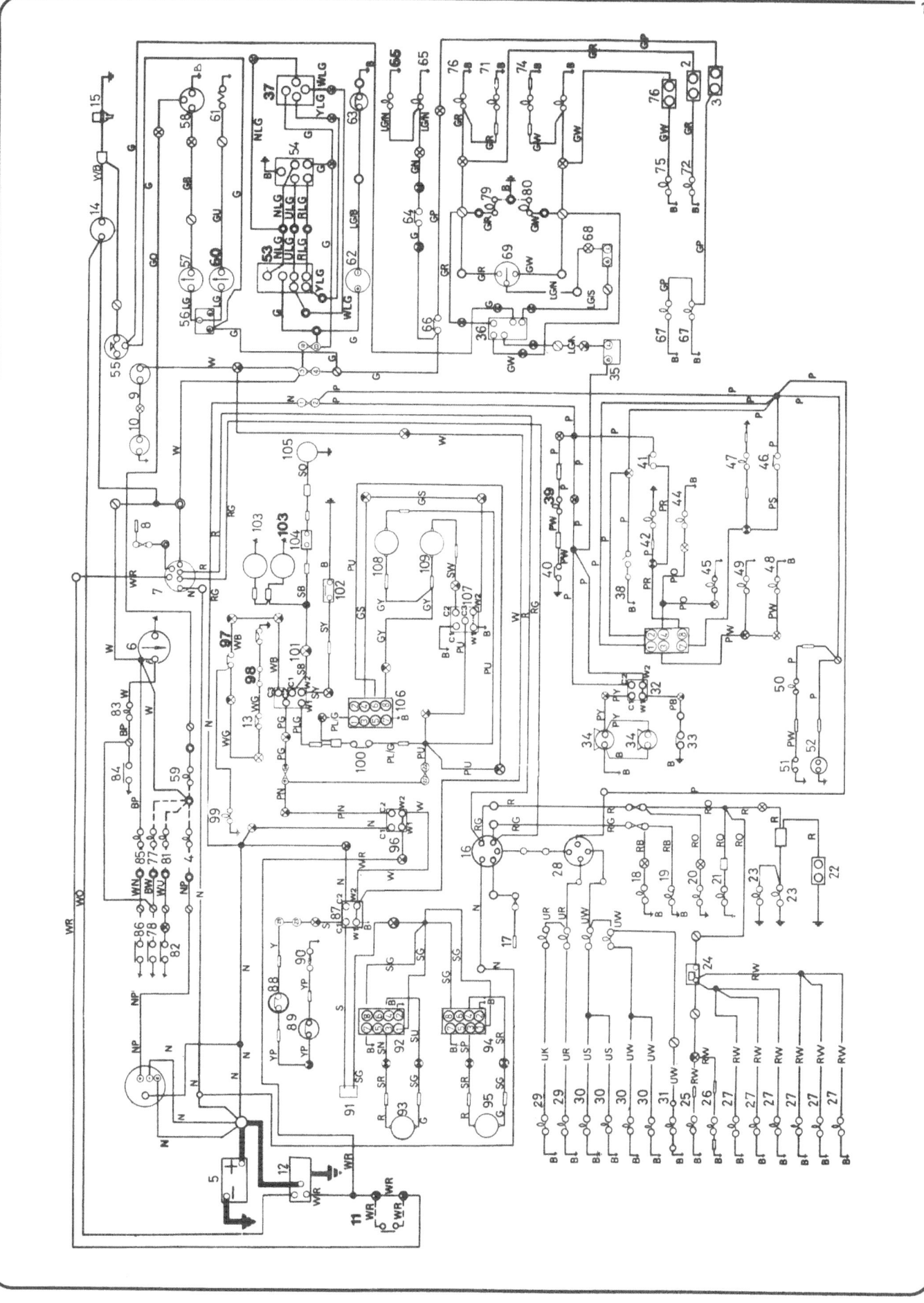

Fig. 10.46 Wiring diagram – USA models with heater (Up to Commission No LE 11276)

1 Alternator
2 Charging system relay
3 Alternator control unit
4 Ignition warning light
5 Battery
6 Battery condition indicator
7 Ignition/starter switch
8 Radio supply
9 Inertia cut-out
10 Petrol pump
11 Inhibitor switch – Borg-Warner automatic only
12 Starter motor
13 Ballast resistor
14 Ignition coil – 6 volt
15 Ignition distributor
16 Master light switch
17 Fog lamp supply
18 LH tail lamp
19 LH front parking lamp
20 RH tail lamp
21 LH front parking lamp
22 RH front parking lamp
23 RH front marker lamp
24 RH rear marker lamp
25 Plate illumination lamp
26 LH rear marker lamp
27 Panel rheostat
28 Cigarette lighter illumination
29 Selector panel illumination – Borg-Warner automatic only
30 Instrument illumination
31 Main/dip/flash switch
32 Dip beam
33 Main beam
34 Main beam warning light
35 Horn relay
36 Horn-push
37 Horn
38 Hazard flasher unit

39 Hazard switch
40 Hazard warning light
41 Cigarette lighter
42 Luggage boot lamp
43 Luggage boot lamp switch
44 RH door switch
45 RH puddle lamp
46 Interior lamp switch
47 RH 'B post' lamp
48 RH console lamp
49 LH door switch
50 LH puddle lamp
51 LH 'B post' lamp
52 LH console lamp
53 Key warning buzzer
54 Key switch
55 Glovebox/map lamp
56 Glovebox/map lamp switch
57 Clock
58 Windscreen wiper switch
59 Windscreen wiper motor
60 Tachometer
61 Voltage stabilizer
62 Fuel indicator
63 Fuel tank unit
64 Fuel warning light
65 Temperature indicator
66 Temperature transmitter
67 Windscreen washer pump
68 Windscreen washer switch
69 Reverse lamp switch
70 Reverse lamp
71 Stop lamp switch
72 Stop lamp
73 Turn signal flasher unit
74 Turn signal switch
75 LH flasher lamp
76 RH flasher lamp
77 Turn signal warning light

78 Handbrake warning light
79 Handbrake switch
80 Temperature warning light
81 Temperature switch
82 Choke warning light
83 Choke switch
84 Brake line failure warning light
85 Brake line failure switch
86 Oil pressure warning light
87 Oil pressure switch
88 Ignition controlled relay
89 Overdrive gear lever switch – optional extra
90 Overdrive gearbox switch – optional extra
91 Overdrive solenoid – optional extra
92 Window lift circuit breaker
93 LH window lift switch
94 LH window lift motor
95 RH window lift switch
96 RH window lift motor
97 Ignition controlled relay
98 Heated back-light switch
99 Heated back-light
100 Heated back-light warning light
101 Heater switch
102 Heater rheostat
103 Heater motor

Colour code
N Brown
U Blue
R Red
P Purple
K Pink
S Slate
LG Light green
G Green
W White
Y Yellow
B Black

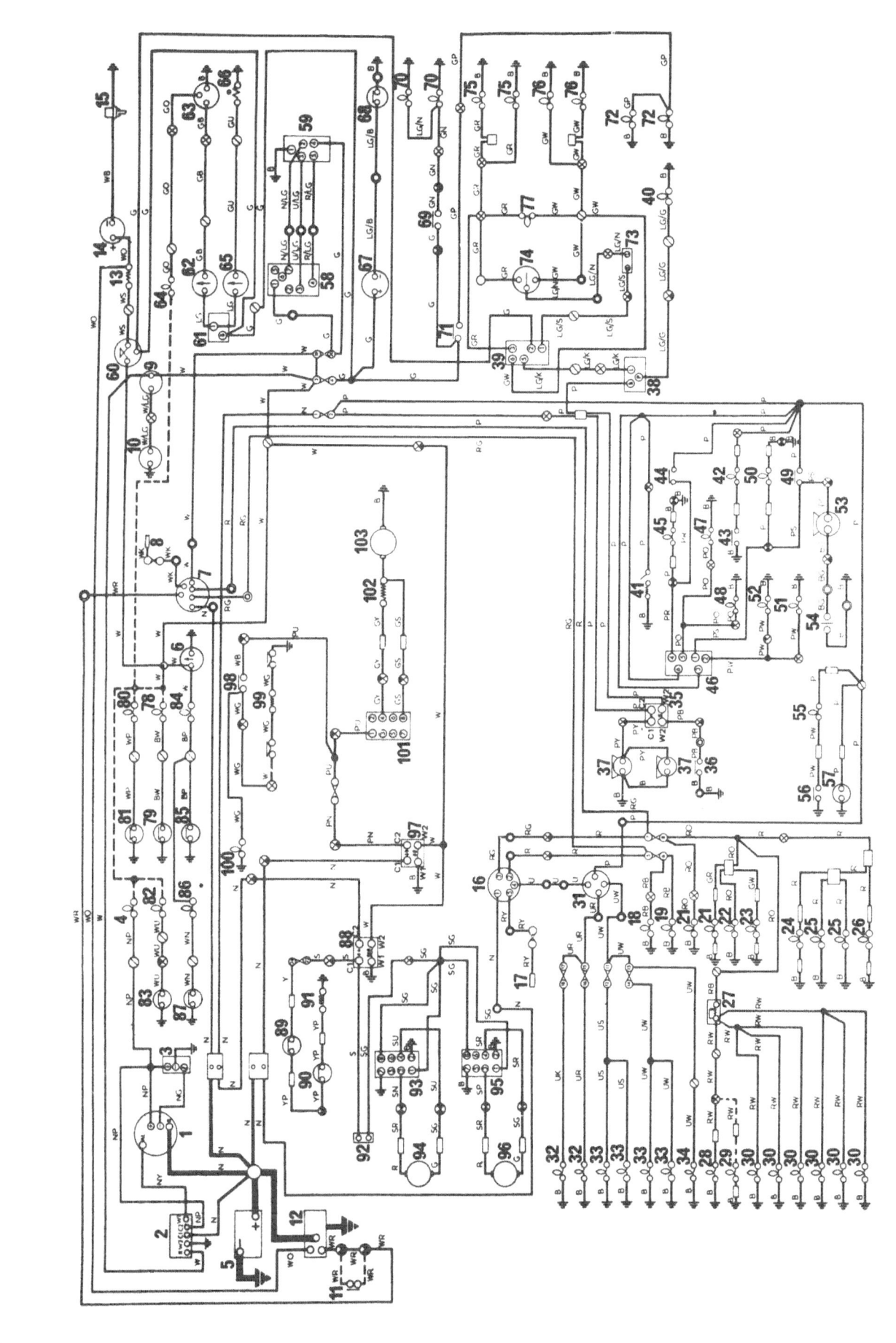

Fig. 10.47 Wiring diagram – USA models with air conditioning (Up to Commission No LE 11276)

1 Alternator
2 Charging system relay
3 Alternator control unit
4 Ignition warning light
5 Battery
6 Battery condition indicator
7 Ignition/starter switch
8 Radio supply
9 Inertia cut-out
10 Petrol pump
11 Inhibitor switch – Borg-Warner automatic only
12 Starter motor
13 Ballast resistor
14 Ignition coil – 6 volt
15 Ignition distributor
16 Master light switch
17 Fog lamp supply
18 LH tail lamp
19 LH front parking lamp
20 RH tail lamp
21 LH front marker lamp
22 RH front parking lamp
23 RH front marker lamp
24 RH rear marker lamp
25 Plate illumination lamp
26 LH rear marker lamp
27 Panel rheostat
27 Cigarette lighter illumination
28 Selector panel illumination – Borg-Warner automatic only
30 Instrument illumination
31 Main/dip/flash switch
32 Dip beam
33 Main beam
34 Main beam warning light
35 Horn relay
36 Horn-push
37 Horn
38 Hazard flasher unit
39 Hazard switch
40 Hazard warning light

41 Cigarette lighter
42 Luggage boot lamp
43 Luggage boot lamp switch
44 RH door switch
45 RH puddle lamp
46 Interior lamp switch
47 RH 'B post' lamp
48 RH console lamp
49 LH door switch
50 LH puddle lamp
51 LH 'B post' lamp
52 LH console lamp
53 Key warning buzzer
54 Key switch
55 Glovebox/map lamp
56 Glovebox/map lamp switch
57 Clock
58 Windscreen wiper switch
59 Windscreen wiper motor
60 Tachometer
61 Voltage stabilizer
62 Fuel indicator
63 Fuel tank unit
64 Fuel warning light
65 Temperature indicator
66 Temperature transmitter
67 Windscreen washer pump
68 Windscreen washer switch
69 Reverse lamp switch
70 Reverse lamp
71 Stop lamp switch
72 Stop lamp
73 Turn signal flasher unit
74 Turn signal switch
75 LH flasher lamp
76 RH flasher lamp
77 Turn signal warning light
78 Handbrake warning light
79 Handbrake switch
80 Temperature warning light
81 Temperature switch
82 Choke warning light

83 Choke switch
84 Brake line failure warning light
85 Brake line failure switch
86 Oil pressure warning light
87 Oil pressure switch
88 Ignition controlled relay
89 Overdrive gear lever switch – optional extra
90 Overdrive gearbox switch – optional extra
91 Overdrive solenoid – optional extra
92 Window lift circuit breaker
93 LH window lift switch
94 LH window lift motor
95 RH window lift switch
96 RH window lift motor
97 Ignition controlled relay
98 Heated back-light switch
99 Heated back-light
100 Heated back-light warning light
101 Blower switch
102 Condenser motor, compressor clutch and rear screen relay
103 Condenser cooling motors
104 Compressor clutch
105 High pressure cut-out
106 Thermostat
107 Micro-switch
108 LH blower motor
109 RH blower motor
110 Blower motor change speed relay

Colour code
N Brown
U Blue
R Red
P Purple
K Pink
S Slate
LG Light green
G Green
W White
Y Yellow
B Black

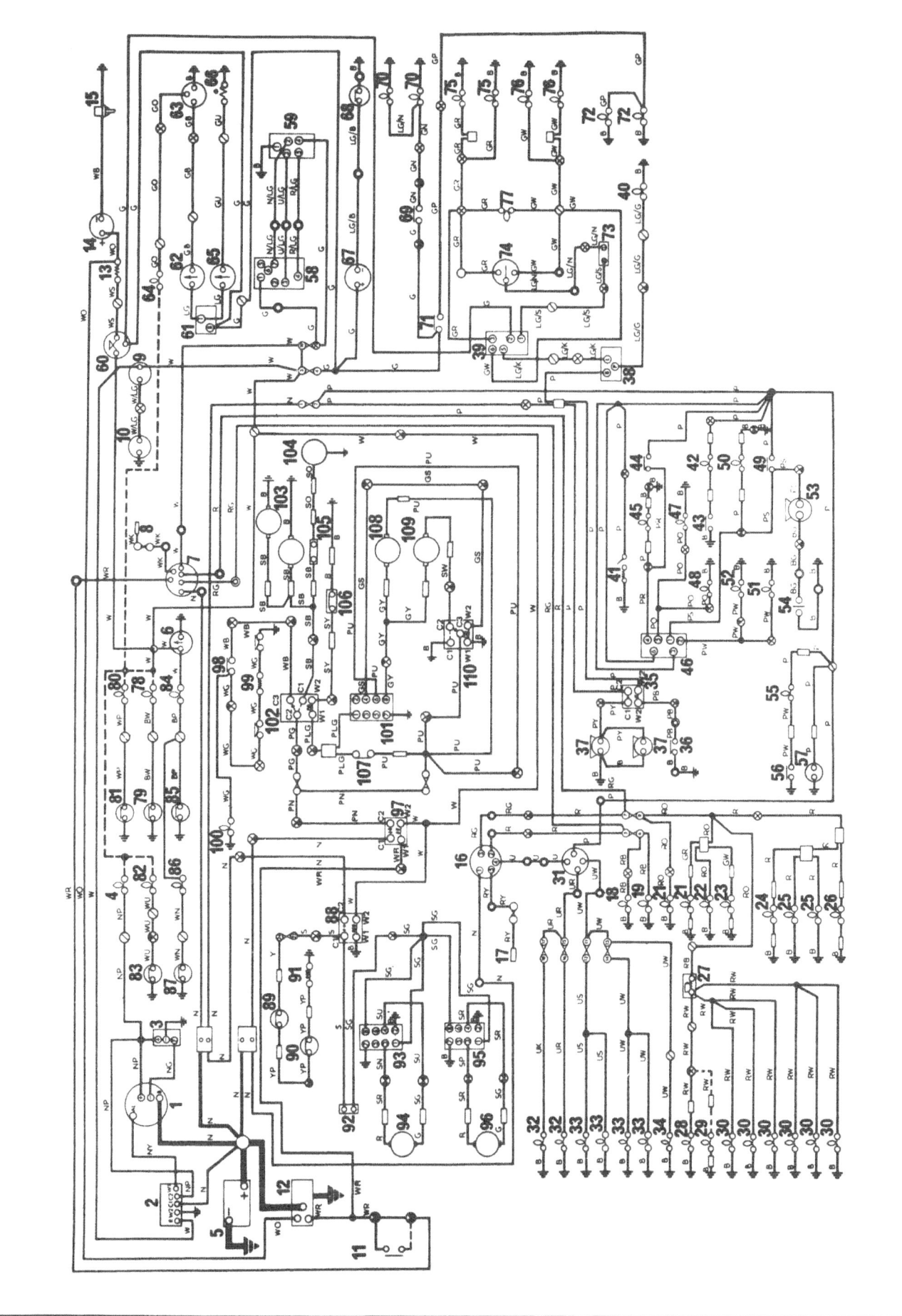

Fig. 10.48 Wiring diagram – USA models with heater (From Commission No LE 11277 to LE 20271)

1 Alternator
2 Ignition warning light
3 Battery
5 Battery condition indicator
6 Ignition/starter switch
7 Radio supply
8 Inertia cut-out
8 Petrol pump
9 Inhibitor switch – Borg-Warner automatic only
10 Starter
11 Tachometer
12 Ignition coil – 6 volt
13 Ignition distributor
14 Master light switch
15 Main/dip/flash switch
16 LH tail lamp
17 LH front parking lamp
18 RH tail lamp
19 LH front marker lamp
20 RH front parking lamp
21 RH front marker lamp
22 RH rear marker lamp
23 Plate illumination lamp
24 Plate illumination lamp
25 LH rear marker lamp
26 Charging relay system
27 Panel rheostat
28 LH outer dip beam
29 RH outer dip beam
30 LH outer main beam
31 LH inner main beam
32 LH outer main beam
33 RH inner main beam
34 Main beam warning light
35 Heater control illumination
36 Ballast resistor
37 Cigarette lighter illumination
38 Instrument illumination
39 Horn
40 Horn relay
41 Horn-push
42 Clock
43 Gearbox/seat belt switch

44 Glovebox lid switch
45 Glovebox lamp
46 Cigar lighter
47 RH console lamp
48 Interior lamp switch
49 Roof lamp
50 RH door switch
51 RH puddle lamp
52 LH puddle lamp
53 LH door switch
54 LH console lamp
55 Roof lamp
56 Ignition key contact
57 Buzzer
58 RH seat switch
59 RH belt switch
60 LH belt switch
61 Fasten seat belt warning light
62 Fuel warning light
63 Fuel tank unit
64 Fuel gauge
65 10V stabilizer
66 Temperature gauge
67 Temperature transmitter
68 Windscreen wiper switch
69 Windscreen wiper motor
70 Alternator control unit
71 RH front flasher
72 RH rear flasher
73 Hazard switch
74 RH flasher warning light
75 Flasher switch
76 LH flasher warning light
77 Flasher unit
78 Hazard unit
79 LH front flasher
80 LH rear flasher
81 Windscreen washer switch
82 Windscreen washer motor
83 Brake lamp switch
84 LH brake lamp
85 RH brake lamp
86 Reverse lamp switch

87 LH reverse lamp
88 RH reverse lamp
89 Choke switch
90 Choke warning light
91 Handbrake switch
92 Handbrake warning light
93 Oil pressure switch
94 Oil pressure warning light
95 Connector blocks
96 Dual brake switch
97 Dual brake warning light
98 Heated back-light warning light
99 Heated back-light
100 Overdrive gear lever switch – optional extra
101 Overdrive gearbox switch – optional extra
102 Overdrive solenoid – optional extra
103 Heated back-light switch
104 LH window lift switch
105 LH window lift motor
106 RH window lift switch
107 RH window lift motor
108 Circuit breaker
109 Window lift relay
110 Ignition controlled relay
111 Heater switch
112 Heater motor
113 Fog lamp supply
114 Boot lamp switch
115 Boot lamp

Colour code
N Brown
U Blue
R Red
P Purple
K Pink
S Slate
LG Light green
G Green
W White
Y Yellow
B Black

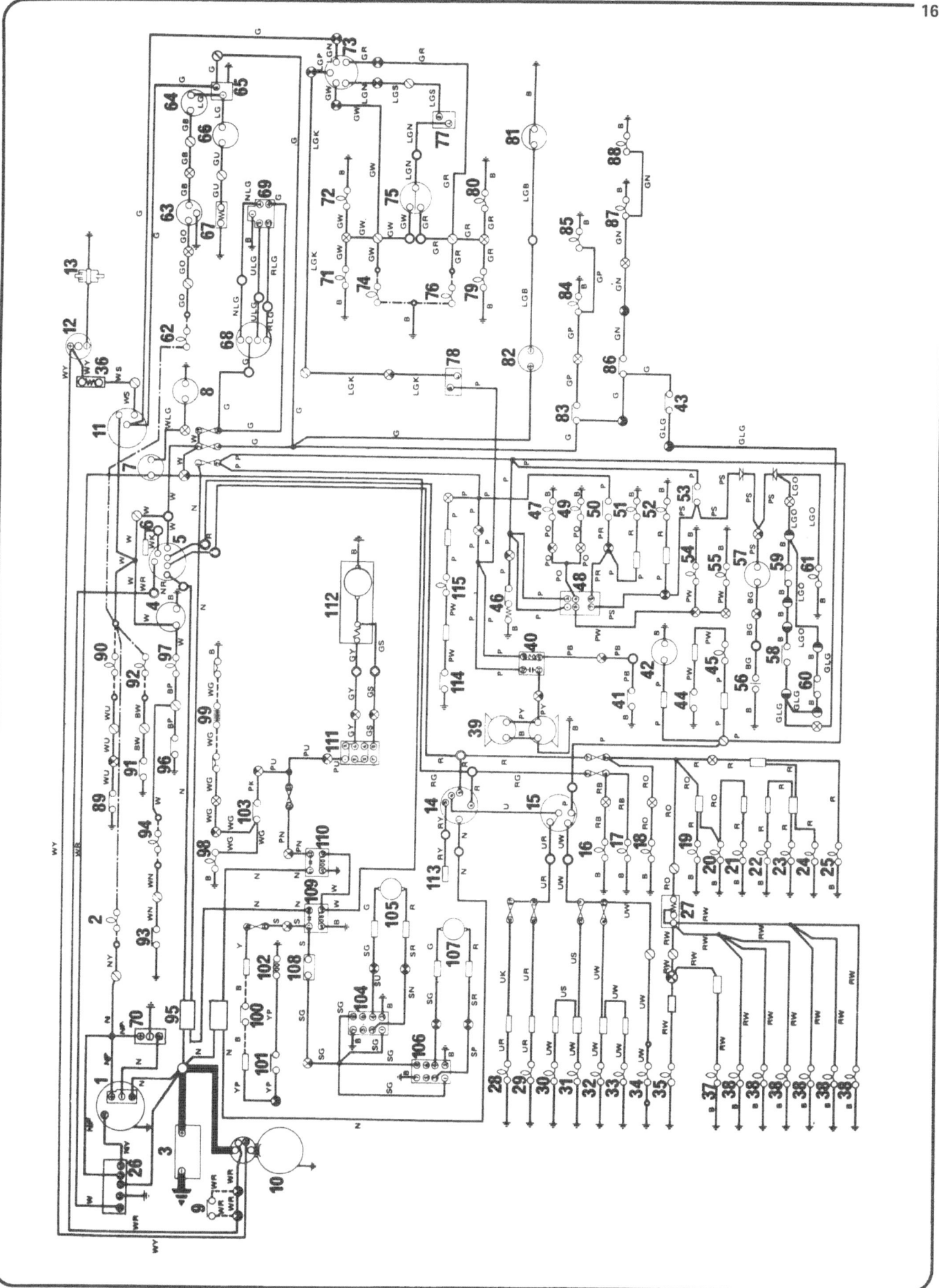

Fig. 10.49 Wiring diagram – USA models with air conditioning (From Commission No LE 11277 to LE 20271)

1 Alternator
2 Ignition warning light
3 Battery
4 Battery condition indicator
5 Ignition/starter switch
6 Radio supply
7 Inertia cut-out
8 Petrol pump
9 Inhibitor switch – Borg-Warner automatic only
10 Starter
11 Tachometer
12 Ignition coil – 6 volt
13 Ignition distributor
14 Master light switch
15 Main/dip/flash switch
16 LH tail lamp
17 LH front parking lamp
18 RH tail lamp
19 RH front parking lamp
20 RH front parking lamp
21 RH front marker lamp
22 RH rear marker lamp
23 Plate illumination lamp
24 Plate illumination lamp
25 LH rear marker lamp
26 Charging system relay
27 Panel rheostat
28 LH outer dip beam
29 RH outer dip beam
30 LH inner main beam
31 LH inner main beam
32 LH outer main beam
33 RH inner main beam
34 Main beam warning light
35 Heater control illumination
36 Ballast resistor
37 Cigar lighter illumination
38 Instrument illumination
39 Horn
40 Horn relay
41 Horn-push
42 Clock
43 Gearbox/seat belt switch
44 Glovebox lid switch
45 Glovebox lamp
46 Cigar lighter

47 RH console lamp
48 Interior lamp switch
49 Roof lamp
50 RH door switch
51 RH puddle lamp
52 LH puddle lamp
53 LH door switch
54 LH console lamp
55 Roof lamp
56 Ignition key contact
57 Buzzer
58 RH seat switch
59 RH belt switch
60 LH belt switch
61 Fasten seat belt warning light
62 Fuel warning light
63 Fuel tank unit
64 Fuel gauge
65 10V stabilizer
66 Temperature gauge
67 Temperature transmitter
68 Windscreen wiper switch
69 Windscreen wiper motor
70 Alternator control unit
71 RH front flasher
72 RH rear flasher
73 Hazard switch
74 RH flasher warning light
75 Flasher switch
76 LH flasher warning light
77 Flasher unit
78 Hazard unit
79 LH front flasher
80 LH rear flasher
81 Windscreen washer switch
82 Windscreen washer motor
83 Brake lamp switch
84 LH brake lamp
85 RH brake lamp
86 Reverse lamp switch
87 LH Reverse lamp
88 RH reverse lamp
89 Choke switch
90 Choke warning light
91 Handbrake switch

92 Handbrake warning light
93 Oil pressure switch
94 Oil pressure warning light
95 Connector blocks
96 Dual brake switch
97 Dual brake warning light
98 Heated back-light warning light
99 Heated back-light
100 Overdrive gear lever switch – optional extra
101 Overdrive gearbox switch – optional extra
102 Overdrive solenoid – optional extra
103 Heated back-light switch
104 Condenser cooling motors
105 Compressor clutch
106 High pressure cut-out
107 Air conditioning relay
108 Circuit breaker
109 Window lift relay
110 Ignition control relay
111 Blower switch
112 Thermostat
113 Blower motors change speed relay
114 LH blower motor
115 LH blower motor
116 LH window lift switch
117 LH window lift motor
118 RH window lift switch
119 RH window lift motor
120 Micro-switch
121 Fog lamp supply
122 Boot lamp switch
123 Boot lamp

Colour code
N Brown
U Blue
R Red
P Purple
K Pink
S Slate
LG Light green
G Green
W White
Y Yellow
B Black

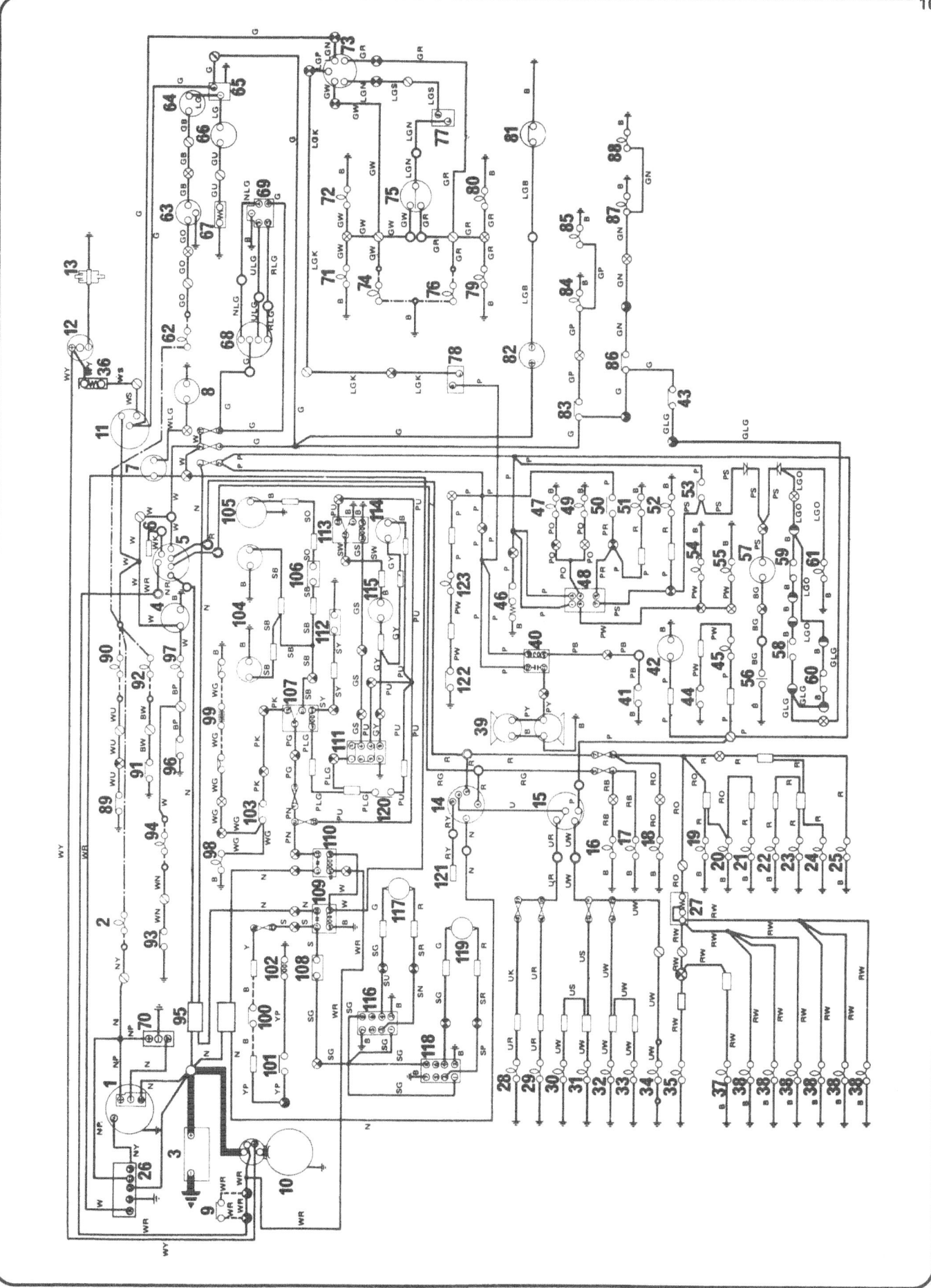

Fig. 10.50 Wiring diagram – USA models with heater (From Commission No LE 20272)

1 Alternator
2 Ignition warning light
3 Battery
4 Battery condition indicator
5 Ignition/starter switch
6 Radio supply
7 Inertia cut-out
8 Petrol pump
9 Inhibitor switch – Borg-Warner automatic only
10 Starter
11 Tachometer
12 Ignition coil – 6 volt
13 Ignition distributor
14 Master light switch
15 Main/dip/flash switch
16 LH tail lamp
17 LH front parking lamp
18 RH tail lamp
19 LH front marker lamp
20 RH front parking lamp
21 RH front marker lamp
22 RH rear marker lamp
23 Plate illumination lamp
24 Plate illumination lamp
25 LH rear marker lamp
26 Hazard warning light
27 Panel rheostat
28 LH outer dip beam
29 RH outer dip beam
30 LH inner main beam
31 LH inner main beam
32 LH outer main beam
33 RH inner main beam
34 Main beam warning light
35 Heater control illumination
36 Borg-Warner illumination – when fitted
37 Cigar lighter illumination
38 Instrument illumination
39 Horn
40 Horn relay
41 Horn-push
42 Clock
43 Gearbox/seat belt switch

44 Glovebox lid switch
45 Glovebox lamp
46 Cigar lighter
47 RH console lamp
48 Interior lamp switch
49 Roof lamp
50 RH door switch
51 RH puddle lamp
52 LH puddle lamp
53 LH door switch
54 LH console lamp
55 Roof lamp
56 Ignition key contact
57 Buzzer
58 RH seat switch
59 RH belt switch
60 LH belt switch
61 Fasten seat belt warning light
62 Fuel warning light
63 Fuel tank unit
64 Fuel gauge
65 10V stabiliser
66 Temperature gauge
67 Temperature transmitter
68 Windscreen wiper switch
69 Windscreen wiper motor
70 Wiper delay unit
71 RH front flasher
72 RH rear flasher
73 Hazard switch
74 RH flasher warning light
75 Flasher switch
76 LH flasher warning light
77 Flasher unit
78 Hazard unit
79 LH front flasher
80 LH rear flasher
81 Windscreen washer switch
82 Windscreen washer motor
83 Brake lamp switch
84 LH brake lamp
85 RH brake lamp
86 Reverse lamp switch

87 LH reverse lamp
88 RH reverse lamp
89 Choke switch
90 Choke warning light
91 Handbrake switch
92 Handbrake warning light
93 Oil pressure switch
94 Oil pressure warning light
95 Vent valve solenoid
96 Dual brake switch
97 Dual brake warning light
98 Heated back-light warning light
99 Heated back-light
100 Overdrive gear lever switch – optional extra
101 Overdrive gearbox switch – optional extra
102 Overdrive solenoid – optional extra
103 Heated back-light switch
104 LH window lift switch
105 LH window lift motor
106 RH window lift switch
107 RH window lift motor
108 Circuit breaker
109 Window lift relay
110 Ignition controlled relay
111 Heater switch
112 Heater motor
113 Fog lamp supply (earlier models only)
114 Boot lamp switch
115 Boot lamp

Colour code
N Brown
U Blue
R Red
P Purple
K Pink
S Slate
LG Light green
G Green
W White
Y Yellow
B Black

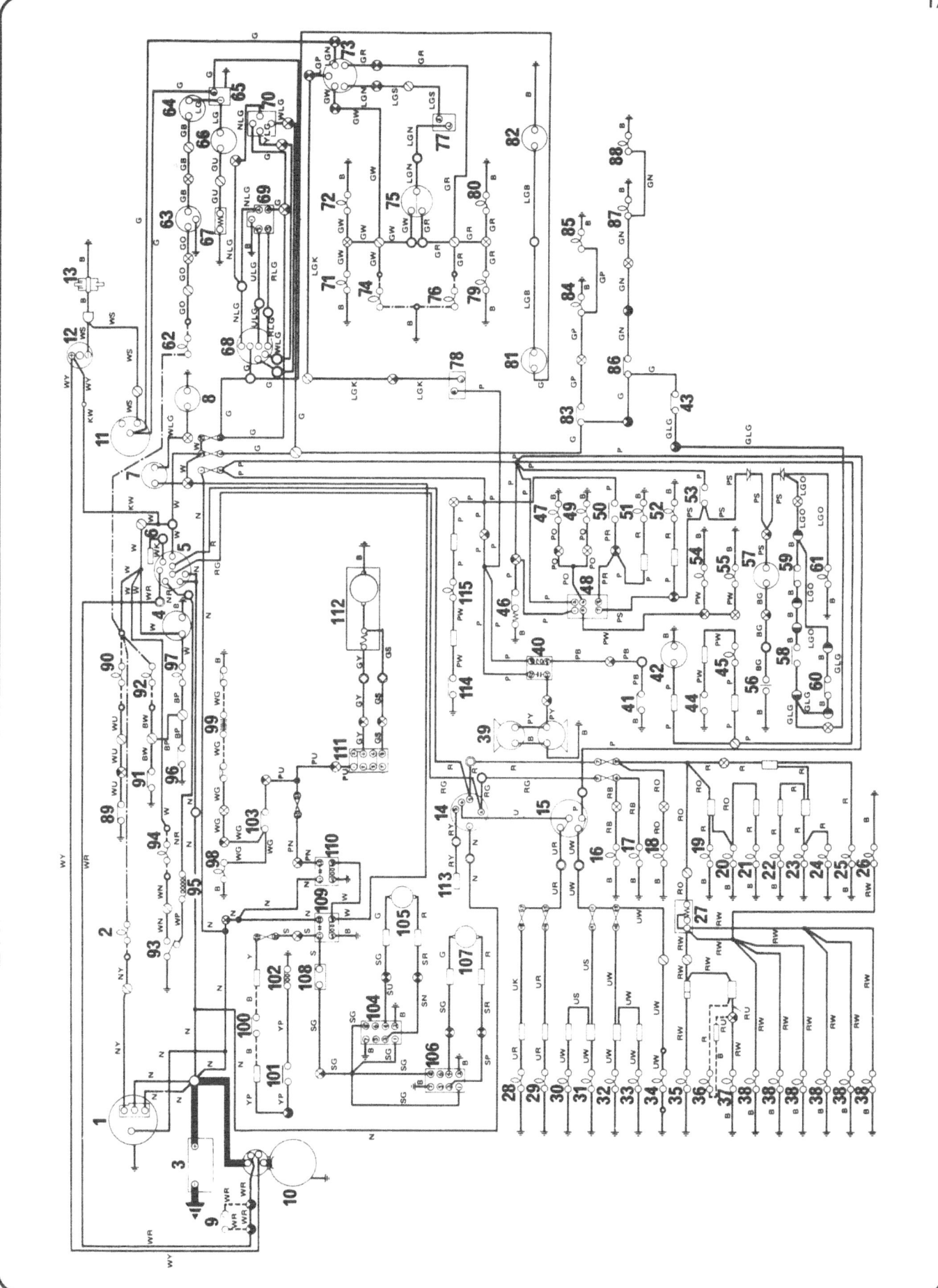

Fig. 10.51 Wiring diagram – USA models with air conditioning (From Commission No LE 20272)

1 Alternator
2 Ignition warning light
3 Battery
4 Battery condition indicator
5 Ignition/starter switch
6 Radio supply
7 Inertia cut-out
8 Petrol pump
9 Inhibitor switch – Borg-Warner automatic only
10 Starter
11 Tachometer
12 Ignition coil – 6 volt
13 Ignition distributor
14 Master light switch
15 Main/dip/flash switch
16 LH tail lamp
17 LH front parking lamp
18 RH tail lamp
19 LH front marker lamp
20 RH front parking lamp
21 RH front marker lamp
22 RH rear marker lamp
23 Plate illumination lamp
24 Plate illumination lamp
25 LH rear marker lamp
26 Hazard warning light
27 Panel rheostat
28 LH outer dip beam
29 RH outer dip beam
30 LH outer main beam
31 LH inner main beam
32 LH outer main beam
33 RH inner main beam
34 Main beam warning light
35 Heater control illumination
36 Borg-Warner illumination – when fitted
37 Cigar lighter illumination
38 Instrument illumination
39 Horn
40 Horn relay
41 Horn-push
42 Clock
43 Glovebox/seat belt switch
44 Glovebox lid switch
45 Glovebox lamp
46 Cigar lighter

47 RH console lamp
48 Interior lamp switch
49 Roof lamp
50 RH door switch
51 RH puddle lamp
52 LH puddle lamp
53 LH door switch
54 LH console lamp
55 Roof lamp
56 Ignition key contact
57 Buzzer
58 RH seat switch
59 RH belt switch
60 LH belt switch
61 Fasten seat belt warning light
62 Fuel warning light
63 Fuel tank unit
64 Fuel gauge
65 10V stabilizer
66 Temperature gauge
67 Temperature transmitter
68 Windscreen wiper switch
69 Windscreen wiper motor
70 Wiper delay unit
71 RH front flasher
72 RH rear flasher
73 Hazard switch
74 RH flasher warning light
75 Flasher switch
76 LH flasher warning light
77 Flasher unit
78 Hazard unit
79 LH front flasher
80 LH rear flasher
81 Windscreen washer switch
82 Windscreen washer motor
83 Brake lamp switch
84 LH brake lamp
85 RH brake lamp
86 Reverse lamp switch
87 LH reverse lamp
88 RH reverse lamp
89 Choke switch
90 Choke warning light
91 Handbrake switch

92 Handbrake warning light
93 Oil pressure switch
94 Oil pressure warning light
95 Vent valve solenoid
96 Dual brake switch
97 Dual brake warning light
98 Heated back-light warning light
99 Heated back-light
100 Overdrive gear lever switch – optional extra
101 Overdrive gearbox switch – optional extra
102 Overdrive solenoid – optional extra
103 Heated back-light switch
104 Condenser cooling motors
105 Compressor clutch
106 High pressure cut-out
107 Air conditioning relay
108 Circuit breaker
109 Window lift relay
110 Ignition controlled relay
111 Blower switch
112 Thermostat
113 Blower motors change speed relay
114 LH blower motor
115 RH blower motor
116 LH window lift switch
117 RH window lift motor
118 RH window lift switch
119 RH window lift motor
120 Micro-switch
121 Fog lamp supply (earlier models only)
122 Boot lamp switch
123 Boot lamp

Colour code
N   Brown
U   Blue
R   Red
P   Purple
K   Pink
S   Slate
LG Light green
G   Green
W   White
Y   Yellow
B   Black

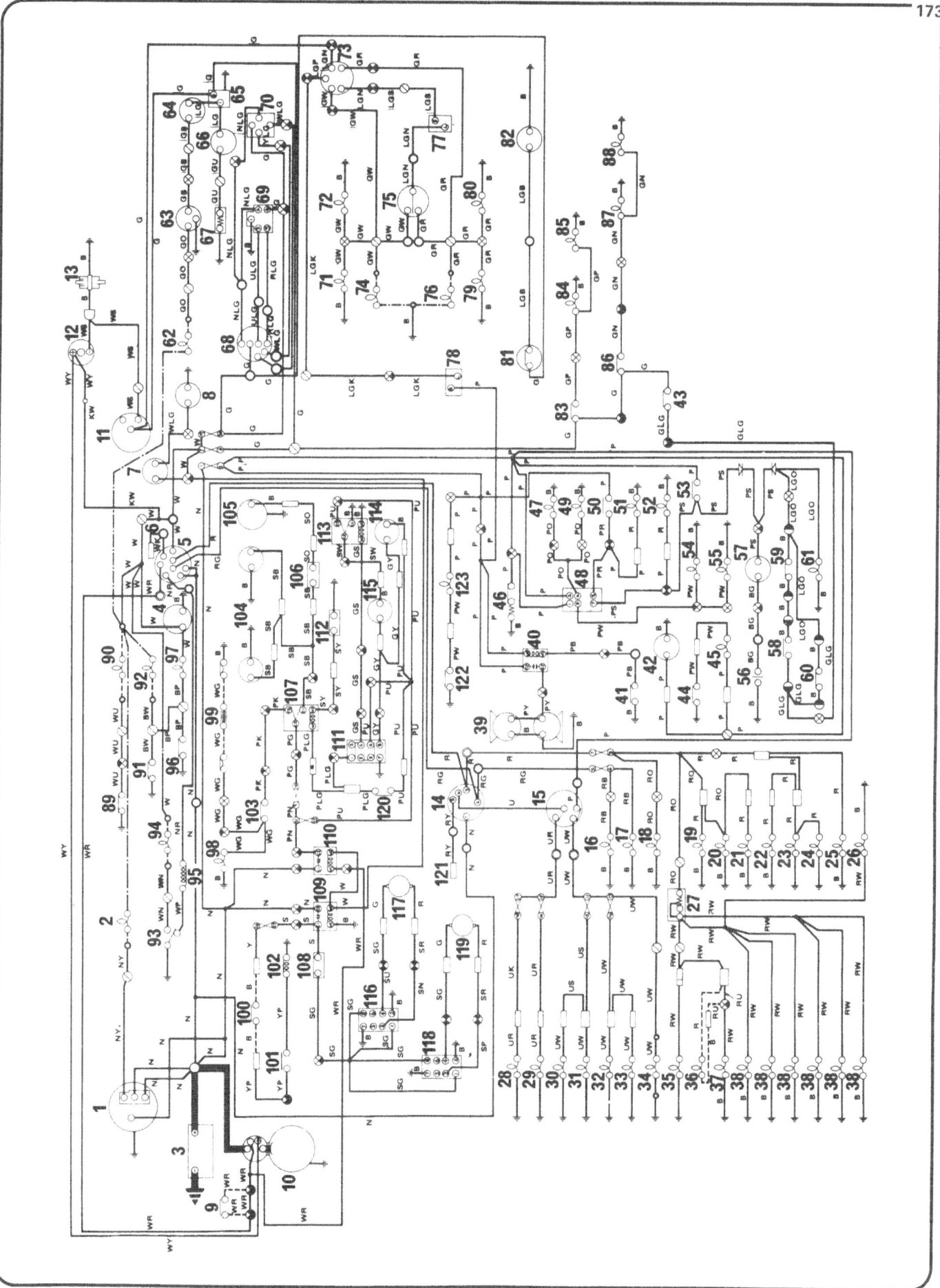

Chapter 11 Suspension and steering

Contents

Specifications

Front suspension
Type .... Independent, single lower suspension arm with combined telescopic damper and coil spring, anti-roll bar

Rear suspension
Type .... Independent, semi-trailing arm with coil springs and telescopic dampers

Rear wheel camber
Up to Commission No LD32670 .... $1\frac{1}{2}°$ negative $\pm\frac{3}{4}°$
From Commission No LD32671 .... $2\frac{1}{2}°$ negative $\pm\frac{3}{4}°$

Rear wheel alignment .... 0 to $\frac{1}{16}$ in (0 to 1·6 mm) toe-in

Steering
Type .... Rack and pinion with integral power assistance

Front wheel alignment (laden):
Toe-in .... 0 to $\frac{1}{16}$ in (1·6 mm)
Castor .... $2\frac{1}{2}° \pm \frac{1}{2}°$
Camber .... $\frac{1}{4}°$ negative $\pm \frac{3}{4}°$
Steering axis inclination .... $11\frac{3}{4}° \pm \frac{3}{4}°$

Wheels and tyres
Wheels .... 14 x 5J steel wheels or 14 x $5\frac{1}{2}$J wire or alloy wheels

Tyres 185/70 HR–14

Tyre pressures
Front .... 26 lbf/in² (1·82 kgf/cm²)
Rear .... 30 lbf/in² (2·11 kgf/cm²)

Torque wrench settings

	lbf ft	kgf m
Front suspension		
Anti-roll bar to link	16	2·2
Anti-roll bar link to radius stay	38	5·2
Balljoint to base of strut	50	6·9
Strut to upper mounting	60	8·3
Strut upper mounting nuts to body	20	2·8
Strut base to vertical link	45	6·2
Disc to hub bolts	34	4·7
Crossmember to body bolts	32	4·4
Lower arm to crossmember	80	11·1
Radius stay to suspension arm	65	9·0
Radius stay to body	38	5·2
Stub axle to vertical link	65	9·0
Steering arms to vertical link	65	9·0
Rear suspension		
Suspension arm to bracket	48	6·6
Suspension arm bracket to bodyframe	32	4·4
Subframe mounting rubber	20	2·8
Subframe strap to floor	65	9·0
Subframe mounting rubber to floor	48	6·6
Frame to axle bolts	80	11·1
Steering		
Rack to crossmember brackets	38	5·2
Steering wheel nut	32	4·4
Track-rod end locknuts	38	5·2
Track-rod end balljoint nuts	45	6·2
Universal joint pinch bolt	20	2·8
Roadwheels		
Steel wheel nuts	80	11·1
Alloy wheel nuts	100	13·9

1 Front suspension – general description

The independent front suspension fitted is of the MacPherson strut design using a single lower suspension arm with a telescopic damper strut mounted to the top of which is a coil spring. The top end of the spring damper unit is positioned in the spring turret housing which is part of the engine compartment side panel construction. The mounting contains phosphor bronze bearing bushes which allow the strut to rotate whenever the steering wheel is turned.

The wheel swivel axle onto which is mounted the disc brake and hub assembly is bolted to the lower end of the suspension strut and pivots on a balljoint positioned in the outer end of the lower suspension arm.

The inner end of the suspension arm is attached to the subframe by a flexible bush. Radius arms are attached at their front ends to the suspension arm by means of a flexible bush whilst at their rear ends they are attached by means of cone shaped rubber mountings.

Steering geometry angles are pre-set during manufacture and cannot be altered without specialist equipment, except for toe-in (see Section 24).

2 Front hubs – adjustment

1   Ensure the handbrake is on, remove the wheel trim, loosen the wheel nuts, jack-up the car, fit axle-stands, and remove the roadwheel.
2   Remove the disc brake friction pads by extracting the split pins and lifting away the two spring plates and the pads.
3   Using a wide bladed screwdriver remove the hub grease cap.
4   Extract the castellated nut retaining split pin and tighten the nut carefully, at the same time rotate the hub to ensure the rollers seat correctly and that the endfloat is eliminated. Care must be taken not to overtighten the nut (maximum of 5 lbf ft [0·691 kgf m] torque). When all endfloat is eliminated turn the nut back until the nearest slot and split pin hole in the stub axle align, then fit a new split pin to lock the nut.
5   Refit the disc brake caliper pads, spring plates and split pins. Refit the roadwheel and remove the axle-stands. Tighten the wheel nuts.

3 Front hubs – removal, inspection and refitting

1   Ensure the handbrake is on, remove the wheel trim, loosen the wheel nuts, jack-up the car, place on axle-stands, and remove the roadwheels.
2   Clean the front hub, disc and caliper and undo the two bolts which hold the caliper to the stub axle and remove the caliper from the disc.
3   Using a piece of wire suspend the caliper so that the flexible hose is not stretched. Do not depress the brake pedal otherwise the pistons will be partially ejected.
4   Refer to Fig. 11.2 and remove the grease cap (41) with a wide bladed screwdriver. Extract the split pin (43) and undo and remove the castellated nut (42). Lift away the washer (44).
5   Carefully withdraw the hub (46) complete with brake disc from the stub axle (39).
6   If new races are to fitted it will be necessary to drive the outer tracks of the two bearings (40, 45) from the hub (46) and the grease seal (38) from the hub using a soft metal drift and working in a diagonal manner.
7   Using a puller extract the inner race (40) from the stub axle.
8   Once the grease seal (39) has been removed a new one should always be fitted as it will distort upon removal.
9   Care must be taken during reassembly otherwise the bearings will be incorrectly adjusted giving poor bearing life. During initial assembly the bearings must be assembled dry.

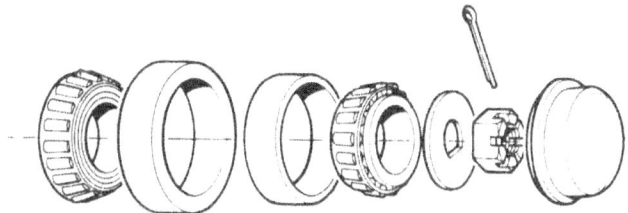

Fig. 11.1 Front hub bearings (Sec 3)

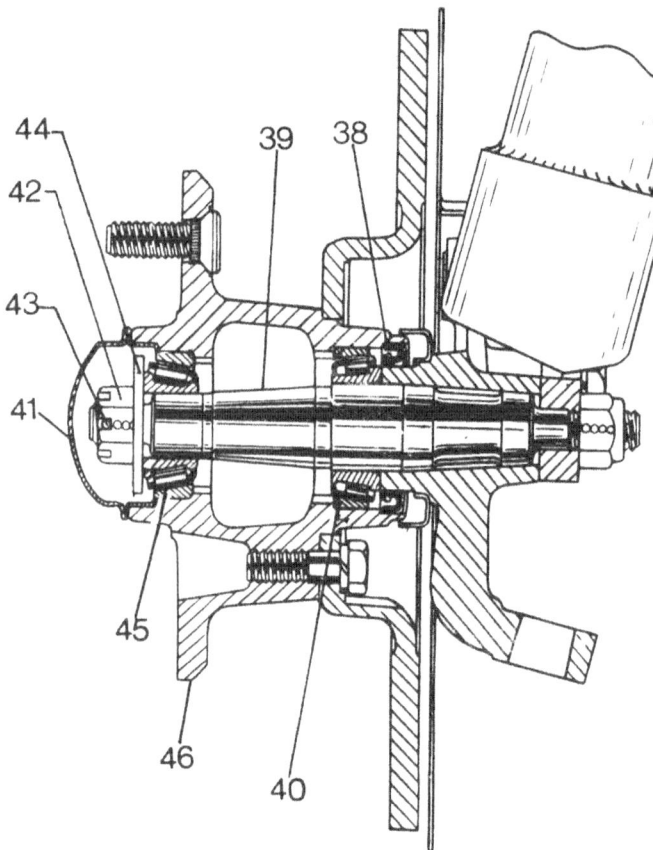

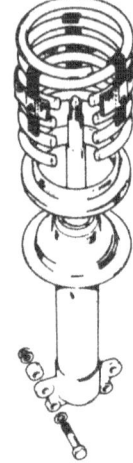

Fig. 11.3 Front spring with hooks in position (Sec 4)

Fig. 11.2 Sectional view through front hub (Sec 3)

38	Grease seal	43	Split pin
39	Stub axle	44	Washer
40	Inner bearing	45	Outer bearing
41	Grease cap	46	Hub
42	Slotted nut		

10　First fit the outer tracks of the bearings to the hub so that the tapers are facing outwards. Using a tube of suitable diameter carefully fit the inner hub race to the stub axle ensuring it is the correct way round.

11　Carefully pack the hub and bearings with grease and then reassemble and adjust as described in Section 2.

12　Install a new split pin and refit the grease cap.

13　Refit the caliper and roadwheel and lower the vehicle to the ground.

4　Front suspension strut – removal and refitting

1　Apply the handbrake and chock the rear wheels.

2　If spring hooks are available fit these over as many coils of each spring as possible. The hooks may be made from $\frac{3}{8}$ in (9·5 mm) diameter rod about 12 in (305 mm) long. Measure the depth of five coils of the spring when compressed and bend over the ends so as to hold the spring in compression. Three hooks are necessary for one coil spring and once in position they should be bound tightly together to stop them flying out (Fig. 11.3). Alternatively use spring compressors.

3　Remove the wheel trim and slacken the wheel nuts. Jack-up the front of the car and place on axle-stands.

4　Undo and remove the nyloc nuts from the top of the spring upper mounting followed by the plain washers (photo).

5　Refer to Fig. 11.4 and undo the four bolts (15, 16) from the vertical link (36). Note that there is a special spacer (53) which must not be mislaid.

6　The spring strut assembly may now be removed from the wheel arch.

7　If the assembly is to be dismantled, thoroughly clean to ensure no dirt contamination.

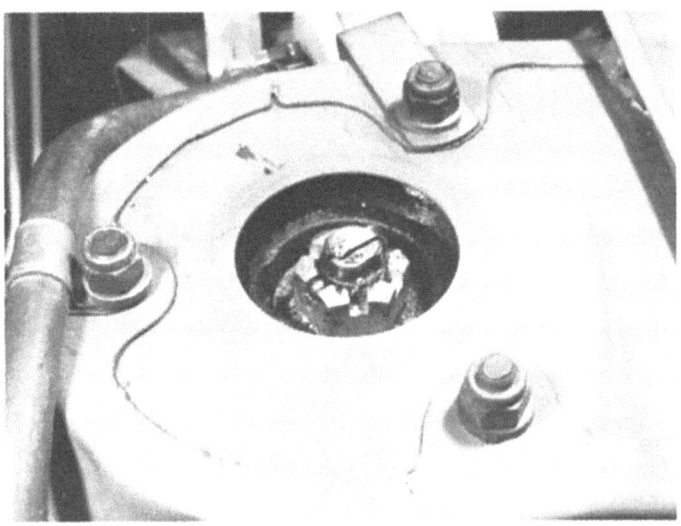

4.4 Suspension strut upper mounting nuts

8　To refit the assembly first clean the inside of each strut housing especially at the top innermost part. Remove all signs of old Plastiseal sealant using a petrol moistened cloth.

9　If there are still signs of sealant on the top of the strut turret this should also be removed.

10　Carefully apply Plastiseal sealant to the top of the strut to ensure a watertight joint when reassembled.

11　Refit the strut to the housing carefully inserting the studs into their holes, then refit the plain washer and loosely tighten the nyloc nuts.

12　Refit the spacer (53) and the four bolts (15, 16) which secure the strut assembly to the vertical link.

13　Refit the roadwheel and when positioned in the straight ahead position, grasp the road spring and rotate it so as to bring its lower extremity directly inboard. The reason for this is to ensure that the spring bows out slightly when loaded so preventing fouling on the wheel arch.

14　Remove the axle-stands and lower the car. Tighten the wheel nuts and refit the wheel trims.

15　Remove the coil spring clips.

16　Tighten the strut retaining nyloc nuts half a turn so compressing the Plastiseal and finally tighten to the specified torque.

5　Front suspension strut – dismantling and reassembly

1　With the assembly clean and placed on a workbench, first extract the split pin (10) (Fig. 11.5) and undo the castellated nut (11).

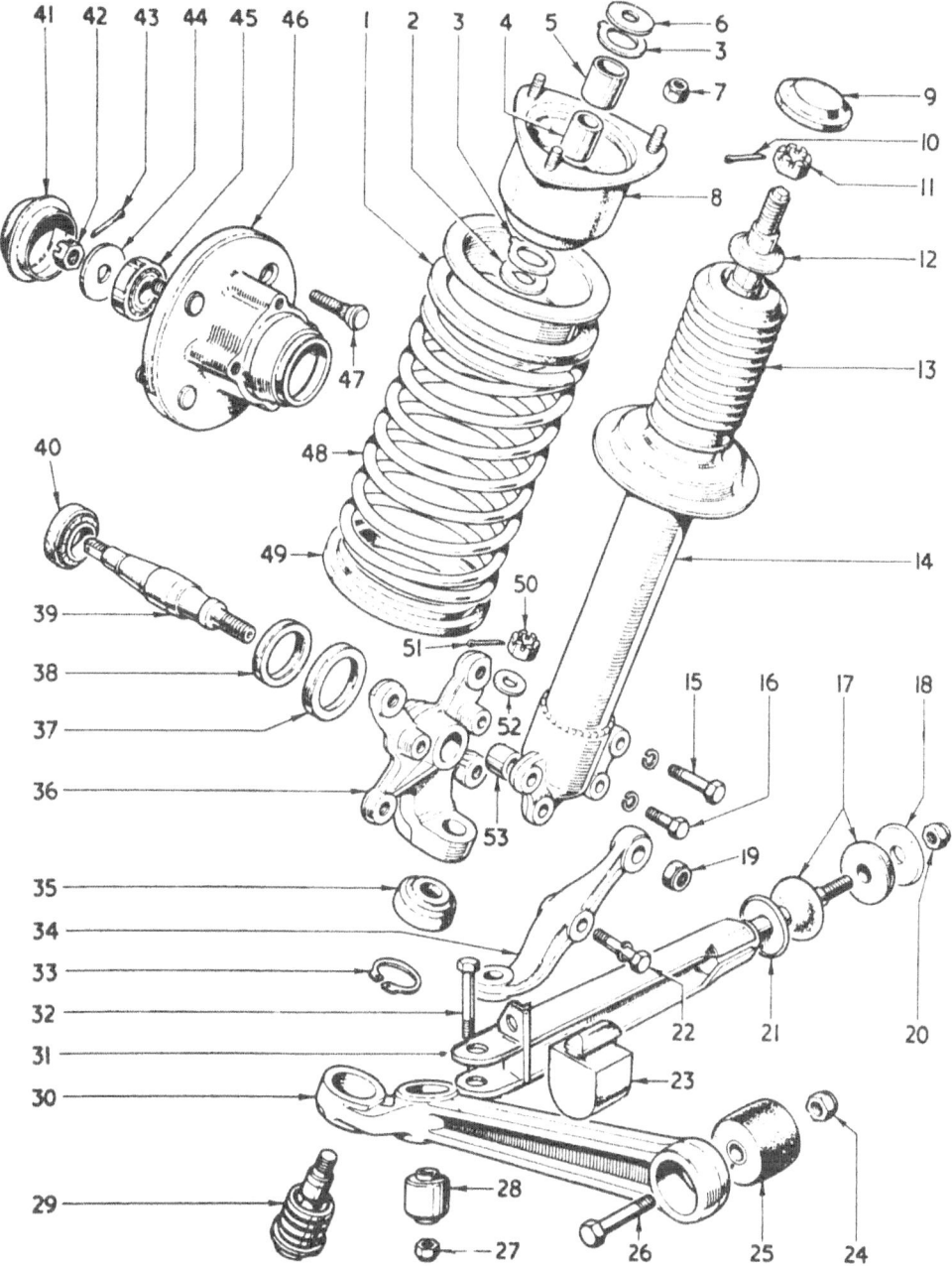

Fig. 11.4 Exploded view of one side of the front suspension (Sec 4)

1	Top rubber insulator, front spring	19	Nyloc nut	36	Vertical link
2	Washer	20	Nyloc nut	37	Water shield for hub seal
3	Thrust washer	21	Thrust washer	38	Seal, grease
4	Sleeve	22	Bolt	39	Stub axle
5	Bearing	23	Bump rubber	40	Inner bearing, hub
6	Washer	24	Nyloc nut	41	Grease cap
7	Nyloc nut	25	Rubber bush	42	Slotted nut
8	Rubber mounting assembly, strut top	26	Bolt	43	Split pin
		27	Nyloc nut	44	Washer
9	Rubber grommet	28	Rubber bush (fitted to vehicles prior to Commission No. MB 8252)	45	Outer bearing, hub
10	Split pin			46	Hub
11	Slotted nut	29	Balljoint assembly	47	Wheel stud
12	Retaining washer, gaiter	30	Suspension arm	48	Road spring
13	Gaiter	31	Drag strut	49	Bottom rubber insulator, front spring
14	Front damper strut	32	Bolt	50	Slotted nut
15	Bolt	33	Circlip	51	Split pin
16	Bolt	34	Steering arm	52	Washer
17	Thrust rubber	35	Gaiter	53	Spacer
18	Thrust washer				

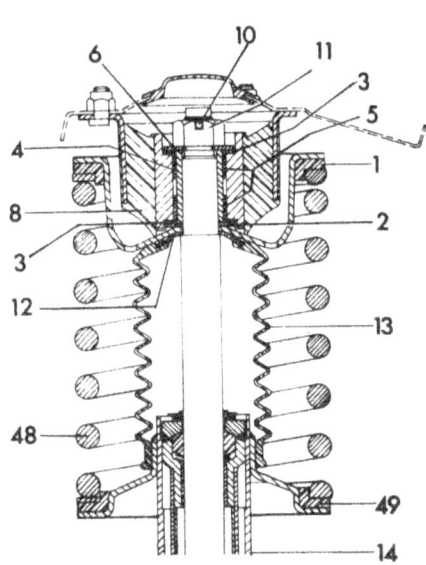

Fig. 11.5 Sectional view of upper end of the suspension strut. For key refer to Fig. 11.4 (Sec 5)

2   Lift away the upper washer (6) and the lower washer (3). The strut top rubber mounting assembly (8) may now be removed from the damper strut (14), followed by the upper rubber insulator (1), spring (48) and bottom rubber insulator (49).

3   Inspect all rubber parts for signs of perishing or damage and fit new parts as necessary. Check that the gaiter (13) is not split or cracked and if suspect renew.

4   If the coil spring requires renewal it is recommended that the original be taken to the local agents and a special tool used to compress the spring and release the clips. The clips can then be fitted to the new spring. Without the special tool it is very dangerous to try to compress or release the spring tension and serious injury could result.

5   To reassemble, insert the washer (12) into the grooved top end of the rubber gaiter (13). Fit the gaiter to the strut (14) easing the lower end of the gaiter over the outer casing of the strut. Position the washer (12) against the shoulder on the top end of the strut.

6   With the coil spring in its compressed state and the clips firmly in position fit the rubber insulators to the top (1) and bottom of the spring (49) and assemble the spring to the strut.

7   Refit the dish shaped mounting onto the top of the spring followed by the washer (2).

8   Lightly smear all rubbing surfaces of the strut assembly with a grease to ensure quiet operation.

9   Refit the distance sleeve (4) into the rubber mounting (8) and position the lower thrust washer (3) onto the lower face of the sleeve ensuring that the plastic covered side is facing downwards.

10 Fit the rubber mounting (8) and relative parts onto the top of the spring and place the second thrust washer (3) on the top face of the sleeve with the plastic covered side facing upwards. Refit the washer (6) and the nut (11) and tighten the nut to the specified torque. Use a new split pin (10) to lock the nut (11).

6   Anti-roll bar – removal and refitting

1   Apply the handbrake and chock the rear wheels. Raise the front of the car and support it on axle-stands.

2   Undo the nut securing the anti-roll bar to the links attached to the radius stay and disconnect the anti-roll bar from the stay (Fig. 11.6).

3   Remove the securing nuts, then withdraw the U-bolts, clamp brackets and distance pieces attaching the anti-roll bar to the body at each side and lift away the anti-roll bar.

4   Examine the rubber bushes on the anti-roll bar and renew them if there are any signs of deterioration.

5   Refitting is the reverse of the removal procedure. Tighten the securing nuts to the specified torque.

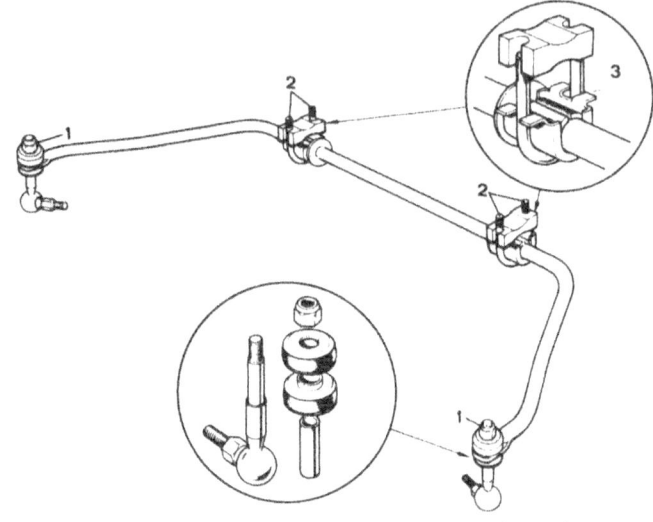

Fig. 11.6 Anti-roll bar attachment points (Sec 6)

| 1 Links | 3 Clamp brackets |
| 2 U-bolts | |

7   Front suspension arm – removal and refitting

1   Apply the handbrake and chock the rear wheels. Raise the front of the car and support it on axle-stands. Remove the wheel.

2   Remove the securing nut and disconnect the anti-roll bar link from the radius stay.

3   Refer to Fig. 11.4 and extract the split pin (51). Undo and remove the castellated nut followed by the washer (52).

4   Part the balljoint assembly (29) and, using a small screwdriver, extract the circlip (33). The balljoint assembly (29) may now be removed.

5   Undo the nut (24) and extract the bolt (26) so that the suspension arm (30) may be detached from the the body crossmember.

6   Undo the nyloc nut (20) and lift away, followed by the washer (18) and thrust rubbers (17). The stay (31) may now be removed (photo).

7   Thoroughly clean the suspension arm and check for signs of damage or distortion.

8   Refitting is the reverse sequence to removal. It is, however, important to note that the washers (18, 21) must be fitted with their rounded sides facing the rubbers (17).

9   Refit the stay bolt (32) so that the head is on the top and the nut (27) is underneath.

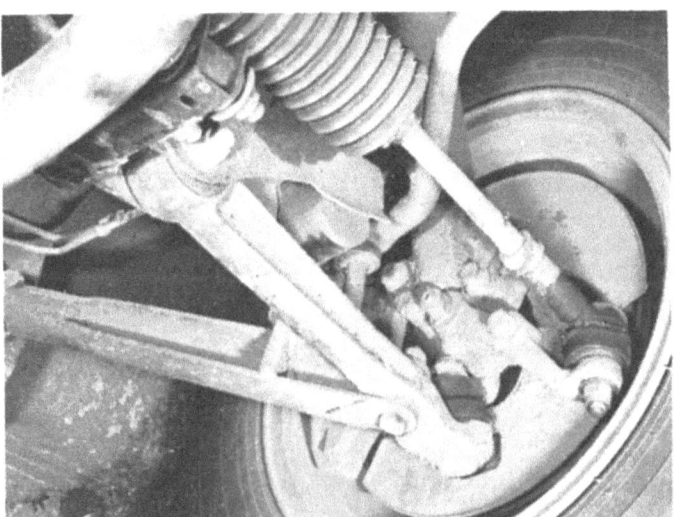

7.6 The front suspension arm and radius stay

10 The bolt (26) and nut (24) must not be fully tightened until the vehicle is off the axle-stands and in the normal static laden condition otherwise the rubber bush (25) will be distorted.

8 Front suspension balljoint assembly – removal and refitting

1   Apply the handbrake and chock the rear wheels.
2   Remove the front wheel trim and slacken the wheel nuts. Raise the front of the car and place on axle-stands. Remove the wheel.
3   Refer to Fig. 11.4 and extract the split pin (51). Undo and remove the castellated nut followed by the washer (52).
4   Part the balljoint assembly (29) from the vertical link (36). Ease off the gaiter (35) and using a small screwdriver extract the circlip (33). The balljoint assembly (29) may now be removed.
5   Refitting is the reverse sequence to removal.

9 Front suspension assembly – removal and refitting

1   Disconnect the earth terminal from the battery. Apply the handbrake and chock the rear wheels.
2   Compress both front coil springs as described in Section 4.
3   Undo and remove the lower steering universal joint coupling pinch-bolt. Mark the position of the coupling relative to the control valve pinion shaft to ensure correct reassembly.
4   Undo and remove the three nyloc nuts (7) (Fig. 11.4) on the top of each spring turret. Lift away the plain washers.
5   Remove the wheel trims and slacken the wheel nuts. Raise the front of the car and place on axle-stands positioned on the chassis side members at the rear of the front wheel arches.
6   Take a thin piece of polythene or plastic sheet and place it under the brake master cylinder filler cap which should be screwed down hard. This will effectively seal the vent holes in the cap and will prevent fluid loss.
7   Wipe round the connections for the two front brake pipes at the pressure differential warning actuator (PDWA) switch and plug the openings to prevent the ingress of dirt.
8   Disconnect the anti-roll bar from the links on the radius stays, refer to Section 6.
9   Disconnect the flexible hydraulic pipes at the power steering control valve, have a container ready to collect the fluid. Plug the ports in the steering assembly and the flexible pipes to prevent the ingress of dirt.
10 Undo the nut (20) (Fig. 11.4) and remove, followed by the plain washer (18) and the rubber abutment (17) from the rear end of the front suspension stay mounting. Repeat the operation on the second side.
11 Place a hydraulic jack under the centre of the crossmember to take the weight of the front suspension units.
12 Undo the eight nuts and bolts – four each side, holding the crossmember to the two main chassis members.
13 Move the front suspension assembly forwards slightly to release the two stays from their mountings and the steering coupling from the pinion shaft.
14 With the assistance of a second person lower the suspension to the ground, tilt backwards and withdraw forwards from the underside of the car.
15 To refit the front suspension assembly first clean the inside of each strut housing, especially at the top innermost part. Remove all signs of old 'Plastiseal' sealant using a petrol moistened cloth.
16 If there are still signs of Plastiseal on the top of the strut turret this should also be removed.
17 Carefully apply 'Plastiseal' sealer to the top of the strut to ensure that a watertight joint is obtained when reassembled.
18 Slide the front suspension assembly into position on the floor and lift onto a trolley hydraulic jack. With the assistance of a second person raise the complete suspension assembly, carefully inserting the strut upper mounting studs into the holes in the top of the strut housing. Refit the washers and nyloc nuts. Do not tighten the nuts.
19 Remove the jack. Carefully manipulate the rear ends of each stay into position and refit the rubber abutments (17) (Fig. 11.4), plain washers (18) and nyloc nuts. Check that the rounded edges of the thrust washers (18, 21) correctly contact the rubbers (17) and that the flat face of the rubbers abut against the body panel.
20 Check that the front wheels are in the straight ahead position. An

assistant should manipulate the steering column intermediate shaft until the universal coupling engages with the pinion splines aligning the previously made marks.
21 Position the four reinforcement strips on the top of the flanges of the two main chassis members and refit the eight nuts and bolts. Note that the two brake hose brackets are held in position by the outer rear nuts.
22 Refit the two front brake pipes to the PDWA switch and connect the two hydraulic pipes to the power steering control valve.
23 Refit the lower steering universal joint coupling pinch-bolt after checking that it engages within the milled groove in the pinion shaft.
24 Clip the brake pipe to the front crossmember.
25 Refit the roadwheels, raise the car, remove the axle-stands and lower the car to the ground. Tighten the wheel nuts and refit the wheel trims.
26 Remove the coil spring clips.
27 Tighten the strut retaining nyloc nuts half a turn at a time so compressing the 'Plastiseal' and finally tighten to the specified torque.
28 Top-up and bleed the brake hydraulic system as described in Chapter 9.
29 Top-up and bleed the power steering system as described in Section 21.
30 Reconnect the battery earth terminal.
31 It is recommended that the front wheel alignment be checked by the local garage to ensure that the original setting has not been altered or, if new parts have been fitted, the necessary adjustments can then be made. (See Section 24).

10 Rear suspension – general description

The independent suspension layout is shown in Fig. 11.7. The rear subframe employs the differential casing as a stiffening member. The suspension consists of semi-trailing arms with coil springs and telescopic shock absorbers.
The suspension arms pivot on rubber bushes mounted on the detachable rear subframe which in turn is attached to the main body shell with flexible rubber mountings.

11 Rear shock absorbers – removal and refitting

1   Raise the rear of the car and place on firmly based stands located under the suspension arms.
2   Undo the lower shock absorber mounting from the suspension arm.
3   Remove the rear compartment trim and undo the upper shock absorber mounting.
4   Compress the shock absorber and lift away.
5   Examine the shock absorber for signs of damage to the body, distorted piston rod, loose mounting or hydraulic fluid leakage which, if

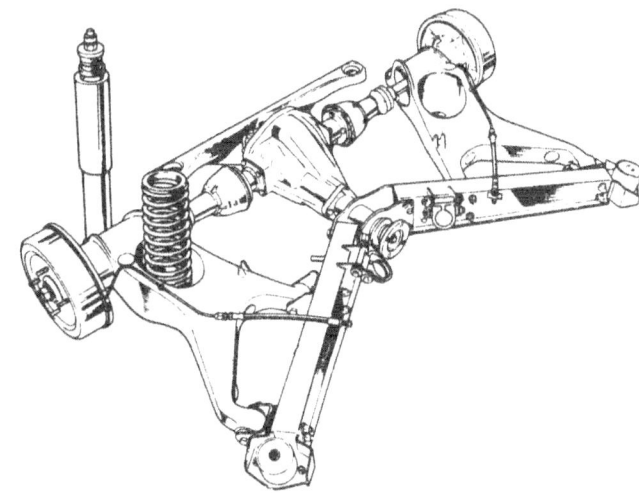

Fig. 11.7 Rear suspension and final drive (Sec 10)

evident, means a new unit should be fitted.

6   To test for shock absorber efficiency hold the unit in the vertical
position and gradually extend and contract the unit between its
maximum and minimum limits ten times. It should be apparent that
there is equal resistance in both directions of movement. If this is not
apparent a new unit should be fitted.

7   Refitting is the reverse sequence to removal.

12 Rear road spring – removal and refitting

1   Remove the wheel trim and slacken the wheel nuts. Jack-up the
rear of the car and support it on firmly based stands or other suitable
supports.

2   Position the saddle of a trolley jack under the suspension arm
spring well and raise the suspension unit to partially compress the
spring. Be careful not to raise the car off the supports (photo).

3   Remove the wheel nuts and lift away the roadwheel.

4   Refer to Chapter 8 and remove the four nuts, bolts and spring
washers holding the driveshaft universal joint flange to the final drive

12.2 Rear road spring – right-hand

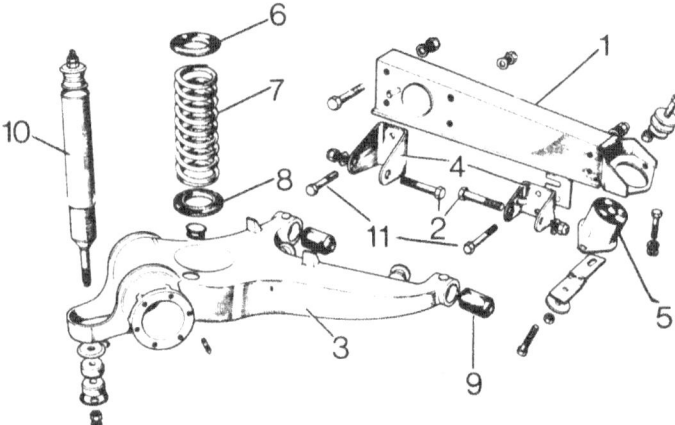

Fig. 11.8 Rear suspension component parts (Sec 12 and 13)

1 Subframe (RH member)	7 Spring
2 Bolts	8 Rubber insulator
3 Suspension arm	9 Flexible bush
4 Support brackets	10 Shock absorber
5 Mounting rubber	11 Bolts
6 Rubber insulator	

unit inner axleshaft flanges. Thread a piece of wire through the two
axleshaft universal joints to stop the shaft parting.

5   Undo the lower shock absorber mounting to suspension arm (Fig.
11.8) by undoing the two nuts and removing together with the washer
and rubber mounting.

6   Very carefully lower the suspension arm until it is just possible to
remove the spring. Do not lower the suspension arm too far otherwise
the brake flexible hose will be strained. Lift away the spring upper
insulator and lower insulator.

7   Inspect the spring for signs of fracturing or excessive rusting. Also
check the free length and if it deviates from the new spring length a
new pair of rear springs should be fitted. Do not fit single springs
otherwise the road holding will be impaired or body position relative to
the road surface will be altered on the one side.

8   Reassembly is the reverse sequence to removal.

13 Rear suspension arm – removal, renovation and refitting

1   Refer to the previous Section and remove the rear suspension
spring. Temporarily reconnect the shock absorber lower mounting.

2   Take a thin piece of polythene or plastic sheet and place it under
the brake master cylinder filler cap which should be screwed down
hard. This will effectively seal the vent holes in the cap and will prevent
fluid loss.

3   Refer to Chapter 9 and disconnect the rear brake flexible hose
from the brake backplate.

4   Extract the split pin from the cotter pin holding the handbrake
cable yoke to the backplate handbrake lever. Lift away the washer and
the cotter noting that the head is towards the top.

5   Disconnect the lower shock absorber mounting.

6   Refer to Fig. 11.8 and undo the four bolts (11). Lift away the bolts
(11), nuts, spring washers and any shims that might be placed
between the support bracket (4) and the subframe member. The
quantity and location of shims should be noted and during reassembly
they should be refitted in their original locations.

7   If the bushes require renewal, the use of a press or large vice will
be required.

8   Obtain a piece of tube with an internal diameter slightly larger
than the external diameter of the bush. Place it behind the bush and
using a piece of rod slightly smaller in diameter than the bush outer
diameter push out the old bush.

9   Using coarse emery cloth clean the eye of the suspension arm and
lubricate with rubber grease.

10 Place a bolt in the tube of the new rubber bush and pull into position using a nut and washer.

11 Repeat this procedure for the second bush.

12 Refitting the suspension arm is the reverse sequence to removal.
The brake system must be bled as detailed in Chapter 9. Also the rear
wheel alignment must be checked as detailed in Section 25 of this
Chapter.

14 Rear suspension subframe – removal and refitting

1   Remove the rear suspension spring as described in Section 12 of
this Chapter.

2   Wipe the end of the rear brake bleed nipple and put a piece of
rubber tubing onto the end. The other end of the rubber tubing should
be put in a clean glass container.

3   Drain the brake hydraulic system by opening the nipple and
operating the brake pedal.

4   Refer to Chapter 9 and disconnect the rear brake flexible hose
from the brake backplate.

5   Extract the split pin from the cotter pin holding the handbrake
cable yoke to the backplate handbrake lever. Lift away the washer and
cotter noting that the head is towards the top.

6   Remove the yokes from the handbrake cables and pull the cables
through the subframe guides.

7   Undo the four bolts holding the propeller shaft universal joint
flange to the rear axle companion flange.

8   Remove the exhaust tail pipes and rear intermediate pipes by
slackening the intermediate pipes-to-silencer clamps and releasing the
tail pipes from the rubber hangers.

9   Position an hydraulic jack under the final drive unit and undo the
four subframe mountings located as shown in Fig. 11.9

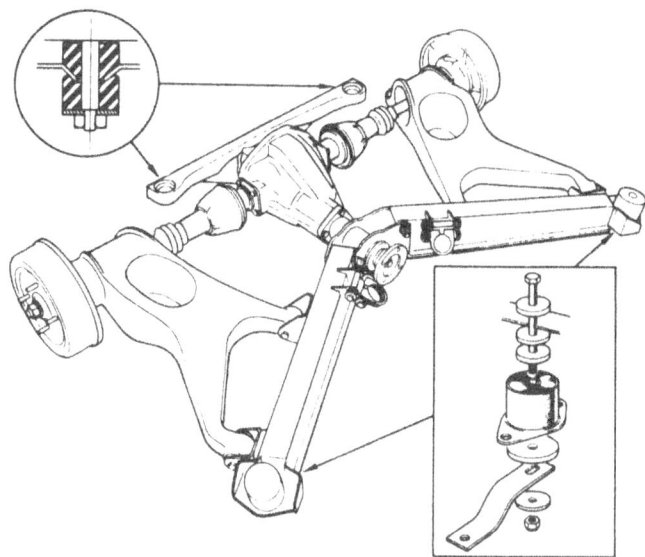

Fig. 11.9 Rear suspension subframe mountings (Sec 14)

10 Carefully lower the subframe assembly and withdraw it towards the rear of the car.
11 Refitting is the reverse sequence to removal. The brake system must be bled as detailed in Chapter 9. Also the rear wheel alignment must be checked as described in Section 25 of this Chapter.

15 Power-assisted steering system – description

With cars having a large power unit in the front the weight on the front wheels can be higher than that for a conventional smaller car, so that a larger tyre section has to be used. These two points can raise the required steering wheel force to a higher than normal level unless a higher reduction ratio is used in the steering system, but, of course, there is a limit to this as too low a geared steering system can be acceptable when parking the car but will necessitate large steering wheel movements for small direction changes on the road. With the fitting of power-assisted steering, therefore, the steering wheel can be turned with little effort. The system basically comprises an hydraulic pump and a special rack and pinion steering gear modified to operate under hydraulic pressure. Overhaul is not considered to be within the scope of the do-it-yourself motorist as specialist knowledge as well as special tools are required. However, there are certain jobs which can be attempted which are described in detail, together with a description of how the system operates.

The special hydraulic pump, (Fig. 11.10) is fitted to a bracket mounted on the timing cover and is of sufficient capacity to give power assistance with the engine at normal idle speed. The hydraulic pump passes fluid from the reservoir to a special valve which contains a spring loaded flow control valve to limit the flow of hydraulic fluid at high speed. The flow is limited by the fluid passing through an orifice causing a pressure drop across the orifice. When a pre-determined flow rate has been reached, the flow control valve uncovers a by-pass port and so allows excess fluid to return to the reservoir. As the flow increases more and more with increasing engine speed, the by-pass port is opened even more, so resulting in a constant flow rate at the steering unit. This valve, although actuated by the rate of flow of hydraulic fluid is not sensitive to pressure fluctuations and a special pressure relief valve is set to control delivery pressure within the range 750 to 850 lbf/in² (52·73 to 59·76 kgf/cm²).

A filter is situated in the hydraulic system so that all fluid returning from the steering unit is filtered automatically unless the filter is blocked due to lack of service, and in this case a spring will operate the filter and unseat it so allowing the returning fluid to by-pass it on its way back to the reservoir.

With the steering wheel in the straight ahead position, hydraulic fluid under pressure created by the pump enters the inlet port and returns to the reservoir without any pressure build up. When the steering wheel is turned slightly on either lock, a reaction from the pinion in

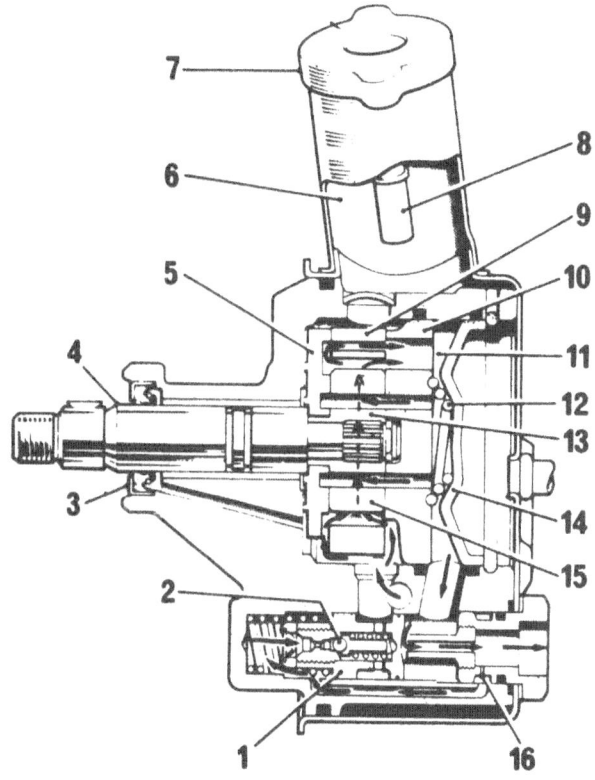

Fig. 11.10 Sectional view of power steering pump (Sec 15)

1 Flow valve	9 Elliptical ring
2 Pressure relief valve	10 Pressure plate
3 Shaft seal	11 Discharge cavity
4 Shaft	12 Spring
5 Thrust plate	13 Rotor hub
6 Reservoir	14 End plate
7 Filler cap	15 Rotor vane
8 Dipstick	16 Orifice

the steering unit moves the pinion housing so that via an operating rod, the control valve spool is moved to direct fluid either to one side of the steering unit rack, or to the other side. Fluid from the steering unit flows back through the control valve to the pump.

When the steering wheel is released the pressure will automatically balance causing the valve spool to centralise itself, and normal castor action of the front wheels will bring the steering wheel back to its straight ahead position.

16 Power-assisted steering – maintenance

1 Maintenance for the power-assisted steering system is straightforward and involves keeping the hydraulic fluid in the pump reservoir topped-up to the level marked on the reservoir using only Automatic Transmission Fluid. It is important to check the level when the fluid is warm (immediately after use) on early models as the fluid expands when warm. On later models the dipstick has a hot and cold level marking (Fig. 11.12). If the reservoir is empty do not run the engine otherwise the pump will be damaged.
2 The pump is driven by a V-belt so it is important that the belt is always correctly adjusted otherwise slippage will occur when the system is in operation.
3 From time to time examine the complete system for signs of leakage. Check that the hose connections are tight and the hoses free from oil or grease and show no signs of cracking.
4 After a very high mileage or if dirty fluid has been used in the system, the filter incorporated in the relief/flow valve should be cleaned or renewed. To do this, disconnect the pump outlet union and

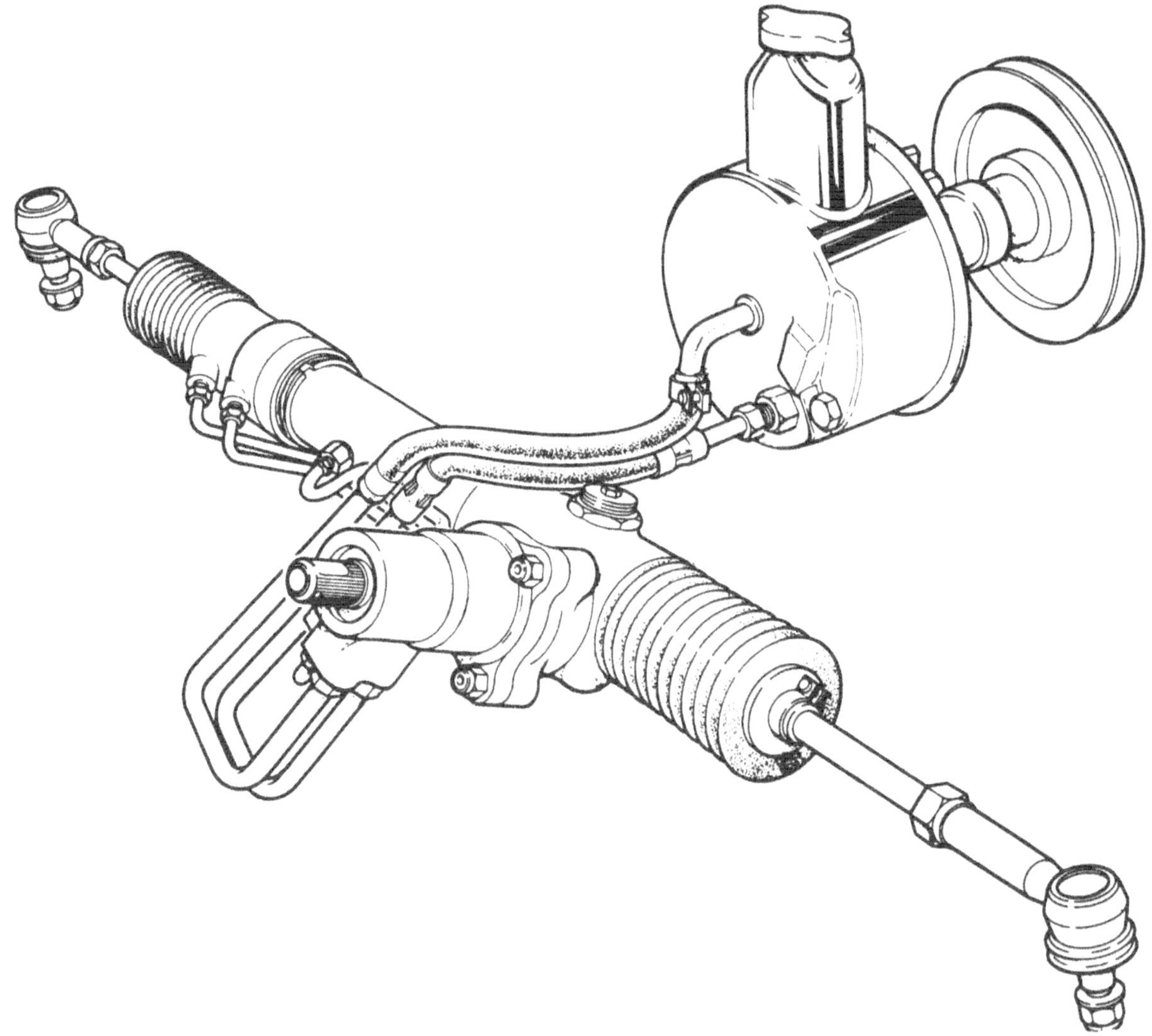

Fig. 11.11 Power steering system (Sec 15)

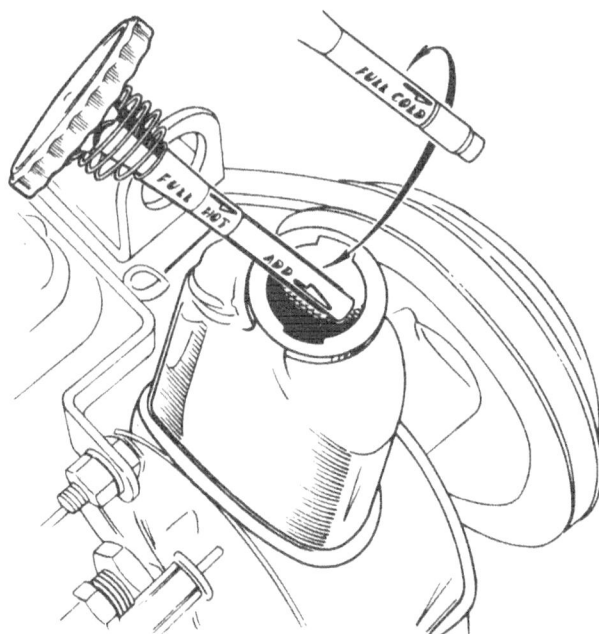

Fig. 11.12 Power steering pump dipstick markings (Sec 16)

withdraw the relief/flow valve and its spring.

5   When refitting, always renew the O-ring and bleed and top-up the system.

6   At the specified intervals (see Routine Maintenance Section), remove the plug from the top of the steering unit. Screw in a grease nipple in place of the plug and then give five or six strokes of a grease gun which has been filled with the specified grease.

17 Track-rod end – removal and refitting

1   Note the relative position of the track-rod end to the track-rod itself (count the number of exposed threads) so that the new track-rod end can be fitted to approximately the same setting.

2   Release the track-rod end locknut (photo).

3   Unscrew and remove the balljoint taper pin nut and remove the washer.

4   Using wedges or a proprietary balljoint separator, disconnect the track-rod end balljoints from the steering arms of the suspension struts.

5   Unscrew and remove the track-rod ends from their respective track-rods.

6   Install the new track-rod ends by reversing the removal process and positioning them in approximately the same positions as the original ones.

7   The front wheel alignment must now be checked and adjusted as described in Section 24.

8   The track-rod end balljoints are of the sealed type and require no lubrication.

17.2 Steering linkage track-rod

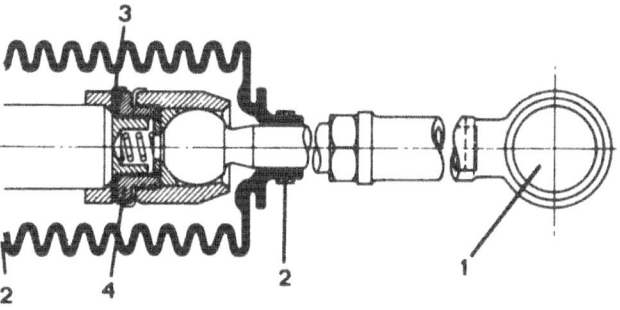

Fig. 11.13 Track-rod removal (Sec 18)

1 Track-rod end
2 Gaiter and securing clip
3 Lockwasher
4 Inner ball housing

19.4 Checking power steering pump drivebelt tension

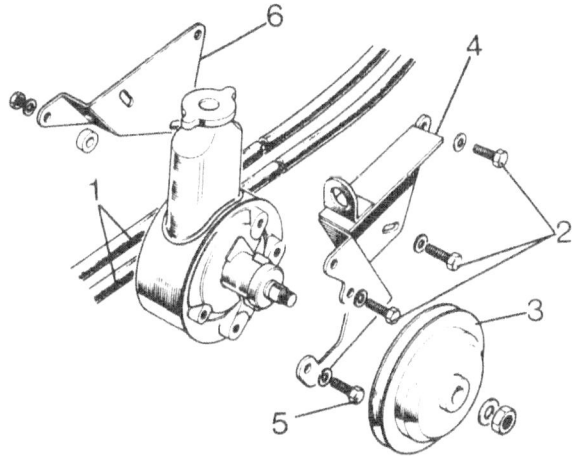

Fig. 11.14 Power steering pump mounting brackets (Sec 20)

1 Flexible hoses
2 Mounting bracket to engine bolts
3 Pump pulley
4 Front mounting bracket
5 Pump to bracket bolt
6 Rear mounting bracket

3   Remove the belt by withdrawing it through the Torquatrol fan blade.

4   Refitting is the reverse of the removal procedure. When tensioning the drivebelt, allow a slight deflection under finger pressure between the pulleys. Excessive belt tension will shorten the life of the pump shaft bearing (photo).

18 Track-rod – removal and refitting

1   Remove the relevant front roadwheel.

2   Disconnect the track-rod outer balljoint from the steering arm as described in Section 17.

3   Slacken the gaiter securing clip then slide the gaiter back along the track-rod to provide access to the inner balljoint (Fig. 11.13).

4   Clean the grease away from the balljoint and straighten the lockwasher tabs securing the balljoint housing to the rack shaft.

5   Unscrew the track-rod and inner ball-housing assembly from the rack shaft.

6   Refitting is the reverse of the removal procedure. When tightening the inner ball and adaptor to the rack shaft, hold the opposite ball end adaptor to avoid putting any stress on the steering rack pinion. Always fit new inner lockwashers and make sure to bend over the tabs.

7   Check the front wheel alignment as described in Section 24.

19 Steering pump drivebelt – removal and refitting

1   Slacken the pump support bracket mounting bolts.

2   Pivot the pump and bracket assembly to release the belt tension, then remove the belt from the pump and crankshaft pulleys.

20 Power steering pump – removal and refitting

1   Obtain a clean dry container of sufficient capacity to accept hydraulic fluid from the reservoir. Clean and then unscrew the outlet hose union from the pump and allow the hydraulic fluid to drain into the container.

2   Disconnect the fluid return hose at the pump union and blank off the ends of the hoses and the pump unions to prevent dirt entering into the system.

3   Slacken off the three bolts securing the pump mounting bracket to the engine and lift off the drivebelt.

4   Remove the securing bolts and lift away the pump and bracket assembly (photo).

5   Remove the pump to bracket securing bolts and separate the pump from the mounting bracket.

6   Refitting the pump is the reverse of the removal procedure. Before fitting the pump to the mounting bracket, rotate the pump by hand to ensure it is completely free and shows no signs of binding.

7   After fitting the pump bleed the steering hydraulic system as described in Section 22.

20.4 Removing the pump mounting bracket bolts

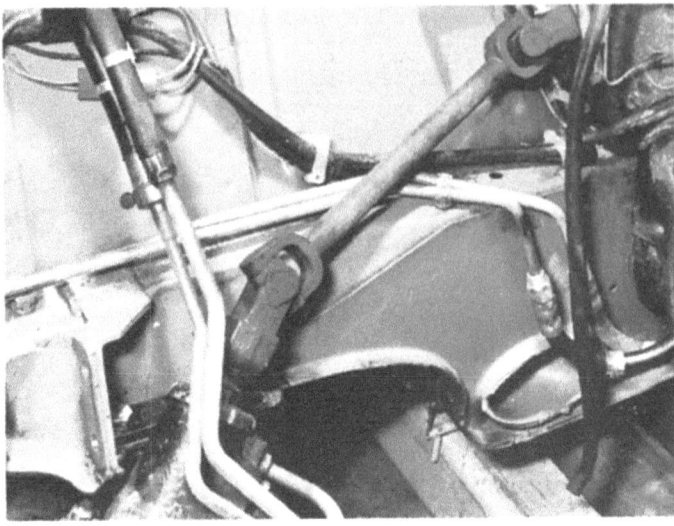

22.3 Remove the intermediate shaft lower universal joint pinch-bolt

22.4 Disconnect the hydraulic pipes from the control valve

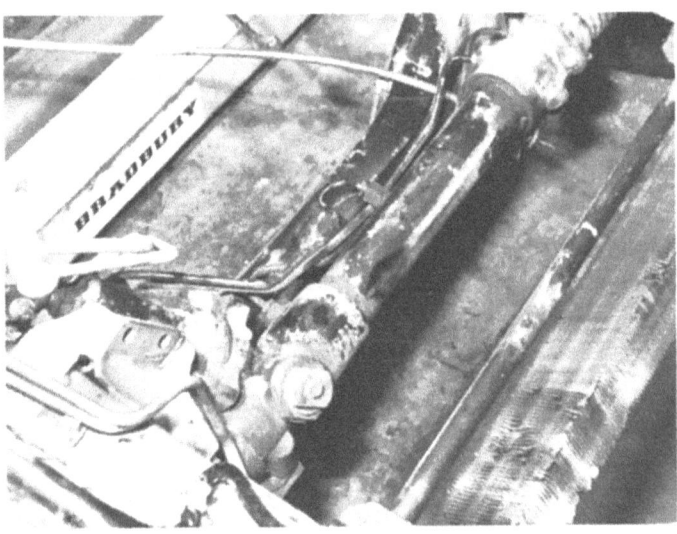

22.7 The steering rack is mounted at the front of the front cross-member

21 Power steering hydraulic system – bleeding

1   This operation will always be required if any part of the system has been disconnected, or the fluid level in the reservoir has been allowed to drop so low that air has been drawn into the pump supply pipe.
2   Fill the reservoir to the correct level.
3   Start the engine and allow it to idle for at least three minutes. Jack-up the front of the car and with the engine still idling, *slowly* turn the steering wheel from lock to lock. Repeat this several times until no air bubbles appear in the reservoir and then top-up with fluid to the correct level.

22 Power steering rack – removal and refitting

1   Chock the rear wheels, apply the handbrake and raise the front of the car and place on axle-stands.
2   Remove the wheel trims, the wheel nuts and lift away the two front wheels.
3   Remove the intermediate shaft lower universal joint pinch-bolt in the engine compartment (photo).
4   Wipe the area around the control valve, where the hydraulic pipes are located, with a clean rag and disconnect the main oil supply and return unions from the control valve housing (photo).

5   Wrap the ends of the hydraulic pipes in a clean non-fluffy rag so stopping dirt ingress. Also plug the ports.
6   Extract the split pins and remove the locknuts securing the track-rod balljoints. Using a balljoint separator or wedges to release the taper, disconnect the balljoints.
7   Remove the four bolts, plain and spring washers and angle plates securing the rack mounting feet to the mounting brackets (photo).
8   Ease the rack forwards so releasing the pinion shaft from the universal joint splines and carefully manipulate the steering assembly away from the underside of the car.
9   Before the steering rack assembly is finally fitted to the car it will facilitate installation if the rack is brought to its central position. This position is easily obtained by turning the pinion from one stop to the other stop and measuring the complete distance the rack has travelled at one end. The rack will be in its central position when it is moved back through half the measurement made.
10   Carefully insert the rack assembly making sure that the setting described in paragraph 9 is not disturbed, locate and insert the pinion splines with the universal joint coupling, checking that the steering wheel spokes are correctly positioned for the straight ahead position.
11   Align the tapped holes in the feet of the rack with those in the mounting brackets and engage the angle plates, bolts, plain and spring washers. Check that the angle plates are in contact with the mounting platform before finally tightening the bolts.
12   Reconnect the track-rod ends to the steering arms using new split

pins to lock the retaining nuts.
13 Tighten the steering intermediate universal coupling pinch-bolt.
14 Reconnect the hydraulic flexible pipe unions to the control valve.
15 Top-up the hydraulic reservoir on the top of the pump and bleed the system as described in Section 22.
16 Finally ensure that the steering rack Bundy pipes do not contact each other or any part of the car as this could cause chafing and premature failure.

23 Power steering units – overhaul

It is not recommended that either the pump or the rack and pinion assembly should be overhauled by the home mechanic due to the need for special gauges and tools.
Either unit should be renewed on a reconditioned exchange basis.

24 Steering angles and front wheel alignment

1 Accurate front wheel alignment is essential for good steering and tyre wear. Before considering the steering angle, check that the tyres are correctly inflated, that the front wheels are not buckled, the hub bearings are not worn or incorrectly adjusted and that the steering linkage is in good order, without slackness or wear at the joints.
2 Wheel alignment consists of four factors:
3 **Camber,** which is the angle at which the front wheels are set from the vertical when viewed from the front of the car. Positive camber is the amount (in degrees) that the wheels are tilted outwards at the top from the vertical.
4 **Castor,** is the angle between the steering axis and a vertical line when viewed from each side of the car. Positive castor is when the steering axis is inclined rearwards.
5 **Steering axis inclination,** is the angle when viewed from the front of the car, between the vertical and an imaginary line drawn between the upper and lower suspension strut swivels.
6 **Toe-in,** is the amount by which the distance between the front inside edges of the roadwheels (measured at hub height) is less than the same distance measured between the rear inside edge of the roadwheels.
7 Due to the need for special equipment, it is recommended that front and rear wheel alignment is left to your dealer. All front wheel angles except toe-in are set in production and cannot be adjusted.
8 For those wishing to check and adjust toe-in, obtain or make up a suitable gauge. This can be made from a length of tubing or rod, cranked to clear the sump or bellhousing and having a screw and locknut at one end. Before making any adjustment place the vehicle on level ground, tyres correctly inflated and the steering set in the straight ahead position. Make sure that all suspension and steering components are unworn and are securely attached.
9 To adjust the toe-in, use the gauge to measure the distance between the two inner wheel rims at hub height at the rear of the front roadwheels.
10 Push the vehicle to rotate the roadwheels through 180° (half a turn) and then measure the distance between the inner wheel rims, again at hub height at the front of the roadwheels. This last measurement should either be the same as the one previously taken or be less by not more than $\frac{1}{16}$ in (1.59 mm) which represents the specified toe-in (0 to $\frac{1}{16}$ in - 0 to 1.59 mm).
11 Where the toe-in is found to be incorrect, loosen the locknut on each track-rod end, also the rubber bellows clips and rotate each track-rod an equal amount until on repeating the complete checking operation, the toe-in is correct.
12 When the adjustment is completed, tighten the locknuts (with the track-rod ends in their correct attitudes) and tighten the bellows clips making sure that the bellows are not twisted.
13 Where new components have been installed, set the track-rods so that their lengths are equal with the steering wheel and front roadwheels in the straight ahead position. This will provide a starting point for precise adjustment as previously described.

25 Rear wheel alignment

These angles are normally set in production and require no adjustment. However, in the event of accidental damage and subsequent major overhaul, it is recommended that camber angles and toe-in are checked by your dealer making sure that they conform to the Specifications. Where necessary, shims can be introduced between the suspension bracket and frame members to correct alignment.

26 Steering wheel – removal and refitting

1 Disconnect the battery earth terminal for safety reasons.
2 Very carefully, to avoid damage, prise off the central steering wheel pad.
3 Undo and remove the six bolts securing the steering wheel to the steering hub and lift the steering wheel off.
4 If it is necessary to remove the steering wheel hub, first remove the central nut and washer then mark the relative positions of the hub centre and the top of the steering column shaft. Now use a suitable extractor to pull the hub away from the column shaft. Note that this operation can be carried out before the steering wheel has been removed from the hub if required.
5 Refitting is the reverse procedure to removal. If the hub was removed make sure that it is correctly aligned on the steering column shaft according to the markings made during removal.

27 Steering column – removal and refitting

1 Disconnect the earth cable from the battery negative terminal.
2 Set the roadwheels in the straight ahead position.
3 Remove the pinch-bolt which secures the upper universal joint on the intermediate shaft to the bottom of the steering column. Working inside the car remove the bolt securing the column lower support tube to the scuttle bracket.
4 Slacken the steering column clamp and then lower the column in the adjustment slots.
5 Disconnect the wiring to the ignition/starter switch, the windscreen wipers and washers, the turn indicators, flasher, horn and the lights by pulling out the four plug-in type cable connectors.
6 Remove the securing nut from the steering column clamp and while supporting the weight of the steering column take out the clamp bolt complete with the lever.
7 Lower the steering column clear of the mounting bracket and withdraw the steering column from the intermediate shaft from inside the car.
8 Refitting is the reverse of the removal procedure. Ensure that the roadwheels are in the straight ahead position and that two of the steering wheel spokes are horizontal when engaging the steering column with the intermediate shaft.

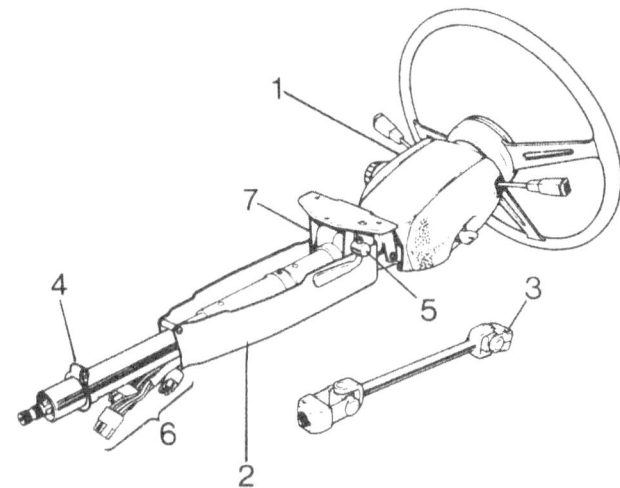

Fig. 11.15 Steering column removal (Sec 27)

1 Nacelle	bracket
2 Lower cover	5 Steering clamp lever
3 Intermediate shaft	6 Plug connectors
4 Support tube to scuttle	7 Steering clamp

28 Steering column – dismantling and reassembly

1   Remove the three screws attaching the nacelle to the steering column and lift away the two halves.
2   Undo the securing bolt then remove the distance piece and the column lower cover. Undo the four securing screws and take off the cable channel guide.
3   Remove the securing screws and lift off the wiper/washer and trafficator/horn stalks.
4   Remove the countersunk screw which locates the steering column mast lower bearing housing, then slide the lower tube towards the steering lock, to provide access to the lower bearing retaining circlip, and remove the circlip and bearing.
5   Undo the upper tube securing bolts and remove the upper and lower tubes.
6   Withdraw the inner tube from the outer tube and remove the two rubber bushes from the outer tube by depressing the locating dowel and then pulling the bushes out of the tube.
7   Examine all the parts for wear and damage, check the rubber bushes for deterioration. Renew any defective parts.
8   Reassembly is the reverse of the dismantling procedure.

29 Intermediate shaft – removal and refitting

1   Remove the upper and lower universal joint pinch-bolts securing the intermediate shaft to the steering column and the control valve pinion (Fig. 11.17).
2   Working inside the car remove the bolt securing the steering column to the scuttle.
3   Ease the lower end of the steering column upwards clear of the intermediate shaft, and then withdraw the intermediate shaft from the control valve pinion.
4   Inspect the shaft for damage and the universal joints for wear. If there is excessive play in the universal joints the shaft must be renewed.
5   Refitting is the reverse of the removal procedure. Remember to have the roadwheels in the straight ahead position and the steering wheel centralised.

30 Steering column lock and ignition switch – removal and refitting

1   Disconnect the battery earth terminal for safety reasons.
2   Remove the ignition key from the steering column lock/ignition switch.
3   Remove the two halves of the nacelle after first removing the three fixing screws.
4   Centre punch the tops of the shear-head screws which secure the steering lock to the column, then remove the screws by using a small chisel to turn them or by drilling them and using a suitable extractor.
5   Disconnect the plug-in connectors to the ignition switch then remove the steering column lock.
6   Refitting the lock is a straightforward operation after aligning the lock with the mounting holes on the column. Tighten the shear-head screws until the heads shear off.
7   The rest of the refitting operation is the reverse sequence to removal.

31 Wheels and tyres

1   The pressed steel, cast alloy or wire wheels are fitted with tyres of crossply or radial construction.
2   Never mix tyres of different construction on the same axle.
3   Check the tyre pressures weekly (including the spare).
4   Periodically, remove any deeply embedded flints from the tyre treads.
5   Periodic movement of the roadwheels round the vehicle in order to even out tyre wear is only to be carried out if the wheels have been balanced *off* the vehicle. In any event, radial tyres should only be interchanged between front and rear and not from side to side of the vehicle during any regular rotational movement.

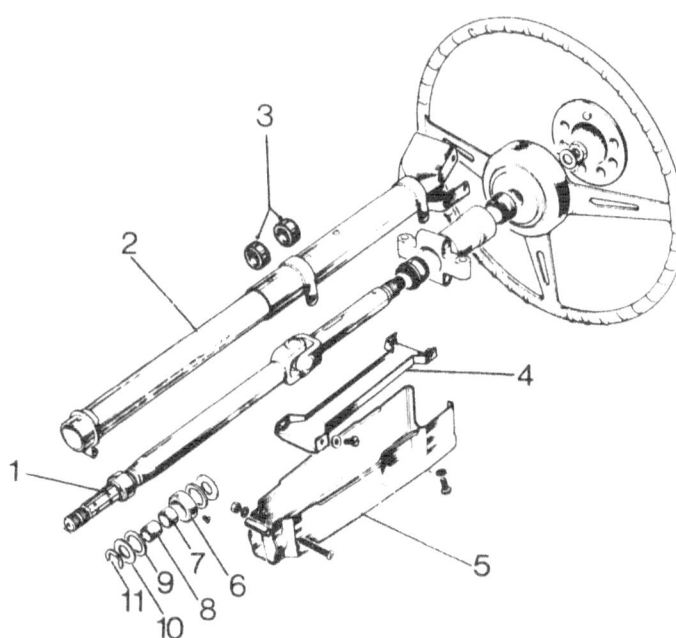

Fig. 11.16 Component parts of the steering column (Sec 28)

1   Steering column
2   Tube assembly
3   Rubber bushes
4   Cable channel guide
5   Lower cover
6   Bearing housing
7   Bearing
8   Spacer
9   Thrust washer
10   Washer
11   Circlip

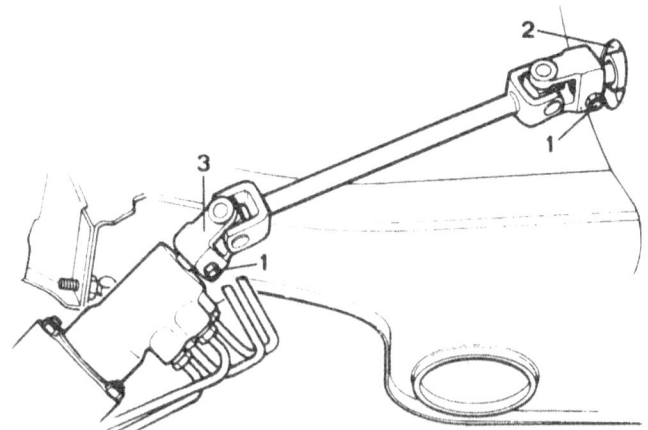

Fig. 11.17 Intermediate shaft removal (Sec 29)

1   Pinch-bolts
2   Scuttle bracket
3   Lower universal joint

32 Fault diagnosis – suspension and steering

Symptom	Reason/s
Excessive play in steering	Worn components
Directional instability	Incorrect tyre pressures Incorrectly adjusted wheel bearings Incorrect castor angle Faulty shock absorber Broken stabilizer bar
Stiff and heavy steering	Lack of lubrication in steering rack Low front tyre pressures Incorrect wheel alignment Power steering inoperative
Wheel shake or vibration	Tyre and wheel out of balance Worn or loose front wheel bearings Worn track-rod ends Worn balljoints Incorrect front wheel alignment Faulty shock absorber
Excessive pitching or rolling on corners	Faulty shock absorber or broken coil spring
'Kick-back' or loose steering	Air in system Gear loose on bodyframe
Jerk in steering wheel when turning	Low oil level Loose drivebelt Flow control valve sticking Insufficient pump pressure
Hard steering	Internal pressure leakage Loose drivebelt Low fluid level Flow control valve sticking
Poor return (centering) of steering	Valve spool plugged or sticking Incorrect steering gear adjustments
Noise from system	Due to loose drivebelt, low oil level or mechanical fault within pump or gear. Hissing noise is normal, particularly evident at full lock or during slow speed turning

Chapter 12 Bodywork and fittings

Contents

1   General description

The two-door body is of unitary, all welded, construction. A sturdy roll-bar, which besides protecting the occupants should the car overturn, also adds to the strength of the body. It is attached to the B posts and also to the header rail between the A posts.

The car can be used either as a hardtop or soft-top; the soft-top is not removed when the hardtop is fitted but is stowed in a compartment behind the rear seat under a rigid cover.

The side windows are electrically operated and the hardtop has a heated rear window. Wiring to the rear window is automatically connected and disconnected when the hardtop is fitted or removed.

The heating and ventilation system has adjustable vents at each end of the dashboard and also in the middle.

The spare wheel is stored under the floor of the luggage compartment.

2   Maintenance – bodywork and underframe

1   The condition of your car's bodywork is of considerable importance as it is on this that the secondhand value of the car will mainly depend. It is much more difficult to repair neglected bodywork than to renew mechanical assemblies. The hidden portions of the body, such as the wheel arches, the underframe and the engine compartment are equally important, although obviously not requiring such frequent attention as the immediately visible paintwork.
2   Once a year or every 12 000 miles (19 000 km), it is a sound scheme to visit your local agent and have the underside steam cleaned. All traces of dirt and oil will be removed and the underside can then be inspected carefully for rust, damaged hydraulic pipes, frayed electrical wiring and similar maladies.
3   At the same time the engine compartment should be cleaned in a similar manner. If steam cleaning facilities are not available then brush a water soluble cleanser over the whole engine and engine compartment with a stiff paint brush, working it well in where there is an accumulation of oil and dirt. Do not paint the ignition system, and protect it with oily rags when the solvent is washed off. As the solvent is washed away it will take with it all traces of oil and dirt, leaving the engine looking clean and bright.
4   The wheel arches should be given particular attention as undersealing can easily come away here and stones and dirt thrown up from the roadwheels can soon cause the paint to chip and flake, and so allow rust to set in. If rust is found, clean down the bare metal with wet and dry paper, paint on an anti-corrosive coating and renew the paintwork and undercoating.
5   The bodywork should be washed once a week or when dirty. Thoroughly wet the car to soften the dirt and then wash the car down with a soft sponge and plenty of clean water. If the surplus dirt is not washed off very gently, in time it will wear the paint down as surely as wet and dry paper. It is best to use a hose if this is available. Give the car a final wash down and then dry with a soft chamois leather to prevent the formation of spots.
6   Spots of tar and grease thrown up from the road can be removed by a rag dampened with petrol.
7   Once every six months, give the bodywork and chromium trim a thoroughly good wax polish. If a chromium cleaner is used to remove rust on any of the car's plated parts remember that the cleaner also removes part of the chromium, so use sparingly.

3   Maintenance – upholstery and carpets

1   Remove the carpets or mats and thoroughly vacuum clean the interior of the car every three months or more frequently if necessary.
2   Beat out the carpets and vacuum clean them if they are very dirty. If the upholstery is soiled apply an upholstery cleaner with a damp sponge and wipe off with a clean dry cloth.

4   Maintenance – PVC external roof covering

Under no circumstances try to clean any external PVC roof covering with detergents, caustic soaps or spirit cleaners. Plain soap and water is all that is required, with a soft brush to clean dirt that may be ingrained. Wash the covering as frequently as the rest of the car.

5   Minor body repairs

The photo sequences on pages 190 and 191 illustrate the operations detailed in the following sub-sections.

Repair of minor scratches in the car's bodywork

If the scratch is very superficial and does not penetrate to the metal of the bodywork, repair is very simple. Lightly rub the area of the scratch with a paintwork renovator, or a very fine cutting paste, to remove loose paint from the scratch and to clear the surrounding bodywork of wax polish. Rinse the area with clean water.

Apply touch-up paint to the scratch using a thin paint brush; continue to apply thin layers of paint until the surface of the paint in the scratch is level with the surrounding paintwork. Allow the new paint at least two weeks to harden; then blend it into the surrounding paintwork by rubbing the paintwork, in the scratch area, with a paintwork renovator or a very fine cutting paste. Finally, apply wax polish.

An alternative to painting over the scratch is to use a paint transfer. Use the same preparation for the affected area, then simply pick a patch of suitable size to cover the scratch completely. Hold the patch against the scratch and burnish its backing paper; the patch will adhere to the paintwork, freeing itself from the backing paper at the same time. Polish the affected area to blend the patch into the surrounding paintwork.

Where the scratch has penetrated right through to the metal of the bodywork, causing the metal to rust, a different repair technique is required. Remove any loose rust from the bottom of the scratch with a penknife, then apply rust inhibiting paint to prevent the formation of rust in the future. Using a rubber or nylon applicator fill the scratch with bodystopper paste. If required, this paste can be mixed with cellulose thinners to provide a very thin paste which is ideal for filling narrow scratches. Before the stopper-paste in the scratch hardens, wrap a piece of smooth cotton rag around the top of the finger. Dip the finger in cellulose thinners and then quickly sweep it across the surface of the stopper-paste in the scratch; this will ensure that the surface of the stopper-paste is slightly hollowed. The scratch can now be painted over as described earlier in this Section.

Repair of dents in the car's bodywork

When deep denting of the car's bodywork has taken place, the first task is to pull the dent out, until the affected bodywork almost attains its original shape. There is little point in trying to restore the original shape completely, as the metal in the damaged area will have stretched on impact and cannot be reshaped fully to its original contour. It is better to bring the level of the dent up to a point which is about $\frac{1}{8}$ in (3 mm) below the level of the surrounding bodywork. In cases where the dent is very shallow anyway, it is not worth trying to pull it out at all.

If the underside of the dent is accessible, it can be hammered out gently from behind, using a mallet with a wooden or plastic head. Whilst doing this, hold a suitable block of wood firmly against the impact from the hammer blows and thus prevent a large area of the bodywork from being 'belled-out'.

Should the dent be in a section of the bodywork which has double skin or some other factor making it inaccessible from behind, a different technique is called for. Drill several small holes through the metal inside the dent area – particularly in the deeper sections. Then screw long self-tapping screws into the holes just sufficiently for them to gain a good purchase in the metal. Now the dent can be pulled out by pulling on the protruding heads of the screws with a pair of pliers.

The next stage of the repair is the removal of the paint from the damaged area, and from an inch or so of the surrounding 'sound' bodywork. This is accomplished most easily by using a wire brush or abrasive pad on a power drill, although it can be done just as effectively by hand using sheets of abrasive paper. To complete the preparation for filling, score the surface of the bare metal with a screwdriver or the tang of a file, or alternatively, drill small holes in the affected area. This will provide a really good 'key' for the filler paste.

To complete the repair see the Section on filling and respraying.

Repair of rust holes or gashes in the car's bodywork

Remove all paint from the affected area and from an inch or so of the surrounding 'sound' bodywork, using an abrasive pad or a wire brush on a power drill. If these are not available a few sheets of abrasive paper will do the job just as effectively. With the paint removed you will be able to gauge the severity of the corrosion and therefore decide whether to renew the whole panel (if this is possible) or to repair the affected area. New body panels are not as expensive as most people think and it is often quicker and more satisfactory to fit a new panel than to attempt to repair large areas of corrosion.

Remove all fittings from the affected area except those which will act as a guide to the original shape of the damaged bodywork (eg headlamp shells etc). Then, using tin snips or a hacksaw blade, remove all loose metal and any other metal badly affected by corrosion. Hammer the edges of the hole inwards in order to create a slight depression for the filler paste.

Wire brush the affected area to remove the powdery rust from the surface of the remaining metal. Paint the affected area with rust inhibiting paint; if the back of the rusted area is accessible treat this also.

Before filling can take place it will be necessary to block the hole in some way. This can be achieved by the use of one of the following materials: Zinc gauze, Aluminium tape or Polyurethane foam.

Zinc gauze is probably the best material to use for a large hole. Cut a piece to the approximate size and shape of the hole to be filled, then position it in the hole so that its edges are below the level of the surrounding bodywork. It can be retained in position by several blobs of filler paste around its periphery.

Aluminium tape should be used for small or very narrow holes. Pull a piece off the roll and trim it to the approximate size and shape required, then pull off the backing paper (if used) and stick the tape over the hole; it can be overlapped if the thickness of one piece is insufficient. Burnish down the edges of the tape with the handle of a screwdriver or similar, to ensure that the tape is securely attached to the metal underneath.

Polyurethane foam is best used where the hole is situated in a section of bodywork of complex shape, backed by a small box section (eg where the sill panel meets the rear wheel arch on most cars). The usual mixing procedure for this foam is as follows: put equal amounts of fluid from each of the two cans provided in the kit, into one container. Stir until the mixture begins to thicken, then quickly pour this mixture into the hole, and hold a piece of cardboard over the larger apertures. Almost immediately the polyurethane will begin to expand, gushing out of any small holes left unblocked. When the foam hardens it can be cut back to just below the level of the surrounding bodywork with a hacksaw blade.

Bodywork repairs – filling and respraying

Before using this Section, see the Sections on dent, deep scratch, rust holes and gash repairs.

Many types of bodyfiller are available, but generally speaking those proprietary kits which contain a tin of filler paste and a tube of resin hardener are best for this type of repair. A wide, flexible plastic or nylon applicator will be found invaluable for imparting a smooth and well contoured finish to the surface of the filler.

Mix up a little filler on a clean piece of card or board – use the hardener sparingly (follow the maker's instructions on the pack) otherwise the filler will set very rapidly.

Using the applicator apply the filler paste to the prepared area: draw the applicator across the surface of the filler to achieve the correct contour and to level the filler surface. As soon as a contour that approximates the correct one is achieved, stop working the paste – if you carry on too long the paste will become sticky and begin to 'pick up' on the applicator. Continue to add thin layers of filler paste at twenty-minute intervals until the level of the filler is just proud of the surrounding bodywork.

Once the filler has hardened, excess can be removed using a Surform plane or Dreadnought file. From then on, progressively finer grades of abrasive paper should be used, starting with a 40 grade production paper and finishing with 400 grade wet-and-dry paper. Always wrap the abrasive paper around a flat rubber, cork, or wooden block – otherwise the surface of the filler will not be completely flat. During the smoothing of the filler surface the wet-and-dry paper should be periodically rinsed in water. This will ensure that a very smooth finish is imparted to the filler at the final stage.

At this stage the 'dent' should be surrounded by a ring of bare metal, which in turn should be encircled by the finely 'feathered' edge of the good paintwork. Rinse the repair area with clean water, until all of the dust produced by the rubbing-down operation has gone.

Spray the whole repair area with a light coat of primer – this will show up any imperfections in the surface of the filler. Repair these imperfections with fresh filler paste or bodystopper, and once more smooth the surface with abrasive paper. If bodystopper is used, it can be mixed with cellulose thinners to form a really thin paste which is ideal for filling small holes. Repeat this spray and repair procedure until you are satisfied that the surface of the filler, and the feathered edge of the paintwork are perfect. Clean the repair area with clean water and allow to dry fully.

The repair area is now ready for final spraying. Paint spraying must

This photographic sequence shows the steps taken to repair the dent and paintwork damage shown above. In general, the procedure for repairing a hole will be similar; where there are substantial differences, the procedure is clearly described and shown in a separate photograph.

First remove any trim around the dent, then hammer out the dent where access is possible. This will minimise filling. Here, after the large dent has been hammered out, the damaged area is being made slightly concave.

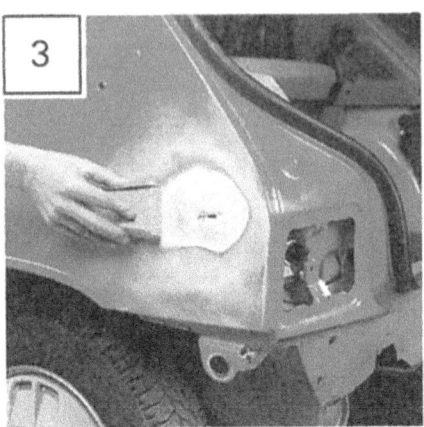

Next, remove all paint from the damaged area by rubbing with course abrasive paper or using a power drill fitted with a wire brush or abrasive pad. 'Feather' the edge of the boundary with good paintwork using a finer grade of abrasive paper.

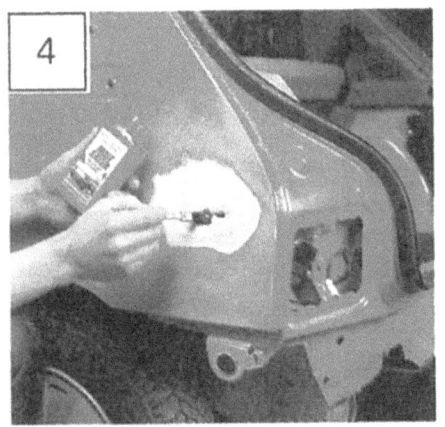

Where there are holes or other damage, the sheet metal should be cut away before proceeding further. The damaged area and any signs of rust should be treated with Turtle Wax Hi-Tech Rust Eater, which will also inhibit further rust formation.

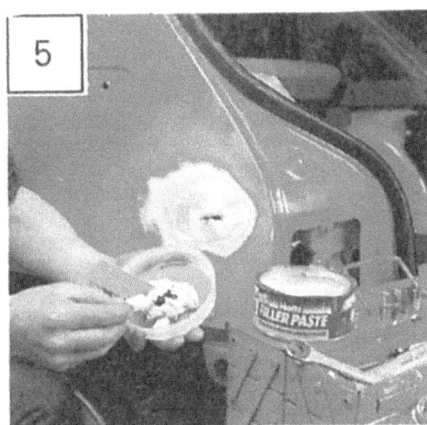

For a large dent or hole mix Holts Body Plus Resin and Hardener according to the manufacturer's instructions and apply around the edge of the repair. Press Glass Fibre Matting over the repair area and leave for 20-30 minutes to harden. Then ...

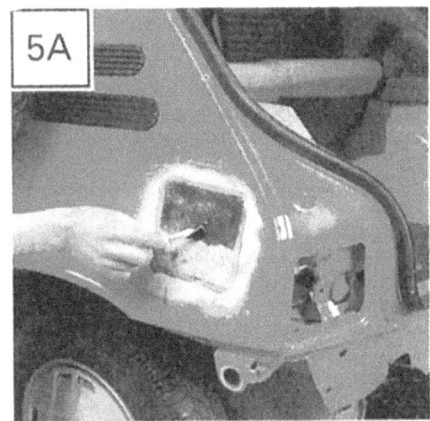

... brush more Holts Body Plus Resin and Hardener onto the matting and leave to harden. Repeat the sequence with two or three layers of matting, checking that the final layer is lower than the surrounding area. Apply Holts Body Plus Filler Paste as shown in Step 5B.

For a medium dent, mix Holts Body Plus Filler Paste and Hardener according to the manufacturer's instructions and apply it with a flexible applicator. Apply thin layers of filler at 20-minute intervals, until the filler surface is slightly proud of the surrounding bodywork.

For small dents and scratches use Holts No Mix Filler Paste straight from the tube. Apply it according to the instructions in thin layers, using the spatula provided. It will harden in minutes if applied outdoors and may then be used as its own knifing putting.

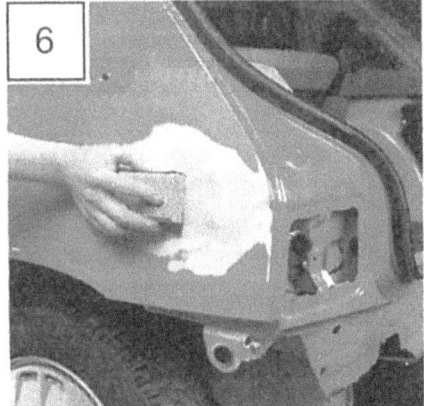

Use a plane or file for initial shaping. Then, using progressively finer grades of wet-and-dry paper, wrapped around a sanding block, and copious amounts of clean water, rub down the filler until glass smooth. 'Feather' the edges of adjoining paintwork.

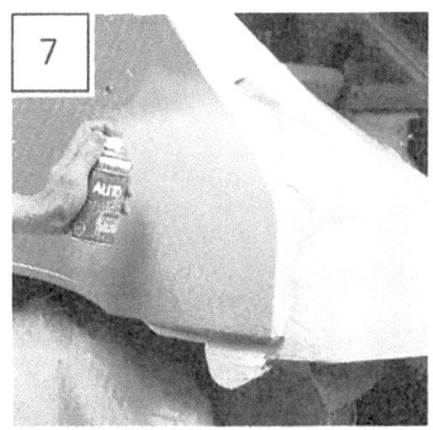

Protect adjoining areas before spraying the whole repair area and at least one inch of the surrounding sound paintwork with Holts Dupli-Color primer.

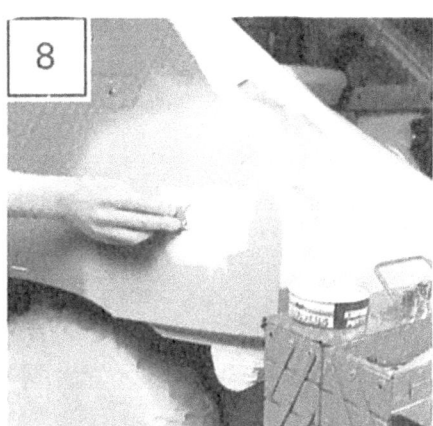

Fill any imperfections in the filler surface with a small amount of Holts Body Plus Knifing Putty. Using plenty of clean water, rub down the surface with a fine grade wet-and-dry paper - 400 grade is recommended - until it is really smooth.

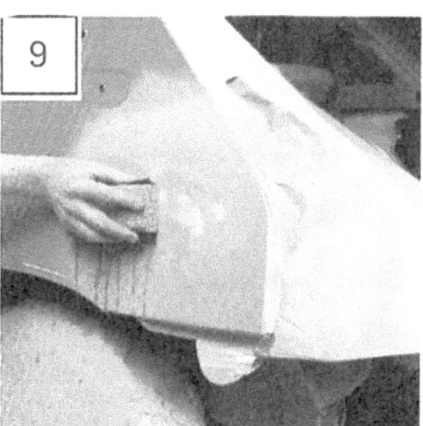

Carefully fill any remaining imperfections with knifing putty before applying the last coat of primer. Then rub down the surface with Holts Body Rubbing Compound to ensure a really smooth surface.

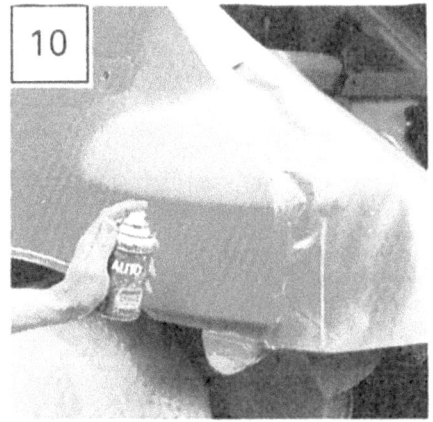

Protect surrounding areas from overspray before applying the topcoat in several thin layers. Agitate Holts Dupli-Color aerosol thoroughly. Start at the repair centre, spraying outwards with a side-to-side motion.

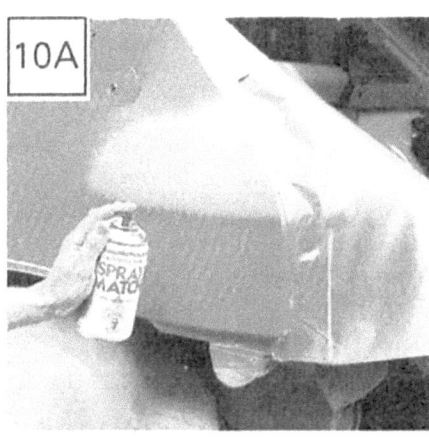

If the exact colour is not available off the shelf, local Holts Professional Spraymatch Centres will custom fill an aerosol to match perfectly.

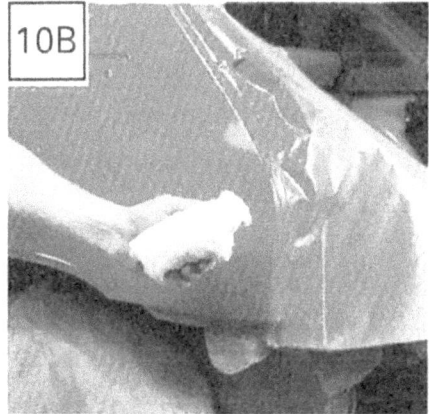

To identify whether a lacquer finish is required, rub a painted unrepaired part of the body with wax and a clean cloth.

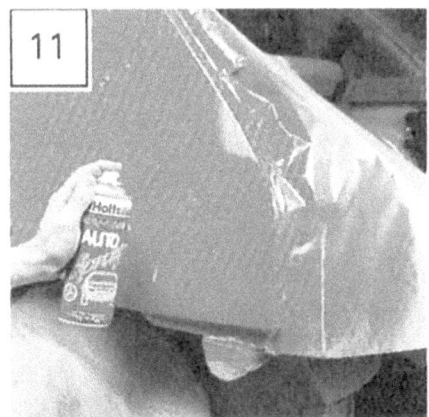

If *no* traces of paint appear on the cloth, spray Holts Dupli-Color clear lacquer over the repaired area to achieve the correct gloss level.

The paint will take about two weeks to harden fully. After this time it can be 'cut' with a mild cutting compound such as Turtle Wax Minute Cut prior to polishing with a final coating of Turtle Wax Extra.

When carrying out bodywork repairs, remember that the quality of the finished job is proportional to the time and effort expended.

be carried out in a warm, dry, windless and dust free atmosphere. This condition can be created artificially if you have access to a large indoor working area, but if you are forced to work in the open, you will have to pick your day very carefully. If you are working indoors, dousing the floor in the work area with water will 'lay' the dust which would otherwise be in the atmosphere. If the repair area is confined to one body panel, mask off the surrounding panels; this will help to minimise the effects of a slight mis-match in paint colours. Bodywork fittings (eg chrome strips, door handles etc) will also need to be removed or masked off. Use genuine masking tape and several thicknesses of newspaper for the masking operations.

Before commencing to spray, agitate the aerosol can thoroughly, then spray a test area (an old tin, or similar) until the technique is mastered. Cover the repair area with a thick coat of primer; the thickness should be built up using several thin layers of paint rather than one thick one. Using 400 grade wet-and-dry paper, rub down the surface of the primer until it is really smooth. While doing this, the work area should be thoroughly doused with water, and the wet-and-dry paper periodically rinsed in water. Allow to dry before spraying on more paint.

Spray on the top coat, again building up the thickness by using several thin layers of paint. Start spraying in the centre of the repair area and then using a circular motion, work outwards until the whole repair area and about 2 inches of the surrounding original paintwork is covered. Remove all masking material 10 to 15 minutes after spraying on the final coat of paint.

Allow the new paint at least two weeks to harden, then, using a paintwork renovator or a very fine cutting paste, blend the edges of the paint into the existing paintwork. Finally, apply wax polish.

6 Major body and underframe repairs

Major chassis and body repair work cannot be successfully undertaken by the average owner. Work of this nature should be entrusted to a competent body repair specialist who should have the necessary jigs, welding and hydraulic straightening equipment as well as skilled panel beaters to ensure a proper job is done.

7 Maintenance – hinges and locks

Once every six months or 6000 miles (9600 km) the door, bonnet and boot hinges should be oiled with a few drops of engine oil from an oil can. The door striker plates can be given a thin smear of grease to reduce wear and ensure free movement.

8 Windscreen glass – removal and refitting

If you are unfortunate enough to have a windscreen shatter, fitting a replacement windscreen is one of the few jobs that the average owner is advised to leave to a body repair specialist.

9 Door rattles – tracing and rectification

1   The commonest cause of door rattles is a misaligned, loose or worn striker plate but other causes may be:-

    (a) Loose door handles, window winder handles or door hinges
    (b) Loose, worn or misaligned door lock components
    (c) Loose or worn remote control mechanism

2   It is quite possible for door rattles to be the result of a combination of the above faults so a careful examination must be made to determine the cause of the fault.
3   If the nose of the striker plate is worn as a result of door rattles renew it and adjust the plate as described later in this Chapter.
4   If the nose of the door lock wedge is badly worn and the door rattles as a result then fit a new lock as described later in this Chapter.
5   Should the hinges be badly worn then they must be renewed.

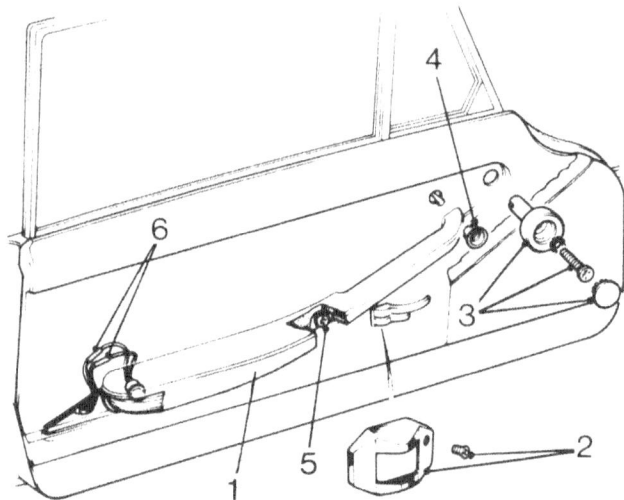

Fig. 12.1 Removing the door trim panel (Sec 11)

1 Arm rest	4 Door mirror control bezel
2 Escutcheon and screw	5 Centre securing screw
3 Quarter vent control knob	6 Puddle lamp leads

10 Door lock striker – removal, refitting and adjustment

1   If a worn striker plate requires renewal, mark its position on the door pillar so that the new plate can be fitted in the same position.
2   Undo the screws securing the striker plate to the pillar, early models three screws – later models two screws, and lift away the striker plate. Refitting is equally straightforward.
3   Adjust, if necessary, by slackening the securing screws and moving the plate as required to ensure that the door closes properly without lifting or dropping and that on the road it does not rattle.

11 Door trim panel – removal and refitting

1   Disconnect the earth cable from the battery negative terminal.
2   Lift the door handle and undo the escutcheon securing screw (photo).
3   Slide the escutcheon to the rear to release the retaining lugs, then remove it from the panel (photo).
4   Prise the bottom off the quarter vent control knob, undo the knob retaining screw and pull the knob from the wheelbox (photos).
5   Unscrew the door mirror control bezel (post 1972 USA cars only).
6   Remove the screw securing the centre of the trim panel.
7   Using a wide bladed screwdriver inserted between the trim panel and the door, carefully release the clips from their holes in the door panel. Start at the bottom and when all the clips are released, lift the panel clear of the three retaining lugs at the top. Disconnect the puddle lamp leads at the push-in connectors. Lift away the trim panel and remove the plastic weather-proofing sheet (photos).
8   Refitting is the reverse of the removal procedure.

12 Door lock – removal and refitting

1   Remove the door trim panel as described in Section 11.
2   Remove the retaining clip and disengage the remote control linkage from the lock.
3   Undo the lock securing screw, three on early models – four on later models, and lift away the lock (photo).
4   Refitting is the reverse of the removal procedure.

13 Door – removal and refitting

1   Remove the door trim panel as described in Section 11.

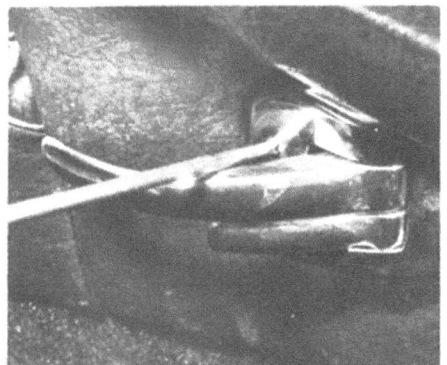

11.2 Removing the inside door handle escutcheon screw

11.3 Lifting away the escutcheon

11.4a Removing the button from the quarter vent control knob

11.4b Pulling the knob from the quarter vent wheelbox

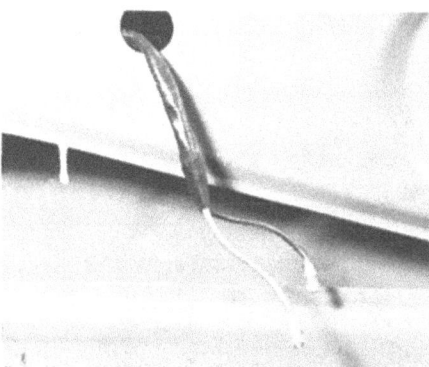

11.7a Puddle lamp electrical leads

11.7b Door with trim panel removed

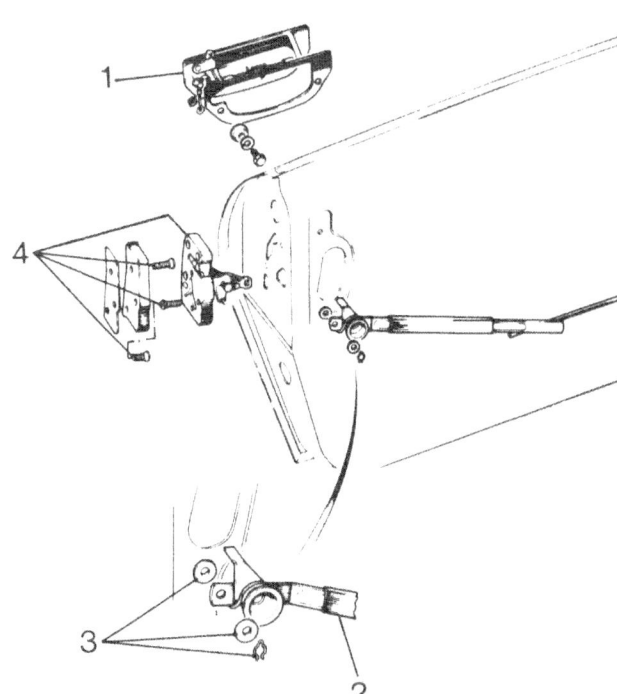

Fig. 12.2 Door lock and remote control linkage (Sec 12)

1 *Outside handle*
2 *Remote control linkage*
3 *Retaining circlip and washers*
4 *Lock and securing screws*

12.3 Door lock securing screws – later models

2   Disconnect the door window regulator motor leads, then release the wiring harness from the clips and withdraw it from the door.
3   Using a pencil, accurately mark the outline of the hinges relative to the A post to assist refitting. It is desirable to have an assistant to take the weight of the door once the two hinges have been released. Remove the seven bolts securing the hinges to the A post and lift away the door. For storage it is best to stand the door on an old blanket and allow it to lean against a wall, with suitable padding between the door and wall at the top to avoid damage.
4   Refitting is the reverse of removal procedure. Before refitting the trim panel check the closing action of the door and adjust, if necessary.
5   To adjust the fore-and-aft position of the door slacken the hinge to

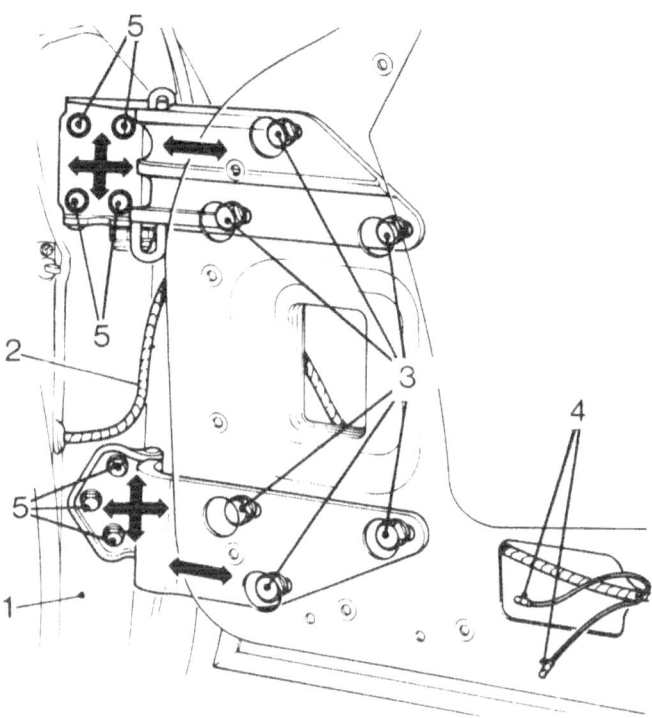

Fig. 12.3 Door removal (Sec 13)

1 'A' post   4 Puddle lamp leads
2 Wiring harness   5 Hinge to 'A' post bolts
3 Hinge to door bolts

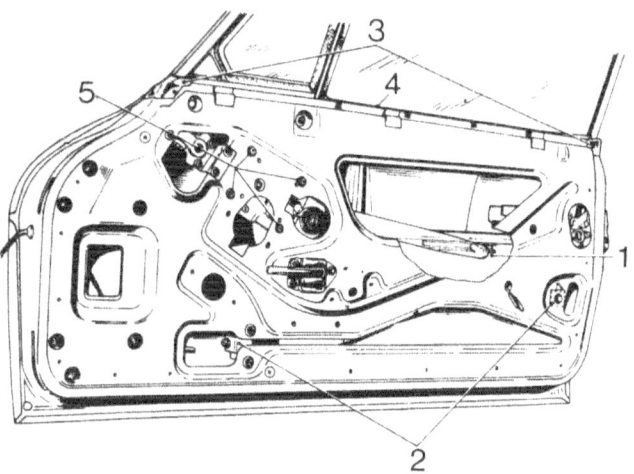

Fig. 12.4 Removing door glass and frame assembly (Sec 14)

1 Window regulator   4 Weatherstrip
2 Brackets   5 Window regulator securing
3 Rivets   bolts

14.3 Window regulator securing bolts

door securing bolts and move the door as required. Vertical adjustment is achieved by slackening the bolts securing the hinges to the A post and repositioning the door as required. When correctly fitted the gap between the door, wing and B post should be parallel.

14 Door glass – removal and refitting

1   Remove the door trim panel as described in Section 11.
2   Using a small hand drill, carefully drill out the two rivets securing each of the door finishers.
3   Remove the four bolts securing the window regulator (photo).
4   Disconnect the window regulator motor leads, disengage the regulator from the glass channel and lower it to the bottom of the door. **Caution**: *Do not separate the motor from the regulator with the components in situ as this may result in personal injury. Refer to Chapter 10, Section 28.*
5   Remove the brackets securing the glass frame to the door, then lift the glass and frame assembly out of the door.
6   Refitting is the reverse of the removal procedure. The bolt holes in the door and brackets are elongated to allow for adjustment of the frame to the door and rubber sealing apertures. **Note**: *The glass and frame assemblies are not interchangeable between the left-hand and right-hand sides.*

15 Quarter vent – removal and refitting

1   Remove the door trim panel as described in Section 11.
2   Undo the three securing bolts and withdraw the wheelbox clear of the quarter vent spindle (photo).
3   Slacken the bolt securing the quarter vent spindle clip then undo the two quarter vent top hinge to glass frame securing screws.
4   Lift the quarter vent, disengage the spindle from its clip and the rubber seal, and remove the quarter vent.
5   Refitting is the reverse of the removal procedure.

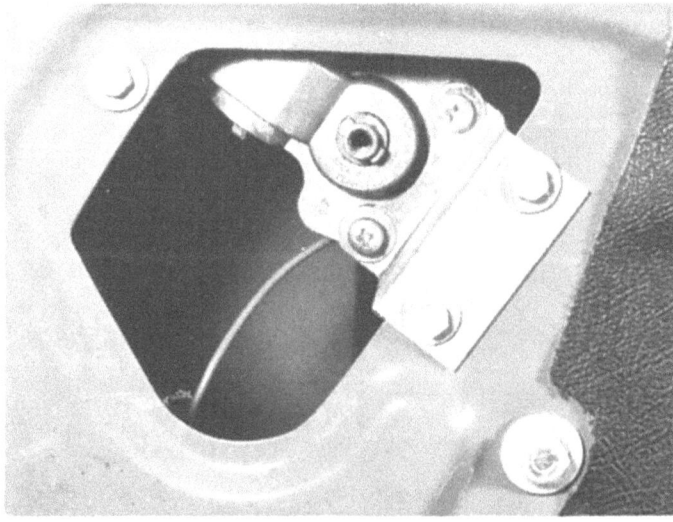

15.2 The quarter vent wheelbox is secured with three bolts

16 Door inside handle and remote control linkage – removal and refitting

1   Remove the door trim panel as described in Section 11.
2   Disconnect the linkage from the door lock by removing the clip and plain washer. Remove the wave washer.
3   Undo the three bolts securing the inside door handle and remove the handle and linkage assembly from the door (photo).
4   Separate the remote control linkage from the handle by springing open the securing clip and withdrawing the linkage from thé nylon bush.
5   Refitting is the reverse of the removal procedure.

17 Door check wire – removal and refitting

1   Remove the door as described in Section 13.
2   Release the door check wire from the door hinge by driving it upwards with a soft-faced hammer.
3   To refit the check wire position it on the hinge with the lower end in its location and the upper end standing clear of the hinge.
4   Get an assistant to hold the door firmly then using a strong screwdriver or suitable bar, rotate the upper part of the check wire

until it is aligned with its locating hole in the hinge (Fig. 12.5).
5   While holding the check wire in this position, drive it downwards, with a soft-faced hammer, to locate the notch in the locating hole.
6   Refit the door, refer to Section 13.

18 Bonnet – removal and refitting

1   Open the bonnet and hold open using the bonnet stay. To act as a datum for refitting, mark the position of the hinges on the front panel using a soft pencil.
2   With the assistance of a second person hold the bonnet in the vertical position and extract the support stay split pin from the cotter pin. Lift away the cotter pin.
3   Undo the three bolts holding the bonnet hinge to the front panel and lift away the bonnet taking care not to scratch the top of the wings (photo).
4   Lean the bonnet up against a wall suitably padded to prevent scratching of the paint.
5   Refitting the bonnet is the reverse sequence to removal, any adjustment necessary can be made either at the hinges or the bonnet catch.
6   Should it be necessary to adjust the bonnet catch first slacken the locknut securing the shaft in position.

16.3 Removing the inside door handle

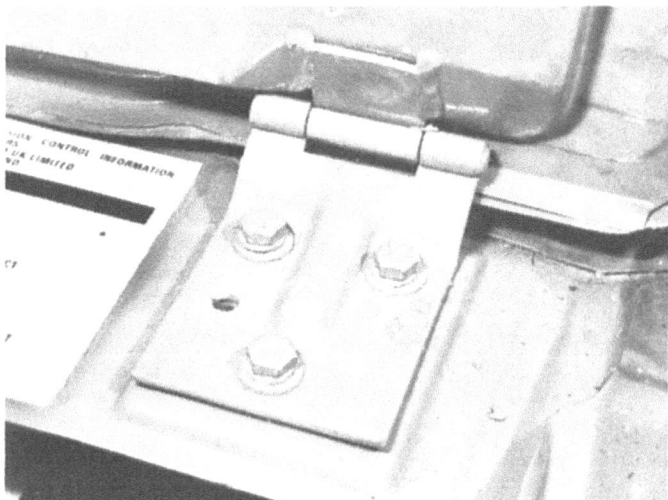

18.3 The bonnet hinges are bolted to the front panel

Fig. 12.5 Use a bar to rotate the check wire (Sec 17)

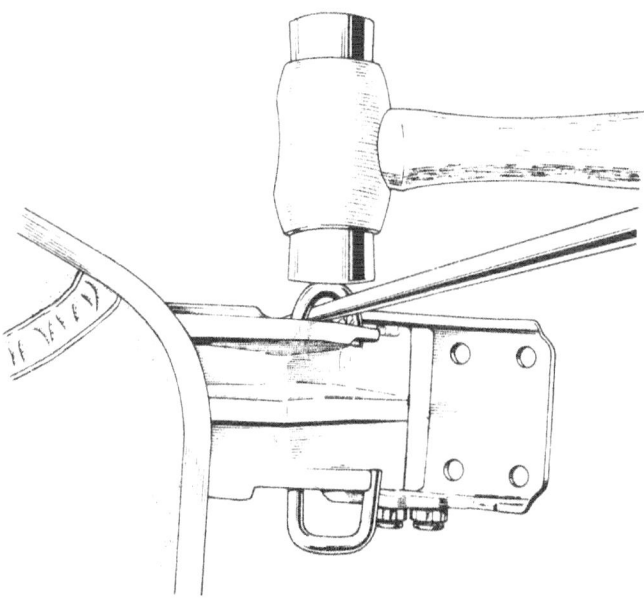

Fig. 12.6 Drive the check wire downwards (Sec 17)

19.2 Remove the bonnet lock release cable

7   Using a wide bladed screwdriver, screw the shaft inwards or outwards and tighten the locknut once the correct position has been
obtained.
8   Test the adjustment by opening and closing the bonnet several
times.

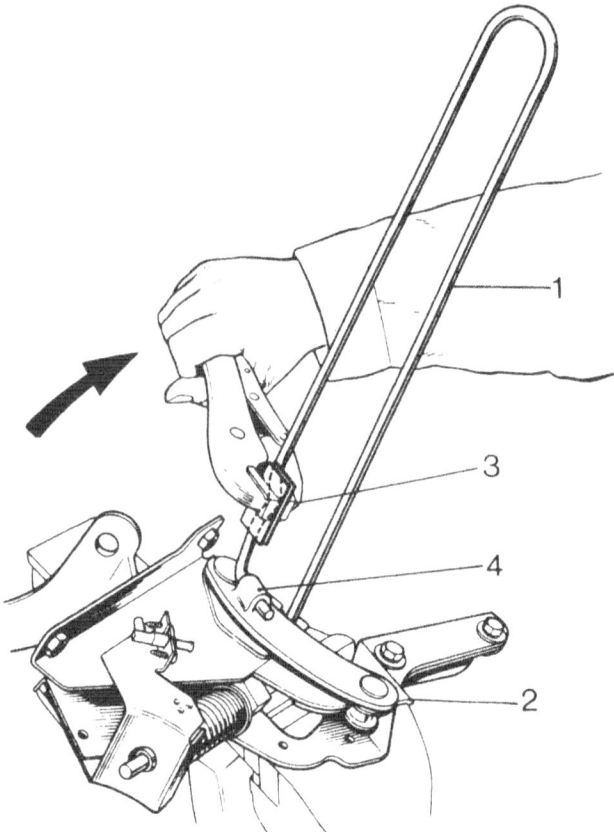

Fig. 12.7 Removing the boot lid spring (sec 20)

1 Spring   3 Grips
2 Hinge assembly   4 Spring anchor point

19 Bonnet lock – removal and refitting

1   Open the bonnet and hold in the open position with the bonnet
stay.
2   Slacken the release cable securing bolts and withdraw the cable
from the trunnions on the lock (photo).
3   Undo the four securing bolts and remove the lock from the
bulkhead.
4   Refitting is the reverse of the removal procedure.

20 Luggage compartment lid springs – removal and refitting

1   Remove the hardtop, refer to Section 24, and/or raise the soft-top
from its storage compartment.
2   On post 1972 cars remove the trim panel from the left-hand side
of the luggage compartment and disconnect the wiring to the number
plate lamps.
3   With the help of an assistant, support the lid and undo the two
bolts each side, which secure the lid to the hinges and lift the lid away
from the car and place it where it will not get damaged.
4   Remove the two bolts securing the catch assembly to the tonneau
cover.
5   Remove the four bolts securing the tonneau cover to its hinges
and then lift the tonneau cover away from the car.
6   Remove the luggage compartment right-hand trim panel and the
trim covering the hinge assemblies.
7   Disconnect the earth cable from the battery negative terminal and
then the leads to the luggage compartment lamp.
8   Undo the securing bolts at each hinge assembly and then remove
the hinges.
9   Mount the hinge assembly in a vice, position the hinges so that the
boot lid hinge spring is in its least loaded position, then using a pair of
grips, grip the spring as shown in Fig. 12.7, and twist the spring as
necessary to overcome the tension, and remove it from its anchorage
point.
10 Release the spring and remove it from the hinge assembly.
11 Refitting is the reverse of the removal procedure.Check the position of the boot lid, the gap should be even all round; if necessary
adjust the position of the lock striker by undoing the three screws
securing the striker plate and shimming or repositioning as required.

21 Luggage compartment lid lock – removal and refitting

1   Remove the two screws securing the pushbutton assembly, then
disengage the pushrod from the bellcrank and lift away the
pushbutton.
2   Undo the four securing screws and remove the cover panel, then
remove the two lock attaching screws and lift out the lock assembly
(photo).
3   Refitting is the reverse of the removal procedure.

22 Bumpers – removal and refitting

Front bumpers
1   Remove the two bolts securing the bumper to the wing mounting
brackets.
2   Undo the four bolts securing the bumper mounting brackets to the
front of the subframe and lift away the bumper complete with over-
riders and number plate.
3   Refitting is the reverse of the removal procedure.

Rear bumpers
4   Lift the luggage boot carpet and remove the floor boards and right-
hand trim panel
5   On cars with the number plate lamps mounted on the bumper,
disconnect the wiring to the lamp at the push-in connectors.
6   Undo the two bolts securing the end sections of the bumper to the
wing and remove the rubber pads located between the bumper and
the wing.
7   Undo the two bolts securing the bumper mounting brackets to the
rear valance and remove the bumper assembly.
8   Refitting is the reverse of the removal procedure.

21.2 Luggage compartment lid lock

23 Console – removal and assembly

1   Disconnect the earth cable from the battery negative terminal.
2   Slacken the gear selector lever knob locking collar, if overdrive is fitted prise out the knob cap and disconnect the switch lead, and then remove the knob and locking collar. On automatic transmission cars prise out the gear selector lever gate.
3   Prise out the door window regulator and interior light switches and disconnect the leads.
4   The console front panel can now be prised out.
5   Pull off the three heater control knobs and remove the heater control panel.
6   Remove the radio or radio aperture cover as applicable.
7   Undo the two screws securing the console to the transmission tunnel and then lift the rear panel off over the gear selector lever.
8   Remove the knobs and bezels from the choke control (spring-loaded pin), heater blower switch and the rear window heater switch.
9   Now disconnect the purple lead from the cigar lighter then unscrew the centre section of the lighter from the outer sleeve and remove the lighter.
10 Disconnect the leads to the lamp on the side of the console and then remove the rear window heater indicator bulb holder. Force the wiring harness from the clips on the console.
11 Withdraw the console backwards from the facia and lift it away.
12 Refitting is the reverse of the removal procedure.

24 Hardtop – removal and refitting

1   Turn the header rail and door pillar levers inwards to release the catches.
2   Release the tonneau catch and with the help of an assistant lift the hardtop up and away from the car.
3   To refit the hardtop, carefully locate it in position, making sure all the catch levers are pointing inwards.
4   Depress the rear edge of the hardtop to engage the tonneau catch, then lock the door pillar catches.
5   Finally lock the header rail catches.
Note: *The heated rear window electrical connections are automatically disconnected and reconnected.*

25 Soft-top – removal and refitting

When refitting the soft-top, two jig bolts machined to the dimensions in Fig. 12.9 are required.

1   Release the tonneau catch then raise the rear of the soft-top and lift the tonneau to the raised position.

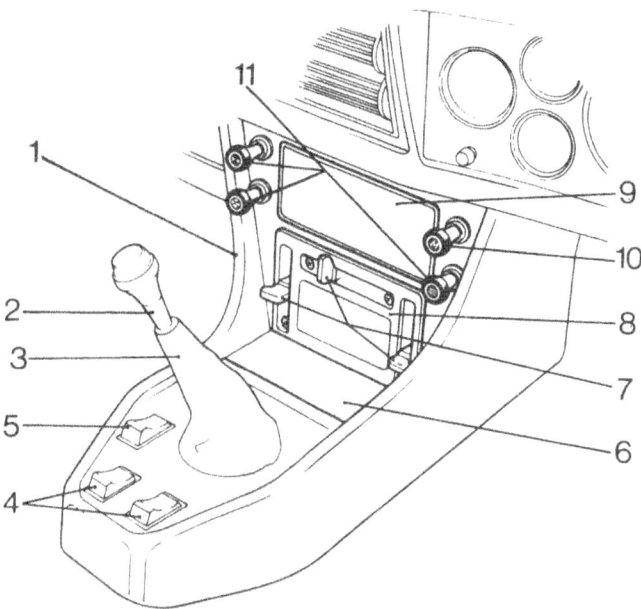

Fig. 12.8 Removing the console (Sec 23)

1 Console	8 Heater control panel
2 Gear lever	9 Radio aperture
3 Gear lever gaiter	10 Cigar lighter
4 Window regulator switches	11 Choke control, blower
5 Interior light switch	switch, rear window heater
6 Console front panel	switch
7 Heater control knobs	

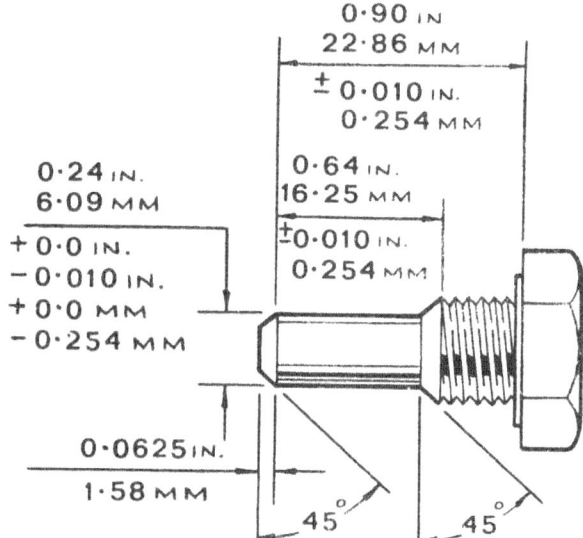

Fig. 12.9 Dimensions of jig bolt for refitting soft-top (Sec 25)

2   Remove the rear seat cushion by pulling the front edge of the seat cushion upwards to free it from between the seat pan flange and the seat squab.
3   Undo the two bolts securing the rear seat squab to the support rail and then lift it clear of the two retaining lugs.
4   Undo the securing nuts and remove the B post covers.
5   Remove the clips attaching the body side trim panels to the seat/trim support rail at each side, then push the trim attachment pegs from their locations in the seat/trim support rail.
6   Remove the two screws securing the body side trim panels to the brackets and lift away the trim panels.
7   Unhook the tension springs.

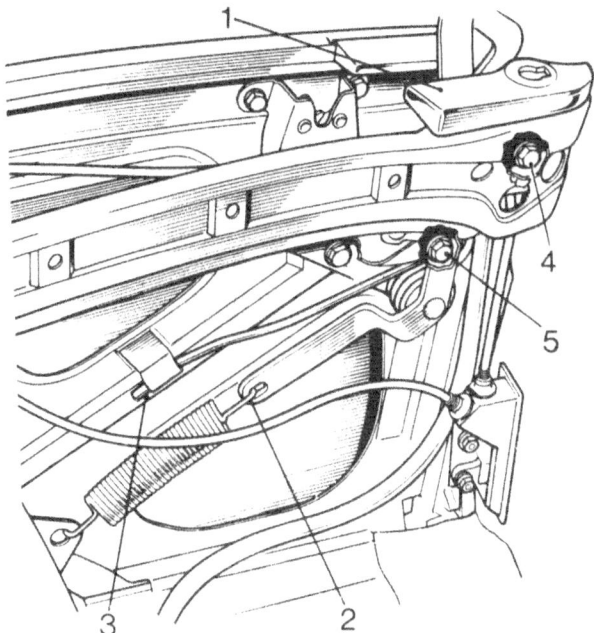

Fig. 12.10 Removing the soft-top (Sec 25)

1 'B' post covers   4 Hod-stick securing setscrews
2 Spring   5 Temporary fitted jig bolt
3 Torsion spring

8   Turn the catch levers and release the front of the soft-top.
9   Lower the soft-top to the folded position and disengage the torsion springs.
10 Undo the six setscrews securing the hood-stick assembly to the body, moving the soft-top as necessary to gain access, remove the screws and lift the soft-top away from the car.
11 To refit the soft-top, open the front section fully and install a jig bolt on each side of the frame, then locate the soft-top in position and lock the front catches.
12 Fit four of the setscrews loosely in position and with the soft-top in the folded position, engage the torsion springs in their anchorage points.
13 Raise the soft-top and lock the front and rear catches, if necessary, adjust the striker pin.
14 Hook the ends of the torsion springs in their locations.
15 Remove the two jig bolts and fit the remaining two setscrews.
16 Adjust the soft-top to remove any slackness by levering the hood-stick assembly, the holes for the setscrews are elongated, then tighten the six setscrews to 15 to 20 lbf ft (2.1 to 2.8 kgf m).
17 Check the operation of the soft-top and adjust, if necessary.
18 The rest of the refitting is the reverse of the removal procedure, refer to paragraphs 1 to 6.

26 Tonneau and soft-top release catches inner cables – removal and refitting

1   Remove the rear seat cushion and the left-hand side body trim panel, refer to Section 25.

Tonneau cable

2   Slacken the lockscrew on the nipple at each tonneau catch, free the inner cable from the control lever and withdraw it from the outer cable.
3   To refit the cable, feed it into the outer cable, fitting one nipple loosely on the cable as it passes through the left-hand tonneau catch. Fit the other nipple loosely at the right-hand catch.
4   Adjust the cable for correct operation of the catches, one end of the outer cable is threaded for adjustment, and secure the cable in the nipples by tightening the lockscrews.

Soft-top cable

5   Slacken the lockscrew and remove the nipple, anti-rattle spring and catch return spring from the inner cable.

6   Release the inner cable from the control lever (it may be necessary to drill out the pivot pin and remove the control lever from its housing) and withdraw it from the outer cable.
7   Refitting is the reverse of the removal procedure, set the nipple to give correct operation of the catch and tighten the lockscrew.
8   Refit the rear seat cushion and the left-hand side body trim panel, refer to Section 25.

27 Heater and ventilation system – description

The heating and ventilation system is designed whereby an air intake located in front of the windscreen passes fresh air to a plenum chamber and it is from this chamber that air is drawn as required by the heater unit. The air is passed through a small radiator matrix which is supplied with hot coolant from the engine cooling system and the warm air is channelled to the windscreen and to the passengers.

During warm weather the system can supply cool fresh air for ventilation purposes. A two-speed blower is used to increase the air supply when required.

28 Heater – removal, servicing and refitting

1   Disconnect the earth cable from the battery negative terminal. Drain the cooling system as described in Chapter 2.
2   Undo the three screws securing the air intake grille and remove the grille.
3   Remove the two screws, accessible with the air intake grille removed, which secure the heater unit to the scuttle.
4   Slacken the securing clips and detach the inlet and outlet heater hoses from the heater at the front of the bulkhead.
5   Undo the four securing screws and lift out the parcel shelf. Pull off the three heater control knobs.
6   Remove the four screws securing the heater control panel and lift away the panel.
7   Remove the radio or radio aperture cover, as applicable.
8   On cars with automatic transmission, prise out the gear selector lever gate panel.
9   Remove the console front cover. Undo the two screws securing the console to the tunnel and pull the console to the rear.
10 Withdraw the air vent hoses clear of the heater, then remove the windscreen demister hoses.
11 Undo the two lower bolts which secure the heater to the scuttle. Remove the four bolts securing the facia support bracket to the facia and the tunnel. Take out the bracket.
12 Disconnect the electrical leads from the blower motor.
13 Remove the three securing bolts and lower the steering column from the facia.

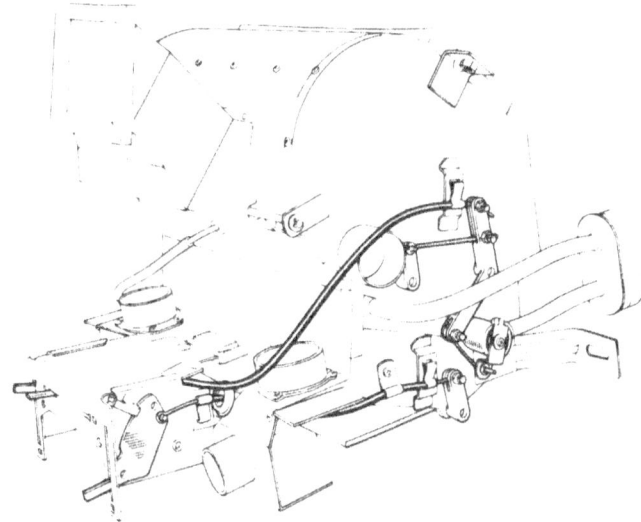

Fig. 12.11 Heater and blower assembly (Sec 27)

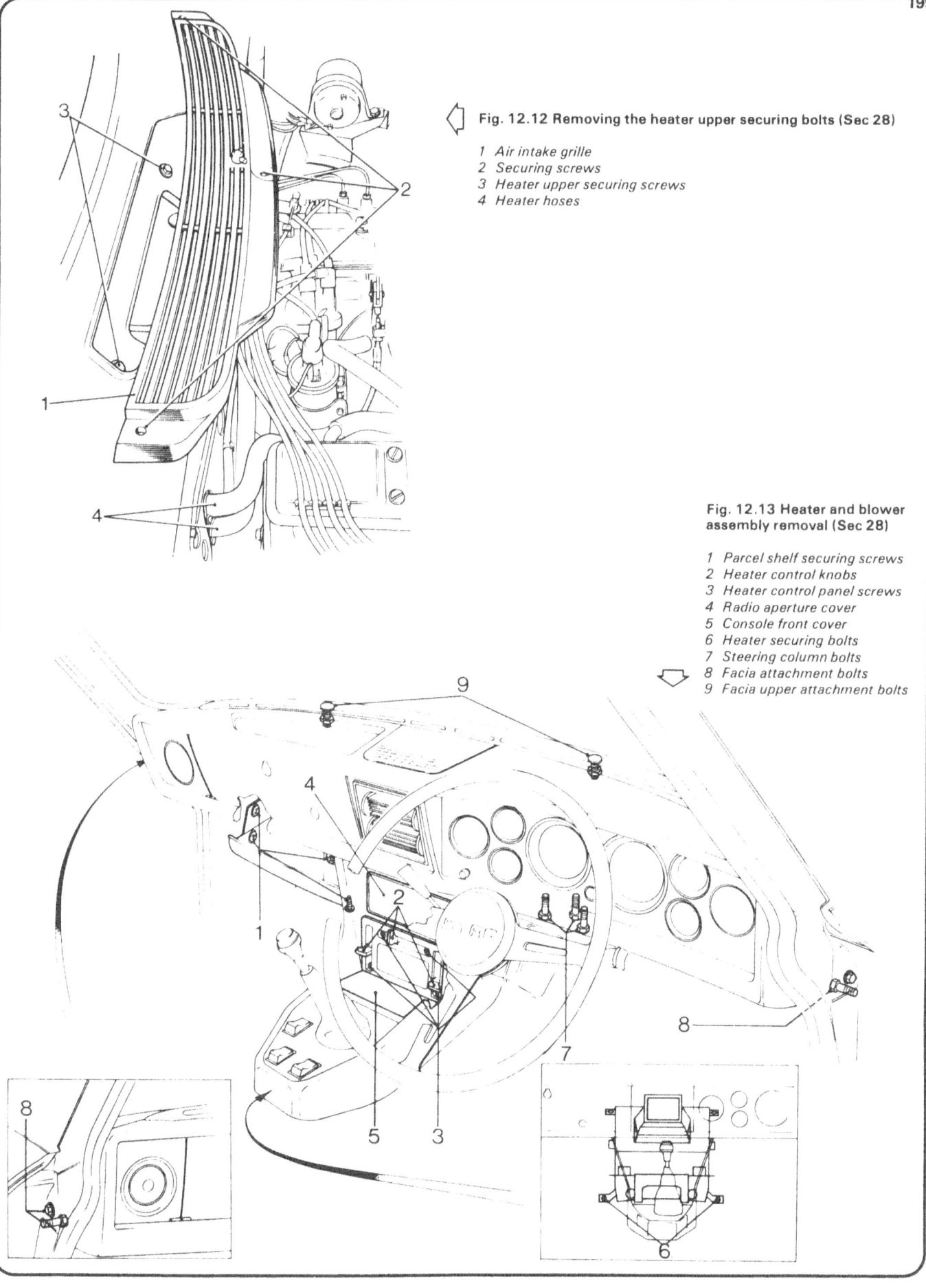

Fig. 12.12 Removing the heater upper securing bolts (Sec 28)

1　Air intake grille
2　Securing screws
3　Heater upper securing screws
4　Heater hoses

Fig. 12.13 Heater and blower
assembly removal (Sec 28)

1　Parcel shelf securing screws
2　Heater control knobs
3　Heater control panel screws
4　Radio aperture cover
5　Console front cover
6　Heater securing bolts
7　Steering column bolts
8　Facia attachment bolts
9　Facia upper attachment bolts

14 Remove the four outer securing bolts from the facia and the two nuts securing the upper edge of the facia. Access to the nut on the passenger side is through an opening in the top of the glovebox.
15 Pull the facia away from the heater and withdraw the heater to the passenger side and lift it out.
16 If the blower motor is faulty, obtain a new one as components to repair it are not supplied individually.
17 If the matrix is blocked, try reverse flushing as described in Chapter 2 for the cooling system radiator. If the matrix is leaking, it is seldom satisfactory to attempt to repair it by soldering as the heat used must be localised, and therefore it is recommended that a new or reconditioned exchange unit is fitted.
18 Refitting is the reverse of the removal procedure. Use sealing compound to reseal those joints and bolts which were previously sealed.

29 Heater and ventilation system controls – adjustment

Heater control

1 Set the heater control to cold. The water valve control lever should now be against its stop with the two matrix flaps closed.
2 Check the position of the flaps by removing the parcel shelf and then pulling the windscreen demister hose away from the heater. The flaps can now be seen through the hose connection.
3 If the flaps are not in the correct position, ie fully lowered against the matrix, slacken the flap lever lockscrew and reset the lever to the correct position.
4 Tighten the lockscrew, reconnect the demister hose and refit the parcel shelf.

Interior air control

5 Set the air distribution control to the car position. The distribution flap, which can be seen at the bottom of the heater, should be fully open.
6 If the flap is not fully open, adjust by loosening the control cable lockscrew on the flap operating lever and moving the flap to the fully open position. Retighten the lockscrew.

Facia air control

7 Set the control lever in the off position and check the position of the cold air flap which can be seen through the air louvres.
8 If the flap is not fully closed, remove the parcel shelf to gain access to the flap operating lever.
9 Loosen the control cable lockscrew, close the flap and then retighten the lockscrew. Refit the parcel shelf.

30 Air conditioning – general

Should an air conditioning unit be fitted and its performance unsatisfactory, or it has to be removed to give access to other parts, it is recommended that this be left to the local Leyland garage. This is because the unit is of a complex nature and specialist knowledge and equipment is required to service the system. Never disconnect any part of the system, due to the danger from the refrigerant which will be released. Your dealer or refrigeration engineer must be employed if the system has to be evacuated or recharged.

General repair procedures

Whenever servicing, repair or overhaul work is carried out on the car or its components, it is necessary to observe the following procedures and instructions. This will assist in carrying out the operation efficiently and to a professional standard of workmanship.

Joint mating faces and gaskets

Where a gasket is used between the mating faces of two components, ensure that it is renewed on reassembly, and fit it dry unless otherwise stated in the repair procedure. Make sure that the mating faces are clean and dry with all traces of old gasket removed. When cleaning a joint face, use a tool which is not likely to score or damage the face, and remove any burrs or nicks with an oilstone or fine file.

Make sure that tapped holes are cleaned with a pipe cleaner, and keep them free of jointing compound if this is being used unless specifically instructed otherwise.

Ensure that all orifices, channels or pipes are clear and blow through them, preferably using compressed air.

Oil seals

Whenever an oil seal is removed from its working location, either individually or as part of an assembly, it should be renewed.

The very fine sealing lip of the seal is easily damaged and will not seal if the surface it contacts is not completely clean and free from scratches, nicks or grooves. If the original sealing surface of the component cannot be restored, the component should be renewed.

Protect the lips of the seal from any surface which may damage them in the course of fitting. Use tape or a conical sleeve where possible. Lubricate the seal lips with oil before fitting and, on dual lipped seals, fill the space between the lips with grease.

Unless otherwise stated, oil seals must be fitted with their sealing lips toward the lubricant to be sealed.

Use a tubular drift or block of wood of the appropriate size to install the seal and, if the seal housing is shouldered, drive the seal down to the shoulder. If the seal housing is unshouldered, the seal should be fitted with its face flush with the housing top face.

Screw threads and fastenings

Always ensure that a blind tapped hole is completely free from oil, grease, water or other fluid before installing the bolt or stud. Failure to do this could cause the housing to crack due to the hydraulic action of the bolt or stud as it is screwed in.

When tightening a castellated nut to accept a split pin, tighten the nut to the specified torque, where applicable, and then tighten further to the next split pin hole. Never slacken the nut to align a split pin hole unless stated in the repair procedure.

When checking or retightening a nut or bolt to a specified torque setting, slacken the nut or bolt by a quarter of a turn, and then retighten to the specified setting.

Locknuts, locktabs and washers

Any fastening which will rotate against a component or housing in the course of tightening should always have a washer between it and the relevant component or housing.

Spring or split washers should always be renewed when they are used to lock a critical component such as a big-end bearing retaining nut or bolt.

Locktabs which are folded over to retain a nut or bolt should always be renewed.

Self-locking nuts can be reused in non-critical areas, providing resistance can be felt when the locking portion passes over the bolt or stud thread.

Split pins must always be replaced with new ones of the correct size for the hole.

Special tools

Some repair procedures in this manual entail the use of special tools such as a press, two or three-legged pullers, spring compressors etc. Wherever possible, suitable readily available alternatives to the manufacturer's special tools are described, and are shown in use. In some instances, where no alternative is possible, it has been necessary to resort to the use of a manufacturer's tool and this has been done for reasons of safety as well as the efficient completion of the repair operation. Unless you are highly skilled and have a thorough understanding of the procedure described, never attempt to bypass the use of any special tool when the procedure described specifies its use. Not only is there a very great risk of personal injury, but expensive damage could be caused to the components involved.

Safety first!

Professional motor mechanics are trained in safe working procedures. However enthusiastic you may be about getting on with the job in hand, do take the time to ensure that your safety is not put at risk. A moment's lack of attention can result in an accident, as can failure to observe certain elementary precautions.

There will always be new ways of having accidents, and the following points do not pretend to be a comprehensive list of all dangers; they are intended rather to make you aware of the risks and to encourage a safety-conscious approach to all work you carry out on your vehicle.

Essential DOs and DON'Ts

DON'T rely on a single jack when working underneath the vehicle. Always use reliable additional means of support, such as axle stands, securely placed under a part of the vehicle that you know will not give way.

DON'T attempt to loosen or tighten high-torque nuts (e.g. wheel hub nuts) while the vehicle is on a jack; it may be pulled off.

DON'T start the engine without first ascertaining that the transmission is in neutral (or 'Park' where applicable) and the parking brake applied.

DON'T suddenly remove the filler cap from a hot cooling system – cover it with a cloth and release the pressure gradually first, or you may get scalded by escaping coolant.

DON'T attempt to drain oil until you are sure it has cooled sufficiently to avoid scalding you.

DON'T grasp any part of the engine, exhaust or catalytic converter without first ascertaining that it is sufficiently cool to avoid burning you.

DON'T allow brake fluid or antifreeze to contact vehicle paintwork.

DON'T syphon toxic liquids such as fuel, brake fluid or antifreeze by mouth, or allow them to remain on your skin.

DON'T inhale dust – it may be injurious to health (see *Asbestos* below).

DON'T allow any spilt oil or grease to remain on the floor – wipe it up straight away, before someone slips on it.

DON'T use ill-fitting spanners or other tools which may slip and cause injury.

DON'T attempt to lift a heavy component which may be beyond your capability – get assistance.

DON'T rush to finish a job, or take unverified short cuts.

DON'T allow children or animals in or around an unattended vehicle.

DO wear eye protection when using power tools such as drill, sander, bench grinder etc, and when working under the vehicle.

DO use a barrier cream on your hands prior to undertaking dirty jobs – it will protect your skin from infection as well as making the dirt easier to remove afterwards; but make sure your hands aren't left slippery. Note that long-term contact with used engine oil can be a health hazard.

DO keep loose clothing (cuffs, tie etc) and long hair well out of the way of moving mechanical parts.

DO remove rings, wristwatch etc, before working on the vehicle – especially the electrical system.

DO ensure that any lifting tackle used has a safe working load rating adequate for the job.

DO keep your work area tidy – it is only too easy to fall over articles left lying around.

DO get someone to check periodically that all is well, when working alone on the vehicle.

DO carry out work in a logical sequence and check that everything is correctly assembled and tightened afterwards.

DO remember that your vehicle's safety affects that of yourself and others. If in doubt on any point, get specialist advice.

IF, in spite of following these precautions, you are unfortunate enough to injure yourself, seek medical attention as soon as possible.

Asbestos

Certain friction, insulating, sealing, and other products – such as brake linings, brake bands, clutch linings, torque converters, gaskets, etc – contain asbestos. *Extreme care must be taken to avoid inhalation of dust from such products since it is hazardous to health.* If in doubt, assume that they *do* contain asbestos.

Fire

Remember at all times that petrol (gasoline) is highly flammable. Never smoke, or have any kind of naked flame around, when working on the vehicle. But the risk does not end there – a spark caused by an electrical short-circuit, by two metal surfaces contacting each other, by careless use of tools, or even by static electricity built up in your body under certain conditions, can ignite petrol vapour, which in a confined space is highly explosive.

Always disconnect the battery earth (ground) terminal before working on any part of the fuel or electrical system, and never risk spilling fuel on to a hot engine or exhaust.

It is recommended that a fire extinguisher of a type suitable for fuel and electrical fires is kept handy in the garage or workplace at all times. Never try to extinguish a fuel or electrical fire with water.

Note: *Any reference to a 'torch' appearing in this manual should always be taken to mean a hand-held battery-operated electric lamp or flashlight. It does NOT mean a welding/gas torch or blowlamp.*

Fumes

Certain fumes are highly toxic and can quickly cause unconsciousness and even death if inhaled to any extent. Petrol (gasoline) vapour comes into this category, as do the vapours from certain solvents such as trichloroethylene. Any draining or pouring of such volatile fluids should be done in a well ventilated area.

When using cleaning fluids and solvents, read the instructions carefully. Never use materials from unmarked containers – they may give off poisonous vapours.

Never run the engine of a motor vehicle in an enclosed space such as a garage. Exhaust fumes contain carbon monoxide which is extremely poisonous; if you need to run the engine, always do so in the open air or at least have the rear of the vehicle outside the workplace.

If you are fortunate enough to have the use of an inspection pit, never drain or pour petrol, and never run the engine, while the vehicle is standing over it; the fumes, being heavier than air, will concentrate in the pit with possibly lethal results.

The battery

Never cause a spark, or allow a naked light, near the vehicle's battery. It will normally be giving off a certain amount of hydrogen gas, which is highly explosive.

Always disconnect the battery earth (ground) terminal before working on the fuel or electrical systems.

If possible, loosen the filler plugs or cover when charging the battery from an external source. Do not charge at an excessive rate or the battery may burst.

Take care when topping up and when carrying the battery. The acid electrolyte, even when diluted, is very corrosive and should not be allowed to contact the eyes or skin.

If you ever need to prepare electrolyte yourself, always add the acid slowly to the water, and never the other way round. Protect against splashes by wearing rubber gloves and goggles.

When jump starting a car using a booster battery, for negative earth (ground) vehicles, connect the jump leads in the following sequence: First connect one jump lead between the positive (+) terminals of the two batteries. Then connect the other jump lead first to the negative (–) terminal of the booster battery, and then to a good earthing (ground) point on the vehicle to be started, at least 18 in (45 cm) from the battery if possible. Ensure that hands and jump leads are clear of any moving parts, and that the two vehicles do not touch. Disconnect the leads in the reverse order.

Mains electricity and electrical equipment

When using an electric power tool, inspection light etc, always ensure that the appliance is correctly connected to its plug and that, where necessary, it is properly earthed (grounded). Do not use such appliances in damp conditions and, again, beware of creating a spark or applying excessive heat in the vicinity of fuel or fuel vapour. Also ensure that the appliances meet the relevant national safety standards.

Ignition HT voltage

A severe electric shock can result from touching certain parts of the ignition system, such as the HT leads, when the engine is running or being cranked, particularly if components are damp or the insulation is defective. Where an electronic ignition system is fitted, the HT voltage is much higher and could prove fatal.

Conversion factors

Length (distance)

Inches (in)	X	25.4	= Millimetres (mm)	X	0.0394	= Inches (in)
Feet (ft)	X	0.305	= Metres (m)	X	3.281	= Feet (ft)
Miles	X	1.609	= Kilometres (km)	X	0.621	= Miles

Volume (capacity)

Cubic inches (cu in; in³)	X	16.387	= Cubic centimetres (cc; cm³)	X	0.061	= Cubic inches (cu in; in³)
Imperial pints (Imp pt)	X	0.568	= Litres (l)	X	1.76	= Imperial pints (Imp pt)
Imperial quarts (Imp qt)	X	1.137	= Litres (l)	X	0.88	= Imperial quarts (Imp qt)
Imperial quarts (Imp qt)	X	1.201	= US quarts (US qt)	X	0.833	= Imperial quarts (Imp qt)
US quarts (US qt)	X	0.946	= Litres (l)	X	1.057	= US quarts (US qt)
Imperial gallons (Imp gal)	X	4.546	= Litres (l)	X	0.22	= Imperial gallons (Imp gal)
Imperial gallons (Imp gal)	X	1.201	= US gallons (US gal)	X	0.833	= Imperial gallons (Imp gal)
US gallons (US gal)	X	3.785	= Litres (l)	X	0.264	= US gallons (US gal)

Mass (weight)

Ounces (oz)	X	28.35	= Grams (g)	X	0.035	= Ounces (oz)
Pounds (lb)	X	0.454	= Kilograms (kg)	X	2.205	= Pounds (lb)

Force

Ounces-force (ozf; oz)	X	0.278	= Newtons (N)	X	3.6	= Ounces-force (ozf; oz)
Pounds-force (lbf; lb)	X	4.448	= Newtons (N)	X	0.225	= Pounds-force (lbf; lb)
Newtons (N)	X	0.1	= Kilograms-force (kgf; kg)	X	9.81	= Newtons (N)

Pressure

Pounds-force per square inch (psi; lbf/in²; lb/in²)	X	0.070	= Kilograms-force per square centimetre (kgf/cm²; kg/cm²)	X	14.223	= Pounds-force per square inch (psi; lbf/in²; lb/in²)
Pounds-force per square inch (psi; lbf/in²; lb/in²)	X	0.068	= Atmospheres (atm)	X	14.696	= Pounds-force per square inch (psi; lbf/in²; lb/in²)
Pounds-force per square inch (psi; lbf/in²; lb/in²)	X	0.069	= Bars	X	14.5	= Pounds-force per square inch (psi; lbf/in²; lb/in²)
Pounds-force per square inch (psi; lbf/in²; lb/in²)	X	6.895	= Kilopascals (kPa)	X	0.145	= Pounds-force per square inch (psi; lbf/in²; lb/in²)
Kilopascals (kPa)	X	0.01	= Kilograms-force per square centimetre (kgf/cm²; kg/cm²)	X	98.1	= Kilopascals (kPa)
Millibar (mbar)	X	100	= Pascals (Pa)	X	0.01	= Millibar (mbar)
Millibar (mbar)	X	0.0145	= Pounds-force per square inch (psi; lbf/in²; lb/in²)	X	68.947	= Millibar (mbar)
Millibar (mbar)	X	0.75	= Millimetres of mercury (mmHg)	X	1.333	= Millibar (mbar)
Millibar (mbar)	X	0.401	= Inches of water (inH₂O)	X	2.491	= Millibar (mbar)
Millimetres of mercury (mmHg)	X	0.535	= Inches of water (inH₂O)	X	1.868	= Millimetres of mercury (mmHg)
Inches of water (inH₂O)	X	0.036	= Pounds-force per square inch (psi; lbf/in²; lb/in²)	X	27.68	= Inches of water (inH₂O)

Torque (moment of force)

Pounds-force inches (lbf in; lb in)	X	1.152	= Kilograms-force centimetre (kgf cm; kg cm)	X	0.868	= Pounds-force inches (lbf in; lb in)
Pounds-force inches (lbf in; lb in)	X	0.113	= Newton metres (Nm)	X	8.85	= Pounds-force inches (lbf in; lb in)
Pounds-force inches (lbf in; lb in)	X	0.083	= Pounds-force feet (lbf ft; lb ft)	X	12	= Pounds-force inches (lbf in; lb in)
Pounds-force feet (lbf ft; lb ft)	X	0.138	= Kilograms-force metres (kgf m; kg m)	X	7.233	= Pounds-force feet (lbf ft; lb ft)
Pounds-force feet (lbf ft; lb ft)	X	1.356	= Newton metres (Nm)	X	0.738	= Pounds-force feet (lbf ft; lb ft)
Newton metres (Nm)	X	0.102	= Kilograms-force metres (kgf m; kg m)	X	9.804	= Newton metres (Nm)

Power

Horsepower (hp)	X	745.7	= Watts (W)	X	0.0013	= Horsepower (hp)

Velocity (speed)

Miles per hour (miles/hr; mph)	X	1.609	= Kilometres per hour (km/hr; kph)	X	0.621	= Miles per hour (miles/hr; mph)

*Fuel consumption**

Miles per gallon, Imperial (mpg)	X	0.354	= Kilometres per litre (km/l)	X	2.825	= Miles per gallon, Imperial (mpg)
Miles per gallon, US (mpg)	X	0.425	= Kilometres per litre (km/l)	X	2.352	= Miles per gallon, US (mpg)

Temperature

Degrees Fahrenheit = (°C x 1.8) + 32   Degrees Celsius (Degrees Centigrade; °C) = (°F - 32) x 0.56

It is common practice to convert from miles per gallon (mpg) to litres/100 kilometres (l/100km), where mpg (Imperial) x l/100 km = 282 and mpg (US) x l/100 km = 235

Index